Politics, Patriotism
and Language

Studies in Modern European History

Frank J. Coppa
General Editor

Vol. 57

PETER LANG
New York • Washington, D.C./Baltimore • Bern
Frankfurt am Main • Berlin • Brussels • Vienna • Oxford

William J. Landon

Politics, Patriotism and Language

Niccolò Machiavelli's "Secular Patria" and the Creation of an Italian National Identity

PETER LANG
New York • Washington, D.C./Baltimore • Bern
Frankfurt am Main • Berlin • Brussels • Vienna • Oxford

Library of Congress Cataloging-in-Publication Data

Landon, William J.
Politics, patriotism and language: Niccolò Machiavelli's "secular patria"
and the creation of an Italian national identity / William J. Landon.
p. cm. — (Studies in modern European history; v. 57)
Includes new English translation of: Discorso o dialogo intorno alla nostra lingua
Includes bibliographical references and index.
1. Machiavelli, Niccolò, 1469–1527—Contributions in political science.
2. Nationalism—Italy—History. 3. Political science—Italy—Philosophy—History—To 1500.
4. Machiavelli, Niccolò, 1469–1527. Principe. 5. Machiavelli, Niccolò, 1469–1527.
Discorsi sopra la prima deca di Tito Livio. 6. Machiavelli, Niccolò, 1469–1527.
Discorso o dialogo intorno alla nostra lingua. I. Machiavelli, Niccolò, 1469–1527.
Discorso o dialogo intorno alla nostra lingua. English. II. Title. III. Series.
JC143.M4L36   320.1—dc22   2004001661
ISBN 0-8204-7275-1
ISSN 0893-6897

Bibliographic information published by **Die Deutsche Bibliothek.**
Die Deutsche Bibliothek lists this publication in the "Deutsche
Nationalbibliografie"; detailed bibliographic data is available
on the Internet at http://dnb.ddb.de/.

The paper in this book meets the guidelines for permanence and durability
of the Committee on Production Guidelines for Book Longevity
of the Council of Library Resources.

© 2005 Peter Lang Publishing, Inc., New York
275 Seventh Avenue, 28th Floor, New York, NY 10001
www.peterlangusa.com

Printed in Germany

For Carla

Table of Contents

೫೦೦೪

A Word on Translations

ഔക

The majority of the translations in this work are the author's. For scholars and students who wish to read the quotations in their original language, the reader will find the corresponding Italian (Latin, etc.) quotations in the endnotes to each Chapter. By the same token, where the author elected to use another scholar's translation, these are also noted for the reader. At times, where the original language is essential to the discussion at hand, the reader will find that language in the text and the translation in the notes.

Acknowledgments

ଞୠ୯ଔ

At the very outset, grateful acknowledgement is hereby made to the copyright holders for permission to use the following copyrighted materials:

MS. Palatino 815, p. 820: Niccolò Machiavelli, *Discorso sopra la lingua volgare, se debba dirsi Fiorentina, o Toscana o Italiana*, in Niccolò Machiavelli, *Zibaldone di lettere e di varie scritture storiche e politiche...raccolte su gli originale da Giuliano de'Ricci*, ms. miscellaneo, sec. XVIII. La Biblioteca Nazionale Centrale di Firenze. "Su concessione del *Ministero per i Beni e le Attività Culturali della Repubblica Italiana.*"

MS. Palatino E.B.15.10 (striscia 1414), cc. 133r, 133v, 137v: Niccolò Machiavelli. *Discorso o dialogo intorno alla nostra lingua*, raccolto da Giuliano de' Ricci, in N. Machiavelli, *Lettere e ragguagli*, ms. miscellaneo, sec. XV–XVI. La Biblioteca Nazionale Centrale di Firenze. "Su concessione del *Ministero per i Beni e le Attività Culturali della Repubblica Italiana.*"

The *Dialogo* in: Benedetto Varchi. *L'Ercolano: dialogo di Messer Benedetto Varchi nel quale si ragiona delle lingue, ed in particolare della Toscana e della Fiorentina*. Milano: Società Tipografica de'Classici Italiani, Contrada di S. Margherita, N.° 1118, 1804. Used by permission of Edinburgh University Library, Special Collections.

Discorso, overro dialogo, in cui si esamina, se la lingua, in cui scrissero Dante, il Boccaccio, e il Petrarca, si debba chiamare Italiana, Toscana, o Fiorentina, in *Opere: Volume Otto: Commedie, terzine ed altre opere*. Cosmopoli, 1769. Used by permission of the Special Collections Department, Glasgow University Library.

I would also like to mention my appreciation for the funding provided to me by Mr. William Oxenbury and the Trustees of the A.M. Dommett Charitable Trust. Their kind and generous support enabled me to pursue and complete key areas of research in this book.

Additionally, of all the people who encouraged me to pursue my studies on Machiavelli, Dr. Richard Mackenney's place is most prominent. While I lived and studied in Edinburgh, Scotland, where the majority of this text was realized, he provided me with constant support, criticism and intellectual stimulation. Our meetings never failed to produce in me, a new curiosity and deeper love of Italian history and culture. In the course of my studies with Richard, I gained a dear friend. Thank you, Richard.

I would also like to extend my gratitude to Professor Susan Meld Shell at Boston College for graciously assisting me. And, Dr. Patricia Allerston also deserves thanks for her help and advice. Respectfully, I would like to thank the late Dr. Peter Laven, who sadly passed away in April of 2004, for his helpful suggestions. And I send regards to Professor Jonathan Usher for his insightful criticism.

Signore Simone Testa, my dear friend and colleague in study at Edinburgh for three years, was always quick to make a pasta and then talk about the philandering of this or that mischievous cardinal before trying my patience with his political views. Somewhere in between all of these perfectly wonderful distractions, we were always able to find time to talk about our ideas and help each other in our quest to make something of the scholarly life we chose to pursue. I wish him the best of luck in the future.

I also send affection to Dr. May-shine Lin, who frequently sent me encouragement from across the Pacific and to Monsieur Philippe Dayan, my old friend, whose hospitality and generosity were appreciated so much more than he knew. I would also like to thank Margaret Angove for her constant support and kindness. Drs. John and Susan Cruickshank deserve special mention because they gave me unwavering support through the most trying of times. The tranquility of their home and my flat on Edinburgh's loveliest street will always hold a cherished place in my memories of Scotland.

To my family, for their boundless provision of encouragement—even if they did think that I was taking a little too long—I give my love. To my Dad and Mom, Dr. George and Mrs. Kathleen Landon, who continued to have faith in me, even when I gave them no reason to do so, I send my deepest love, respect and thanks.

Finally, I want to thank my dearest wife who out of the kindness and gentleness of her heart, took my dreams and made them her own. For the past ten years, through unexpected trials and the most wonderful escapades, she has been and continues to be my best friend and most exquisite treasure. This book is unreservedly and lovingly dedicated to my wife, Carla.

Introduction

❧❧❧

Federico Chabod described *Il Principe* as, in a sense, "primordial," detailing the ultimate character of this world."[1] One might suggest that Machiavelli and the historiography dedicated to studying his writings have also become something "primordial." Indeed, from that amorphous matter a different Machiavelli evolves and rears his head depending upon who is searching for him. One might find a cynic, a realist, a master of simulation and dissimulation, the father of the Italian nation, or the founder of modern political science.[2] Apparent shock and horror greeted his work in the sixteenth and seventeenth centuries, then came the apologists of the eighteenth, nineteenth and early twentieth centuries. There was further disquiet in the wake of the Second World War and more recently, he has come to be viewed as the zenith of republican virtue. Machiavelli's reception has been nothing if not varied.

English playwrights, French philosophers, Italian and Anglophone historians and political scientists have each put forward their version of Machiavelli—and each is decidedly different.[3] While it is beyond the scope of this investigation to present a complete historiographical survey of works dedicated to the study of Machiavelli, one should mention: Christopher Marlowe, William Shakespeare, Jean-Jacques Rousseau, Francesco de Sanctis, Federico Chabod, Ernst Cassirer and Maurizio Viroli. Why these one might ask? Each of these writers represents defining characteristics of Machiavelli's reception. Beginning with the earliest of these, Marlowe and Shakespeare, one will find a distillation of sixteenth-century views of Niccolò Machiavelli—the advisor and friend of tyrants, the master of murder and deception.

The two great English playwrights, Marlowe and Shakespeare, conjured a vision of a shadowy Florentine whose very name was meant to provoke fear and revulsion in their audiences.[4] Playing upon English insecurities and Francophobia, Marlowe's "Machevill" brought to mind everything that the theater-goer hated and feared about their "untrustworthy" neighbors from across the channel. Bringing the "Machevill" into local, more familiar and therefore more terrifying surroundings, Richard of Gloucester, in Shakespeare's *Henry VI, Part III*, dares to surpass the "murderous

Machiavel's" penchant for blood.[5]

Marlowe and Shakespeare certainly portrayed Machiavelli in an unfavorable light. However, their vision of Machiavelli did not rely upon his printed words (*Il Principe* was not translated in English until 1640), but upon the rumor that followed his name as a result of the banned status of his work.[6]

Written in an age dominated by Ciceronian political morality, Machiavelli's frank depiction of the "verità effettuale" stood out in glaring opposition to the norm.[7] However, during his lifetime, he was never rebuked for passing comment on the "way things are." Indeed, such stark rhetoric regarding the actions of princes may have been forgiven him after his death if he had not so relentlessly assaulted the Roman church.[8] These assaults, combined with the depictions of him in Shakespeare and Marlowe, as the secretive and bloodthirsty villain, had a lasting impact on the historiography concerned with Machiavelli's work and life. Such was Machiavelli's association with un-Christian, immoral cabals, that Rousseau—in the eighteenth-century—read *Il Principe* as though it contained a hidden message. Underneath the apparent advocacy of tyranny, Rousseau argued that Machiavelli was actually a republican.[9]

So, one might surmise from Rousseau's reading of Machiavelli that his reputation was no fault of his own, but due to the corruption of the Medici regime which forced him to couch his republican idealism in the language of tyranny. By the time of Italian unification and in its aftermath, a much different picture of Machiavelli came to the fore. Indeed, some viewed Machiavelli's final Chapter of *Il Principe* as a prophetic foreshadowing of the rise of Charles Emmanuel I.[10]

When Francesco de Sanctis rose to a place of prominence in Italian scholarly circles Italian unification was, for all practical purposes, complete. Arguably the most famous historian of that era, de Sanctis reserved for Machiavelli praise rather than disdain. For de Sanctis, Machiavelli was one of the first to expound upon the "modern science" of politics.[11] Furthermore, he readily acknowledged Machiavelli's secularism and he embraced it. Indeed, it seems that de Sanctis re-appropriated Machiavelli's *cinquecento* ideas, fitting them quite comfortably within the new framework of a united Italy, all the while refusing to entangle himself in questions about the morality of Machiavelli's writings. To de Sanctis, Machiavelli's political thought appeared to be tailor-made for the romantic nationalism of the *Risorgimento*. This may be why he, unlike many scholars before or since, paid attention to Machiavelli's patriotism and his use of *patria* of which more will be said in due course. However, such continuous praise of the Florentine faded in Italian scholarship, to be replaced by a more balanced approach to Machiavelli. The most famous of these studies was written by Federico Chabod.

In his *Machiavelli and the Renaissance*, Chabod presented a human portrait of Machiavelli. He painted a "ritratto" to which many readers could relate and an interpretation of his works which dealt not only with the genius, but also with the inaccuracies of Machiavelli's works.[12] In other words, Chabod contextualized Machiavelli's political thought, tracing its evolution to *cinquecento* Italy rather than trying to re-shape it to fit into a twentieth-century framework. By the same token, Chabod does not attempt to excuse or condemn Machiavelli's "immorality." Rather he addressed the ideas contained in *Il Principe* with their historical and political importance in mind without passing judgment thereon. Or, one might conclude, Chabod examined meticulously Machiavelli's historical inaccuracies, not his moral inadequacies.[13] The same cannot be said of the writings of Ernst Cassirer.

In his influential collection of essays, *The Myth of the State*, Cassirer summoned once again the long-dead shade of the "murderous Machevil". Persuasively, Cassirer argued, "that Machiavelli's *Prince* contains the most immoral things and that Machiavelli has no scruples about recommending to the ruler all sorts of deception, perfidy and cruelty is incontestable."[14] That such unscrupulousness played into the hands of despots and tyrants, Cassirer had no doubt. Where Chabod strove to view Machiavelli within the context of early *cinquecento* Italy, Cassirer examined Machiavelli's political thought in terms of the political absolutism and tyranny which he had so recently witnessed during the Second World War.[15] Indeed, his points were well-argued and persuasive, and Machiavelli's reputation suffered as a consequence. Yet, Cassirer's contemporaries, J.H. Whitfield, Felix Gilbert and Hans Baron, to varying degrees sought to repair the old wounds which Cassirer's arguments had re-opened in Machiavelli's reputation.[16] They succeeded to such an extent, one might argue, that they had more in common with the idealism of de Sanctis than the moralism of Cassirer.

In recent scholarship, Maurizio Viroli has published a great deal on Machiavelli's political thought.[17] Bridging the gap between Italian and Anglophone scholarship, Viroli has published most of his works in both languages. Approaching the "problem" of Machiavelli and political morality, Viroli has illustrated, following Chabod, that *Il Principe* must be viewed as a product of its time. Of equal importance, building upon Allan Gilbert's work on *Il Principe*'s genre, Viroli has set forth that *Il Principe* is not a political work—at least in terms of traditional Florentine republican values—but a book about the "art of the state". This explains, according to Viroli, the differing foci of *Il Principe* and the *Discorsi*, the former being a devastating critique of contemporary humanist views and the latter being a handbook for republicans.[18]

From the sixteenth century until the present, views and interpretations of Machiavelli and his political works have changed dramatically. However, there is a certain consistency. Whether viewed as a demonic and crafty personage, a friend of tyrants, or as the pinnacle of *cinquecento* republican political theory, Machiavelli has undoubtedly been viewed as a genius. Drawing upon and highlighting divergent strands in his political thought, each of these ways of viewing the Florentine can be justified, but are there other aspects of his political thought and personality which have yet fully to be developed?

If one casts one's gaze back to the *cinquecento*, one might argue that Francesco Guicciardini's commentary on his friend's political works allows for a different picture of Machiavelli to emerge.[19] Genius he was, schemer and friend of tyrants he might have been, but was he a naïve and romantic idealist? Our study seeks to illustrate that Machiavelli's political thought has significant traces of those attributes. Indeed, an examination of his call for Italian liberation and unification may help to demonstrate this.

The first two Chapters of this study examine Machiavelli's theory of the "secular *patria*," which drew on aspects from the ancient sources with which he was familiar. However, he drained those sources—Cicero and Livy specifically—of all references to religion. An examination of Machiavelli's "secular *patria*" may help to demonstrate, contrary to the assertions of prominent scholars such as Baron, that *Il Principe* and the *Discorsi* are united by this concept of the "secular *patria*."[20] If Machiavelli wanted a united Italy, as those Chapters will argue, then it appears that he wanted it to be a united *patria* free from religion in the temporal sphere. More specifically, it seems that he wanted Lorenzo de' Medici to use the resources of the Church to liberate and unite Italy, but thereafter he wanted religion and politics to go their separate ways—a theory which Guicciardini recognized and at which he scoffed.

When, in 1515, Lorenzo was named *Capitano* of Florence, his uncle Giovanni de' Medici sat on the papal throne as Pope Leo X. This linking of Florentine and Roman interests provided Italy with a brief window of opportunity—a special *occasione*—with a chance to throw off the yoke of foreign oppression and unite itself under a secular republican government.[21] The final Chapter in Machiavelli's *Il Principe* seems to indicate that Machiavelli hoped Lorenzo and Leo X, following the example of Cesare Borgia and his father, Pope Alexander VI, would use their familial bond and the link this afforded between Florence and Rome to undertake a drive for Italian liberation and unification. Having achieved this, Lorenzo, following the example of the Roman dictator, would magnanimously lay aside his all-powerful office, allowing Italians to unite themselves under a secular republican regime—as Cesare Borgia had done in the Romanga in Chapter VII of *Il Principe*. But, one might argue, such a plan is too simplistic, too naïve for the great Machiavelli. Indeed, one might also argue, the extent of his knowledge of the ins-and-outs of Italian politics more generally, and the Medici family more specifically would rule out his drawing up such a plan. That he was perhaps more knowledgeable than most regarding the details related to these is likely, but this study will argue that his desire to see Italy united blinded him to the practicalities of uniting a politically and culturally diverse peninsula. Guicciardini's role in this is central, for he passed judgment on Machiavelli's plan for liberation and unification—and that judgment was altogether unfavorable.

Guicciardini argued that, for example, even if Lorenzo loved the united *patria* he helped to create, that love would not be enough to cause him to lay aside his all-powerful office. Indeed, for Guicciardini, Machiavelli's plan was laughable.[22] One might say the same about the actual means by which, Machiavelli argued, Italian unification could be achieved. Chapters Three and Four, for example, illustrate that Machiavelli's concept of a "national citizen army" was flawed, and his concept of ending the practice of exile so idealistic, that he lost touch with the practicalities of what was actually happening in Italy. How, for example, could a united Italian army which—according to Machiavelli—should refuse to use artillery, be successful against the military might of a German or Swiss mercenary army, let alone the hardened regular troops of Spain or France? It seems that his study of classical sources and the contemporary society that led him to "secularize" his theory of *patria* also drained practicality from his military considerations.[23]

If one turns to a work that many think was written by Machiavelli—the *Discorso o dialogo intorno alla nostra lingua*—one might find that the concept of the secular *patria* is present, and that, interestingly, it is linked with linguistic unification. The author of the *Dialogo* sets forth the Florentine/Tuscan dialect as the superior language in Italy. Indeed, the author argues for Florentine linguistic hegemony. These interesting similarities, along with similarities in vocabulary and other political ideas found in works definitely written by Machiavelli, are not enough to *prove* his authorship. However, that short work, which is discussed in detail in Chapters Five through Seven, *could* have been written by Machiavelli, and at a particular time—the *vendemmial* of 1515, the same time, this examination argues, that Machiavelli wrote the final rousing Chapter of *Il Principe*. Perhaps the similarities between the *Dialogo* and works by Machiavelli are mere chance, or perhaps the author of the *Dialogo* knew the works of Machiavelli well.

Nevertheless the call in the *Dialogo* for Florentine linguistic hegemony seems to complement Machiavelli's call for Florentine political superiority. Indeed, the way in which the *Dialogo* appears to mirror Machiavelli's political views shaped the way in which that work is studied in this study.

Traditionally, the *Dialogo*, whether viewed as a work of Machiavelli or not, has been studied as a linguistic treatise. Literary elements of that *Dialogo* have been "done to death." Some of the greatest Italian scholars of the twentieth century paid particular attention to those. One might cite the works of Sergio Bertelli, Fredi Chiappelli and Bortolo Tommaso Sozzi as but three examples.[24] Recently, however, something of a "renaissance" of interest has taken place in which the *Dialogo* has been studied by political scientists as well as historians: Susan Meld Shell, Maurizio Viroli, and Angelo Codevilla to name but a few.[25] Each of these have examined to varying degrees the presence of political considerations in the *Dialogo*. Shell for example compared the *Dialogo* with Machiavelli's *Istorie fiorentine*. This study compares it with *Il Principe* and the *Discorsi*.[26] Because we lack an autograph copy of the *Dialogo*, it cannot be ascribed to Machiavelli with total certainty. However, following Shell, Viroli and others, there certainly seems to be enough similarities between that work and much of Machiavelli's political *opere* to examine it as a likely product of his pen. Indeed, the *Dialogo* may provide insight into Machiavelli's plan for Italian unification as set out in *Il Principe* and the *Discorsi*.

Politics, patriotism and perhaps language combine in Machiavelli's plan for Italian liberation and unification to make a potent concoction at once impractical and prophetic. His plan, which appeared to his friend Guicciardini to be laughable, proved indeed to be out of place in the early years of the *cinquecento*. Rather, one might argue, Machiavelli's call for Italian unification, its idealism and even naiveté found a home in the romantic nationalism of Italy's *Risorgimento*.

CHAPTER ONE

Patria in the Context of Niccolò Machiavelli's *Il Principe* and the *Discorsi*

വ‍ോ

"How could the faithful secretary of the Florentine republic, the author of the *Discourses on the First Ten Books of Titus Livy*, also be the author of *The Prince*?"[1] In the realm of Machiavelli studies, rarely has such a loaded question been posited, as its author, Hans Baron himself readily admitted. In this Chapter, we will seek to unpack Baron's query, thereby examining issues related to the date of Machiavelli's *Il Principe* and the *Discorsi sopra la prima deca di Tito Livio* and the relationship of one to the other in time, content and political vocabulary. This will place our investigation firmly within the confines of existing Machiavelli scholarship.[2] However, rather than focus on words such as *stato*, *fortuna*, or *virtù*, we will suggest that the term *patria* is also a central, though neglected, word in Machiavelli's *opere*.[3]

That is not to say that *patria* has been entirely neglected in historical and political discourse relating to Machiavelli. On the contrary, J.H. Hexter and Maurizio Viroli have given particular attention to the term in Machiavelli's political works, although their investigations make up only small parts of articles or treatises concerned with Machiavelli's political thought.[4] This Chapter, and indeed the entirety of this work, aims to emphasize that *patria* may be helpful in interpreting Machiavelli's political works, especially *Il Principe* and the *Discorsi*.

Utilizing the substantial electronic tools available, the author has mapped Machiavelli's use of the term *patria* across his political and literary output.[5] This compendium may prove useful for future studies of the term *patria* and its importance in Machiavelli's political vocabulary. Every occurrence of *patria* and its related derivatives are found in the Appendices of this study. The focus of this Chapter and the following three are upon *patria* in *Il Principe* and the *Discorsi*. This is for two principal reasons. The first is that one will find from a cursory inspection of the attached Appendices on *patria* that, generally, Machiavelli does not use it in his literary output. While there are exceptions which are noted, they are few. The second, and more important reason for limiting the scope of this investigation into *patria*, is that it may prove helpful in interpreting the relationship between Machiavelli's two most famous works—the goal of this Chapter.

In examining *patria* and the relationship between *Il Principe* and the *Discorsi*, one possible reading came to the fore; *patria* may be that which mediates between the themes of principality and dictatorship in *Il Principe* and the republicanism of the *Discorsi*. This proposed mediation may have interesting implications. Did Machiavelli have a coherent plan for the creation of a united Italy and of a national identity? It seems that he did and an understanding of his use of *patria* may help to interpret the different facets of that plan.

By seeking to set out the aspects of this plan, this Chapter will examine the uses of the term *patria* in *Il Principe* and the *Discorsi*, first separately, then in comparison with one another to see whether there is a distinct political shift from one work to the other as Baron implied in his question. Then, based upon the outcome of this investigation, we may better be able to ascertain whether the hypothesis stated above is valid. The interpretation of Machiavelli's plan for Italian unification is only discussed briefly in this Chapter, keeping the focus firmly on the uses of *patria* in *Il Principe* and the *Discorsi*. The specifics of the plan that Machiavelli appears to have formulated will be dealt with in the following Chapter along with an examination of Machiavelli's sources.

Having set out the *modus operandi*, and the basic outline of this Chapter, it is helpful to begin to unpack Baron's question. The first component which is essential in laying the groundwork for the investigation is the date of *Il Principe* and the *Discorsi*.

The Date of *Il Principe* and the *Discorsi*

There is much controversy concerned with the date of *Il Principe* and the *Discorsi*. Baron suggested, and this Chapter accepts, that *Il Principe* predates the *Discorsi* by two years. This date structure may help to diminish the apparent problem with their simultaneous evolution. For example, *Il Principe* contains specific advice for a new prince while the *Discorsi* set out parameters for the proper functioning of a republican government. Therein may be one of the problems with examining *Il Principe* and the *Discorsi* together. They are seemingly irreconcilable with one another, for the apparent advocacy of princely rule in *Il Principe* and the almost continuous praise of republican government in the *Discorsi* do not make comfortable bedfellows. Indeed, the differing foci of *Il Principe* and the *Discorsi* have caused some historians to view Machiavelli's work as disjointed and even incoherent.[6] The use of the term *patria* may, however, mediate and reconcile these apparent contradictions.

There are certain facts related to the date of *Il Principe* which need not be debated. For example, there is a consensus among most that *Il Principe* was written in 1513.[7] In 1515 or 1516, most agree, Machiavelli returned to his treatise on principalities to amend its introduction as a result of the death of Giuliano de' Medici, to whom it was originally dedicated. He re-dedicated *Il Principe* to Lorenzo, Giuliano's successor. While re-dedicating *Il Principe*, it is likely that Machiavelli edited and added further sections to his work, including the last Chapter (see below).[8]

It has been assumed that Machiavelli's *Discorsi* originated at around the same time as *Il Principe*. For, the first sentence of the second Chapter in *Il Principe* suggests that Machiavelli developed *Il Principe* and the *Discorsi* simultaneously. In Chapter Two of his *Il Principe*, Machiavelli wrote: "I will leave behind the discussion of republics, because I reasoned about them at length at another time."[9] Machiavelli's statement prompts several possibilities. The first is, that the *Discorsi* were indeed written at the time of *Il Principe*. The second is that the *Discorsi* were written in two distinct stages; the first stage along with *Il Principe* and the other, at a later date, when Machiavelli would have had recourse to the *Histories* of Polybius, particularly book VI.[10] A third argument, supported by Baron and John Hale, relies upon the idea that Machiavelli went back to *Il Principe* in 1515, after the *Discorsi* were underway, to update and add to his treatise on principalities.[11] Hale's and Baron's theory accounts for Machiavelli's reference to a work on republics in the passage from Chapter Two of *Il Principe*. This date structure allows for a 1513 dating of *Il Principe*, with amendments made in 1515, and more, it also allows for the *Discorsi* to date from late 1515.[12] But, what of the arguments that date the works together?

Felix Gilbert suggested that the *Discorsi* were written in two separate stages, the first concurrent with *Il Principe* and the second after *Il Principe* was completed. This first stage, Gilbert hypothesized, was not the *Discorsi*, but another work on republics.[13] This treatise on republican government, according to Gilbert, provided an interesting solution to the "altra volta" passage in *Il Principe*, for it explains how Machiavelli could refer to a previous work on republics, *before* he began work on what was to become the *Discorsi*. The second, or final version of the *Discorsi*, while based on this earlier treatise on republics, evolved well after *Il Principe* was finished.[14] He acknowledged the theoretical and conjectural nature of his work on the dating of the *Discorsi*. While Gilbert's theory manages to locate *Il Principe* in 1513 and the *Discorsi* in 1515, this theory is not demonstrable—as Gilbert himself indicated—particularly in light of what he calls the "first stage." There is no evidence at hand to illustrate that Machiavelli wrote a separate work on republics. Gilbert hypothesized that this work must have been lost, but there is no concrete evidence to back up his answer to the *Il Principe-Discorsi* date controversies. It must be said that those who are most critical of Gilbert—J.H. Whitfield for instance—do not replace his conjectures with theories of their own.[15]

J.H. Hexter, on the other hand, placed the date of the *Discorsi* somewhere between 1510 and 1520, following the date structure set forth by Gilbert in the above-mentioned arguments.[16] He subscribed to Gilbert's hypothesis that the *Discorsi* were written in two separate stages, but here their theories diverge. Hexter illustrated that the *Discorsi* could not have been anywhere near their polished form until sometime after 1515 at the earliest, for Machiavelli could not have come into contact with any portions of Polybius VI until at least 1515.[17] Furthermore, Hexter illustrated that Polybius VI, unlike the other books of his history, was not available in either Latin or Italian. The final version of the *Discorsi* relied heavily on sections of Polybius' book VI, but in 1515 it was only available in Greek. Machiavelli did not know Greek. So how could he have used Polybius VI?

Hexter posited an intriguing answer to this unexplained problem. It is likely that Machiavelli met with Janus Lascaris, a native Greek speaker, at the *Orti Oricellari* in 1515, or perhaps later. This meeting, Hexter proposed, allowed Lascaris and Machiavelli to discuss Polybius, particularly book VI, and it may have spawned a partial translation of Polybius VI into Latin. Hexter's thesis explains how Machiavelli was able to rely on Polybius VI in his *Discorsi* and it also moves the date of at least the second half of the work to 1515 or later, allowing for a smoother transition between *Il Principe* and the *Discorsi*. However, like Gilbert's arguments mentioned above, Hexter's hypotheses have come under attack because they are not clearly demonstrable. Again, Hexter's critics do not propose an alternative answer to the problems that he raised. Gilbert and Hexter agree that the *Discorsi* were written in two stages, separated by several years at the least. Paradoxically, their hypotheses were attacked and shown to be undemonstrable despite the fact that they, to a large extent, agree with the view that the *Discorsi*, in some form, developed concurrently with Machiavelli's *Il Principe*.[18] The most experimental of the theories set forth concerning the dating of *Il Principe* and the *Discorsi* is reserved for last because the implications of this theory may shed light on the development of the term *patria* in *Il Principe* and the *Discorsi*.

Baron posited an alternative explanation to those set forth by Gilbert and

Hexter. Like Gilbert and Hexter before him, Baron focused attention on Machiavelli's reference to republics in Chapter Two of *Il Principe*, or the "altra volta" passage. Baron explains the dilemma presented by Machiavelli's reference by theorizing that when Machiavelli went back to *Il Principe* in 1515 or 1516 to re-dedicate it to Lorenzo, he also added several passages, including the "altra volta" passage. This theory not only explains Machiavelli's statement, but it also goes some way toward explaining the differing nature of *Il Principe* and the *Discorsi*. Baron suggests that *Il Principe* was written in 1513, following the greatest scholarly consensus, but he moves the bulk of the *Discorsi* to late 1515 and the following years.[19] When two years are placed between them, the problem of justifying the simultaneous evolution of these two seemingly diametrically opposed political works is diminished and perhaps abolished.[20] Baron concluded his argument by writing: "Believers in the customary chronology of Machiavelli's works would have to explain better than has been done in the past, how Machiavelli could have written even a portion of the *Discorsi*, or have advocated some of their guiding ideas, under the conditions of 1513."[21]

When the arguments of Baron, Gilbert and Hexter are placed together, their scholarship is formidable. However, Baron's assertion that *Il Principe* was amended after Machiavelli had either completed the *Discorsi* or had them well under way is especially intriguing; for his scholarship allows for a smoother transition from the focus on principalities in *Il Principe* to the republicanism of the *Discorsi*.

Despite the differing views represented therein, from the wealth of scholarly debate concerned with the dates of *Il Principe* and the *Discorsi*, one can conclude that both works, written concurrently or at diverse times, evolved in a completely different manner. This evolution and the disparity between their respective subjects, gives, we suggest, greater weight to those theories which separate the dates of composition. Therefore, following Baron and Hale, we date *Il Principe* as a work of 1513 with additions being added in 1515 or 1516, and the *Discorsi* to a date no earlier than late 1515. Even if one sets aside the above mentioned arguments, there remains compelling evidence which suggests that Machiavelli began the *Discorsi* in 1515, adding amendments to *Il Principe* at that time.

The simplest, and perhaps most conclusive confirmation which separates the dates of *Il Principe* and the *Discorsi* can be found in two related pieces of evidence. The first may be found in the dedicatory letter of the *Discorsi*.

> If this is so, I do not know which of us would have to be less obligated to the other: either I to you, who forced me to write that which I never would have written on my own; or you to me, if (my) writing has not satisfied you.[22]

Machiavelli dedicated his *Discorsi* to Zanobi Buondelmonti and Cosimo Rucellai. The three became fast friends at Rucellai's scholarly gathering which he hosted in his gardens, the *Orti Oricellari*.[23]

Machiavelli only became associated with Buondelmonti and Rucellai after going to these meetings. Furthermore, he first referred to the *Orti* in a letter dated 17 December 1517.

> I know that you find yourselves there the whole day together with the Most Reverend de'Salviati, Filippo Nerli, Cosimo Rucellai, Cristofano Carnesechi, and sometimes, Antonio Francesco delli Albizi; and you devote yourselves to eating well, and you remember little of us here, poor oafs (dying from cold and lack of sleep). However, so that we are able to live a little, we get together sometimes, Zanobi Buondelmonti, Amerigo Morelli, Batista della Palla and I, and talk about that trip to Flanders with such energy...[24]

In light of this letter, it is possible that Machiavelli did not begin attending the *Orti* until 1517, pushing the date of the *Discorsi* back to that year, if one believes that his friends "forced" him to write the work. This late date is not probable. On the contrary, it seems likely that Machiavelli began visiting the *Orti* in 1515, almost two years after his expulsion from political life, when he finally may have felt comfortable walking the streets of his beloved Florence[25]. From this evidence and that set forth above, it appears that the *Discorsi* are a work of late 1515 or early 1516.

Such a date structure for *Il Principe* and the *Discorsi* may open interesting possibilities. For example, if *Il Principe* was written in 1513, a period of two years intervened before he began his treatise on republics, the *Discorsi*. In that time period, one might argue, Machiavelli's political thought became more expansive. And more precisely, a particular *occasione*—or brief window of opportunity—was at hand, that would allow Italy to be free from foreign occupation and united politically under a republican government. This could see a temporary unification of Florentine and Roman interests; Medici *Capitano*, Lorenzo at Florence, and Leo X, Medici Pope, at Rome. Indeed, it seems that Machiavelli extensive coverage of Cesare Borgia's and Alexander VI's action in Chapter VII of *Il Principe* was meant to be a blue-print of sorts for Lorenzo and Leo. The united interests of the Medici family and the opportunity this presented for Italian unification, could have led Machiavelli, in the intervening period between writing *Il Principe* and the *Discorsi*, to add a final Chapter to the former.[26]

Famously, this Chapter calls for the liberation of Italy from the barbarians at the hands of a swift, papal sanctioned, dictatorial prince. Perhaps Peter Laven's words sum up this point best:

The necessity of the times limited the possible field of effective action. Machiavelli's desperate solution was the emergence of a tyrannical law-giver, who would be prepared to adopt extreme measures such as those of Cesare Borgia in order to force his will on Italy, and, having done so, would be willing to hand on his dictatorially-ordered state to a republican government based on the example of the Roman republic. With the Papacy and Florence under the control of the Medici, he looked to that family for such a leader, especially to Leo X.[27]

Laven then argued that Machiavelli did not in reality believe that a unifying prince would actually give up his power after such a successful drive to free Italy from foreign invaders.

However, we propose that the reason the prince would relinquish his power, was out of duty to the *patria*.[28] In this interpretation, Machiavelli may be viewed, not as a cynical realist, but as an idealist who wanted to see his *patria*, Florence, and the whole of Italy, free and united under a republican government. This must be tested against the texts that Machiavelli wrote.

La Patria and Il Principe

In examining *patria* in *Il Principe* one must consider first, for whom it was written and second the genre in which it resides. Machiavelli's work was written for a specific—and limited—audience and his work fits squarely into a particular genre of political treatise. Regarding intended audience, Machiavelli gives the reader a good guide by offering an introduction to its intended recipient. This can be found in the work's dedicatory epistle to Lorenzo de' Medici. For this reason, as we hypothesized above, Machiavelli's call for Italian liberation and perhaps unification was aimed primarily at Lorenzo, and also to Leo X as Laven argued. We know that some of Machiavelli's closest friends were asked to read an early draft of *Il Principe*, but other than these few, we cannot know for sure who read it, or how far its audience extended.[29] Given that *Il Principe* was not published until 1532, anything beyond the minimal data presented above would be speculation and is therefore not pursued. On the other hand, genre considerations are much easier to map and have been studied by prominent scholars, particularly Allan Gilbert.

In his *Machiavelli's Prince and Its Forerunners*, Gilbert argued meticulously that Machiavelli's short treatise on principalities was indeed one treatise in an exceedingly long line of advice books for princes or *de Regimine Principum*.[30] At first glance, Gilbert's attention to historical detail appears to devalue Machiavelli's genius, but on closer inspection, he merely contextualizes and historicizes Machiavelli's genius in order to illustrate from whom he borrowed and indeed from which historical trends and values he deviated.[31] To develop each of these topics would require another volume. What one must take away from Gilbert's magisterial assessment is that Machiavelli's *Il Principe* developed within an evolving continuum of advice books. However, where others sought to carry on the long tradition of advice books to princes, Machiavelli sought to turn the whole subject on its head, pulling the philosophical rug from under the feet of his humanist predecessors and Cicero in particular.[32]

Il Principe, according to Maurizio Viroli, lacks all the language normally associated with politics in the *Quattro* and *Cinquecento*. For example, one will not find any "*politico*-rooted words" therein, because "*Il Principe* is not a discourse on the city," which would entail, according to Viroli, a distillation of republican political language.[33] J.H. Whitfield came to a similar conclusion when he noted that the *Discorsi*—not *Il Principe*—are built upon words such as "il vivere civile" and "il vivere politico"; republican vocabulary and language.[34]

Viroli's measured judgments of *Il Principe* help to illustrate that there is a distinct difference between the aims of *Il Principe* and the *Discorsi*. For example, the former is intended for a prince. Therefore, one will find words that relate to a prince and the maintenance of his personal "stato" or the "stato" over which he lords. The *Discorsi*, as a treatise on republics and republican values are concerned with the public good and the "bene comune."[35] In analyzing words such as "stato" and "*politico*-rooted terms" Viroli's considerations on *Il Principe* and the *Discorsi* successfully demonstrated their different use of language, thus pulling the works apart. We propose that this separation should be maintained, both in time, genre and content, but that it need not be an unbridgeable chasm.[36] On the contrary, *patria* may be the link between these two works. Keeping these ideas in mind, let us turn to the text of *Il Principe* itself and analyze how and where Machiavelli used the term *patria*.

Machiavelli's use of *patria* in *Il Principe* may correspond with the goal which one might argue he desired to achieve—the liberation and unification of Italy. Perhaps the rousing conclusion of the piece illustrates this. Here, however, it may prove helpful to illustrate where Machiavelli used *patria* in *Il Principe*. The work is 27,860 words in length, including Chapter headings. The treatise is divided into twenty-six Chapters. One will find *patria* in only four of these twenty-six Chapters; twice in Chapter six, three times in Chapter eight, twice in Chapter nine and once in Chapter twenty-six for a total of eight occurrences. Each occurrence may, however, be far more important than this small frequency would indicate.

The author has taken the editorial decision to include all references to *patria* in *Il Principe* in the Appendix to this Chapter. Each reference to *patria* below will contain a number in "parentheses" to guide the reader to the appropriate quotation in the Appendix. Keeping this in mind, it may prove helpful to define *patria* in the context of *Il Principe*. George Bull translated *patria* as "country" and "native city," which are conventionally accepted and satisfactory translations, but one may be able to add nuance to these accepted translations.

"Fondatore" (1), "ne fu nobilitata" (2), "diventa principe" (3) and (6), "libertà" (4), "vivere...sicuro" (5), "difese contro" (7): these words are linked with *patria* in the first seven occurrences of *patria* in *Il Principe*. Interestingly, each occurrence refers to an exceptional *virtuoso* who successfully founded, freed, or defended their *patria* by their own means, or by popular consent.

Might these instances suggest that Machiavelli wanted to illustrate that radical action could produce not only a free, but a new, united *patria* in Italy? The examples that Machiavelli set forth, could show the new Florentine prince how to seize the *occasione* as Romulus and Nabis had done before him. Add to this the possibility of papal funding and cooperation, and one may have highlighted Machiavelli's plan to unite Italy. Here, we suggest, the last Chapter of *Il Principe* finds an intriguing place. Therein Machiavelli wrote that "questa *patria* ne sia nobilitata." When Machiavelli wrote "questa patria," was he referring to his *native*, or local *patria*, Florence, or Italy—a *communal patria*? The answer is difficult and may indicate that Machiavelli was speaking of both.

Denys Hay once observed that:

> For most Italians, *patria* meant, not the entire peninsula, but those narrower localities with which they had immediate sentimental and political ties. Yet, however oblivious in practice to the demands of larger loyalties, literate Italians were forever referring to the land as a whole. It is hard to find a poet or historian, or writer of any kind, who does not offer observations or reflections which might be used to illustrate a view of Italy.[37]

Machiavelli, like all Italians, had "immediate sentimental and political ties" with Florence—his *patria*—but, particularly after the French invasions of 1494, as Hay pointed out, loyalties, especially noticeable in Machiavelli, expanded to include all of Italy and its need for freedom.[38] In 1515, the year in which Machiavelli may have authored the last Chapter to *Il Principe*, what was the situation in Florence and in Italy?

Machiavelli's regional *patria*, which he loved, was under the control of the Medici, and Italy as a whole was divided into three spheres of influence:

the French, the papacy, and the Spanish.[39] For all practical purposes, the papacy was the last Italian institution capable of dealing with either foreign power on a level footing. Yet it was the papacy's involvement in political affairs that brought foreign powers into Italy in the first place.[40] Machiavelli's local *patria* was, due to Medici control, linked with a peninsular and an international power—the papacy. The fragile and brief *occasione* which Machiavelli presented to Lorenzo in the last Chapter of *Il Principe*, was the unique link between Florence and Rome provided by the Medici. Lorenzo was prince and *capitano* of Florence and his uncle, Leo X sat on the papal throne. According to Machiavelli, "The opportunities given them enabled these men to succeed, and their own exceptional prowess enabled them to seize their opportunities."[41] Thus, with clever rhetorical ambiguity, which we propose related *patria* to Florence and Italy, he called on Lorenzo to "ennoble" both; Florence, by making it the centre of a united Italy, and Italy itself by expelling and defeating Spain and France.

   Patria, as used the first seven times it appears in *Il Principe*, set out historical examples which Lorenzo and Leo X could imitate. Seizing the *occasione* which united the interests of Florence and Rome, Lorenzo could, one might argue, set out not only to expel Italy's foreign oppressors, but also unite the peninsula, creating a united Italian *patria*—under a republican government.

La Patria and the *Discorsi*

Like *Il Principe*, the *Discorsi* were not published until 1532, five years after Machiavelli's death. Given this date of publication, we cannot be sure of the extent of the readership of the text or when individuals read the *Discorsi* before that date. There are, however, three notable exceptions to this statement. The *Discorsi*, like *Il Principe*, contain a dedicatory epistle. The former is not to a prince, but to two of Machiavelli's friends in scholarship— Zanobi Buondelmonti and Cosimo Rucellai. A portion of this letter has already been cited. Given that the work was dedicated to them, and that they perhaps gently coerced Machiavelli to put his ideas in writing, we can be fairly sure that they read the manuscript. One might also conclude that Francesco Guicciardini not only read, but produced a commentary on the *Discorsi*, in 1528, one year after his friend's death.[42] With the exception of these three, one cannot be sure to whom Machiavelli extended the privilege of reading his treatise on republics.

   In terms of genre, the *Discorsi* are at once a history and a political handbook, rather more like a work of Florentine civic humanism than the voracious attacks thereon in *Il Principe*.[43] Maurizio Viroli demonstrated that unlike *Il Principe*, the *Discorsi* are filled with "*politico*-rooted" words, which in the Florentine context placed the *Discorsi* in a similar genre as those histories written by Bruni and Salutati. While some of the ideas present in *Il Principe* are present in the *Discorsi*, the expansiveness of the latter and its source materials along with its political vocabulary differ from *Il Principe*. Furthermore, as Viroli illustrated, the *Discorsi* are first and foremost a book concerned with the language and practicalities of civic life, political life and republicanism, markedly different from *Il Principe* and its focus on the language of the advice books to princes.[44] These different sources and indeed, subject matter, one might suggest, enacted changes upon the term *patria* in the *Discorsi*, expanding it, yet retaining certain qualities. This expansion and continuation, may add weight to the hypothesis that *patria* is a link between the starkly contrasting subjects of Machiavelli's two most famous treatises.

Patria and its derivatives appear in the *Discorsi* seventy-nine times. The work, including Chapter headings, is 118,693 words in length. They are divided into three *Libri*. The first is divided into sixty individual *discorsi* about a given subject. *Libro* II is divided into thirty-two *discorsi* and the third book contains forty-nine. *Patria* occurs 17 times, in twelve of the first book's sixty Chapters; 20 times in ten of book two's thirty-three and forty-two times in book three's forty-nine. Given the length of the *Discorsi*, *patria*'s frequency of occurrence is minimal, though marginally more frequent than in *Il Principe*. Perhaps Machiavelli's writing took on a greater patriotism as he developed a plan for Italian unification. The way in which *patria* is used in the *Discorsi*, in comparison with its counterparts in *Il Principe* seems to bear this out.

Where *patria* in *Il Principe* focused specifically on founding or uniting a *patria*, the *Discorsi* present a different and more varied picture. Therein, one might generalize, Machiavelli associated *patria* with a different set of verbs and modifiers. Like the occurrences of *patria* in *Il Principe*, the reader will find a complete list of those occurrences found in the *Discorsi* in the Appendix to this Chapter. The selected references cited below will also include a number indicating to the reader where the full quotation may be found in the Appendix.

At this point, it may prove helpful to examine those instances of *patria* in the *Discorsi* which are similar to those used in *Il Principe*. In *Il Principe*, *patria* was associated with those who "defend"—"difendere" or its conjugations—and those who "become," "diventare, diventa, etc." founders or princes of their *patria*. These words are also used in the *Discorsi* in relation to those who seize, under exceptional circumstances, power, in order to found a republic or a principality.

One will find that these occur four times in the *Discorsi*. As these are cited in the Appendix to this Chapter, please refer to the following numbers there: (*Patria* in the *Discorsi* 18, 20, 70 and 72). When those occurrences are compared with occurrence (7) in *Il Principe*, one will find that there is some continuity between the works; at least where *patria* is used, but not where other political language is concerned as Viroli's research, previously cited, helped to illustrate. Keeping that in mind, one will find that the continuity provided by *patria* does not end with those references. Again, for the sake of simplicity, please use the bracketed numbers that follow to find their corresponding quotations in the Appendix to this Chapter.

Compare *Discorsi* (3, 11 and 31) with *Il Principe*'s (1, 2 and 6). Each of those references contain historical examples to illustrate how one "diventa" king, prince or founder of a republic. Again, this provides a certain sense of continuity to these works, which Viroli and Baron appear to have overlooked. This continuity is limited, but it is important because it is provided by the term *patria*. What one may find from further investigation into the term *patria* in the *Discorsi*, is that it not only occurs with greater frequency, but that given the republican nature of the *Discorsi*, one should expect it to be linked with words that encourage or exhort citizens to promote or protect the "bene comune."[45]

Most often—seven times—as the compendium in the Appendix illustrates, Machiavelli cited actions which were "contro" the good or survival of the *patria*. (See Appendix One, "*Patria* in the '*Discorsi*,'" numbers 10, 41, 43, 50, 51, 54 and number 1 in the final section "*Patrie* in the *Discorsi*"). Machiavelli may have wanted to illustrate what not to do in order to bring honour, prosperity and indeed, unity to one's *patria*. The verb which is most associated with *patria* is "liberare" or its conjugated derivatives; used five times. (See "*Patria* in the *Discorsi*," numbers: 37, 44, 46, 48, 49.) Taken at face value the combination of these two words and the frequency of their use seem to indicate that Machiavelli wanted to teach his readers, and we propose that he wanted Lorenzo to be one of them, how to act in a manner that would not only heap honour upon their local *patria*, Florence, but also liberate their common *patria*, Italy; protecting and expanding the "comune patria" and the "bene comune."

Along with "liberare" one will find "difendere" (discussed above) in numbers 18, 20, 70(x2) and 72. That verb is followed closely in numbers of occurrences by "occupare" (45, 52, 53, 66), "salute" (39, 59, 67, 74) and "rovinare" (14, 42, 58, 69). "Abbandonare" (8, 23, 78), "amore della patria" (9, 56, 76), and "congiure" (50, 51, 53) appear three times each respectively (Again, full quotations in Appendix to this Chapter). From this interesting collection of words, it seems that Machiavelli desired to show how one should act in order to bring honour to one's *patria* as well as the contrary.

It seems that those who bring honour to their respective *patrie* are praised in the *Discorsi*, whereas those who act selfishly, putting private interests before the "comune patria" and the "bene comune" are shown for what they are—traitors against the *patria*. Traitors against the *patria* also betray the common good, which for Machiavelli, entails rebellion against that form of government which best protects the "bene comune"—a republican government.

> Because it is not the particular good (*bene particulare*) but the common good (*bene comune*) that makes cities great. And without doubt this common good is not observed if not in republics: because all that promotes it is done and, even though this or that private citizen is condemned, there are so many who benefit from such good, that they are able to overcome the disposition of those few who are oppressed by it. [46]

Then, if one recalls that Machiavelli specifically linked the common good, the common *patria* and a prudent orderer of a republic, the hypothesis regarding Lorenzo and Leo X is increasingly probable:

> Therefore, a prudent organizer of a republic, who has this spirit—who desires to govern not for himself but for the common good (*bene* comune), not for his own succession, but for the common fatherland (*comune patria*)—should strive to have authority alone; neither will a wise man reprove one who takes some extraordinary action, which is used in order to found a kingdom or constitute a republic. [47]

If Machiavelli did devise a plan for the expulsion of the barbarians and the unification of Italy, one must ask two further questions: how shall one define "republic" within the context of the *Discorsi*, and what would cause a successful unifying prince to resign his dictatorial powers to a republican government?

Machiavelli is clear in his definition of republican government. Following the Roman example, Machiavelli theorized that a republic should consist of three groups: Consuls, Senators and Tribunes each bound by strict constitutional limitations. [48] The Consuls were constitutionally sanctioned to take command of the government, should crisis dictate, whereas the Senate and Tribunes would, in more peaceful times, legislate and uphold the rule of law as dictated by the constitution. That is not to say that Machiavelli believed Rome was a place of peace and tranquility. On the contrary, the Roman republican system was, according to Machiavelli, filled with tension and strife that, perhaps paradoxically, led to and promoted greater freedom. [49]

The Senate was balanced and held in check by the Tribunes.[50] The latter were democratically elected by the Plebeians. It was their duty to plead the case of the populace during legislation. This careful balance of constitutionally sanctioned power and discord between the Senate and the Tribunes, Machiavelli proposed, led to an uninterrupted period of Roman freedom and liberty.[51] Later, after periods of internal struggles and external wars, the office of dictator was created. Constitutionally sanctioned, through an amendment, for decisive and necessarily limited action, the dictator was appointed, carried out his duties to the *patria* and the *bene comune*, then resigned his office.[52] We shall return to a discussion of this office in the following Chapter. As we saw above, the common good is best protected by a republican government and the common good is, in Machiavelli's works, linked with the common *patria*.

Conclusion

If Lorenzo were to take the steps that it seems Machiavelli was calling him to take, he would find, in his *patria*, the reasons to give up his dictatorial powers. "Amore della patria" and the desire to promote the "bene comune," which is best protected by a republican government may have been that which would cause Lorenzo to resign his all-powerful office. Having done so, his name would find a place within the hallowed halls of history along with such prudent orderers as Lycurgus and Brutus, two of Machiavelli's favorite historical examples.

To conclude, *patria* seems to be a term which provides continuity between *Il Principe* and the *Discorsi* and goes some way toward answering the problems highlighted by Hans Baron at the outset of this Chapter. If the last Chapter of *Il Principe* did, indeed, call for Lorenzo to seize the *occasione* and expel the barbarians from Italy, then unite all of Italy into a single *patria*, the *Discorsi* set out what Machiavelli hoped he would do next. He wanted Lorenzo to be the Italian Lycurgus, a latter-day Brutus—but he did not want the united Italian *patria* to be founded upon religion.

CHAPTER TWO

Machiavelli's *Secular Patria*: His Sources, A Contemporary's View and the Call for Italian Unification

80C3

Machiavelli's view of religion in *Il Principe* and the *Discorsi* continues to provoke a wide spectrum of reactions. In 1559 for example, both works, along with every other product of Machiavelli's pen were placed on the *Index librorum prohibitorum*, or the Index of Prohibited Books, by the Roman Inquisition which deemed them anti-Christian, and particularly anti-papal.[1] In 1640 the first Anglophone translator of *Il Principe*, with great eloquence, produced this subtle commentary:

> Everything hath two handles, as the firebrand. It may bee taken up at one end in the bare hand without hurt: the other end being laid hold on, will cleave it to the very flesh, and the smart of it will pierce even to the heart. Sin hath the condition of the firy end, the touch of it is wounding with griefe unto the soule: nay it is worse; one sinne goes not alone, but hath many consequences. Your Grace (James Duke of Lenox, Earle of March, Baron of Setrington, etc.) may find the truth of this in your perusal of this Author.[2]

In 1950, Father Lesley Walker wrote that he found Machiavelli's "advocacy of paganism...not only repulsive but absurd."[3] Others, such as J.H. Whitfield, excuse Machiavelli's most subversive and morally questionable political language. Maurizio Viroli recently wrote that Machiavelli's views are compatible with Christianity, and indeed are part of the legacy of Christian politics handed down to the Florentines from such monumental individuals as St. Augustine and St. Thomas Aquinas.[4]

This Chapter avoids any attempt to reprove or censure Machiavelli's political view. Instead, it argues that Machiavelli's use of the term *patria* in *Il Principe* and the *Discorsi* is secular and that his "secular *patria*" may be the foundation of the new united Italy. The investigation into each work will include examples from Machiavelli's sources that will illustrate how he borrowed the term *patria* from his ancient Roman ancestors and how he modified their definitions; in effect, secularizing a term sometimes associated with religion. Machiavelli's Roman sources, particularly the writings of Cicero and Titus Livy, were scoured for the term *patria* and its derivatives with the same tools utilized for the production of the Appendices which map the term in Machiavelli. In order to provide *cinquecento* context to Machiavelli's use of *patria*, we will examine a particular work written by one of his contemporaries.

Contemporary source materials are purposely limited to Francesco Guicciardini's *Considerazioni intorno ai Discorsi del Machiavelli sopra la prima deca di Tito Livio* (1528). He was both a close friend and, conveniently for this discussion, a staunch critic of Machiavelli's approach to history and of his ideas concerned with Italian unification. We hope to show that Guicciardini was also secular in his approach to *patria*, but that he did not share in Machiavelli's dreams of a united Italy. On the contrary, he argued that Italy should remain divided.[5] There is precedent for examining Machiavelli and Guicciardini side by side. Felix Gilbert's famous *Machiavelli and Guicciardini*, is, perhaps, the best example of this precedent and has not been surpassed.[6] However, Gilbert's work was criticized for not comparing the differences between Machiavelli and Guicciardini sufficiently.[7] By examining specific elements in Machiavelli's and Guicciardini's political thought which are related to Italian unification, Gilbert's scholarship may be rounded out. For these substantive reasons, this investigation is limited to Guicciardini's *Considerazioni*, as a means of measuring Machiavelli's use of *patria* within the context of the first 30 years of the *cinquecento*.

After examining a selection of Machiavelli's sources, we will seek to build upon and test more searchingly the hypothesis stated in the previous Chapter; namely, that Machiavelli may have devised a plan for Italian liberation and unification which could only come to fruition if "amore della patria" was at its heart. This, the previous Chapter argued, would cause Lorenzo, Italy's unifying prince, to resign his dictatorial powers and allow for the creation of a united Italian republic. What follows sets out more of the specifics of Machiavelli's plan for this unification and also illustrates that it was secular in nature.

Il Principe and *De officiis*

As the previous Chapter illustrated, *patria* in *Il Principe* is not used in connection with religion of any sort, pagan or otherwise. On the contrary, it is used in association with things human and corporeal, particularly the "fondatore" who becomes prince of his *patria* by using any and every means available, moral or immoral, just or bestial.[8]

Cicero on the other hand advised those who led their *patria* to act in a way which would be decorous and human in very respect; *virtus* in other words—a ruler or citizen ought to avoid acting like a beast and provide a good example to those whom he leads or wishes to lead.[9] Much has been written of Machiavelli's undoing of Cicero's arguments, particularly relating to the famous passages on the "fox" and the "lion" in *Il Principe*. This altercation with Ciceronian political and ethical philosophy provided one of the most lively passages in Machiavelli's treatise (see below Chapter Five).[10] Here, there are more pressing issues to entertain. Given that Machiavelli was familiar with Cicero, it may prove helpful to analyze how Cicero used *patria* and its related terms in *De officiis* in order to understand whether Machiavelli altered and secularized the Ciceronian understanding of *patria*.[11]

As in the case of *Il Principe* and the *Discorsi*, it may be helpful to provide basic statistical information regarding *patria* and its derivatives in *De officiis*. The treatise is 34,200 words in length. It is divided into three books (*libri*). The first of these is divided into forty-five chapters (*capita*); the second, twenty-five; and the third, thirty-three. *Patria* and its derivatives occur in Cicero's treatise twenty-five times. In Book I, the words appear nine times and are distributed throughout five of the forty-five *capita*. Book II on the other hand only contains one reference to a derivative of *patria*, in *caput* twenty-three. Book III on the other hand contains fifteen references to *patria* or a synonymous derivative; and these are present in nine *capita*. Marginally, Book III contains the highest frequency of *patria*. This is particularly true of *Liber* III, *caput* 23. Therein one may see that *patria* and its derivative are used four times. Having examined the occurrences and distribution of *patria* in Cicero's *De officiis*, it may prove helpful to enquire into how Cicero used the term(s) (*patria*, *patriam*, *patriae*) and how, if at all, Machiavelli's use deviated from it. Each occurrence of *patria* is catalogued in an Appendix to this Chapter, following the method adopted in Chapter One.

As an inspection of that Appendix will illustrate, Cicero used *patria* in a manner which linked it with societal and moral obligations. Among these obligations, Cicero most often placed *patria* either above or equal to that obligation which one has to honour one's parents, family and friends.[12] Given that *De officiis* was written by Cicero to his son, one would expect to find such advice in its pages. How then, does Cicero's use of *patria* differ, if at all, from that of Machiavelli in *Il Principe*?

Machiavelli, contrary to Cicero, does not place any moral obligation on the prince to whom he addressed his advice book. By the same token, Machiavelli—in *Il Principe*—brushed aside Cicero's and the humanists' morality. He undermined the Ciceronian notion of what "ought" to be the truth and replaced it with the "verità effettuale."[13] These words have been translated as the "effectual truth," the "real truth," "what really happens" and "the effective truth."[14] Each of these possible translations, in its own way, helps to illustrate that Machiavelli was not concerned with ideals, but with realities (See below, Chapter Five). Furthermore, it also appears that Machiavelli purposely avoided linking his uses of *patria* with religion, where Cicero, at least one time in *De officiis* placed the citizen's obligation to the *patria* below that of the "diis immortalibus," or the "immortal gods."[15]

In contrast, it seems that Machiavelli had no time for religion—or morality for that matter—in politics. That which would free his *patria* and perhaps unite all of Italy, he recognized, would require steps traditionally viewed as unjust or immoral.[16] Indeed, political action in *Il Principe* appears to be based upon whether or not a prince is successful, not whether his actions are moral. In this case, could Machiavelli be proposing that the prince do whatever was necessary to obtain two goals: the liberation and unification of Italy? As the discussion of Machiavelli's anti-ciceronian rhetoric makes up a large part of a later Chapter, we will not pursue it further here. The goal of presenting Cicero's uses of *patria* and its derivatives was to illustrate that he, at times, subjugated his Roman *patria* to religion. For Machiavelli, by way of contrast, his *patria* was that which was to be ennobled, not by religion, but by itself.[17] Viewed in this way, the *Discorsi* present an expanded definition of *patria*; one which details how a new prince could liberate and unify Italy and then resign his dictatorial authority to an elected republican government. We sought to illustrate that Machiavelli secularized the Ciceronian definitions of *patria* in *Il Principe*, but did he do the same with Titus Livius in the *Discorsi*?

Patria in Titus Livius's *Ab urbe condita*

Much has been written on Machiavelli's sources, the structure of the *Discorsi* and how it conforms to the structure of Livy's history.[18] Scholars such as Father Lesley Walker, Felix Gilbert and J.H. Whitfield have all produced studies on this facet of Machiavelli's treatise on republics.[19] However, where political vocabulary is concerned, *patria* has been overlooked in favor of other terms such as "bene comune, il vivere politico and constituzioni."[20] As the previous Chapter illustrated, the latter words do not appear in *Il Principe*, because its subject does not call for the use of such language. They appear in the *Discorsi* because, Maurizio Viroli argued, one cannot speak of republican values, at least in sixteenth century Florence, without having recourse to the words which underpinned its vocabulary.[21] *Patria* on the other hand appears in both works, providing, one might suggest, greater continuity to them. For this reason, we shall continue to examine the term and its derivatives in the *Discorsi* in relation to the source materials from which it was drawn in order to see whether Machiavelli secularized *patria* in the *Discorsi* as he did in *Il Principe*. This may help one to understand and perhaps reconcile the differing views of *Il Principe* and the *Discorsi* and in turn it may help to illustrate that Machiavelli had a plan for Italian unification.

At this point, it may prove useful to proceed to Livy's use of the term *patria* in order to illustrate how, if at all, Machiavelli's appropriation, or re-appropriation of the given terms differs from that of Livy. The first ten books of Livy's history are 159,656 words in length, somewhat longer than Machiavelli's commentary (118,693 words). Livy's ten Books are divided thus: Book I, sixty *capita*; Book II, forty-five; Book III, seventy-two *capita*; Book IV, sixty-one; Book V, fifty-five *capita*; Book VI, forty-two *capita*; Book VII, forty-two *capita*; Book VIII, forty *capita*; Book IX, forty-six *capita*; and Book X, forty-eight *capita*. One will find *patria* and its synonymous derivatives in each book with the exception of Book X, which has none. In Book I on the other hand one will find this term or terms, fifteen times. These are distributed in six of the book's sixty *capita*. In Book II these terms occur thirteen times in five of the book's forty-five *capita*. Book III contains these terms eight times, and they are distributed in five out of seventy-two *capita*. The frequency of occurrence continues to decline in Book IV, with only six uses in three of sixty-one *capita*. The low ebb of Book IV is followed by Book V which contains the highest rate of occurrence; thirty-one times distributed in six of fifty-five *capita*. Book VI once again has a very low frequency of occurrence, similar to that of Book IV; six occurrences, distributed in three of forty-two *capita*. Book VII contains thirteen occurrences of *patria* distributed in four of forty-two *capita*. Book VIII on the other hand contains only seven references to *patria* or a related term in four of the book's forty *capita*. Finally, in Book IX, one will find these terms used nine times; distributed in three out of forty-six *capita*. Book X contains no reference to any of these terms. These rather dry statistics are drawn from the Appendix to this Chapter which provides context to each of the terms in Livy's history. Following the precedent of the previous Chapter, in the text below, the reader will finds numbers drawn from the Appendix to this Chapter. These will guide the reader to specific quotations and examples.

In numbers (5) and (6), for example, Livy linked the *patria* with religion. In the former, he reaffirmed the divinity of Rome's founder, Romulus while in the latter, Livy recounted how the gods withdrew their support from the Romans for a brief time, hoping to regain their admiration and praise. These examples from Livy provide a distillation of *patria* in Livy's *Ab urbe condita*. Livy's use of the term, a careful reading of the Appendix may confirm, is most often associated with those who act either for or against their *patria*. These examples seem to indicate that Cicero's definitions of *patria* which linked, or subordinated this term to religion and Livy's definitions are similar. This may also illustrate that Machiavelli differed from both in his secular interpretation of *patria*.

An interesting reference to *patria* in the *Discorsi* was purposely set aside until this point in the discussion. This single occurrence appears to link *patria* with religion in Machiavelli's *Discorsi*.

> Because, if they considered how religion permitted us the exaltation and the defense of the fatherland (*patria*), they would see how it also wishes that we love and honor it, and prepare ourselves to be such that we are able to defend it.[22]

How shall we deal with this example? Is it an aberration or a symptom of larger religious influences in Machiavelli? Maurizio Viroli certainly thought the latter to be true. Referring to the quotation cited above, Viroli wrote, "while the political writings of the scholastics were not among his favorite reading and he rarely went to church, even Machiavelli recognized the existence of a Christian patriotism in which the Roman themes lived."[23] In another of his works, Viroli mentions that in Florence, religion was usually viewed as subordinate to, and separate from politics.[24] Guardedly, it may prove interesting to take issue with Viroli on the former point, for the latter appears to confirm the hypothesis that Machiavelli's *patria* was secular in nature. Rather than present Machiavelli as an itinerant supporter of religion, one might suggest that the passage cited above and those who with gall enough to follow it, deserve the title, "Machiavellian."[25] In order to illustrate this point we shall examine a portion of Polybius's *Histories*, particularly Book VI. 56, which Machiavelli used as a source for *Discorsi* I. 12 and the passage cited above.

Polybius, over a millennium before Machiavelli's birth, dared to suggest that the Roman religions had no basis in fact or reality; on the contrary, they were created by those in power in order to control those who were not; instilling in the masses a fear not only of temporal punishment for the breaking of laws, but of eternal damnation that would follow.

But as the masses are always fickle, filled with lawless desires, unreasoning anger and violent passions, they can only be restrained by mysterious terrors or other dramatizations of the subject. For this reason I believe that the ancients were by no means acting foolishly or haphazardly when they introduced to the people various notions concerning the gods and belief in the punishment of Hades, but rather that the moderns are foolish and take great risks in rejecting them.[26]

Discorsi I. 12, along with II. 2, read in light of this passage from Polybius, makes one think once again of the temporary union of Rome and Florence. Is Machiavelli referring to the papal sanction under which Lorenzo would operate in order to liberate and unify Italy? Did he want Lorenzo to operate under the cloak of religion?[27]

With those questions still fresh, one may turn to a contemporary of Machiavelli's, Francesco Guicciardini. What, if anything, did he have to say about *patria*, religion and Machiavelli's proposals for a liberated and united Italy?

Patria in Guicciardini's *Considerazioni*

Guicciardini's friendship with Machiavelli provides some of the most memorable literary exchanges of the *cinquecento*. Through letters the two would meet and discuss topics as varied as playwriting and the challenges facing the Italy of their day.[28] After Machiavelli's death, and the sack of Rome, Guicciardini's political life came to a bitter end. Having made crucial errors leading up to the sack of Rome and having lost his governorship of the Romagna, Guicciardini retreated, for a time, into the study and writing of histories.[29] Might one be tempted to ask whether the "unified Romagna" which Machiavelli lauded in *Il Principe* and which Guicciardini governed had, in reality, returned to its lawless roots just after Cesare Borgia's death?[30] Perhaps this personal experience with the brigands of the Romagna tainted Guicciardini's assessment of Machiavelli's political theory with a hint of bitterness. This may prove to be the case. In 1528, for example, he produced a commentary on Machiavelli's *Discorsi*. As they provide a first-hand account of Guicciardini's opinions, untainted by the thought of bringing offence to his friend, we shall examine how *patria* and religion are viewed therein, and what, if anything, Guicciardini had to say about Italian liberation and unification. But before progressing to this, it will be helpful to provide statistical information regarding the *Considerazioni*.

Guicciardini's commentary on Machiavelli's *Discorsi* is a short work, 19,375 words in length.[31] Rather than provide a comment or critique of each of Machiavelli's *Discorsi*, Guicciardini selected thirty-nine discourses on which to pass judgment. For example, he commented on twenty-eight out of the sixty Chapters of Machiavelli's first book; eight out of thirty three from book two; and only three of forty-nine in the final book of the *Discorsi*. So, it appears that Guicciardini did not have in mind to write an exhaustive commentary on his recently deceased friend's *Discorsi*. On the contrary, it may be that he selected certain chapters for specific reasons. In particular, one might suggest, Guicciardini sought to undermine Machiavelli's arguments relating to Italian unification and liberation by a dictatorial lawgiver. Guicciardini's use of *patria* appears to bear this out. *Patria* appears in the *Considerazioni* eight times and in only three of its chapters. All of these are listed in the Appendix to this Chapter. (See 1, 2, and 6 particularly). Those examples from Guicciardini's *Considerazioni* may indicate that he understood the "verità effettuale," where Machiavelli was deluded. According to Guicciardini, the very idea that a dictatorial lawgiver would resign his office after unification, was little more than wishful thinking. It seems that Machiavelli was speaking about things as they were in his imagination, not as they were in reality and Guicciardini was not about to let him get away with it.

That said, however, Guicciardini's use of *patria* is not altogether different from Machiavelli's use thereof. This is not surprising in that Guicciardini's work is a commentary. One will find similar adjectives and modifiers used in conjunction with *patria* in Guicciardini and in Machiavelli's *Discorsi*. "Rovina" (1, 3, 4, 5, 8) and words and phrases which amount to "ruin" (i.e. "occupa la tirannide nella *patria*" to cite one example); "libertà" (6, 7), "amore della patria" (2) are all present in the *Discorsi* and were discussed in the previous Chapter (All numbers correspond to the Appendix to this Chapter). Here, however, the similarities between Machiavelli and Guicciardini come to an end.

We suggest that Guicciardini was familiar with, and indeed recognized Machiavelli's plan for Italian liberation and unification, but that he thought it was impossibly impractical in reality. The thought of Lorenzo acting as unifying prince and magnanimously laying aside his dictatorial powers, even taking into consideration "amore della patria," Guicciardini thought laughable. If one keeps this thought in mind and turns to Guicciardini's comments on Book I, Chapter Twelve of Machiavelli's *Discorsi*, one may find this developed by Guicciardini.

> It is impossible to speak so much ill of the papal court that it does not deserve worse: it is a disgrace, an example of all the ignominy and opprobrium in the world. And I also believe that the Church's greatness that is, the power that religion has given it, has been the reason why Italy has not fallen into a monarchy, because on

the one hand it has had such influence that it has been able to become the leader and summon foreign princes when necessary against those who were going to attack Italy, and on the other hand, since the Church lacked its own armies, it did not have enough forces to enable it to establish temporal dominion aside from what others were willing to grant it. But I do not really know whether Italy's not coming under a monarchy has been fortunate or unfortunate for this land. For if this might have brought glory to the name of Italy and fortune to the city that dominated, it would have been disastrous for all the others; oppressed by the shadow of one, they would have had no means of achieving any greatness whatever, since it is the custom of republics not to share the fruits of their freedom and power with any but their own citizens. [32]

Even in Guicciardini one finds the transition from a single ruler ("una monarchia") to that of a republic ("republiche"). However, as the quotations above illustrated, for Guicciardini, the thought of a unifying prince or dictator laying down his arms was simply not possible in reality. His assessment of Machiavelli, though stinging, sheds light on the hypothesis which we are seeking to demonstrate—Machiavelli believed that the special *occasione* which linked the interests of Florence and Rome could see Italy liberated and united

Guicciardini's sentiments have much in common with Peter Laven's arguments (above, Chapter One). Nevertheless one can seek to illustrate that Machiavelli believed—perhaps naively—that his plan for unification would work. By so doing, one might be able to view Machiavelli in a different light. The picture that is beginning to emerge is of an idealist who clung so desperately to the idea of an ennobled Florence and a united Italy, that he became blind to the impracticalities of his goals. This naiveté has, for the most part, gone unnoticed, with the majority of scholars seeking to uncover in Machiavelli the first glimpse of modern political realism. That is not to say that Niccolò Machiavelli's ideas do not contain tantalizing hints of such realism and its shocking excuses for immorality for which he has been much maligned. Indeed, by the very same token, the political necessity in Machiavelli's plan for Italian unification would cause the princely unifier to reject all morality for the sake of the common good—the liberation and unification of Italy.

Necessità and the *Secular Patria*

In Machiavelli's concept of political necessity, which is at the heart of *Il Principe* and the *Discorsi* both, Christian and pagan morality are left by the wayside to be replaced by a new type of morality that focuses completely on the maintenance of the common good and thus, the *patria*.[33] In Machiavelli's new morality, any action that benefits the *patria* must be considered a political good and therefore a political necessity. In *Il Principe*, Machiavelli used the examples of two Spaniards, Ferdinand of Aragon and Cesare Borgia, to illustrate that concept. Both men used religion to attain a secular goal—political unification.[34] Ferdinand used the "cloak of religion" to unify Spain swiftly and mercilessly. Borgia's unification—with the financial backing of his father, Pope Alexander VI—of the Romagna cannot be compared in scale with Ferdinand's unification of Spain, but because the goals and outcomes were identical, and Machiavelli admired their successes, both must be examined. While the *Discorsi* provide an excellent example of Machiavelli's belief in political necessity, drained of all forms of religious consideration; it is necessary, in order to lay the foundations for the discussion of the *Discorsi*, which conclude this Chapter, to examine political necessity in *Il Principe*.

Any deed that benefits the *patria* can be judged to be good, as the examples of Ferdinand of Aragon and Cesare Borgia in *Il Principe* indicate.[35] Do Ferdinand and Cesare provide examples that Machiavelli hoped Lorenzo would imitate? This seems to be the case. The *occasione* was there to be seized, if only Lorenzo would ask Pope Leo X to support his drive for unification as the papacy had done in the Spanish *reconquista*. After Ferdinand achieved his goals he turned on the papacy. Thereafter, the Spanish monarchy often insisted on its independence of the Roman Church.[36] Machiavelli did not want Lorenzo to replace the Roman Church with religious institutions answerable to him as Ferdinand had done with the establishment of the Inquisition. On the contrary, it seems that he wanted Lorenzo to remove religion from politics and thus the *patria* altogether. The protection of the *patria* and bringing honour to it formed the centerpiece of Machiavelli's notion of political necessity. He knew that in order to unite Florence and Italy, Lorenzo would have to act in a manner that went against Christian and pagan morality.[37] The new prince would have to fashion himself after Cesare Borgia.

Borgia united the Romagna with the money and prestige of Pope Alexander VI—his father.[38] After he achieved unification, Cesare completely removed the Church from his political considerations. The Church had no place in Cesare's united Romagna. It was replaced by political necessity as the means of promoting the common good as the savage execution of Remirro de' Orco illustrates.[39] Machiavelli went on to write that, "non saprei reprenderlo" ("I cannot possibly censure him"). Despite all of his brutality, Borgia's understanding of political necessity brought about his rise to power and more importantly the unification of the Romagna.[40] The famous examples of Ferdinand and Borgia in *Il Principe* contain Machiavelli's explicit advice for the new prince. Is there similar advice to be found in the *Discorsi*?

Vickie B. Sullivan recently wrote that in Machiavelli's *Discorsi* and the definitions of political necessity therein, Machiavelli "suggests there is an excuse for the harshness of his teaching."[41] Sullivan's study is a measured analysis of Machiavelli's secular notion of politics. However, *patria* does not play a role in her study and it is worth adding it as a new dimension.[42]

Sullivan intently focuses on Book Three, Chapter Twelve of the *Discorsi* entitled "Come uno capitano prudente debbe imporre ogni necessità di combattere a' suoi soldati, e a quegli degli inimici, tòrla." (That a Prudent General should make it absolutely necessary for his own Troops to fight, but should avoid forcing the enemy to do so).[43] She notes that Machiavelli "entirely ignores the divine realm."[44] Necessity, as detailed by Machiavelli and expanded upon by Sullivan, in Book Three, Chapter Twelve of the *Discorsi*, is the necessity not only of brutal warfare, but also the condition of constant preparedness that enables an army instantly to take the offensive. Only in preparedness, brutality and strength does a soldier have the chance of keeping himself alive. Patriotic sentiment, in the *Discorsi* as in the closing Chapter of *Il Principe* enables and intensifies selflessness and heroism in warfare. One can juxtapose this scenario and place the same form of necessity on the *patria*. Preparedness and on occasion, brutality, are political necessities that enable the *patria* to survive. Yet, Machiavelli is not calling for a consistently bloodthirsty citizenry, but a citizenry that is willing to die to protect its *patria*.

Military preparedness is a constant in Machiavelli's theory, yet brutality is only necessary when the survival or the unification of the *patria* is in question. Therefore, Machiavelli's political necessity is strictly bound by political morality; moral in the sense that "good" is that which benefits the *patria* and "evil" is that which brings harm to it. So, Machiavelli sets up a distinct contrast between that which is perceived as "good" or "evil" in Christian and pagan morality and that which is "good" or "evil" in his concept of political necessity.[45]

Political necessity in Machiavelli's political works requires a certain measure of "azione straordinaria" (extraordinary action) but it does not require a thirst for blood.[46] On the contrary, it requires a thirst for the security and prosperity offered by a unified secular *patria*. Paradoxically, Machiavelli's prince needed to accept the necessity of brutality to achieve peace. The question that needs to be addressed at this point is, why did Machiavelli hope that Lorenzo, after unification, would completely remove the church from the political arena?

The answer Machiavelli provides is as follows:

The Church, not being, therefore, powerful enough to occupy the whole of Italy, nor having allowed another to occupy it, has been the cause why it (Italy) is not able to come under one headship, but has been under many princes and *signori*, from which is born such disunion and such weakness that is has been the prey, not only of barbarian powers, but of anyone who assaults it. [47]

This passage, perhaps an intensification of similar sentiment set out in Chapter of XI of *Il Principe*, sums up Machiavelli's view of the mingling of politics and religion. Such a mixture, he argued, was the root cause of Italy's disunion and despair because successive popes had not only refused to cease meddling in the secular world, but had invited looting and plundering hordes and invasion after invasion across the Alps. The papacy was, according to Machiavelli, politically as well as geographically responsible for the division of Italy.

Garrett Mattingly's classic survey of Renaissance diplomacy summed up the root causes of Machiavelli's distaste for the papacy as follows: "each pope was compelled, in pursuit of his ambitions, to employ the arms of foreigners against Italians, so that each left Italy weaker than he found it." Echoing Guicciardini, Mattingly went on to describe the contradiction in papal politics, for each, while working with foreign powers, was simultaneously struggling to keep the central papal states free from foreign control. The popes referred to are Alexander VI (1492–1503), Julius II (1503–1513), and Leo X (1513–1521). Machiavelli admired all of them to a varying degree, due to their political cleverness, military strength, or because they offered a chance for Italy to be freed from the barbarians. Yet, he hated them precisely for these same reasons, because they, working like instruments of the barbarians, allowed Italy to be further shattered. All these sought to extend the temporal power of their own office. The papacy did nothing for the good of Italy. This concept of the papacy as an instrument of foreign power is a key concept that must be discussed. [48]

The early sixteenth century popes, all to a varying degree, worked with the foreign occupiers, Spain and France; sometimes with one or with both. This at once made the office an "evil" cohort of the barbarian, yet it also made the papacy the only office in Italy capable of maintaining a balance of power in the peninsula. Machiavelli, realizing the opportunity this presented for freeing Italy, seized upon both notions. Lorenzo and Leo, working in tandem, mirroring Cesare Borgia and Alexander VI, could bring about successful Italian unification centered at Florence. However, Machiavelli was careful to list the reasons for Borgia's and Alexander's failure; almost all of which were, according to Machiavelli, due to faith in the power of the pope.[49] One might be tempted to ask, did he want to instruct Lorenzo and Leo how to avoid repeating the same mistakes while at the same time far surpassing the Borgia's successes?

From Dictatorship to Republic? Theory and Practice

Scrutiny of Machiavelli's republican political theory may help one to understand the significance of the transitional phase, from principality to republic, within Machiavelli's overall political theory for Italian unification. By the same token, such a line of investigation may help to answer the questions asked above. It has been argued previously that the new Italian *patria*, and the new prince's obligations to it, would cause him to renounce his position, thereby returning political power to a new, unified Italian citizenry. In theory, such a plan sounds plausible, particularly in light of the persuasive and stirring rhetoric in which Machiavelli couched his theory.[50]

When one reads the final Chapter of *Il Principe*, it becomes clear that Machiavelli tried to draw attention to the Florentine/Church link. Such a union, and the *occasione* it represented, would necessitate a temporary melding of Florentine and Church interests for the purpose of unification. However, after unification in his theory, Machiavelli makes no mention of a united church and *patria*. On the contrary, there is evidence in *Il Principe*'s epilogue that Machiavelli desired the opposite.

For Machiavelli, Italian unification was a cause supported by "iustizia grande." Because, as Livy wrote, "iustum enim est bellum quibus necessarium, et pia arma ubi nulla nisi in armis spes est." (Because a necessary war is a just war and where there is hope only in arms, those arms are holy).[51] Machiavelli's hope was not in the divine but in *arms*; the arms of a united Italian citizen army, captained by Lorenzo de' Medici. The special *occasione* that existed in Lorenzo and Leo X's familial bond, along with the wealth and prestige such a bond offered, appear to be the only reasons that Machiavelli introduced the church into his plan for Italian unification. As the previous Chapter argued, it appears that Machiavelli wanted Lorenzo's unificatory push to work in cooperation with Leo X, effectively making Lorenzo a dictator. The specifics of the dictator's role articulated in the *Discorsi* may help further to illustrate the secular nature of Machiavelli's *patria* and Lorenzo's role in the unification process, but it may also illustrate that Machiavelli's theory was hopelessly idealistic. The following quotation from the *Discorsi*, when read in light of the epilogue to *Il Principe* may demonstrate this:

> And those Romans who created the office of the Dictator in Rome are condemned by some writers as the cause of the time of tyranny in that city; citing as the first tyrant the one who commanded it with this title, "Dictator," saying that, if that office had not been created, Caesar would not have been able—under any public title—to make his tyranny appear honest. This case was not well examined by the one who held this opinion, and it was believed against all reason.[52]

Machiavelli clearly viewed the office of dictator as beneficial rather than detrimental to the Roman republic: "perché e' non fu nome né il grado del Dittatore che facesse serva Roma, ma fu l'autorità presa dai cittadini per la lunghezza dello imperio" ("For it was neither the name nor the rank of the dictator which made Rome servile, but the loss of authority of which the citizens were deprived by the length of his rule").[53] Machiavelli continued with the discourse on dictatorships:

> One sees that as long as the Dictatorship was given by public order, and not by his own authority, that it was always good for the city. Because magistrates who are made and authority given by extraordinary means, not those given by ordinary means, hurt republics; one sees that in Rome—for such a long period of time—a Dictator never did anything if it was not good for the republic.[54]

Machiavelli made a clear distinction between Caesar—the tyrant—and the appointed office of dictator. The dictator, while his office possessed extensive powers, was bound by his obligation to the rule of law, the common good and therefore, the *patria*; and that office was only appointed for a short time.[55] Again, Machiavelli specifies that the dictator's role is necessary, yet limited by duty to the republic and to his *patria*: the exact opposite of a tyrant who spurns the rule of law, the common good and the *patria* for his own selfish interests. The dictator, as a prudent orderer, in stark contrast to the tyrant, acknowledges that the common good and the republic are directly linked with the common *patria*. This sentiment placed Machiavelli's republican writings squarely in line with the Ciceronian tradition.[56] Indeed, Machiavelli clearly separates the true dictator and the tyrant masquerading as dictator.

> The reasons for this are most evident. First, if a citizen who wishes to, is able to commit offense and steal extraordinary authority, it happens that he has many qualities, which in an uncorrupted republic it is impossible for him to have: because he needs to be rich and to have many adherents and partisans, which one is not able to have where the laws are observed.[57]

This brief passage appears to be a concise condemnation of the Medici and of Florence. The fact that this quotation appears in Machiavelli's discourse on dictators presents a dilemma. How can one reconcile such an admission with Machiavelli's theory for secular Italian unification which is based upon the Medici *occasione*?

Machiavelli was painfully aware of the Medici family's penchant for machination, which either kept them in power or consistently close to it in Florence. Indeed, with their powerful connections and the prestige attached to their name, the Medici came to power, each time, in precisely the manner that Machiavelli described above.[58] This highlights a definite problem in Machiavelli's theory for Italian liberation and unification. Why would Machiavelli expect Lorenzo to act any differently if he attempted to re-order Florence and then all of Italy? In order to get around this problem, it seems that, naively, Machiavelli reasoned that the new prince, or orderer, would be bound like every citizen to his *patria*. This would cause him to resign his all-powerful office once unification was complete allowing for the creation of a united Italian republican government under a united "secular *patria*."

Conclusion

The *occasione* of a Medici pope and Florentine *Capitano* provided, according to Machiavelli, the best opportunity for such unification since Cesare Borgia and Alexander VI had unified the Romanga. In light of the epilogue to *Il Principe* and the passages in the *Discorsi* which deal with the office of the dictator, it seems that Machiavelli thought that Lorenzo and Leo, after unification, would separate Church and *patria*. Such a separation, combined with Lorenzo's abdication of dictatorial powers would allow for the creation of a united Italy under a "secular *patria*" and a republican regime as detailed in the *Discorsi*. Furthermore, with the end of Lorenzo's office, the *occasione* would end. The interests of Florence and Rome would diverge. Such a departure would allow for the separation of Church and *patria*, creating a religious centered Church and a politically based "secular *patria*"; the two would never again be mixed. This vision, despite its genius, was flawed. Guicciardini, ever the realist, recognized this, and pulled the rug from under his friend's feet.

If Lorenzo and Leo achieved such success, Guicciardini argued that there was nothing that could induce a unifying prince—particularly a Medici—to give up his arms other than force. John Hale gave later voice to Guicciardini's concerns in his *Florence and the Medici*.[59] When had a Medici prince ever willingly given up headship of the Florentine government out of goodwill and feelings of duty toward Florence's citizens? Never. This time, the "verità effettuale" appears to have escaped Machiavelli the realist. Rather, he appears increasingly to be the idealist whose plans were based more on theory than fact; more on hopes than realities. Machiavelli's political vision, as made manifest in *Il Principe* and the *Discorsi*, was not applicable to the context in which it was formulated. While this may ultimately illustrate the naivety of his vision, paradoxically, it also highlights his genius.

The "modernity" of Machiavelli's theory which separated Church and *patria*, one might argue, is a daring and precocious conceptual experiment in the history of secular nationhood, recognizable to contemporary historians and political scientists, but utterly alien to his contemporaries. By what means was Lorenzo to prosecute Italian unification? Machiavelli's answer was a citizen army. Here too, his blindness or aloofness to present Italian circumstances in the *cinquecento*, induced perhaps, by overzealous patriotism, led him to theorize about equally recognizable, though thoroughly impractical solutions to Italy's ills.

CHAPTER THREE

The Secretary and the Citizen Army: Theory and Practice

૪୬୯୫

Building upon the discussions of Chapters One and Two, which illustrated the secularism of Machiavelli's view of *patria* in *Il Principe* and the *Discorsi*, and also the impracticality of his plan for unifying Italy under that *patria*, it may prove helpful to examine additional aspects of that plan. Hans Baron pointed out that Machiavelli's two works appear to be irreconcilable with one another due to their content.[1] This is, as was demonstrated previously, an unfounded concern. Rather, *Il Principe* and the *Discorsi*, while different in the majority of their political vocabulary, are united by Machiavelli's concept of the "secular *patria*."[2] One might be tempted to ask whether the similarities between *Il Principe* and the *Discorsi* end there.

In seeking to answer this question, it may prove beneficial to demonstrate that Machiavelli's two most famous works, *Il Principe* and the *Discorsi*, appear to be linked further by military considerations and particularly the subject of the citizen army. Indeed, this continuity seems to indicate that "the citizen army," in Machiavelli's theory, would provide the means for Italian liberation and unification under a secular *patria*; but it also may shed light on a further short-coming of his political vision.

In a further assertion of Machiavelli's lack of realism, one might argue that he had lost contact with what was actually happening on the battlefields of Italy. It seems that he developed such an infatuation with the idea of the citizen army and how such an army could unify Italy that he became blinded to the practicalities and realities of warfare in the first quarter of the *cinquecento*. This is borne out in the pages of the *Arte della guerra*, written just after the *Discorsi*. In the *Arte* Machiavelli argued that a citizen army provided superior defensive and offensive capabilities, but he absurdly discounted the necessity of artillery and gunpowder on the battlefield.[3]

This Chapter shall examine Machiavelli's ideas concerned with the citizen army in *Il Principe*, the *Discorsi* and the *Arte*, demonstrating a distinct continuity in his political works—and a further shortcoming of his political vision. The greatest emphasis will be placed on *Il Principe*; particularly Chapters VII, XII, XIII and XXVI because they are central to Machiavelli's military considerations in that book and the groundwork upon which similar considerations in the *Discorsi* and *Arte* are based. The chief protagonist in these Chapters is Cesare Borgia. His ruthless, secular unification of the Romanga which operated under the guise of Church cooperation, provided a blueprint of sorts by which a new prince could unify Italy. Borgia's success, Machiavelli argued, could be traced to his reliance on a citizen army, not mercenary troops. One might suggest that Machiavelli wanted Lorenzo de' Medici to follow Borgia's example, but on a national scale. The last Chapter of *Il Principe*, read in light of Chapters VII, XII and XIII, which focus upon Borgia, appears to demonstrate this point. After the examination of *Il Principe*, it may prove helpful to examine passages from the *Discorsi* and the *Arte* which are complementary to those in Machiavelli's treatise on principalities. These passages will demonstrate a distinct continuity between these three works, while also exemplifying Machiavelli's inability to come to terms with the warfare of his day. Indeed, all of these examples may illustrate that Machiavelli's theory for the creation of a citizen army, at least on paper, appeared to be practicable, but in reality, laughable.

Utilizing the scholarship of Michael Mallett, Sydney Anglo, and Machiavelli's contemporary Guicciardini, it may be shown that Machiavelli's writings concerned with the citizen army were not grounded in practice, but only in theory.[4] This may be because all of his major works, *Il Principe*, the *Discorsi* and the *Arte*, were written after he was sent into exile, cutting him off from the ins-and-outs of politics in Florence (the subject of the following Chapter). It is equally probable that his unending praise of ancient sources which he studied relentlessly in exile, led to the exclusion and derision of modern (*cinquecento*) warfare, its practicalities and its tactics in exchange for outdated and outmoded musings.

Moreover, Machiavelli's refusal to acknowledge the importance and successful deployment of mercenary troops in the Italian wars proves to be all the more shocking when one realizes that Prato and the Florentine Republic, under Soderini, fell to Spanish mercenaries acting under the auspices of the Pope Julius II and the Medici family. When one adds to this bloody concoction that Florence and poor Prato were "defended" by a Florentine citizen army which Machiavelli was instrumental in constituting, the absurdity of his vision is brought to the fore.[5] It may have been Machiavelli's and Florence's experience during the Pisan wars (1498–1509) that mercenary troops in *their* employment were cowardly, but the Florentine citizen army proved to be equally unreliable when faced with a small band of well-trained Spanish mercenaries (1512).[6] This defeat led to the Medici restoration and eventually to Machiavelli's exile. Disaffected and detached from political life in Florence, his political and military theory filled "il capo di castellucci."[7]

The Theory of the Citizen Army in *Il Principe*, the *Discorsi* and the *Arte della guerra*

Chapters VII, XII, XIII and XXVI of *Il Principe* contain specific advice on why one ought to place one's hopes in a citizen army rather than in mercenary or auxiliary troops. On examination, it seems that Machiavelli's theory for the citizen army begins with his discussions of Cesare Borgia and reaches a crescendo in the work's final Chapter. Did Machiavelli want Lorenzo to follow Cesare's example on a national scale? Given the conclusions of the previous Chapters and the attention paid—in *Il Principe*— to Cesare's successes and his ultimate failure, it seems that Machiavelli indeed desired Lorenzo to follow Cesare's example. However, Machiavelli did not want Lorenzo to repeat Cesare's mistake of relying for too long on the prestige afforded him by the papacy. An examination of *Il Principe* will help to illustrate this.

Chapter VII of *Il Principe*, "De' principati nuovi che s'acquistano con le armi e fortuna di altri," or "New Principalities Acquired with the Help of Fortune and Foreign Arms," contains Machiavelli's description of Borgia's rise to power.[8] The title of the Chapter is somewhat misleading. Machiavelli does not praise Borgia's use of foreign arms—mercenary or auxiliary—but his recognition that in order to be successful he would need arms of his own. The reasons Machiavelli set forth for this switch in Borgia's military strategy are, to Machiavelli at least, evident: Borgia relied on his own arms rather than the hired arms of others.[9] Based upon Machiavelli's conclusions in that Chapter, one may be led to believe that the army which Borgia later used was entirely made up of citizens from the provinces and cities that he had conquered and re-ordered. As a result—according to *Il Principe*—the Romagna became so loyal to Borgia that even as he lay stricken with syphilitic complications in Rome, "the Romagna waited for him more than a month."[10] Borgia never returned and his armies dissolved, but his example, as set forth by Machiavelli, nonetheless may provide a good place from which to develop this investigation.[11]

Indeed, it may be helpful to examine why, in *Il Principe*, Machiavelli viewed mercenary troops as utterly undependable. He provides the answer in Chapter XII of the treatise.

The reason for this is, they have neither love, nor any other cause to keep them on the battlefield, except that little stipend, which is not sufficient to make them want to die for you. [12]

According to Machiavelli, mercenaries are cowardly as XIII of *Il Principe* indicates and their counterparts—auxiliary soldiers—are too brave; "In summation, in mercenaries cowardice is more dangerous, and *virtù* with auxiliaries."[13] Machiavelli makes a point of differentiating between mercenary and auxiliary troops. His distinction between these is not altogether clear.

For example, mercenaries are those troops for which one pays as the quotation above illustrated. But are the means by which auxiliary troops are obtained any different from mercenary troops? Machiavelli defined auxiliary troops as follows; "Auxiliary armies, which are the other sort of useless armies, are involved when one calls a (great) power which, with its arms, comes to help and defend you."[14] In both cases, the host is being made to pay in one form or other for the services of an army. With mercenaries a government is forced to pay the army directly; with auxiliaries, a government is forced to pay that government which lent the troops with allegiance or cash. Given this consistency, there does not seem to be a need to provide separate definitions for mercenary and auxiliary troops in Machiavelli's theory; and this seems to be illustrated in *Il Principe*.[15]

If we return to Borgia, we will see that according to Machiavelli, he only became famous and respected after he had assembled his own armies. Indeed, as a variety of the passages cited from *Il Principe* imply, Borgia and the Romagna prospered because both placed their trust for common defense as well as military offence in the hands of a citizen army. Such solid military foundations, at least according to Machiavelli, are the precursors to an equally solid set of laws[16]. Providing a distinct contrast to his definitions of hired troops, Machiavelli elaborated on "good arms" or "buone arme."

And by experience one sees that only princes and armed republics make the greatest progress and that mercenary armies bring nothing if not damnation—and with what difficulty a republic that possesses its own army comes under the subjugation of one of its own citizens compared with one which is armed with foreigners (or foreign arms). [17]

With the example of Cesare Borgia still fresh in his mind, it may be that Machiavelli hoped another prince would arise and succeed where Cesare had failed, by successfully throwing off the yoke of reliance on foreign arms, for native Italian troops. Chapter XXVI of *Il Principe* certainly seems to call for such a prince.[18] Machiavelli's theory did not end there. On the contrary, he exhorted the reader of his *Il Principe*, perhaps Lorenzo (as discussed in Chapter One), to rely on "la virtù italica" to liberate Italy. The following passage remains in the Italian to illustrate the importance of that term. The reader will find the translation in the note.

> Volendo dunque la illustre casa vostra seguitare quelli eccellenti uomini che redimirno le provincie loro, è necessario, innanzi a tutte l'altre cose, come vero fondamento d'ogni impresa, provvedersi d'arme proprie; perché non si può avere né più fidi né più migliori soldati. E, benché ciascuno di essi sia buono, tutti insieme diventeranno migliori, quando si vedranno comandare dal loro principe, e da quello onorare et intrattenere. È necessario, per tanto, prepararsi a queste arme, per potere con la *virtù italica* defendersi dalli esterni.[19]

By carefully choosing to use "italica", which in itself carries connotations of antiquity, Machiavelli introduced the idea of regaining or restoring what had been lost since the Romans dominated the Italian peninsula. Interestingly, this occurrence of "italica" is unique among the political and literary works written by Machiavelli.[20] Such deliberate word selection prepares the reader for the call to unite Italy with a citizen army and also the quotation from Petrarch which ends *Il Principe*. Both of these, Machiavelli's "virtù italica" and Petrarch's "virtù" and "antico valore," act as reference points, drawing the reader's mind back to the glory of ancient Rome. Could such glory be regained under Lorenzo's leadership? It seems that Machiavelli thought so.[21]

It appears that Machiavelli's belief in the citizen army, which was rooted in his belief of the inherent strength and *virtù* of Italians, led him to deride all other types of soldiers. It may be that he wanted Lorenzo to adopt a similar approach to warfare. However, it is clear that Machiavelli wanted Italy's new unifier to avoid Cesare's mistake of putting too much trust in the power of the papacy.[22]

While Cesare's father Pope Alexander VI lived, he succeeded in unifying the Romagna and advancing his own cause across the peninsula; causing the Spanish and French to take notice of his actions.[23] However, after his father's death, and the unexpected death of his successor Pope Pius III, Cesare panicked, allowing Giuliano della Rovere to ascend to the papal thrown as Julius II. With this election, might one suggest that the Borgia *occasione* ended?

After Julius's election, Cesare was squeezed from power and forced into obscurity. Any chance for further secular unification was crushed by the Church, leaving Julius in a position of ever-increasing strength. Julius took up the cause of liberating Italy from foreign oppression, re-imbuing Cesare's secular drive for unification with a distinct religiosity. As "esempli freschi," these men and their actions may have informed Machiavelli's own theory concerning the citizen army, and the liberation and unification of Italy. Could it be that in the last Chapter of *Il Principe* that Machiavelli was exhorting Lorenzo to act quickly while the union of Medici Pope and Florentine *Capitano*—the Medici *occasione*—lasted?[24]

In light of the previous Chapter's conclusions, this appears to be the case. Indeed, Machiavelli's secular notion of *patria* appears to have prompted him to exhort Lorenzo to rely, not on religion or the Church, or upon money, but upon "buoni soldati" as the liberators and unifiers of Italy. One may find this sentiment in the *Discorsi* where Machiavelli carried on disparaging the use of mercenary soldiers and exhorting a prince or temporary dictator to use his own troops to gain wealth and reputation for his *patria*.

Book Two, Chapter 10 of his *Discorsi*, entitled "I danari non sono il nervo della guerra, secondo che è la comune opinione," ("Money is not the Sinew of War, as is Common Opinion") provides one of the most concentrated discussions of mercenary troops and their shortcomings in Machiavelli's *oeuvre*.[25] Therein, Machiavelli attempted to set aright those who "mistakenly" believe that money is the "sinew of war" and thus that mercenaries or gold can buy peace, liberty or victory. He set himself the difficult task of trying to change "common opinion."[26]

According to Machiavelli, and his source for this discourse, Titus Livy, the victorious Romans—under the Republic—were successful precisely because their army was made up of their own native and naturalized citizens and not the hired arms of others.[27] The discourse in Book Two, Chapter 10 of the *Discorsi* seems to indicate that Machiavelli's theory of the citizen army crosses the boundaries between the *Discorsi* and *Il Principe* drawing them together. In both works, Machiavelli exhorted his reader to abandon the practice of hiring troops to wage war. One may conclude that Machiavelli hoped Lorenzo, following Cesare Borgia's example on a national scale, would raise a native Italian army, liberate Italy and unite it. One may find that a similar theme links these works with the *Arte della guerra*.

Written in 1519, the *Arte* provides a complementary picture to that which came to the fore in *Il Principe* and the *Discorsi*. It is dedicated entirely to unpacking Machiavelli's plan for restoring a citizen army in Italy and shunning the practice of hiring troops. Written in the form of a dialogue, its protagonists include: Cosimo Rucellai, Fabrizio di Colonna, Zanobi Buondelmonti, Battista della Palla and Luigi Alamanni. Cosimo, Zanobi, Battista and Luigi act as sounding boards off which Colonna (Machiavelli's voice in the *Arte*) reflects upon the virtues of the ancients and the superiority of a citizen army. A quotation from the *Arte* will demonstrate that it expands upon the topic of the citizen army introduced in *Il Principe* and the

Discorsi.[28]

For example:

> So, when a prince or a republic will endure toil and will place diligence in these
> orders and in these armies, he will always have in his country, and there always will
> be, good soldiers; and they will be superior to their neighbors. Indeed, they will be
> those that give rather than receive laws from other men. But, as I have said to you,
> the disorder in which we live at present is that which cuts us off from the past—and
> these things are not esteemed. Therefore our armies are no good; and if there were
> leaders or natural virtuosos among us, they would not be able to demonstrate it.[29]

Four years after he completed *Il Principe*, Machiavelli continued to praise
the citizen army as this quotation illustrates. However, when one reads the
final line cited above, it becomes clear that he realized Lorenzo would never
do what he hoped. Indeed, the young Medici died in 1519, the year
Machiavelli wrote the *Arte*. When one reads the closing lines of the *Arte* in
this knowledge, they sound as much like a lament at an *occasione* lost, as a
hope of things to come.[30]

It seems that the conclusion of the work draws together *Il Principe*, the
Discorsi and the *Arte* as Franco Fido intimated:

> The clear relationship between *The Prince*, the *Discourses on Livy*, and the *Art of
> War* may tempt one to see them as panels of a triptych on the art of founding,
> governing, and defending the state, respectively. In fact, in this sense, the *Art of War*
> represents a conciliation of the first two, inasmuch as, like the *Discourses on Livy*, it
> extols the harmonious and lawful cooperation of all the components of the social
> organism and, at the same time, stresses the necessity of a unified military command
> that is reminiscent of the concentration of all power in one person expounded in *The
> Prince*.[31]

Fido is right to point out the relationship between Machiavelli's works. But
as well as acting as a conciliatory work, the *Arte* is as much Machiavelli
grasping for legitimacy through ancient texts. Indeed, the originality of *Il
Principe* and the *Discorsi* gave way to exceedingly long, often unaltered
quotations from the ancients in the *Arte*. Might one suggest that Machiavelli,
rather than communing briefly and fruitfully with the ancients, as in *Il
Principe* and the *Discorsi*, gave himself over to them completely in the *Arte*?
In their company, perhaps, he found solace for the *occasione* lost, and
possible vindication for his own failed political career.

A particular passage in the text may provide a brief glimpse into
Machiavelli's personal experience with the failed citizen army at Florence.[32]
Referring to that army which he helped to create at Florence, and perhaps
trying to excuse its cowardice and failure, Machiavelli linked Florence's

citizen army with those of ancient Rome and Carthage.[33] It seems that Machiavelli's reliance on the ancients may have provided him with some comfort. Since Rome's and Carthage's citizen armies could fail then rebound, surely Florence's could do the same. Perhaps the young Medici could have united Italy with a citizen army, as the final Chapter of *Il Principe* suggested. If only Lorenzo had successfully implemented Machiavelli's theory, might Italy have been liberated and united and the exiled Secretary restored? (See below, Chapter Four) However, Machiavelli's hopes proved to be misplaced. By the time he sat down to write the *Arte*, Lorenzo was dying, along with the Medici *occasione* and Machiavelli's chance for political redemption. It seems that Machiavelli's fixation with grand dreams and speculations about liberation and unification caused his political and military vision to break away from reality.

Practice versus Theory in *Il Principe*, the *Discorsi* and the *Arte*

The work of Machiavelli's contemporary, Francesco Guicciardini, and, in our own time, of Michael Mallett and Sydney Anglo enables us to compare Machiavelli's theories with the actual practice of warfare in the Italy of his day. Mallett commented upon Machiavelli's *Il Principe*, Guicciardini commented upon the *Discorsi* and Anglo wrote about military considerations in the *Arte*; and we shall set out their assessments in that order.

As the quotations cited above from *Il Principe* indicated, Machiavelli actually *believed* that Cesare Borgia shunned the hiring of mercenary troops and preferred to use his own troops. Michael Mallett reflected that such views were terribly misguided and not based in reality:

> Machiavelli was a Florentine whose experience of the *condottieri* was largely limited to the one army in Italy which had failed to achieve the permanence and professionalism of those of the other major states. He admired the army of Cesare Borgia but believed mistakenly that its strength lay in a high proportion of militia, whereas the bulk of Borgia troops were mercenaries like any other army.[34]

Indeed Mallett went so far as to suggest that Machiavelli's views were "anachronistic and his solutions unrealistic… his preoccupation with a national militia as the solution to the problem of national strength blinded him to the more realistic alternatives of the time"; namely the use of mercenary troops.[35] As Mallett indicated, Borgia did use *some* native troops, but the *majority* were mercenaries. This assessment of Machiavelli's theory of the citizen army in *Il Principe* starkly set out Machiavelli's lack of realism in military matters. It also suggests that Machiavelli's theory for the liberation and unification of Italy as set out in *Il Principe* was fatally flawed. May one say the same of the *Discorsi*?

According to Francesco Guicciardini, undoubtedly, one must answer "yes." As the previous Chapter illustrated, Guicciardini reserved intense criticism for Machiavelli. This instance is no different. As an individual who had experienced the horrors of war first-hand, Guicciardini was perhaps better able to comment on the effectiveness of mercenary troops and the "common opinion" which states that money is the sinew of war.

> Whoever was the author of the maxim that the sinews of war are money and those who later repeated it did not mean that money alone was enough to wage war, or that it was more necessary than soldiers, for that would have been not only a false belief but also a quite ridiculous one. It meant that those who waged war had a very great need of money and that without money it was impossible to keep it going, because it is necessary not only for paying soldiers but for providing weapons, provisions, spies, ammunition, and much equipment used in warfare. These things are required in such superabundance that it is impossible for those who have not experienced it to imagine it. Although an army lacking in money sometimes provides it by its *virtù* and with the aid of victories, nevertheless, such examples are extremely rare, especially in our day; in every case and at all times money does not run after armies until after they have won. I grant that those who have their own soldiers wage war with less money than those who have mercenaries; nevertheless, those who wage war with their own soldiers also need money, and not everyone has his own soldiers; it is much easier to get soldiers with money than to get money with soldiers. So anyone who construes the maxim according to the meaning of the one who said it, and according to how it is commonly understood, will not be surprised by it or in any way condemn it.[36]

Guicciardini's *Considerazioni intorno ai Discorsi del Machiavelli sopra la prima deca di Tito Livio*, his commentary on Machiavelli's *Discorsi*, contain a systematic unraveling of Machiavelli's discourse on money and war.[37] Each instance that Machiavelli set forth, Guicciardini refuted. For example, where Machiavelli said that it was easier for soldiers to get or find money, Guicciardini countered with advice to the contrary. Perhaps Machiavelli's unrealistic approach to mercenaries and citizen armies was linked to his lack of experience in actual warfare. This may help to explain why he held on to his beliefs in the face of the failure of Florence's citizen army, and indeed why he held on to those beliefs until the end of his life.

The *Arte della guerra* provides a later and altogether more startling glimpse into Machiavelli's perverse clinging on to the theory of the citizen army. One might suggest, as Sydney Anglo has, that this may be explained by his dreams and desires for a united Italy; "Machiavelli...concentrates upon the means whereby conditions might be established which would enable such a (republican) government to develop from the ruins of contemporary Italy."[38] However, the means which Machiavelli set forth were completely impracticable. In seeking to devise a plan to save Italy from the barbarians and give it greatness with a united republican government, Machiavelli lost sight of the realities of warfare in the *cinquecento*.

This "blindness" as Mallett called it, may be traced to Machiavelli's over-reliance on classical source materials. Indeed, Machiavelli's almost slavish cribbing of writers such as Vegetus and Frontinus in the *Arte* led Anglo to conclude that "this classical tradition compromised every one of Machiavelli's major "discoveries" in the realm of civil-military relations, and purely military organization....(which) had not escaped the attention of commentators—even as early as the thirteenth century."[39] That is not to say that Machiavelli's method of copying the ancients, sometimes verbatim, was out of the ordinary for writers of his time. In fact,

> In employing such a technique, Machiavelli is following in the footsteps not merely of his Italian predecessors, Valrutius and Cornazano, but also of such transmontane and "medieval" barbarians as Christine de Pisan, the authors of *Le Livre de Iouvencel* and *Le rosier des guerres*, and indeed of almost every writer who had attempted to deal with military affairs.[40]

However, in applying the ancient methods of warfare, unchanged, to Italy of his day, Machiavelli's theory for the creation of a citizen army began to sound out-of-touch and impracticable. One might cite his shunning of artillery and gunpowder as a prime example of this. The reason for Machiavelli's lurch away from reality, Anglo argued, was down to one central reason: "Machiavelli was blinded to military realities by his colossal antipathy to the mercenary captains whom he deemed responsible for most modern ills."[41]

Such blindness led to passages like that which follows:

> There is nothing that causes greater confusion in an army than impairing its vision; from whence the bravest armies are routed, by the impairment of their sight by dust or the sun. And, there is nothing which impairs the vision more than the smoke which is produced by artillery. Wherefore, I believe that it would be more prudent to allow the enemy to blind themselves, than for you, blind, to have to find them. So, I would not use artillery, or (because this would not be met with approval, in respect to the reputation which artillery has) I would place it on the corners of the formation, so that, when fired, the smoke would not blind the front of the ranks; which is where the eminent soldiers would be.[42]

As if such an admission was not damaging enough to his credibility, Machiavelli went on to discuss how he would organize his troops in order to deal best with incoming artillery volleys.

He advised his readers that their troops should be tightly organized and well-armored. If one were trying to protect one's troops from the ravages of arrows or pikes or cavalry charges, such advice would have been sound. To suggest that a similar arrangement would protect against an artillery barrage is absurd. Indeed, one might conclude that Machiavelli had never actually seen artillery in action, or the carnage that a well placed canon ball could do to a tightly grouped infantry unit. Nor, one can conclude, had he ever taken part in trying to secure the enemy's artillery in either siege or open warfare.[43]

The great realist, the father of modern political science, and many of his other appellations, at least in this respect, seem to be misplaced.[44] Rather, Machiavelli appears to be a romantic, a dreamer, anything but realistic. Why else would a man of his genius dare to compare Florence's measly military might with the grandeur of ancient Rome and Carthage as illustrated above, or brush aside artillery as a hindrance to warfare?

It may be that his belief in a citizen army, which has become so central to national identities and security in the present, was well before its time as some scholars have argued.[45] However, within the context of the early *cinquecento* his ideas, while apparently sincere, are absurd. On the fields surrounding Pisa, among the crumbling walls of Prato and in the aftermath of the Medici restoration, Machiavelli had been witness to the *effects* of war and he detested them, as his poem on *Ambizione* indicates:

> Let him turn his eyes here (to Italy) who wishes to behold the sorrows of
> others, and let him consider if ever before now the sun has
> looked upon such savagery.
> A man is weeping for his father dead and woman for her
> husband; another man, beaten and naked, you see driven in
> sadness from his own dwelling.
> Oh how many times, when the father has held his son tight in
> his arms, a single thrust has pierced the breasts of them both!
> Another is abandoning his ancestral home, as he accuses cruel
> and ungrateful gods, with his brood overcome with sorrow.
> Oh, strange events such as never have happened before in the
> world! Every day many children are born through sword cuts
> in the womb.
> To her daughter, overcome with sorrow, the mother says: "For
> what an unhappy marriage, for what a cruel husband have I kept you!
> Foul with blood are the ditches and streams, full of heads, of
> legs, of arms, and other members gashed and severed,
> Birds of prey, wild beasts, dogs are now their family tombs—
> Oh tombs repulsive, horrible and unnatural!

> Always their faces are gloomy and dark, like those of a man
> terrified and numbed by new injuries or sudden fears.
> Wherever you turn your eyes, you see the earth wet with tears
> and blood, and the air full of screams, of sobs, and sighs.[46]

It is doubtful that he had ever seen a battle, particularly one in which artillery played a significant role, first hand. The following anecdote, though possibly apocryphal, may help to illustrate this point. Matteo Bandello recalled watching Machiavelli's botched attempt to drill Giovanni de Medici's troops—the "bande nere." The story goes that Machiavelli stood in the blazing sun for two hours trying to order Giovanni's men. After that time, Niccolò had not even begun to organize them, so Giovanni stepped in and organized his 3,000 troops in a matter of minutes.[47] Surely this story illustrates Machiavelli's military incompetence. If Machiavelli had been anything other than an "armchair soldier" it would have been hard to imagine him speaking with such nonchalance about the relative ease with which one could take an enemy's cannon; and he would have been able better to organize Giovanni's troops.[48]

Conclusion

The sincerity and the naivety of some of Machiavelli's thinking are brought to the fore when one examines his theory of the citizen army. Given that this subject appears in each of the three works examined in this Chapter, it appears that he wholeheartedly believed in what he wrote. In turn, the appearance of the subject in *Il Principe*, the *Discorsi* and the *Arte*, provides the three works with a distinct continuity. Indeed, the subject of the citizen army adds nuance to his theory for the creation of an Italian national identity which was discussed in the previous Chapters. Perhaps, as the final Chapter of *Il Principe* indicates, Machiavelli wanted Lorenzo and Leo to unite Italy politically and militarily, following Borgia's example in the Romagna, which was detailed so thoroughly in Chapter VII. However, Machiavelli's vision of Cesare's success was based upon a false premise. Native citizens made up only a small percentage of his army; the majority, as was standard practice at the time, were mercenary troops.

Machiavelli's over-reliance on classical sources may have blinded him to the realities of *cinquecento* warfare. Might one ask whether in his exile, stripped of standing and office in the Florentine Chancery, he became so desirous to end the *otium* of his existence that the tenuous *negotium* he conjured drew more and more from the world of the ancients and detached him further and further from the realities of Italian politics and warfare?

CHAPTER FOUR

Machiavelli's Road to Exile

ಬಂಡ

The theme of exile is woven tightly throughout Machiavelli's writings after his expulsion from Florence by the restored Medici in 1513. Randolph Starn and more recently Christine Shaw have focused on exiles in Italy, but Machiavelli does not figure prominently in their research.[1] John Najemy, on the other hand, dedicated a chapter in his recent work to Machiavelli's life in exile just after his expulsion.[2] Najemy focuses on Machiavelli's letters to Vettori, which provide many insights into Machiavelli's view of exile in the time leading up to his writing *Il Principe*. This Chapter, following Najemy's lead, investigates whether part of Machiavelli's theory for Italian liberation and unification may have been an end to the practice of exile. In order to illustrate this it may be helpful to focus on Machiavelli's life in exile as he described it in his letters. Then, we shall proceed to the dedicatory letter and epilogue of *Il Principe*, which may have been written, as was proposed previously, just before Machiavelli began his *Discorsi*.

Written from his small farm at Sant'Andrea, Machiavelli's letters from exile span roughly a two-year period.[3] They reveal an intensely political individual stripped of everything: political office, standing and the meager wealth that he was able to accumulate in service to his *patria*. But then, it appears that something happened to Machiavelli. His personal letters only reflect this change to a certain extent, but his major political works seem to mirror it more precisely.[4]

Although Machiavelli was no longer the Second Chancellor to the Florentine Republic, he was, through his academic pursuits in exile once again rendering service to his *patria*. While he was unable to return to direct political service through participation in its government; through his own pursuits and diligent scholarly labor (his *otium*) he was able to serve his *patria*, thus restoring his relationship with it. This may have laid the groundwork for his return to active political service which he craved (*negotium*) This Chapter will argue that it is essential to keep these two aspects of Machiavelli's exile in mind when thinking of how he dealt with his life on the farm at Sant' Andrea.

With that in mind, this Chapter begins with a detailed history of Machiavelli's political downfall and subsequent exile, which forms the necessary backdrop for the whole discussion. Here, Peter Godman's research is fundamental.[5] His scholarship is utilized in the first part of this Chapter in order to contextualize the history of Machiavelli's political descent from successful and favored Second Chancellor to lowly exile. This first section will attempt to demonstrate that Machiavelli was as much a victim of his own poorly thought through actions in the Chancery as he was of the restored Medici's desire for political vengeance. This history of Machiavelli's descent into personal crisis is followed by an examination of several key letters that Machiavelli wrote while in exile. These letters provide a possible window into how he perceived his own exile and how Machiavelli may have sought to end the practice of exile in Italy. In turn, that would be an essential part in the unification process broadly outlined in the epilogue of *Il Principe*.

In order to understand how Machiavelli's view of his exile changed it is necessary to study his fall from political grace in Florence. Godman's work has shed new light on an important figure in Machiavelli's political life; his superior at the Florentine Chancery, Marcello Virgilio Adriani. Adriani played an important part in bringing about Machiavelli's banishment.[6] His actions and spiteful attitude toward Adriani early in their service together cemented Adriani's dislike, which, combined with Machiavelli's outspoken and perhaps misguided patriotism, ultimately led to his downfall and exile. During his years in exile, Machiavelli retreated into the corridors of his mind, peopled with the ancients and their secrets while Adriani remained in the Palazzo Vecchio; the Florentine halls of power, filled with the Medici and their supporters.[7]

Machiavelli and Marcello Virgilio Adriani

Adriani and Machiavelli were appointed Chancellors to the Florentine Republic in 1498; Adriani on 16 February and Machiavelli on 2 June.[8] Adriani was named the *primo segretario fiorentino*, or "First Chancellor," and Machiavelli was installed under him, as the *secondo segretario fiorentino* or "Second Chancellor." Over a 14-year period both Chancellors worked together until Piero Soderini's increasingly unstable republican government collapsed in 1512, under intense pressure from Julius II. This led to the restoration of the Medici. Machiavelli's political career did not survive the transition, yet Adriani came through the tumult unscathed with his position and honor intact. Why did Adriani succeed where Machiavelli failed?

Roberto Ridolfi argued that Adriani was successful because he remained "neutral."[9] Ridolfi's assessment is complemented by Giuseppe Prezzolini's biography of Machiavelli. Now dated but still useful, it contains a vivid depiction of Adriani's appearance as well as his sense of self-importance. Prezzolini wrote:

> This Marcello (Adriani) of ours was called in for baptisms and funerals or for any other eloquent or semaphoric occasion...Lungs he had, and a belly abundant to ply the bellows; a face impressively void, wreathed in a patriarchal beard, and all the appearances with none of the substance of dignity. Doughty, with a broad forehead, a pair of fine eyebrows, transparent and obtuse, behold him; behold that forearm and its sweeping gestures reaching to the last row, farther than his words can carry, behold how it fires applause, when at the end of a peroration it smites the table resoundingly, and through your spyglass you note the mouth closed and the face uplifted in expectation of the forthcoming and irresistible cheers.[10]

More recent scholarship has illustrated that Adriani did indeed like to "ply the billows," but he was far from neutral, indeed he was self-serving and egocentric.[11] Along with his high self-opinion, Adriani possessed a large measure of astute political savvy; knowing precisely when and where to voice his opinions. By contrast, Machiavelli often found it hard to keep his opinions to himself.[12] His patriotic, zealous and outspoken character was not conducive to political survival in Soderini's teetering republic or under the restored Medici government. If one traces the relationship between these two individuals, the differences between them are startling and it may become easier to see why Machiavelli lost everything he loved and why Adriani prospered even after the Medici restoration.

As Second Chancellor, Machiavelli was, in theory, Adriani's subordinate. However, in practice, Machiavelli, not Adriani, was given the duties usually afforded to the First Chancellor. Therefore, he was "dubbed Soderini's "mannerino" or puppet."[13] While the First Chancellor was left poring over papers in the Palazzo Vecchio, Machiavelli was sent on diplomatic missions. In a letter dated 14 October 1502 Agostino Vespucci in Florence, wrote to Machiavelli at the court of Cesare Borgia, about Adriani. Vespucci jested: "Niccolò, greetings. I do not know whether to write or not. If not, I shall be accused of negligence, but if I do write, I fear that I shall be called a slanderer, especially against Marcello (Virgilio Adriani) and Ricci."[14]

In these opening lines Vespucci begins to poke fun at Adriani, but he saved the joke for the next line: "Marcello, the negligent one in the matter (that is, of your duty), has refused the burden of writing."[15] In this "aside," Vespucci slipped in a jab at Adriani that must have caused both him and Machiavelli to laugh at the thought of Adriani having to do Machiavelli's work. That Adriani was feeling overworked and abused as a result of Machiavelli's absence is evident in a letter he wrote to Machiavelli shortly after Vespucci's letter on 7 November 1502.

> Notable man, etc. The *gonfalonier* told me this morning that it does not seem right in any way to him that you should depart, since he does not feel it is time, and leave that place devoid of any representative of our city; since he would have to send someone else there, he does not know who could be more suitable, in respect to many things. Therefore he has told me to write you thus and advise you not to leave; the Lord knows whether I do so willingly, since I find myself with my business, *yours, and my teaching on my hands*. Whether you have to follow the duke or not when he goes to Rimini, you will be told more precisely by (through) public (channels) later.[16]

The words in italics above, "yours, and the teaching on my hands," or "con le tue e con la lezione addosso," may be the central reasons as to why Adriani was not only jealous of Machiavelli, but also reasons why Adriani was able to remain in the service of the Medici while Machiavelli was exiled.

Not once did Adriani say what *he* thought about Machiavelli. Adriani only related to Machiavelli what he was instructed to say. Yet, Adriani slipped in conspicuous references to his personal views. His distaste and jealousy at having to do the work of his subordinate, as well as his own, clearly wore on Adriani's patience. Despite Adriani's protests and bluster, one can only imagine what the political ramifications might have been if Adriani, rather than Machiavelli, had been sent on the first Florentine mission to Cesare Borgia. One cannot help but feel thankful that he remained trapped in the Palazzo Vecchio while Machiavelli was traveling to the most prestigious courts in Italy. However, Adriani would have been more comfortable, despite his jealousy, when Machiavelli was away on diplomatic missions. For when Machiavelli and Adriani were in Florence together, matters were even worse for the First Chancellor.

Adriani was left out of the circle of friends in the Palazzo Vecchio; "a clique of three facetious wags, headed by Machiavelli along with Vespucci and Biagio Buonaccorsi."[17] The three friends were united in their dislike of Adriani, often making their superior the butt of ill-humored jokes, which amounted to little more than personal attacks on Adriani.[18] Machiavelli, Vespucci and Buonaccorsi began these "jokes" as early as 1499, which Adriani left unrequited, until November 1512, when all three of the "wags" were stripped of their political offices and exiled. Godman's recent research has uncovered important factors that may have led Machiavelli and his friends to be exiled and all of them can be traced to Adriani.

Along with the figurative knives that Machiavelli, Vespucci and Buonaccorsi slid into the back of Adriani, they were also outspoken critics of prominent Florentine citizens. As Godman puts it:

> Like Marcello Virgilio (Adriani), Machiavelli was an elected official who depended on the approval of the Signoria for renewal of his post. That, in the eyes of the cautious colleague (Adriani), ought to have entailed a discretion that (Machiavelli), with his two confederates in satirical provocation flouted.[19]

In silence, Adriani was forced to follow Machiavelli around putting out all of the fires that his subordinate had started. Ominously, perhaps, for Machiavelli, Adriani often instigated Machiavelli into fanning the embers of political discontent in Florence.

For example, in 1504 Machiavelli wrote a "comedy" entitled *Le Maschere* in which many of Florence's leading citizens were the recipients of provocational satire, which caused a great deal of embarrassment to the First Chancellor.[20] Unfortunately, little is known of the now lost work beyond a comment on it which survives in Giuliano de' Ricci's *Priorista*.[21] A portion of the *Priorista* was printed by Pasquale Villari. It may be helpful to see what he and Ricci's work have to say about *Le Maschere*.

> It would seem that Machiavelli frequently amused himself at this period by mingling irony and satire with his official daily work and his political meditations, for it was now that he must have composed a second literary work, which has unfortunately perished. This was an imitation of "The Clouds" and other comedies of Aristophanes, entitled "Le Maschere." All that we know of it is that it was written at the insistence of Marcello Virgilio , and together with other papers and compositions of his came into the hands of Giuliano de'Ricci, who, though he had transcribed many other unpublished writings of his illustrious grandfather, declined to copy this, not only because it was reduced to barely legible fragments, but because the author had attacked in it, "under feigned names, many citizens who were still living in the year 1504." ...In all his compositions, Niccolò indulged in much license, as well as in blaming great personages, lay and ecclesiastical, as in reducing all things to natural or fortuitous causes. Certainly this stinging satirical spirit of his produced him many enemies, and helped to embitter his life....[22]

Adriani, it seems, put up with the embarrassment (of which he was the original cause and instigator, knowing the sharp-witted character of Niccolò) for a time, preparing his revenge—Machiavelli's exile. It appears that Adriani was prepared to bide his time, suffering and scheming in silence; for even though Adriani was an outsider at the Palazzo Vecchio, he went out of his way to act in a prudent manner so as not to offend anyone in Soderini's government. More precisely, his actions, it appears, were carefully weighed and balanced so as not to be offensive to the powerful Florentine families that still quietly supported the Medici—those same families who he had only recently encouraged Machiavelli to slander.

For years Adriani had not only held the post of First Chancellor, he had also held the distinguished Professor's Chair at the Florentine Studio, once held by Angelo Poliziano, which was the "teaching on my hands."[23] According to Godman, Adriani used his lectern as a "private pulpit, (where) he transformed his lectures into sermons for future rulers of the Republic."[24] His students included the best and brightest sons of Florence's leading families—almost all of whom were, although quietly, Medici supporters.[25] Adriani's lectures were republican in content, yet they were subtly tinged with support for the Medici. This did not go unnoticed by his students, who it seems, told their parents about the marvelous Adriani.[26] The sorely abused first Chancellor, despite his office, could make no headway in Soderini's government, so he contented himself to bide his time in his lectures and studies, there preparing a place for himself in the next government, should Soderini's fall.

It did, and Adriani was not only well positioned to continue his political and scholarly service, he was at last able to take revenge on the three men who had tortured him for 14 years: Vespucci, Buonaccorsi and Machiavelli. "Among the factors that contributed to Machiavelli's "dismissal, deprivation and total removal from and out of the Chancery," one may have been neglected: the push, concealed but comprehensible, that came from within."[27] The likely push came from Adriani, but certain events transpired that made his revenge upon Machiavelli and friends relatively easy.

One of Adriani's most famous students, Francesco Guicciardini, wrote in his *Ricordi* a brief reflection that summarized Adriani's success in Florence after the Medici restoration. Tellingly, it also encapsulated the reasons for Machiavelli's downfall.

> I say that a good citizen and lover of the fatherland (*patria*) should seek to stand well with a tyrant, not only for his own security—for he is in danger when he is suspected—but also for the benefit of the fatherland (*patria*). For to govern thus, he comes to the occasion with counsel and with works which favor (the implementation of) many useful measures and disfavoring many that are harmful; and those who blame him are fools, because they and their city would be ripe for the taking if the tyrant had none but wretches around him.[28]

Compare Guicciardini's with Machiavelli's words:

> Because this is a general rule which is never false—a prince, who is himself unwise,

cannot be well advised, unless he places his trust in a most prudent person who governs everything. In this case, a prince may be able to abide well, but endure for only a short time, because his governor would soon usurp his state.[29]

As has been illustrated in the previous Chapters, Guicciardini had a talent for undermining his friend's assertions. More than summarizing Machiavelli's poor political maneuverings, the ever-observant Guicciardini is directly undermining Machiavelli's assertion that flatterers should be shunned, thereby beating Machiavelli at his own political game.[30] Machiavelli's true, impassioned character came to the forefront when he and his republic were tested.

Machiavelli, unlike Adriani, could not sit idly by and watch his beloved Republic fall. His deep love for his *patria*, underlined by his love of republican liberty, caused him to take action. He remained at Florence, the heart of his *patria*, to organize the militia against the Spanish army, while they were still some distance away.[31] As we saw in the last Chapter, the Spanish army besieged Prato, which was defended by 3,000 infantrymen. Of the 3,000-strong infantry, Machiavelli's militia made up one third of their total number. The defenders managed to turn away the first wave of the Spanish attack, but they miserably failed during the second assault when the Spanish troops were able to breach Prato's walls and pour into the city. The Florentine infantry, including Machiavelli's militia, fled in terror, leaving Prato in the merciless hands of the starving Spanish. Under the watchful eyes of Giovanni de' Medici who accompanied the Spanish troops, "countless murders, sacrileges and rapes were committed" in Prato.[32]

In Florence, Piero Soderini's government was collapsing as the Medici armies approached its gate. Machiavelli's hastily gathered Florentine militia was no match for the battle-hardened Spanish troops who came to greet them. Ill-prepared and outclassed, the militia faltered, Soderini fled to Siena under the cover of night and the Republic fell.

After Soderini's government collapsed, Machiavelli was dismissed from the Chancery on 7 November 1512 for his outspokenness against the Medici, his intensely patriotic views and for his part in the city's defense. Only three days later, the Signoria "sentenced (Machiavelli) to be restricted within the Florentine territory for a year, obliging him to pay a caution of 1,000 gold Florins."[33] Unable to produce such a large sum of money, Machiavelli was forced to ask three friends to help him pay his fine.[34] Crushingly, Machiavelli was barred from crossing the threshold of the Palazzo Vecchio, the place where he had served the Republic for the past 14 years. Yet, this was only the beginning of Machiavelli's personal tragedy. Less than three months later, every last vestige of his political life was destroyed.

In February 1513, a list of 18 or 20 names fell from Pietro Paolo Boscoli's pocket. Boscoli was a young Florentine who held openly anti-Medicean views.[35] The list was discovered by Bernardino Coccio, a Medici supporter, who quickly turned it over to the Florentine Balìa of Eight.[36] The list, the Eight concluded, named anti-Medicean conspirators. Boscoli and his close friend Agostino Capponi were arrested and thrown into prison on 18 February 1513, but the Eight were not yet content.[37] Machiavelli's name was also found on the list.[38] Already stripped of his office and exiled from the Palazzo Vecchio for his anti-Medicean views, the Eight now had Machiavelli arrested.

Amid this turmoil, Adriani remained seemingly aloof and unaffected, yet hardly "neutral," at the Palazzo Vecchio as the First Chancellor. "Within and without the Chancery, the interests of members of the ruling house and of Marcello Virgilio (Adriani) converged."[39] The Medici wanted to stamp out any vestige of a possible conspiracy to overthrow their newly restored rule, as did Adriani, who probably wanted to rid Florence of Machiavelli. Furthermore, Cardinal Giovanni de' Medici, soon to be Pope Leo X, was so intent on crushing the possible conspiracy that he refused to leave Florence for the Conclave at Rome, even though he expected to be elected pope, until a suitable sentence was passed.[40] Boscoli and Capponi were sentenced to death. Neither man implicated Machiavelli, but both were beheaded on the morning of 23 February 1513 for their part in the conspiracy.[41] Machiavelli escaped the executioner's axe, but he did not avoid the torturer's ropes. He had nothing to do with the "conspiracy"—if in fact, one ever existed—but whether the conspiracy was real or contrived, the Medici made their presence known quickly and Adriani carried on in their service. Machiavelli's fall was complete—as was Adriani's revenge.[42]

Cardinal Giovanni de'Medici was elected Pope on 11 March 1513. Florence was enraptured to have gained such an honour. The following day, as an act of good will, Florence's prisons were emptied. Ironically, Machiavelli the patriot was allowed to go home—along with accused murderers and petty thieves.[43] But where was home for Machiavelli?

Machiavelli's Letters from Exile

"Deciding where exiles would be ordered to go was an important matter. Those making the decision had to take into account what the element of punishment (other than being banished from home) was intended to inflict."[44] The Signoria, guided by their Medici overseers seem to have thought of the perfect punishment for Machiavelli. They expelled him from political service in Florence, but they sent him only a maddeningly short distance away from his beloved Palazzo Vecchio. Then, his home in exile was at a small villa in Sant' Andrea in Percussina, "a little village on the old Roman postal road, seven miles from Florence and two from San Casciano."[45] He had little or no money to support himself, or his family, so he was forced to work his small farm. All the while Machiavelli knew that Adriani, the architect of his exile, was situated comfortably in the service of the Medici and at the Studio in Florence, while he was an outcast, poor and without any political leverage.

Machiavelli appears to have descended into a depression that lasted for several months, but he did not sink into bitterness, as had so many exiles before him, Petrarch and Dante in particular.

> As their (Florentine exiles) voices crack and come apart in anger, they change from connoisseurs of sadness into masters of malediction. Dante let taunts fly with a sure sense of target—proud Florence.[46]

Machiavelli, despite his hurt and heartbreak, never attacked Florence. On the contrary he sank himself into study that focused on educating Florence's citizens by praising their *patria*. Machiavelli wrote and studied, not simply as Starn said, to "keep—or find—a voice through all (his) losses," but as a means of transformation and restoration; a means of serving his *patria*, even though he was no longer employed by her government.[47] It seems that Machiavelli was then able to overcome the *otium* of his life in the country.[48] Machiavelli's study appears to have been much more than a "compulsion," which helped to "mask" his pain. Through his study, he restored his relationship with his *patria*, balancing to some degree, the *otium* that he endured and *negotium* he yearned for.[49]

The change in Machiavelli's outlook began in the late months of 1513 with *Il Principe* but it did not reach its maturity until the second year of his exile, particularly around the vintage season of 1515 in the dedicatory letter and epilogue to *Il Principe*. We can begin to trace the change in his letters written as an exile.

Perhaps the *occasione* of Medici Pope and Medici *Capitano* at Florence opened his eyes? Seizing the opportunity would bring together Italy's many *patrie* into one united *patria*, and it would no longer be possible to be exiled within it. The barbarians would at last be driven from Italian soil; the exiled Sienese citizen, the banished Genoese and the disgraced Florentine, among others, would be united in a single *patria*, under the leadership of a *principe*. If one doubts that triumphal unification could bring an end to exile, there are examples from the *quattrocento*, albeit on a smaller scale, that illustrate just such a phenomenon. Borso d'Este, in 1452, celebrated his triumphal entry into Reggio as its new lord by canceling every sentence passed against exiles, thus allowing all of Reggio's exiles to return home.[50] A unifying prince, in Machiavelli's theory, could, like d'Este, only on a grander scale, end the practice of exile in Italy, with *one* decree. Might one argue that the "secular *patria*" provided the means of ending exile by restoring in each citizen, exile or otherwise, "virtù italica" with which to identify? This possibility is a neglected implication of Machiavelli's political thought.

Machiavelli's thought may never have come to such a distinct conclusion had he not been sent into exile. His exile may help one to understand how his political thought grew and matured. Indeed, what were the surroundings of Machiavelli's exile in which he developed his mature political vision?

For Starn, in order to understand the person as well as the process of exile, one must begin with an analysis of Italy's geography:

> Rivers from the Alps cut their way through mazes of valleys and steep gullies that mark the courses of the Tiber, the Arno, the tributaries of the Po, and the ten parallel streams, from the Taro to the Biferno, of the eastern Apennine slope. In the plains, water has piled up silt in fertile places or seeped through trackless lowland stretches, like those reclaimed only in recent times on the delta of the Po...physical connections are limited within such an environment.[51]

Machiavelli was exiled into the western reaches of the Apennine mountain chain, which are clearly visible from Florence. He lived only seven miles from Florence, but as Starn said, he would have been almost completely cut off from life in the city both in terms of business and, more important, in terms of politics. Samuel Cohn has also pointed to the distinction between the city—Florence—and the surrounding towns, countryside and mountainous regions—the *contado*.[52] Even if, as Cohn asserts, "the society and culture of the mountains did not differ so dramatically from the plains as historians have supposed," Machiavelli most definitely saw a difference.[53] For business, Machiavelli cared little, but for political service he pined, as his letter of 9 April 1513 indicates:

> Wherefore, if I were able to speak with you, not being able to do otherwise, I would fill you head with "little castles," because Fortune has decreed that, not knowing how to discuss either the wool trade or profits or losses, it happens that I discuss politics, and I need either to take a vow of silence or discuss this. If I were able to emerge from the (Florentine) dominion, I would like then, to go down there and find out if the pope is at home.[54]

This letter is filled with subjunctives. Emphasizing the sorrowful and perhaps fanciful nature of his life in exile, Machiavelli's letter is filled with "se's" or "if's": "if" he could talk to his friend, "if" he could leave the Florentine territories. His punishment was well executed. Exile within the boundaries of Florence, within an easy ride of the city-centre, may have been worse for Machiavelli than being exiled outright and sent abroad. This letter seems to illustrate the grief and frustration Machiavelli felt during his exile. He could not *physically talk* to his friend. He could only write letters to Vettori because he was unable to leave the "dominio" or dominion of Florence for a year as part of the punishment of his exile. Machiavelli was alone, stripped of even the simplest pleasure of speaking to friends. His letter continues as follows: "But, among so many requests for pardon, mine fell to the floor because of my negligence. I shall wait until September."[55] Machiavelli knew that the help Vettori could offer him was more psychological than physical. He knew that Vettori could, in reality, make little headway for him with the Pope. The sense of self-doubt continued in a letter of 1513.

> I hear that Cardinal Soderini is busying himself a lot with the pontiff. I should like you to advise me whether or not you think it would be appropriate for me to write him a letter requesting a recommendation to His Holiness. Or would it be better for you to speak on my behalf directly with the cardinal?[56]

He did not know where to turn. Machiavelli was searching for every possible avenue and every open door to the pope, but he found all of them closed. Soderini was no help to him and in the end, Vettori, in turn, failed.[57] Machiavelli was alone in his exile in the mountains, estranged from his beloved Florence, and so time passed.

He did at times begin to venture back into Florence as the letter of 16 April indicated. An unscrupulous friend, one Tommaso del Bene, harassed Machiavelli for money, while he crossed the Arno via the Ponte Vecchio. The rest of the time he spent between his home in the mountains and with various friends, to whom he referred as the "brigata" or the "gang."[58] Machiavelli's friends and his use of the term "brigata" highlight the criminal connotations that were associated with exiles. In a unified Italy, true criminals who deserved exile would not be allowed to roam the countryside, stirring up trouble, they would be banished to a place outside of the peninsula.[59]

So went Machiavelli's life in exile. At various intervals Vettori asked for Machiavelli's advice on grave matters at Rome, such as the treaty between the Spanish and the French, which threw all of Italy into fanciful speculation about the intentions of the French and the intelligence of the Spanish King.[60]

> I got up early and wrote so that when you find it convenient you may tell me what you think was the fancy of the king of Spain in this truce. I shall agree with your

> judgment because, to tell you the truth without flattery, I have found it more sound in these matters than that of any other man that I have spoken with.[61]

Whether Vettori passed on Machiavelli's advice is doubtful, or if he did, it fell on deaf ears. So, the summer passed with Machiavelli involved in studies and responses to Vettori's questions. Even if Vettori neglected to pass Machiavelli's advice to the appropriate persons at Rome, he nevertheless helped Machiavelli by giving him a means to vent his political views. Then, somewhere between 26 May and 4 August the Machiavelli family was struck by tragedy.[62] Machiavelli managed few words:

> I have gotten your letter of 26 May, to which I have nothing more to say than that we are all well; Marietta gave birth to a baby girl, who died after three days; Marietta is well.[63]

His wife lost a child and this was all he could say. Without the distraction of Vettori's letters it is hard to imagine Machiavelli surviving the first summer of his exile. Then, quite suddenly something began to change in his letters to Vettori. On 26 August, his bewilderment still evident, a foretaste of *Il Principe* leapt off the page, but not before Machiavelli told Vettori how life in exile was weighing on him. Machiavelli wrote to Vettori:

> Your letter of the twentieth dismayed me: its organization, its countless lines of reasoning, and all its other merits entangled me in such a way that at first I was bewildered and confused.[64]

Through his not-so subtle sarcasm, perhaps the briefest of glimpses into Machiavelli's life as an exile is stolen. Without mentioning his exile, Machiavelli clearly described his feelings. He was "entangled, bewildered and confused" in exile. Machiavelli's word choice makes it sound as though he lost his way in a dense forest, where he would remain hopelessly lost, but that was not to be the case. One cannot help but recall the opening lines of Dante's *Inferno* where he described his surroundings. Dante wrote: "In the middle of our life's walk / I discovered myself in a dark wood / Where the straight way was lost."[65] Unlike Dante, for Machiavelli redemption came through political service, not through divine intervention. In this letter to Vettori, Machiavelli was taking the first steps toward overcoming his exile. He continued:

> Had I not been able to collect my wits somewhat by rereading it, I would have given up the game and would have answered you by going on to something else. But as I became more familiar with it, the same thing happened to me as it did the fox when he saw the lion: the first time he almost died of fright; the second, he halted behind a

clump of bushes to take a look; the third he chatted with him. And so I, having collected my wits by becoming more familiar with your letter, shall answer you. [66]

John Najemy suggested, and we concur, that Machiavelli's "confusion seems oddly out of place." [67] One might conclude then, that Machiavelli was not bewildered as a result of Vettori's letter. On the contrary, it may be that Machiavelli painted a picture of himself and his changing relationship to exile. At first he was terrified, then more familiar, and at last triumphant. Furthermore, this letter also presents the first instance where Machiavelli used the "fox" and the "lion," made famous in *Il Principe* Chapter 18.[68] It is becoming clear that Machiavelli was coming to terms with the *otium* of his pastoral exile.

More cynically, it may appear that Machiavelli simply wanted to be re-instated or given a new office in the Medici government—an interpretation often bestowed upon *Il Principe*.[69] Such a conclusion is unfounded, for all of the evidence at hand suggests that Machiavelli truly believed in the ideas he was formulating. The idealism that helped have him thrown from office not only permeated his political service, but more importantly his scholarly service to the Florentine *patria*.

The next letter that Machiavelli wrote to Vettori is dated 10 December 1513, and is his most famous letter. Therein, he described to Vettori his life on the farm; the day-to-day drudgery of exile and survival, but there amidst the mud and filth of his country life, he transformed himself. He came to grips with the forced *otium* of his pastoral life:

> When evening comes, I return home and enter my study; on the threshold I take off my workday clothes, covered with mud and dirt, and put on the garments of the court and palace. Fitted out appropriately, I step inside the venerable courts of the ancients, where I nourish myself on that food that *alone* is mine and for which I was born; where I am unashamed to converse with them and to question them about the motives for their actions, and they, out of their human kindness, answer me. And for four hours at a time I feel no boredom, I forget all my troubles, I do not dread poverty, and I am not terrified of death. I (take or transform)[1] [*transferisco*] myself into them completely. And because Dante says that no one understands anything unless he retains what he has understood, I have jotted down what I have profited from in their conversation and composed a short study, *De principatibus*.[70]

As Godman states, at the heart of this letter is the verb "transferisco" or transform and a subtle metaphor that it contains:

> The metaphor is less one of movement than of metamorphosis. A total transformation of the self and the present that arises from immersion in the past is Machiavelli's meaning; and witty but unrecognized allusion to a cultural concept

well known in the Middle Ages and Renaissance. That concept is *translatio atrium/studii*: the theory of the transmission and progress of scholarship from Greece to Rome, from France to Italy, culminating ...on the farm of San Casciano.[71]

So, Machiavelli detailed and declared to Vettori his total transformation. He was no longer forced to look to Vettori as his intercessor or savior. Through introspection and study, Machiavelli affected a *real* transformation in his life. He took the first steps toward mastering the *otium* of his life in exile. Machiavelli was on the way to restoring his personal relationship with his *patria*. Najemy wrote: "in politics, in exile...(Machiavelli's) evening dream (the letter above) represents the months in which he turned inward to a "dialogue" all his own."[72] His inward dialogue brought about this transformation as well as his redemption from exile, which only began with the writing of *Il Principe* in December 1513. Might this inward dialogue also have found an outlet in a dialogue on language? (This is discussed in the following Chapter).

Machiavelli's letters to Vettori and his other friends over the next two years detail the life of a man still struggling with his exile. *Il Principe*, still without its epilogue or re-written dedication, did not bring about his complete restoration. In fact, Machiavelli's literary output, with the exception of *Il Principe*, was almost non-existent between the end of 1513 and the two years that followed, but some time around the late months of 1515 the floodgates opened.   Machiavelli wrote the dedicatory letter and epilogue to *Il Principe*, he began the *Discorsi*, he wrote several plays and poems, he wrote the *Arte della guerra* and he was commissioned by Pope Clement VII to write the *Istorie Fiorentine*.[73]

That Machiavelli's exile from political service still affected him is seen in the language he adopted in the dedicatory letter to *Il Principe*. His language highlights all the more the importance that the theme of exile had in Machiavelli's political works; so much so that his language evokes the landscape that encompassed his life in exile.

The mountainous landscape of his exile also formed the basis for one of his most famous analogies, which is contained in the dedicatory letter to *Il Principe*. In the second to last paragraph of the letter Machiavelli's tones are sweeping, like those of the artist sketching the landscape that he wishes to paint:

> Nor I hope will it be reputed (as) presumptuous if a man of base and lowest status dares to discuss and reason about the governing of princes; because, just as some who draw the countryside place themselves low in the plain to consider the mountains and the high places, and to consider that which is low, place themselves high on a mountain, similarly, to thoroughly understand the nature of people, one

needs to be a prince, and to know fully that of princes, one needs to be of the people.[74]

In the closing paragraph of the dedicatory letter Machiavelli's tone changes completely. Gone are the sweeping tones, replaced by a specific and impassioned plea from a man who knew the life of an exile all too well.

> Take, therefore, your Magnificence, this little gift in the spirit with which I send it; from which, if you diligently consider and read, you will know my urgent desire that you reach that greatness which Fortune and your other qualities promise. And, if your Magnificence, from the auspices of your great height, will sometime look to these low places, you will know how much I undeservedly endured the great and continuing malignity of Fortune.[75]

Although he was able to manage the *otium* of his life in exile, he still desperately craved an official restoration. In the last paragraph of the dedicatory letter Machiavelli is no longer a painter of political landscapes, he is the lonely despised hermit; alone for everyone to see, who wants nothing more than to be restored to his former position. Yet, there is a still subtler allusion beneath his plea.

Machiavelli had no desire to view the world from the mountain top, no desire for princely status, but more importantly he had no desire for religious redemption. Machiavelli's letter is not an appeal to the divine for deliverance, but an appeal to an earthly prince. In his mind, he traveled in time, to various places, so that he could carry on political discourses with those whom he admired. Machiavelli's fanciful dialogues took him on a secular pilgrimage. On his journeys, it may be that he sought political, not religious, salvation for himself and for Italy. In order to illustrate this point it is perhaps helpful to cite a portion of one of Petrarch's most famous letters, with which Machiavelli may have been familiar.[76] By way of contrast, compare Machiavelli's words above with those of Petrarch's letter:

> Being so befooled, I sat down in a hollow. My thought quickly turned from the material to the spiritual, and I said to myself in approximately these words: "What you have experienced so often today in the ascent of this mountain certainly happens to you and to many who are striving for the blessed life. But the spiritual straying is not so easily to be perceived, for the movements of the body are in the open, whereas those of the soul are hidden and invisible. The life that we call blessed is situated on a high place; and narrow, we are told, is the way that leads to it; and many hills stand in the way, and we must advance from virtue to virtue up shining steps. The summit is the ultimate goal, the terminus of the road on which we journey. Everyone wishes to arrive there, but, as Ovid says: "To wish is not enough; to gain your end you must ardently yearn." You, certainly, both wish and ardently yearn, unless you are fooling yourself, as you so often do. What then holds you

back? Surely nothing but the level road that seems at first easier, amid base earthly pleasures. But after much wandering you will either have to climb upward eventually, with labors long shirked, to the heights of the blessed life, or lie sluggishly in the valley of your sins. And if—I shudder at the thought!—the darkness and the shadows of death find you there, you will spend an eternal night in perpetual torture.[77]

Machiavelli's familiarity with Petrarch and his well-documented history of citing him may have influenced the opening letter of *Il Principe*. Unlike Machiavelli, however, Petrarch sought to climb to the divine summit. Petrarch's redemption, guided by St. Augustine whom he read while atop the mountain, was divine; for Machiavelli redemption came through political service, not through religious redemption.[78] He undermined Petrarch's overtly Christian themes, stripping them of all religious connotations, leaving only the bare bones of political service. Machiavelli was happy to "ipsius peccatorum tuorum segnem procumbere" or "lie in the sluggish valley of your sins," as Petrarch referred to it, as long as he could continue to serve his *patria* as a scholar. However, Machiavelli desperately wanted to end his time in exile and once again serve his *patria*. It may be that he placed all his hopes, for personal as well as Italian unification and restoration, in Lorenzo, the Medici *Capitano* of Florence and his uncle, Pope Leo X.

In a land of petty states littered with desperate exiles, Machiavelli provided a possible solution to their, and his, restoration. In the epilogue of *Il Principe*, Machiavelli carefully chose the "oppressed" and the "oppressors." Every group mentioned is either pagan or Jewish—Christianity does not fit into Machiavelli's plans.

And if, as I said, it was necessary, in order to see the *virtù* of Moses, for the people of Israel to be enslaved in Egypt, and to understand the greatness of Cyrus's spirit, the Persians had to be oppressed by the Medes; and the excellence of Theseus, the Athenians had to be dispersed; so, at present, wanting to know the *virtù* of the Italian spirit, it was necessary for Italy to be lowered to this extremity, as it is in the present; that it be more enslaved than the Hebrews, more servile than the Persians, more dispersed than the Athenians, leaderless, lawless, torn, overrun, and she had to have endured every sort of ruin.[79]

Every historical group of peoples mentioned by Machiavelli was led out of political oppression into exile by their respective leader and then out of exile into prosperity and fame; out of exile into peace; from peace to prosperity and supremacy. If Lorenzo, with the cooperation of Pope Leo, could unite Italy, he would out of necessity bring into fellowship all of her exiles, with their new *patria*—centered in Florence. One might argue that Machiavelli's secular vision for Florentine supremacy and centrality in a united Italy stands in stark contrast to the Florentine experience under Savonarola.[80] Perhaps this was Machiavelli's dream: a united Italy free from the practice of exile and also from religion in the sphere of politics. It seems that he endured the *otium* of his exile, but he also craved political restoration and this could only come through political unification. If one moves beyond the confines of *Il Principe* one may yet glimpse how Machiavelli's exile affected his other political works.

In the *Discorsi*, Machiavelli re-stated and re-iterated the theme of exile. He remained an exile from the Florentine political world when he wrote the *Discorsi*, but he still craved restoration. Furthermore, Machiavelli wanted to be politically reunited with his *patria*, not through his own maneuverings, but by the political workings of a prince and eventually a republican government. He wrote:

> It may not be amiss amongst other topics to show how dangerous it is to trust those who have been driven from their country, since this is a matter with which everyone who holds office has to deal...One should reflect, therefore, on the unreliability of agreements and promises made by men who find themselves shut out from their country, because in determining what such men's word is worth it must be borne in mind that, once they get a chance of returning to their country without your help, they will desert you and turn to others in spite of any promises they may have made to. While in regard to the vain promises and hopes, so intense is their desire to get back home that they naturally believe much that is false and artfully add much more: so that between what they believe and what they say they believe they fill you with a hope which is just that, if you rely on it, either you incur expense in vain or take up what will ruin you.[81]

Machiavelli, it seems, wanted Lorenzo to open the doors to Italy's exiles so they would unite with him, against the "others": the French, Spanish and Swiss. This brief citation from the *Discorsi* may be another glimpse of "Niccolò's Smile" as Viroli called it, but more likely this is a heartfelt statement from a man who viewed his exile, at least in part, as over.

Conclusion

We have attempted to investigate how Machiavelli was able to manage the *otium* of his pastoral prison, which, in turn, we proposed, laid the theoretical groundwork for the ending of his exile, and that of every other exiled Italian, as called for in the epilogue to *Il Principe*. As the study of Machiavelli's life in exile illustrated, he began that new life as a depressed and desperate man, but he refused to take revenge as others had done before him. On the contrary, he remained true to his greatest love—his Florentine *patria*—and he was able to come to terms with the forced *otium* of his life in exile. The first signs of this manifested themselves in his letters to Vettori written late in 1513. Perhaps, Machiavelli saw a brief window of opportunity in Florence that could not only unite Italy and expel the barbarians, but also end and reconcile his political divorce from Florence, which would bring him back to the Palazzo Vecchio in Florence as its Second Chancellor. Lorenzo, the Medici *Capitano* at Florence and his uncle, head of the Church, Pope Leo X, and their temporarily united interests made up the *occasione*. Indeed, Leo's interests in Florence and its politics were such that he remained in Florence for the outcome of the Capponi-Boscoli trials which took place during his own papal election.[82]

In order to attain such a glorious goal, Italy would need, according to Machiavelli, to rely not on mercenaries, but on its own resources. The impracticalities of his theory for a citizen army do not lessen its genius. Indeed, the vision of a united citizen army, encompassing Italians from every corner of the peninsula, including restored exiles conjures visions of triumph and Italian success. A desire to honour Machiavelli's "secular *patria*" would be that which could provide the impetus for Italy's uniting prince—like a Roman dictator—to resign his office, handing power over to an elected republican government. Such freedom and liberty, perhaps, would aid in the creation of a united Italy. In examining these aspects of Machiavelli's political thought, a certain implicit naiveté may have been uncovered, but in so doing one may better see how deep his sincerity ran, permeating every aspect of his life. However, a work which many scholars attribute to Machiavelli may be able to add nuance to his theory for the creation of a united Italy and its identity. Even if it is not the work of Machiavelli, it gives insights into preoccupations with a national identity that Machiavelli may well have shared. It is titled the *Discorso o dialogo intorno alla nostra lingua*.

CHAPTER FIVE

Niccolò Machiavelli,
Author of the *Discorso o dialogo*
intorno alla nostra lingua?

ℬℭ

Il Principe and the *Discorsi* seem to be more closely related in terms of content than many scholars were willing to admit. The presence of *patria*, the citizen army and the theme of exile in both works may be indicative of this close relationship. Furthermore these elements may indicate that Machiavelli devised a plan for Italian liberation and unification as discussed in previous Chapters. It is likely, given the expansiveness of the *Discorsi*, in comparison with the concise prose and rhetoric of *Il Principe*, that these works are united in content, though divided by date of authorship as Chapter One argued. *Il Principe* for example was written in 1513 and amended perhaps in the autumn of 1515. Following closely on the heels of these additions, Machiavelli may have begun his *Discorsi* in late 1515 or early 1516, helping to explain the continuity between the two works as well as the differences in their length. Is there anything which may help one to understand how Machiavelli's thought became increasingly patriotic, or which helps one to appreciate how his political thought became more expansive in the intervening years?

An answer may be found in the pages of a work entitled the *Discorso o dialogo intorno alla nostra lingua*. However, such an answer is not without its difficulties. For example, the authorship (discussed in this Chapter) and date (the subject of the following Chapter) of the *Discorso o dialogo intorno alla nostra lingua*, are contested. The large majority of scholars, both Italian and Anglophone believe it to be a product of Machiavelli's pen, but there are enough holes in its provenance to hinder proof of its authorship. However, one might argue that there is enough textual, intertextual and contextual evidence to suggest that Machiavelli may have authored the text. The text seems, tantalizingly, to "fit" between Machiavelli's *Il Principe* and *Discorsi*.

Patria in the *Dialogo*

The *Dialogo*, as it is abbreviated for the remainder of this study, is a short treatise, 4,513 words in length. In the treatise, its author sets forth the Florentine/Tuscan dialect as the superior Italian vernacular, hence, the scholarly attention given to the *Dialogo* as a linguistic treatise. However, it may be that the underlying reason that its author defends his native dialect is only partly due to his linguistic investigations. Could it be that the *Dialogo* is as much a political treatise as it is linguistic?

It is toward an understanding of the politics behind the language of the *Dialogo* that this Chapter seeks to move. And this may be illustrated by examining the term *patria* in the *Dialogo*. Perhaps this may help to demonstrate Machiavelli's authorship and it may show that the *Dialogo* is important in helping to interpret Machiavelli's plan for Italian liberation and unification. That said, the author recognizes and acknowledges the historical trend of examining the *Dialogo* in the context of the *Questione della lingua*, but wishes to deviate from this precedent and focus on its political implications. In so doing, the author is following a relatively new approach to the *Dialogo*, which has recently been studied by political scientists and historians, not linguists.[1] Before moving to the examination of *patria*, it may prove helpful to the reader to provide a brief synopsis of the work.

The *Dialogo*, written in the form of a letter to an unknown recipient, is, it seems, its author's defense of his native Florentine/Tuscan dialect. The letter is divided into three parts. The first part contains a *discorso* on the author's beliefs in the superiority of that dialect against the notion that Italy's great writers, namely Dante, Petrarch and Boccaccio wrote in a "courtly tongue" rather than in their native Florentine. This patriotic defense is followed by a *dialogo* with Dante, who set out in Latin in his *De vulgari eloquentia* the belief that all learned Italians wrote and spoke in a courtly language.[2] The third part comprises a return to a *discorso*, addressed to Dante who remains silent and attentive. But what caused the author to write the treatise in the first place?

It seems that the *Dialogo* was sparked by Gian Giorgio Trissino's visit to Florence where he took up Dante's view of the courtly tongue and expounded thereon.[3] Flying in the face of Trissino's and Dante's assertions, the *Dialogo*'s author set out to correct them. Here, the political implications inherent in the *Dialogo* are perhaps felt most deeply, for its author, it seems, not only desired that other Italians should adopt his *lingua della patria*, but he also likened Trissino's and Dante's attacks on the language of his *patria* to political treason. However, the author seeks to re-educate Dante, not banish him into the nether regions of Hell. Indeed, at the conclusion of the

Dialogo, Dante goes so far as to confess his sins against the *patria*, not heaven, and is forgiven and restored by the author. Beyond these apparent textual facts, nothing is known of the *Dialogo*'s intended audience or readership. One might be tempted to guess at these, but that is all that is possible. Therefore, it may prove helpful to see how the term *patria* is used in the *Dialogo* in order to see whether its use therein corresponds with Machiavelli's use of *patria* in *Il Principe* and the *Discorsi*. If there are similarities, may these be used to strengthen the case for Machiavelli's authorship?

Patria in the *Dialogo* is used sixteen times, *patrie* once and *patrium* once. Given that the work is only 4,513 words in length, *patria* and its derivatives appear therein with greater frequency than either *Il Principe* or the *Discorsi*. The occurrences are as follows.

Capoverso 1: *Patria* appears four times.
Capoverso 7: Once.
Capoverso 10: Twice.
Capoverso 64: Once.
Capoverso 93: Twice.
Capoverso 94: Twice.
Capoverso 95: Three times.
Capoverso 97: Once.
Capoverso 94: *Patrie* appears once.
Capoverso 93: *Patrium* appears once.[4]

In capoverso 1, for example, the author links *patria* with verbs and modifiers such as *onorare, hanno sortito… più nobile, lacerare, fa nimico*. The words with which *patria* is linked seem to indicate that the author is exhorting those who love their *patria* to continue honoring it and despite events within it never to seek to "strike" it or become an enemy thereof. Of these occurrences, that which may catch the reader's eye is the second occurrence, "hanno sortito patria più nobile."[5] It seems that the author of the *Dialogo* viewed his *patria* as the noblest, at least in terms of its language, in all of Italy. One might be tempted to compare this sentiment with what Machiavelli says in *Il Principe*.

In *Il Principe*, as Chapter One set out, *patria* was used in conjunction with derivatives of *nobile*, twice. "Donde la loro patria ne fu nobilitata e diventò felicissima" and "questa patria ne sia nobilitata." Perhaps the author of the *Dialogo* wanted his *patria*, Florence, to be *più nobile*, politically as it was linguistically. So, there may be at least some similarity between the two works. But do the similarities end there?

"Lingua" is used in conjunction with *patria* five times in the *Dialogo* and one time in conjunction with *patrie*. "Scrissono nella lingua patria; ma quella lingua si chiama d'una patria; tu vuoi vedere la dignità della tua lingua patria; disaiutandoli la lingua patria; a dimenticare quella lor naturale barbaria nella quale la patria lingua li sommergeva"; and "perché e' dicano che tutte le lingue patrie son brutte s'elle non hanno del misto di modo che veruna sarebbe brutta."[6] At times—as in this instance—*patria* is used as an adjective to describe the author's "father" or "native" tongue. In the context of the *Dialogo* this "native tongue" refers to Florentine or Tuscan. If we turn to the writings of Machiavelli, one may find that he recognized the distinctiveness of his native Tuscan dialect.

Il Principe provides an interesting example in which Machiavelli does not use *patria*, but he defined his language as Tuscan.

> E questo è, che alcuno è tenuto liberale, alcuno misero (usando uno termine toscano, perché *avaro* in nostra lingua è ancora colui che per rapina desidera di avere, *misero* chiamiamo noi quello che si astiene troppo di usare il suo).[7]

Machiavelli unmistakably refers to "nostra lingua" or "our language," as *toscano*. This seems to indicate that he was cognizant of his relationship to Tuscany, linked by citizenship in Florence as we saw in the previous Chapters and that Machiavelli was aware that part of his identity, culturally and politically was the language of his *patria*, Florentine and Tuscan. The *Discorsi*, it seems, present an even clearer linkage between language, politics and patriotism.

In the *Discorsi* Machiavelli, referring to the ancient inhabitants of Tuscany before they fell under the sway of Rome, wrote, "aveva i suoi costumi e la sua lingua patria."[8] It seems that Machiavelli recognized the relationship between customs and language, particularly in relation to his native Tuscany. An attack on the language and customs of his *patria* could perhaps have caused Machiavelli to come to its rhetorical rescue. This does not seem improbable. There is another interesting similarity between the *Dialogo* and another of Machiavelli's works; notably the *Istorie fiorentine* (1521). The author has taken an editorial decision not to include all references to *patria* in the *Istorie* as this would make this exercise inordinately lengthy. However, these occurrences are carefully compiled in the Appendix to this Chapter for the reader's inspection. Therefore, we have limited our examination to one important example.

In the *Istorie*, Book One, Chapter Five, Machiavelli discussed the decline of Rome, the "barbarian" invasions and the mixing of cultures and languages that followed, which created, new languages and cultures.

From among these ruins and new peoples sprang new languages, as appears now in France, Spain, and Italy: the native language (*lingua patria*) of the new peoples mixed with the ancient Roman to make a new order of speech.[9]

One may find a more expansive and complementary line of argument in the *Dialogo*. Therein its author wrote:

And here it follows, that languages enrich themselves from the beginning, and become more beautiful as the they become most copious; but is it very true that with time, through the multitude of these new words, they are bastardized and become something different; but this happens over hundreds of years; which others do not perceive until it has descended into an extreme barbarism. This change is very quick when it happens that a new population comes to live in a province. In this case it makes its change in the course of an age of a man. But in whichever of these two ways the language is changed, it follows that if there is the will, the lost language can be regained by good writers who have written in that language, as has been done and is still being done with the Latin language and the Greek.[10]

In both cases, new peoples and new customs are introduced and similarly, new languages are created. In the former, Machiavelli referred to the foundations of the French, Spanish and Italian languages and customs. In the latter, responding to an attack on his language, the author is trying to illustrate that the Florentine language is able dexterously, to re-appropriate foreign words into itself, retaining its original beauty while becoming more copious. Perhaps the similarities which have been illustrated are more than superficial.

Machiavelli, the Provenance of the *Dialogo* and the Inquisition

The Church banned the works of Machiavelli in 1564. In that year his writings were added to the "first class" on the Index of banned books, which meant that lay-persons were strictly forbidden from reading or possessing anything written by Machiavelli, unless they were sanctioned by the Church to do so. Giuliano de' Ricci and Niccolò Machiavelli the younger—Machiavelli's grandsons—were given such a sanction by the Church to compile, edit and purge Machiavelli's *opere* of all anti-Church or anti-papal rhetoric in order to make the "new and improved" Machiavelli suitable for public consumption. Their work lasted from 3 August 1573 until 17 May 1578.[11] During that time, in 1577, Ricci and Machiavelli the younger discovered the *Dialogo*, which they believed to have been written by their grandfather (discussed below).

The author of the *Dialogo* neglected to provide a title for the short treatise, so Ricci and Niccolò the younger provided one—*Discorso o dialogo intorno alla nostra lingua.*[12] Then, in 1579 after nearly five years of work, Ricci and Niccolò the younger refused, in protest, to publish their edited version of Machiavelli's *opere* anonymously, or under a fictitious author's name as the Church at Rome sought to compel them to do.[13] So, along with the rest of their work, the *Dialogo* slipped into obscurity.

The *Dialogo* was once again brought to light in a 1726 copy, made from Ricci's manuscript.[14] Four years after this copy was produced Giovanni Bottari published the *Dialogo* for the first time.[15] Interestingly, and troublingly to some, Bottari did not attribute the *Dialogo* to Machiavelli and he carefully removed and edited all negative references to the papacy in the treatise. These references are few but abrasive (cited below). Despite Bottari's omissions, his 1730 edition continued to be the text on which other subsequent editions of the *Dialogo* were based, even after it was accepted as a work of Machiavelli in 1769.[16] It was not published in its entirety until 1929—199 years after its original publication and a full 414 years after it was written in 1515.[17] The checkered and varied history of the *Dialogo* has produced an equally colorful historiography. In order to present an orderly and precise history of the historiography concerned with the *Dialogo* it is helpful to assess each point of view chronologically.

Scholarship published since 1960 takes the place of prominence in the following historiographical assessment because recent and contemporary scholarship has subsumed nineteenth century arguments both for and against Machiavelli's authorship into itself. Furthermore, a careful plan of investigation into the historical debates concerned with the *Dialogo* will facilitate in attaining to the goal of this Chapter which is to suggest that Machiavelli may have written the *Dialogo*. It is best to divide the historians and historiography concerned with the *Dialogo* into two camps: those who believe Machiavelli is the author of the *Dialogo* and those who do not. Cecil Grayson represents best those who doubt Machiavelli's authorship and Hans Baron those who support Machiavelli's authorship. Interestingly, and perhaps this is indicative of the *Dialogo*'s own diverse history, scholars periodically jump from one camp to the other, muddling its historiography.

Confusingly both Grayson's 1960 essay "Lorenzo, Machiavelli and the Italian Language," and Baron's 1961 essay titled "Machiavelli on the Eve of *Discorsi*: The Date and Place of His *Dialogo intorno alla nostra lingua*" point to Machiavelli as the author of the *Dialogo*.[18] While Baron remained firm in his assertion that Machiavelli authored the text, Grayson, after re-thinking his position, changed his mind, choosing instead to rule out Machiavelli as the author of the *Dialogo*. In an essay entitled "Machiavelli and Dante," published in 1971, Grayson compiled many of the earlier arguments against Machiavelli's authorship set forth by distinguished nineteenth-century Italian scholars such as Filippo Luigi Polidori and Oreste Tommasini among others.[19] Grayson prefaced his article with the following:

> This article is a revised version of the paper read at the Italian Institute, London, on 14 May 1969, during a symposium organized by the Society for Renaissance Studies to celebrate the quincentary of Machiavelli's birth. I am grateful to Professor Carlo Dionisotti whose intervention in discussion on that occasion led me to qualify my earlier conclusions regarding the attribution of the *Dialogo* to Machiavelli. In dedicating this article now to my friend Hans Baron, I am conscious of removing the ground from beneath his feet, as well as my own. If I am right in doing so, I hope that he will not mind if we fall together![20]

It is interesting to point out that Grayson attributes his change of mind to Carlo Dionisotti. Grayson's comments seem to indicate that Dionisotti did not believe that Machiavelli authored the *Dialogo*. Given the fact that Grayson's article is a summation and expansion of most of the earlier arguments against Machiavelli's authorship, one can conclude that Dionisotti held similar views at that time. However, Dionisotti also had a change of mind, for he attributed the *Dialogo* to Machiavelli in a lecture delivered in the autumn of 1969, only months after he criticized Grayson's lecture.[21] Confusingly, it appears that Dionisotti changed Grayson's mind and *vice versa*.

Dionisotti went on to publish his research into Machiavelli and the *Dialogo* in several books and articles. All of these came to the same conclusion—Machiavelli authored the *Dialogo*. Most importantly, Dionisotti's ideas appear in his 1980 book *Machiavellerie* and more recently in a 1993 article entitled "Machiavelli, Man of Letters."[22] Grayson's and Dionisotti's "changes of mind" are representative of the larger historiographical framework that both inform and hamper studies into the *Dialogo*.

Maurizio Viroli's influential 1998 essay on patriotism, *For Love of Country*, includes references to the *Dialogo* as a work of Machiavelli, and Susan Meld Shell, in her essay published in 2000—"Machiavelli's Discourse on Language"—re-opened research into the *Dialogo*.[23] Shell's and Viroli's recent additions to the *Dialogo*'s historiography are important because both scholars insist that Niccolò Machiavelli wrote the *Dialogo*. Their recent acceptance of the *Dialogo* as a work of Machiavelli adds weight to the proposals and historical analysis of the treatise's text that follows in due course.

In recent years Italian scholars have produced three critical editions of the *Dialogo*. Bortolo Tommaso Sozzi published his Einaudi critical edition in 1976 entitled *Discorso o dialogo intorno alla nostra lingua: Edizione Critica* and Ornella Castellani Pollidori published two critical editions: one in 1978 entitled *Niccolò Machiavelli e il "Dialogo intorno alla nostra lingua." Con una edizione critica del testo*, followed by her 1981 *Nuove Riflessioni sul Discorso o dialogo intorno alla nostra lingua di Niccolò Machiavelli.*[24] All three editions defend Machiavelli's authorship. These critical texts and the historiographical arguments concerned with the *Dialogo* focus on two basic arguments: first, (this Chapter's focus), whether or not Machiavelli wrote the short treatise, and second, (the subject of the next Chapter), the date in which the text was written.

The question of authorship itself encompasses many arguments. The most potentially damaging argument concerning authorship focuses upon the author's treatment of Dante in one particular passage of the *Dialogo*. Those who seek to remove the *Dialogo* from Machiavelli's *oeuvre* seize on this fact, believing that Machiavelli was always reverential toward Dante in his other works. The *Dialogo*'s author, Machiavelli or not, *is* critical of his famous Florentine ancestor. Three scenarios may help to show why. First, the author's harshness is necessary when viewed in the patriotic context of the entire *Dialogo*. Second, he may have used Dante's exile to point out the irony of his own exile. Third, it is also likely that the author was expressing contemporary, republican humanist views that left little room for Dante's trust in a world empire.[25] These three possibilities, which are complementary rather than mutually exclusive, along with a study of the *Dialogo*'s surviving manuscripts, strengthen the case for Machiavelli's authorship.

The history of the *Dialogo*, first in manuscript form, and then much later in printed form is intriguing. This history, along with the author's treatment of Dante in the text, has led some to believe that Machiavelli could not have written the treatise. However, an analysis of the *Dialogo*'s provenance suggests that Machiavelli could have written it. Moreover, the treatment of Dante inherent in the treatise is by no means out of character for Machiavelli. Could the *Dialogo* be symptomatic of Machiavelli's increasing patriotism which found its first outpouring in the epilogue of *Il Principe*, followed by the lengthy *Discorsi*? An examination of the *Dialogo*'s manuscripts may help to answer this question.

Four *apografi*, or copies of the *Dialogo* survive; three are complete and of the other, only a fragment remains. The reader will find that three of these are discussed below, while the fourth manuscript, for reasons of scholarly practicality, is detailed in the notes.[26] Until Bortolo Tommaso Sozzi published his critical edition of the *Dialogo* in 1976, it was always assumed that at least one, but more than likely two, of the four surviving manuscripts had their roots in Giuliano de' Ricci's apograph—a copy from an original manuscript—of 1577.[27] As Sozzi illustrated, there are perhaps too many differences between the texts to justify this position.[28] However, Sozzi does not have a response or theory to fill the gap created by his enquiry. This is one of the many intriguing elements associated with the surviving manuscripts of the *Dialogo*.

The first—and perhaps most reliable—manuscript of the *Dialogo* can be traced to 1577. It was copied from a manuscript that is itself now lost. Giuliano de Ricci, grandson of Niccolò Machiavelli, was the first to discover and copy the *Dialogo*. The manuscript from which Ricci copied lacked Niccolò Machiavelli's signature, but Ricci was assured by Bernardo Machiavelli, Niccolò's son, that he had seen his father with such a work and that he recalled hearing his father speak about the topics included in the *Dialogo*. Bernardo, in 1577, was 74 years of age; quite old, but Ricci felt that the eyewitness account provided by Niccolò's son was sufficient to attribute the work to Bernardo's father. Ricci did not find a copy of the yet untitled *Dialogo* in Machiavelli's personal papers. In fact the *Dialogo* that he had in his possession was given to him by a donor, whose name Ricci did not mention. The anonymous donor assured Ricci that the small treatise was a product of Niccolò Machiavelli's pen. That Bernardo's memory and the donor's assurance corroborated each other provided Ricci with further confirmation.[29]

However, the manuscript that Ricci had in his possession was lacking more than Machiavelli's signature. It also lacked a title. Ricci provided the title that has, over time, become the most accepted: *Discorso o dialogo intorno alla nostra lingua*. This manuscript is not without its own sense of intrigue, for it is obvious that it was copied by two different people. After describing the manuscript, Sozzi noted:

> The transcription of the *Discourse* by Ricci, in beautiful and dark cursive of a chancelloresque type, does not extend to the whole of the work, but it covers only the first page and is partially cut on the second part of the page; the remainder, in an atypical cursive, almost certainly from the late *cinquecento*, is from another hand.[30]

Ricci's handwriting, the better of the two, comprised only one and a half pages of the manuscript. More will be said about the "altra mano" in due course.

Of the remaining manuscripts, which are central to our discussion, one survives in complete form. The Vatican manuscript, like the Borghini fragment discussed below, is not easily dated. Some have only gone as far as to venture that it is a later copy than that of Ricci, while others have assigned the Vatican manuscript's origins to the seventeenth century.[31] While the Vatican manuscript is similar to the Ricci manuscript, it goes by a different title, *Messer Niccolò di Bernardo Machiavelli: discorso over dialogo circa la lingua fiorentina*, but it was thought by Mario Casella, editor of the first complete, edition of the *Dialogo*, to have come from Ricci's apograph.[32] However, Sozzi's edition of the *Dialogo* illustrated that there are perhaps too many differences between the two texts to trace, with any degree of certainty, the Vatican text to Ricci's apograph.[33] This fact adds more problems to the history of the *Dialogo*, but as the title of the Vatican manuscript indicates, that whoever copied the text no doubt agreed that the *Dialogo*'s origins could be traced to Machiavelli.[34]

The final surviving manuscript is a part of the Borghini collection in Florence.[35] Unlike the Ricci manuscript, the Borghini manuscript is incomplete, ending at the mid-point of the author's exchange with Dante.

N. By my faith you do guard yourself well against Florentine words![36]

The Borghini fragment is interesting in that it, like the Vatican manuscript, also names Machiavelli as its author; *Discorso di Nic⁰. Machiavelli nel quale si tratta [della lingua]*.[37] The section of the title in brackets is not in the same handwriting as the rest of the title. It is not clear who provided this amendment. Sozzi wrote that "the final specification is by another and much later hand."[38] Giovanni Bottari, the first to publish the *Dialogo* in 1730, may have added this "specification," while he was preparing his text for publication. As with the Vatican text, it is uncertain whether or not the Borghini fragment was copied from the Ricci apograph. There is no scholarly consensus concerning either the date or the origin of the Borghini fragment. However, it was found hidden, without a date, between Borghini's papers from the mid-1570's, which led Grayson to the following conclusion:

> The Borghini fragment [...] probably found its way into this collection without Borghini's knowledge or even after his time. It is difficult otherwise to explain Borghini's silence about a work on language here bearing the name of Machiavelli. The (manuscript) is not in Borghini's hand; it lies between works of the mid-70's, though it is not necessarily a guide to the actual date of the (manuscript). Dr. John Woodhouse tells me there are no allusions to Machiavelli among them (apart from the occurrence of his name in a list of Florentine writers)—a silence which may well be explained by the interdict on Machiavelli's works, though it is questionable whether Borghini would have felt this to inhibit reference to a work on language.[39]

This appears strained. It seems that Grayson did not take into account the Index of Prohibited Books which included all of Machiavelli's works.

Indeed, the ban on Machiavelli's work was strict and it seems quite possible that it would have inhibited all and any reference.

Recent scholarship, although not explicitly tied to the *Dialogo*, has shed new light, not only on Machiavelli's status as a banned author in the 16th century, but also on the relationship of Giuliano de' Ricci and Vincenzo Borghini to the *Dialogo*'s provenance. Machiavelli's "heretical" and banned status in the last quarter of the 16th century could quite easily have led a collector to "forget" to mention owning a work penned by Machiavelli. A papal ban provided more than enough impetus to hide a work written by Machiavelli, particularly when the short treatise on language contained scathing criticism of the papal court.

Peter Godman's scholarship on the Inquisition in Italy and its relationship to the Congregation for the Index brings some possible answers to several of the *Dialogo*'s historiographical puzzles. It is necessary to trace several of Machiavelli's larger political works in order to illustrate where and how the *Dialogo* fits into this scenario. In *From Poliziano to Machiavelli*, Godman, having recourse to texts made recently available by the Vatican, recounts the history of Machiavelli's political works and their relationship to the Inquisition and the Congregation. Here it must be noted that the Inquisition was the first body sanctioned by the Church to oversee the editing of Machiavelli's work. Later, the Congregation, established on 5 March 1571 by Pope Pius V, was set up to deal exclusively with the editing and banning of books. Machiavelli's work, along with Boccaccio's, was embedded in the subsequent debates concerning which authors were troubling or subversive to the doctrines of the Roman Church.[40] Machiavelli's name was originally placed in the "first class" on the Index of questionable or troubling authors in 1559. By 1564, his name was placed on the index of heretical authors.[41] Lay-persons were thus strictly forbidden to possess his work. Only those who were sanctioned or commissioned by the papacy to "edit" or purge the work were allowed to possess it. This is a brief summary of the history of Machiavelli's posthumous standing in the eyes of the papacy. A detailed analysis of the years 1559 to 1564 illustrates not only the precariousness of Machiavelli's standing on the Index of banned authors and with the Congregation who prepared the Index during these years, but it also helps to show why the intricacies of the provenance of the *Dialogo* have been uncertain for so long.

The papacy found itself in a difficult position when it banned Machiavelli's *Istorie Fiorentine*, for Machiavelli was commissioned to write the work on 8 November 1520 by Cardinal Giulio de'Medici; the future Pope Clement VII.[42] Not wanting to appear contradictory, the Inquisition, under the guidance of Pope Paul IV, commissioned Girolamo Muzio to prepare edited versions of the *Discorsi* and the *Arte della Guerra*.[43] Godman's research illustrates that Muzio had in his possession his newly purged versions of the *Discorsi* and the *Arte* at the Council of Trent in 1562.[44] Later, an edition of the *Istorie* was to be produced and overseen by the Congregation at Rome.[45] At this point Machiavelli's work was set aside because he was soon to be placed on the Index of Heretical Authors (in 1564)—the Index was designed to list and categories the works of heretical authors.[46] During the pontificate of Gregory XIII, in 1573, a full nine years later, the papacy commissioned Cosimo de'Medici to organize censors in Florence to produce all of Machiavelli's works in purged form. Two men were given this task, Niccolò Machiavelli's grandsons: Giuliano de' Ricci and, as Godman refers to him, Niccolò Machiavelli's "homonymous canon," Niccolò Machiavelli the younger.[47]

One can surmise that Ricci's and Machiavelli's refusal to publish Machiavelli the elder's work without his name attached, stemmed from the fact that their edition of the *Istorie fiorentine*, was, despite the fact that they omitted the author's name, shelved and deemed unfit.[48] Amid all of this turmoil, the *Dialogo* may find its place.

Ricci discovered the *Dialogo* in 1577 when he and Machiavelli were nearing the end of their aforementioned editing tasks. Here, one of the questions concerning Ricci's apograph is answered. The identity of the "altra mano," may, with some degree of certainty, be ascribed to Niccolò Machiavelli the younger. Given that he was Ricci's assistant, he would have had the responsibility of copying texts at Ricci's command.

Ricci and Niccolò the younger refused to edit the text, and this may explain why the harsh references to the papacy remain in Ricci's apograph. It may be more fitting, after applying Godman's research to the *Dialogo*'s provenance, to re-name the apograph as that of Ricci/Machiavelli. There are two likely reasons why Ricci and Niccolò the younger did not publish the *Dialogo*. First, given that Machiavelli's grandsons were involved in the preparation of the manuscript, it is not surprising that Niccolò the younger and Ricci refused, not only to publish Machiavelli's work under another name, but also, as the facts at hand seem to indicate, they chose to suppress rather than purge the *Dialogo*. Was this the same method they used with Machiavelli's *Le Maschere*?[49] The second reason for their decision to hide the *Dialogo* could have resulted from the awkward position that Niccolò the younger would have found himself in, as a Church canon and as the "infamous" Machiavelli's namesake; a telling example of "the family perspective" on the problem.[50] Their actions, whether for the sake of their grandfather, or for the sake of the reputation of Niccolò the younger, saved the *Dialogo* from the Inquisition, allowing it to remain hidden and obscure.

This is an attractive solution to several of the problems surrounding the early manuscripts of the *Dialogo*. Yet, others remain; the survival of the Borghini fragment is linked to the censorship of Machiavelli by the Inquisition and the Congregation. Vincenzo Borghini, like his fellow Florentines Niccolò the younger and Ricci, was also employed by the papacy to produce an "edited" version of Machiavelli's *opere*.[51]

Borghini was the head of the Florentine Academy. He was responsible for delegating to his *deputati* the task of editing Boccaccio's work, but he was also to oversee the editing of Machiavelli's work at the Florentine Academy. He, unlike Ricci and Niccolò the younger, was very serious about adhering to papal requirements. In 1542 he went so far as to remove Machiavelli's *Discorsi* and the *Istorie* from his personal library, predating by some time the official ban placed on Machiavelli's work.[52] However, Godman's scholarship illustrates that Borghini was not afraid to undertake delicate and semi-secretive work. For example, when Borghini was reminded that all of Machiavelli's works were under formal ban, unless a papal commission was given, he allowed the preparation of censored versions of Machiavelli's work to begin, hoping that the Inquisition would be lenient.[53]

By 1572, Borghini's *deputati* were preparing Machiavelli's work—along with Boccaccio's *Decameron*—for censure.[54] However, Borghini was more interested in producing a censored version of Boccaccio, so the Florentine Academy's "corrected" Machiavelli was never completed. Yet his work on the *Decameron* was allowed to continue, culminating in a new "authorized edition" that "was published by the Giunta in Florence in 1573."[55] Frustratingly for Borghini and his *deputati*, their censored Boccaccio was subsequently banned in 1573 after Gregory XIII was elected pope, in succession to the more lenient Pius V.[56] Referring to Gregory XIII's views of Machiavelli, Godman wrote that he "regarded that author as a damnable heretic."[57] John Tedeschi pointed to this change of mind on the part of the papacy, as "a fine example of confusion in Roman censorship practice."[58] It is in this ever-changing and uncertain world of censorship that Ricci and Niccolò the younger completed the task of preparing censored versions of Machiavelli's work where Borghini and the Academy failed.[59] Borghini's involvement in the censoring of Machiavelli's work is not great, but the fact that he was involved in the early stages of the "editing" process directly links him with Machiavelli's work and it helps to explain how he could have come into contact with the *Dialogo*, particularly when one considers that he, Ricci and Niccolò the younger—all Florentines—were moving in the same scholarly and "editorial" circles.[60]

Given that the manuscript found in Borghini's papers is only a fragment, he could easily have overlooked this small treatise, but it is more likely, as was stated earlier, that he suppressed his copy of the *Dialogo*. Might one suggest that it would be beneficial for a scholar of his standing to try and suppress Machiavelli's authorship of the *Dialogo*? Interestingly, the fragment he kept ends—conveniently—before the author proceeded to his criticism of the papal court. As already stated the Borghini manuscript was found, without a date, between personal papers from the mid-1570's—the exact period in which Borghini, Ricci and Niccolò the younger were working on "editing" Machiavelli. But was the threat of prosecution enough to cause Ricci, Niccolò the younger and Borghini to suppress their respective copies of the *Dialogo*?

Machiavelli's work remained under strict ban long after Gregory XIII's pontificate. In 1600, the Inquisition forbade even the Medici to own a copy of the *Discorsi*.[61] Furthermore, as late as 1605, one of the lesser Academies at Florence was denied permission to possess any works written by Machiavelli, even for the purposes of censoring them, as the following letter illustrates:

Reverend Father.

In reply to the letter of your reverence of 4 December, I want to say that these most illustrious and reverend cardinals, my colleagues have not seen fit to grant a license to the Regent of the Academy of the Spensierati to possess and read the works of Machiavelli, Boccaccio and Castelvetro for the purpose of correcting them so that new editions can be published...

Rome, 12 February 1605, The Cardinal Borghese[62]

This short letter, written by Camillo Borghese in response to a Florentine request, shows that Machiavelli's work, listed first among the three banned authors, was not tolerated by either the Inquisition or the Congregation. Borghese was elected Pope Paul V later in the same year. This evidence supports the premise that Borghini suppressed his manuscript. It seems that Machiavelli's work was considered so dangerous, that by 1610 the Inquisition and the Congregation denied permission even to those of highest rank to read it. For example, "Baron de Fucariis, the imperial ambassador in Venice" was denied permission to *read* Machiavelli's work even in censored form.[63] And individuals who, despite the ban placed on Machiavelli's work, were found to have private copies, could expect arrest, torture and possible excommunication at the least, as was the case for the unfortunate Cesare di Pisa.[64] It is no wonder, considering that Machiavelli's work was completely banned from 1579, and that penalties for possessing his work were stiff, that Borghini neglected to mention owning even a portion of work attributed to that author. Indeed, there may have been advantages to *not* attributing the *Dialogo* to Machiavelli. One could safely keep the work in one's library and one could avoid prosecution by the Inquisition for owning a work by a banned author.

If the original manuscript had survived, from which Ricci and Niccolò the younger made the first copy, perhaps, this discussion would be less problematic. Yet, even in the absence of the original, a good deal of information can be gained. The Ricci/Machiavelli apograph is the first and perhaps most reliable manuscript of the *Dialogo*. The Vatican manuscript is consistent with the Ricci/Machiavelli manuscript, but it contains enough variations in the text to cast doubt on the idea that its origins can be traced to the Florentine transcription. If the Vatican manuscript was not copied from Ricci's apograph, then new possibilities may arise. Although not provable, perhaps there was another manuscript that is now lost from which the Vatican transcribers copied? The Borghini fragment's origins are equally cloudy, but the fact remains that four manuscripts of the *Dialogo* survive and that they were, in one form or another, kept from both the Inquisition and the Congregation.[65]

There was a single copy of the Ricci/Machiavelli apograph produced in 1726, a full 149 years after Ricci discovered the *Dialogo*. This gap can be explained by the fact that Ricci, as well as Borghini, was working for the Church. Borghini may have hidden his copy. It is probable that Ricci chose a similar path. Ricci did not publicize the fact that he possessed an unpurged text which he believed to have been written by Machiavelli, given the stringent penalties for possessing a work by a banned author. The copy of the Ricci/Machiavelli manuscript, the *Palatino* manuscript, like its predecessor, is located in the Biblioteca Nazionale in Florence.[66] The unknown copyist was central in bringing the *Dialogo* back to the attention of Italian historians and scholars. However, those who chose to reintroduce the *Dialogo* to the Italian public must be held accountable for the next stage of its curious history.

At this point, the circumstances surrounding the history of the *Dialogo* become even more intriguing. In 1730, the *Dialogo* appeared for the first time as a printed work in a collection compiled by Giovanni Bottari, a Florentine scholar and prolific editor. He chose to print the work without an author's name attached, ignoring the historical precedent set by Ricci and Niccolò the younger in 1577, the Vatican transcribers and subsequent 1726 copy, which placed the work firmly in Machiavelli's *opere*. Bottari's reasoning for this editorial license is not clearly demonstrable. Moreover, Bottari chose not to attribute the work to anyone. Instead, he placed the *Dialogo* in the appendix of Benedetto Varchi's *L'Hercolano dialogo nel quale si ragioni generalmente delle lingue, ed in particolare della Toscana e della Fiorentina.* The British Library has a copy of this 1730 edition.[67] The Edinburgh University Library has the Milanese edition of 1804 in its special collections.[68] Although not edited by Bottari, the 1804 editors chose to use Bottari's 1730 introduction. Furthermore, as the 1730 and 1804 editions indicate, Bottari was not happy with the name that Ricci and Niccolò the younger had given to the work, choosing instead to title it; *Discorso over dialogo sopra il nome della lingua volgare: dialogo in cui si esamina se la lingua in cui scrissero Dante, il Boccaccio e il Petrarca si debba chiamare italiana, toscana, o fiorentina.*[69]

It is strange that Bottari's edition has enjoyed so much respect. Sozzi described it as "con aggiunta di molti arbitrii ed errori."[70] Perhaps the most blatant of Bottari's omissions concerns the references to the papal court at Rome. Again, Sozzi's scholarship makes this point clear.[71] The following passage is complete, relying upon the Ricci/Machiavelli apograph of 1577 and the Vatican manuscript. The italicized portion of the quotation represents the section that Bottari chose to omit.

> Ma se tu parli della corte di Roma, tu parli d'un luogo dove si parla di tanti modi, di quante nazioni vi sono, né se li può dare in modo alcuno regola. *Di poi io mi maraviglio di te, che tu voglia, dove non si fa cosa alcuna laudabile o buona, che vi si faccia questa; perché dove sono i costumi perversi conviene che il parlare sia perverso e abbia in sé quello effeminato lascivo che hanno coloro che lo parlono.* Ma quello che inganna molti circa i vocaboli comuni è che, tu e gli altri che hanno scritto essendo stati celebrati e letti in varii luoghi, molti vocaboli nostri sono stati imparati da molti forestieri e osservati da loro, tal che di proprii nostri son diventati comuni.[72]

This discussion of the papal court is prefaced by a discussion of the "courtly tongue." This is, according to Dante's character in the *Dialogo*, the common tongue of learned Italians.[73] The *Dialogo*'s author is quick to dispense with the idea of a courtly tongue, by stating that court languages reflect their localities, nothing more. While the discussion is focused on courts, the *Dialogo*'s author takes the opportunity to attack the papal court at Rome. The complete reference to the papal court, quoted above, is found in every complete manuscript before Bottari's.[74] However, in Bottari's 1730 edition and subsequent editions until 1929, the reference is missing.[75] Here, it is important to mention that the references to the papal court are underlined in the Vatican manuscript and set off with brackets in the *Palatino* manuscript of 1726[76]. An analysis of the latter seems to indicate that the brackets were added after the *Palatino* manuscript was copied. A similar examination of the Vatican manuscript has not been able to determine whether the references to the papacy were underlined while it was copied, or after. While no additional information can be gleaned from the Vatican manuscript regarding this point, it seems probable that Bottari was responsible for adding the brackets to the *Palatino* manuscript. Although not underlined, the Ricci/Machiavelli manuscript, while it is hastily transcribed throughout, becomes exceedingly sloppy where the author discusses the papacy. (See Figure 4 below)

Cecil Grayson gives Bottari's 1730 edition an interesting place of precedence over other early printed editions that name Machiavelli as the author.[77] Grayson seizes upon Bottari's edition because Bottari was the first to reject Machiavelli's authorship. Surprisingly, Grayson neglected to mention Bottari's omissions. Here Godman's scholarship provides possible answers: first, as to why Bottari edited the text and changed its name, and second, why he chose not to attribute the work to Niccolò Machiavelli.

What follows may be conjecture, but it is not merely speculative. Giovanni Bottari's 1730 edition of the *Dialogo* was purged of all critical references to the papacy. The facts at hand seem to indicate that Bottari followed the sixteenth-century guidelines set forth by the Inquisition and later the Congregation of the Index regarding the editing and purging of Machiavelli's work. He acted as a censor, and unlike Ricci and Machiavelli the younger, he did not have any problem publishing the *Dialogo* without the author's name attached, choosing instead to include it in an obscure appendix without any indication of authorship. Despite Bottari's censorship, his edition of the *Dialogo* was the central text on which subsequent editions were based until a complete version was published by Casella and Mazzoni in 1929.[78]

In 1769, the *Dialogo* was published for the first time as a work of Niccolò Machiavelli.[79] The Special Collections Department at the Glasgow University Library possesses a copy of this edition. The title used by the 1769 edition's editors is the same as Bottari's, but they removed this portion of the title "*sopra il nome della vulgar lingua*," calling it the *Discorso, overro dialogo, in cui si esamina, se la lingua, in cui scrissero Dante, il Boccaccio, e il Petrarca, si debba chiamare Italiana, Toscana, o Fiorentina.* An examination of this text illustrated that Bottari's omissions remained. The extent to which these omissions affected the *Dialogo* can be seen in that the italicized reference to the papal court—cited earlier in the Chapter—was not included in editions throughout the eighteenth, nineteenth and early twentieth centuries. Even those editions that claimed to seek the purest version of the text somehow overlooked this omission. Examples from a few of the editions are enough to demonstrate this.

The *Opere Complete di Niccolò Machiavelli, con molte correzioni e giunte rinvenute sui manoscritti originali,* published in Florence in 1843, does not include the references to the papal court that Bottari deleted.[80] The same omission is repeated in Giuseppe Zirardini's *Opere di Niccolò Machiavelli* of 1851.[81] This version, printed in Paris, like the above Florentine *Opere* of 1843, followed the example set forth by Bottari. Indeed his text, despite its obvious omissions, remained the standard until Casella's and Mazzoni's 1929 edition. Why would Italian scholars perpetuate and pass on a flawed text?

The first possible answer to this question is that these nineteenth-century scholars may not have considered the text to be flawed if they adhered to conservative Catholic policy. Second, it is most likely that generations of scholars continued to publish the flawed Bottari text because they failed to examine the manuscripts themselves. This seems likely in light of the title of the above-mentioned Florentine texts of 1769 and 1843. The editors of this 1843 edition, for example, adopted the 1769 edition's title; *Discorso over[o] Dialogo in cui si esamina se la lingua in cui scrissero Dante, il Boccaccio e il Petrarca si debba chiamare Italiana, Toscana, o Fiorentina.*[82] The information at hand seems to indicate that the editors of the 1769 edition relied on Bottari's text—not the manuscripts—and the editors of the 1843 edition, in turn, relied on the 1769 edition.

Those editors who followed Bottari may have exercised "self-censorship" for religious reasons. The Roman Church—at least in Italy—was not in a position of strength in the mid 19th century, so "self-censorship," as opposed to a Church mandated censorship is more likely, given that by February 1849, Pope Pius IX was in exile in Gaeta.[83] Further complicating matters, archival research was not formally developed until the late 19th and early 20th centuries. The editors who adopted Bottari's edition may not have checked the manuscripts of the *Dialogo,* despite the fact that many claimed to have done so.[84] Whatever the case may be, the harshest references to the papacy in the *Dialogo* were left in unpublished manuscripts in two of Italy's great libraries.

The *Dialogo* was not published in its complete form until the early twentieth century. The Guido Mazzoni and Mario Casella edition of 1929 contains the first complete edition of the *Dialogo.*[85] The editors were aware of their contribution to the study of the *Dialogo.* Casella wrote, "'*Il Dialogo circa la lingua Fiorentina*' è qui dato per la prima volta nella sua integrità, con quel passo contro alla Curia romana che il Bottari aveva soppresso nella sua edizione del 1730."[86] The *Dialogo* was thus first published in censored form in 1730 and in its entirety only in 1929. It took 199 years for the full text to be printed—astounding considering that after 1769 it was thought to be a work of Machiavelli.

The history of the manuscripts and early editions of the *Dialogo* is colorful and puzzling. Its history and certain details in the text itself have caused some scholars to question the *Dialogo*'s authorship. Grayson and others have suggested that the knowledge inherent in the *Dialogo* is beyond that which could be expected of Niccolò Machiavelli. Furthermore, and perhaps more troubling to scholars, is the way in which the author of the *Dialogo* deals with his counterpart in the verbal exchange within the treatise. This point would not be so disconcerting if the author had selected a less famous Florentine than Dante Alighieri with whom to debate. The next section of this Chapter seeks to illustrate that the author's treatment of Dante in the *Dialogo* is consistent with the treatment of Dante in some works by Machiavelli. By the same token, the attitude that the author of the *Dialogo* and Machiavelli often adopted toward Dante is, perhaps representative of the Florentine humanists' struggle to re-appropriate Dante's "antiquated" political vision, centered on universal monarchy or remove it altogether from the new Florentine framework of republicanism.

Machiavelli and Dante

The *Dialogo*'s author is critical of his counterpart, Dante. Grayson asserted that Machiavelli had always been reverential toward Dante in his other works, which meant that he could not be the *Dialogo*'s author.[87] There is more than enough textual as well as contextual evidence and current scholarship to do away with Grayson's argument. For example, Maurizio Viroli does not doubt that Machiavelli wrote the *Dialogo*. Susan Meld Shell's recent work on the *Dialogo*, unlike Viroli's, focuses intently on the authenticity of the work and specifically on Machiavelli's treatment of Dante in the *Dialogo*.[88] The argument to which Shell is responding had its origins in 1883. Then, Oreste Tommasini argued that there was no historical precedent in Machiavelli's work to justify his critical treatment of Dante. On the basis of this argument, Tommasini questioned Machiavelli's authorship.[89] This argument was later followed and developed by Cecil Grayson. He, like Tommasini, did not think that one could reconcile the critical treatment of Dante with any of Machiavelli's other works.

Machiavelli often quoted from Dante, though not always correctly, over a period spanning roughly 25 years.[90] These quotations and references can be found in some of Machiavelli's most famous letters and public works. It is apparent that Machiavelli made attempts to copy Dante's *terza rima* in his *Prima decennale* as well as the *secondo*.[91] This history of apparent emulation does not, despite Grayson's views, lessen the possibility of Machiavelli's authorship of the *Dialogo*. An important part of this puzzle is missing: Machiavelli's poem, *L'Asino*. There is no doubt over authorship, and it owes a great deal to Apuleius' *Metamorphoses*—and to Dante's *Commedia*.[92]

Scholars have paid little attention to the mockery of Dante inherent in Machiavelli's *L'Asino*.[93] The similarities between Dante's *Commedia* and Machiavelli's *L'Asino* are more than superficial and far from flattering. At the beginning of *L'Asino*, Machiavelli speaks these words to introduce his readers to the poem's main character—himself: "The varied chances, the pain and the grief/ that under an Ass's form I suffered, / I shall sing if fortune allows."[94] The first segment of the poem, although interesting, is not important in this context. However, the second section of the poem changes tone and setting from the first, here following the story of Machiavelli's adventures while still in human form. For as Roberto Ridolfi lamented: "unfortunately, the promise of the first chapter is not kept, because the poem stops short at the best point before the metamorphosis."[95] *L'Asino* is thought to have been written no earlier than the autumn of 1515 and not later than 1519.[96] *L'Asino*, despite its unfinished state offers an interesting insight into Machiavelli's literary relationship with Dante.

In that poem, Machiavelli describes his surroundings. Mimicking—or mocking—Dante's *Inferno*, Machiavelli begins his journey in a dark wood. Unlike Dante's intricate depiction of an afterlife based upon a theology that attempts to reconcile pagan antiquity with Christian doctrine, Machiavelli depicts the underworld in terms that are wholly pagan; entirely drained of Christian connotation and devoid of redemption.[97] He finds himself alone and helpless, in an unfamiliar world. However, he is discovered by a beautiful young woman, a servant of Circe; the Homeric character who changed Odysseus' men into swine. The young woman, or "la mia duchessa," as Machiavelli calls her, is fond enough of him to take him into her bed.[98] After a night of bliss the duchess proceeds to give Machiavelli a tour of the many spheres of Circe's animal kingdom. Along the way the duo meet a pig. This pig was at one time a man—a victim of Circe. Interestingly, Shell notes that he speaks like Epicurus.[99] The pig rises from the mud in which it was wallowing, so that it may speak to Machiavelli and the Duchess, mirroring Ugolino in Dante's *Inferno*. This is how Machiavelli described their meeting. The speaker is Machiavelli:

> As we came near, that hog raised his snout all smeared with
> turd and mud, such that to look at him made me sick.
> And because long before I had been known to him, he turned
> toward me with a show of teeth, remaining otherwise quiet and
> without motion.
> So I said to him, in the most gracious tones: "May God give you

a better fate if it seems to you good; may God support you
if you desire support."[100]

Compare Machiavelli's words with those of Dante's when he and Virgil
come upon Ugolino in the Ninth and lowest circle of Hell:

> ....I saw two frozen in one hole
> so close that the head of the one was a hood for the other;
> and as bread is devoured for hunger,
>   so the upper one set his teeth upon the other where the
> brain joins with the nape.
> Not otherwise did Tydeus gnaw
>   the temples of Menalippus for rage
> than this one was doing to the skull and the other parts.
> "Oh you who by so bestial a sign show
>   hatred against him whom you devour, tell
> me the wherefore," I said, "on this condition,
> that if you with reason complain of him,
>   I knowing who you are and his offence, may
> yet require you in the world above, if that
> with which I speak does not dry up.[101]

Thus, the pig's response was diametrically opposed to that of the sorrowful
and wretched Ugolino.[102] The pig, unlike Ugolino, does not want his name or
position restored in the human world above. When given the chance to return
to its human form it rejects the notion, preferring its life in the mud.
Machiavelli continues:

> "On her part she (the duchess) also wants me to tell you that she will free you
> from such great evil, if you wish to return to your early shape."
> Erect the boar stood on his feet when he heard that, and in great
> excitement the muddy beast made his reply:
> "I know not whence you come or from what region, but if you
> have come for nothing else than to get me away from here, go
> off about your business.
> I have no wish to live with you; I refuse. I see clearly that you
> suffer from the error which long bound me too.
> So much your self love deceives you that you do not believe
> there is any good apart from human existence and its worth[...]
> Without the least doubt I assert and affirm that superior to
> yours is our condition[...]."[103]

Harvey noted that the pig would rather "found his notion of the good on
nature," freely accepting its pleasures and troubles, without the interference
of human greed and lust.[104] Redemption in *L'Asino*, unlike Dante's
Commedia, is found in nature, not in things divine.

Shell comments, "Machiavelli naturalizes and bestializes the *Commedia*, translating its spiritual ascent into the worldly meanderings of an ass. In Machiavelli's Circean barnyard the sublime figures in the *Commedia* become ludicrous."[105] Her scholarship provides a thoroughly different picture of Machiavelli and his relationship to Dante from that which is painted by Tommasini and others, but she is by no means alone in her interpretation of Machiavelli's *L'Asino*. Harvey, in his poetic analysis of Machiavelli's *L'Asino*, adds: "Like Dante's journey, this will be a spiritual descent and a reckoning of human affairs and human lives, but unlike Dante, Machiavelli presents a pagan vision of the underworld, and there will be no redeeming ascent afterward.[106] It seems that Machiavelli, while imitating Dante's famous poem, went out of his way to transform the *Commedia*'s heavenly subject into that which was anything but sublime. It may prove helpful to return to a subject discussed in Chapters One and Two: Machiavelli's subversion and re-appropriation of other writers.

The way in which Machiavelli went about changing the backdrop and meaning of Dante's poem to fit his own agenda is in character with the way in which he subverted and re-wrote other authors.[107] Machiavelli used animals—a secular symbol of nature—in *Il Principe*, as he had in *L'Asino* to undermine the authority of republican Rome's illustrious patriot and prolific writer, Marcus Cicero. The most famous of these rejections focuses on the Ciceronian tradition of the virtuous man, particularly when he discusses the "fox" and the "lion." Quentin Skinner illustrated the great lengths to which Machiavelli went in order to turn the Ciceronian conception of proper republican government on its head.

> To the classical moralists and their innumerable followers, moral virtue had been the defining characteristic of the *vir*, the man of true manliness. Hence to abandon virtue was not merely to act irrationally; it was also to abandon one's status as a man and descend to the level of beasts. As Cicero had put it in Book I of *Moral Obligation*, there are two ways in which wrong may be done, either by force or by fraud. Both, he declares, "are bestial" and "wholly unworthy of man"—force because it typifies the lion and fraud because it "seems to belong to the cunning fox."[108]

The Ciceronian passage to which Skinner refers is as follows:

> Wrong may be done, then, in either of two ways, that is, by force or by fraud, both are bestial: fraud seems to belong to the cunning fox, force to the lion; both are wholly unworthy of man, but fraud is the more contemptible. But of all forms of injustice, none is more flagrant that that of the hypocrite who at the very moment when he is most false, makes it his business to appear virtuous.[109]

Skinner, using examples from Chapter 18 of *Il Principe*, illustrated how far Machiavelli was willing to go in order to discredit and disavow the classical and humanistic approaches to princely virtue. He wrote that, "To Machiavelli, by contrast, it seemed obvious that manliness was not enough...one of the things a prince therefore needs to know is which animals to imitate." He continues, "Machiavelli's celebrated advice is that he will come off best if he 'chooses among the beasts the fox and the lion,' supplementing the ideals of manly decency with the indispensable arts of force and fraud."[110] As this example is the most telling of Machiavelli's willingness to attack and reject authors where at other times he accepts their writings wholeheartedly, it is helpful to quote from Chapter 18 of *Il Principe* at length:

> You must know, therefore, that there are two means of fighting: one with laws, the other with force: the first manner is specific to man, the second to beasts: but because the first is often times not enough, one must have recourse to the second. So that for a prince, it is necessary to know how to use both "the beast" and "the man," well....Since, therefore, being a prince necessitates the knowledge of how to make good use of "the beast," of these he ought to imitate the fox and the lion; because the lion cannot defend himself from traps, the fox cannot defend himself from wolves. He needs to be the fox, therefore, to recognize traps and the lion to dismay the wolves. Those who act simply like lions lack understanding. A prudent ruler is not able therefore, neither must he, observe his promise, when such an observance turns against him, and the reasons which caused him to promise are extinguished.[111]

As if these words were not enough to discredit thoroughly the Ciceronian concept of political virtue and princely rule, Machiavelli adds a brutal, anti-Ciceronian flourish. He went on to write:

> Alexander VI never did, nor thought of, anything other than deceiving men, and he always found a victim who he was able to deceive. And there was never a man who possessed greater efficacy in asseveration, or with such great readiness to swear to a thing, who observed (or honoured) it less.[112]

As Skinner concluded, Machiavelli had the Ciceronian passage quoted above in mind when he wrote Chapter 18 of *Il Principe*. These examples illustrate Machiavelli's willingness to reject a given author in one work, while he, in other works, accepts the beliefs of the author he once rejected. This is particularly the case where Cicero is concerned.

In Machiavelli's other works, contrary to the picture presented by *Il Principe*, the focus is almost solely upon the Ciceronian definition of a properly ordered republican government. Cicero's influence is profoundly felt throughout Machiavelli's *Discorsi*.[113] Machiavelli was ready to adopt the

theories set forth by his famous Florentine or Roman ancestors, when doing
so would support his current and evolving political thought. However, he
was as quick to disavow the theories of well-respected predecessors in order
to make a contrary point.

In *Il Principe*, Machiavelli dismissed much of Cicero's political thought
whereas, throughout the *Discorsi*, Cicero's patriotic and republican theories
are central.[114] The glaring examples of anti-Ciceronianism in *Il Principe*
cited above do not render Machiavelli's treatise un-"Machiavellian"—unlike
Machiavelli—nor do historians question Machiavelli's authorship because
Cicero is viewed favorably in his other political works.

The same logic may be applied, gently, to the *Dialogo*. Those who deny
Machiavelli's authorship of the treatise do so, partly because the author of
the *Dialogo* is critical of Dante, where he was favorable toward him in other
works. The earlier study of *L'Asino*, a work undoubtedly written by
Machiavelli, demonstrated that he was not always favorable to Dante. So, the
mockery of Dante in the *Dialogo* does not necessarily remove the work from
his *oeuvre*. It is true that on most occasions, Machiavelli is well disposed
toward Dante, for Machiavelli mentions him often in his personal letters and
he often copied Dante's *terza rima*. Where favorable treatment was required,
Machiavelli was unwavering in his support of Cicero and Dante, but where
subversion was deemed necessary, Machiavelli was likewise unwavering. He
sought to undermine Cicero's authority in *Il Principe*, while in the *Discorsi*
Machiavelli emulated him. Similarly, the author's treatment of Dante in the
Dialogo, appears to mirror Machiavelli's treatment of Cicero in *Il Principe*.

There are several passages often referred to, but the most often quoted of
these passage focuses upon Dante personally. Grayson refers to this passage
as definitive evidence of the un-"Machiavellian" nature of the *Dialogo*.[115]
Therein, Machiavelli refers to Dante as a "pazzo" or a "lunatic," for
defaming his native Tuscan tongue. If that passage is taken out of context it
seems that the author was dealing perhaps too severely with his famous
Florentine ancestor; but when the passage which deals stiffly with Dante is
set against the backdrop of the patriotism inherent in the *Dialogo*'s short
preface, the author suggests that these harsh words, or "attacks" fit squarely
into the citizen's obligations to protect the *patria*. This interpretation goes
some way to meeting objections raised about the un-"Machiavellian" nature
of the attack leveled at Dante. The patriotism inherent at the outset of the
Dialogo is written seriously and earnestly. Such language in the *Dialogo* sets
up the attack that is leveled at Dante, but it also allows the writer to play with
the reader's emotions by its use of irony.

One cannot help but think that the *Dialogo*'s writer was thinking of his
own predicament when he attacked Dante. Would the use of this sort of irony

be out of character with Machiavelli? The answer is an emphatic "No." Florence had a history of exiling those who loved her most; Dante being one example. Machiavelli, himself an unjustly exiled patriot, knew this all too well. Was the author, perhaps Machiavelli, referring to his own exile?

It is likely that instead of being one or the other, this passage is a combination of patriotic indignation and severe irony, both of which were familiar to Machiavelli as the dedicatory letter and epilogue of *Il Principe* illustrate. Roberto Ridolfi and Maurizio Viroli point to Machiavelli's use of irony and humor, which he often deployed at the strangest times, to alleviate his heartbreak over his exile from Florence.[116] Despite the heartbreak he felt, Machiavelli often used his biting sense of irony to humorous ends. The *Dialogo* contains a telling example of this sort—a notable example that Grayson and others overlooked.

Keeping the focus firmly on the author's treatment of Dante in the *Dialogo*, the text provides further examples of his ironic sense of humor. Here, it is helpful first to cite the passage to which Grayson and others referred:

N. My Dante, I hope that you will amend your ways, and that you will consider better the Florentine idiom and your work, and that you will see that if anybody is to feel shame, Florence will know it better than you; because, if you will consider carefully that which you have said, you will see that in your own verses you have not escaped awkwardness, as in:

> *Then we left...and we went on a while*;
> You have not escaped dirty words, like this:
> *That makes shit of that which is eaten*;
> You have not escaped obscenity, such as:
> *He raised his hands with both the figs.*[117]

The last example that Machiavelli cites from Dante's *Commedia* includes references to "fiche" or figs. In Italian *fico, fichi,* or *fiche* are not only the words for the fruit, "fig," they are also directly related to vulgar hand gestures and sex organs. In this instance, irony combines with obscenity—to which Machiavelli was no stranger.[118]

This is perhaps a further example of "Niccolò's Smile" as Maurizio Viroli wrote in the most recent biography of Machiavelli, published in 2000. This is an ironic smile; one that covered his pain and longing for political service, but also a smile that existed even before his exile revealing his love of life and humor.[119] When viewed in this context, the author's "shock" over Dante's "obscenity" is not so much proof against, but rather support for Machiavelli's authorship of the *Dialogo*. The passages above provide telling

examples of Machiavelli's use of irony as well as humor. Machiavelli's
acknowledged writings present many additional opportunities to study his
use of irony. For the problem at hand these ironic and emotive writings are
best illustrated by Machiavelli's prison poems. Concerning these troubling
poems, Maurizio Viroli writes:

> It may seem strange that Machiavelli should have written two sonnets asking for
> mercy from the Medici. In prison, one writes to seek a meaning or reason for one's
> punishment, or to rediscover oneself, or to search the depths of one's soul for the
> resources with which to resist. Above all, as was the case with Machiavelli, one
> writes to ask those who can help to do so, but then one does this with a serious letter,
> not with a sonnet making light of oneself, of the misery, the prison, and the
> torture.[120]

It is helpful to include the entirety of Machiavelli's first poem to
illustrate Viroli's point.

> I have, Giuliano, a pair of shackles on my legs
> With six hoists of the rope on my shoulders:
> My other miseries I do not want to talk about,
> As this is the way poets are to be treated!
> These walls exude lice
> Sick with the heaves no less, that (are as big as) butterflies,
> Nor was there ever a stench in (the massacre of) Roncesvalles.
> Or among those groves in Sardinia,
> As there is in my dainty inn;
> With a noise that sounds just as if at the earth
> Jove was striking lightning, and all Mount Etna (too).
> One man is being chained and the other shackled
> With a clattering of keyholes, keys, and latches;
> Another shouts that he is (pulled) too high off the ground
> What disturbed me most
> Was that close to dawn while sleeping
> I heard chanting: "Per voi s'ora."
> Now they can go their own way;
> If only your mercy may turn toward me,
> Good father, and these criminal bonds be untied.[121]

This poem provides its readers with an interesting insight into Machiavelli's
thought. He was a survivor, in every sense of the word, strong enough to
overcome six rope drops (*sei strappadi*). These drops involved the prisoner's
hands being tied, at the wrist, behind his or her back. The wrists were then
tied to a much longer rope that ran through a pulley connected to the ceiling.
At the other end of the rope, the individual or individuals responsible for
carrying out the *strappado* would lift the prisoner off the ground, sometimes

to the height of several meters. As if this were not enough pain, the torturers would then release the rope, letting the prisoner fall. Then, just before the individual's feet hit the ground, the torturer would violently stop the rope, causing the prisoner's shoulder joints to carry the entire weight of their body. The prisoner could at least expect to have his or her arms dislocated at the shoulder, or worse. Machiavelli underwent six such drops, all the while maintaining, as he asserted, his composure and his innocence. In fact, he was proud of the way in which he dealt with his imprisonment and torture. Machiavelli, writing to Francesco Vettori on 18 March, 1513 stated: "I should like you to get this pleasure from these troubles of mine, that I have borne them so straightforwardly that I am proud of myself for it and consider myself more of a man than I believed I was."[122] His self-debasing humor, and the irony of his situation, combined to form the basis of the poem. He was clearly struggling with his predicament and this was causing him to ponder how he came to be in such a situation, when he knew that no other Florentine citizen loved his *patria* more.

Machiavelli often used irony when he was in emotional turmoil or physical pain. The irony used in Machiavelli's prison poem of 1513 is similar to the apparent criticism of Dante in the *Dialogo* in that both works sprang from an immediate sense of injustice and wrongful exile from that which he loved most—political service to his *patria*. In both circumstances, in 1513 and the autumn of 1515, he used the irony of his imprisonment to illustrate the absurdity of his predicament. From 12 February to 12 March 1513 Machiavelli was imprisoned in Florence and in the autumn of 1515 he was figuratively imprisoned on his farm, removed from political life, his friends and the city that he loved most. Maurizio Viroli, using excerpts from Machiavelli's letters vividly described this pastoral prison:

> "I am living on the farm" are the words with which Niccolò begins his account. For other Florentines of his and earlier times, to live "on the farm" meant getting away from the business and noise of city life, finding peace in study, thought, and rustic pastimes. For Niccolò, it was a forced renunciation of the life he loved best. Literary leisure, philosophical and religious meditation, rural peace were of no interest to him; he loved the city, with its streets, squares, porticoes, and benches; he enjoyed being in company, laughing at the happenings of everyday life, and taking part in the great affairs of state. To convey to his friend (Francesco Vettori) how little country life suited him, he writes that for a while he amused himself by "snaring thrushes with my own hands," the technique being to spread birdlime on elm switches, where once having lit on them, the birds were trapped, for the more they struggled to escape, the more they were caught: "I would get up before daybreak[...] prepare the birdlime, and go out with such a bundle of birdcages on my back that I looked like Gaeta when he came back from the harbor with Amphitryon's books." Machiavelli, until recently a secretary of the Florentine Republic, leaving his house before sunrise

to catch thrushes, so loaded down with birdcages that he is like Geta, Amphitryon's servant in the fifteenth-century novella—one would be hard pressed to imagine anything at once so absurd and heartbreaking.[123]

Machiavelli's life was filled with toil; some to pass the time and some necessary. Sebastian de Grazia described the topography and terrain on which Machiavelli's farm was located:

> Tuscany, an ancient region of central Italy, where Florence holds its territories, is one-third mountains, one-third hills, and the rest plains. The soil is thin, much of it rocky and sandy; the climate offers not enough spring rain and too much summer dryness for foraging livestock. Niccolò's farming can be classified as intensive hill agriculture.[124]

Everything about Machiavelli's country life was hard, detached from city life in every way struggling to find a balance between *otium* and *negotium*. Against the background of this pastoral exile, Machiavelli penned his *Il Principe*—and perhaps the *Dialogo*. It would be no surprise if a sense of irony were to pervade the author's treatment of Dante in the *Dialogo*—Machiavelli, like Dante before him, was in exile.

The attack on Dante in the *Dialogo*, is easily reconcilable with the patriotism inherent to the treatise and to the Florentine political context. Far from standing alone, the author of the *Dialogo* is one of a long line of Florentines who scrutinized and criticized Dante's writings. This general opposition to Dante had its roots in the late *trecento* and the early *quattrocento*, under the leadership of Florentine humanist scholars such as Leonardo Bruni. Hans Baron's *The Crisis of the Early Italian Renaissance* provides a good place from which to begin an investigation into *quattrocento* views of Dante in Florence.[125]

Dante, perhaps more than any other poet or philosopher of his time, embodied the ideals that have since become central to defining the Middle Ages. Baron wrote on this subject:

> If a full acquaintance with ancient literature and command of Ciceronian language are accepted as the measure of genuine culture, dark shadows are bound to fall on Dante and his work. And since, furthermore, his political and historical views had been shaped by the medieval idea of universal monarchy, which in Florence's struggle for liberty was beginning to look obsolete, Dante, too had to be included in the indictment against centuries soon to be called the Middle Ages.[126]

Baron mentioned one of Dante's many contributions to the culture of the Middle Ages, that which must be placed before any other in this specific context, his belief in universal monarchy.

Interestingly, Dante's *De Monarchia* focuses on the role of the papacy whose divine mandate he dismisses. Divine authority rests upon the shoulders of the Emperor alone; the truly divine office ordained by God to rule man. These beliefs and the differences in them, formed the foundation of the Guelph/Ghibelline dispute that divided Florence and much of Italy during the late thirteenth and early fourteenth centuries.[127] Although much more complicated, each group can be roughly defined as follows: the Guelphs supported the Church and city-state independence whereas the Ghibellines supported the Holy Roman Empire and universal monarchy.[128] The Guelph faction managed to outmaneuver its foe. As a result, Dante and many other Ghibelline sympathizers were forced into exile.[129] These tumultuous times saw the ushering in and rebirth of Roman republican theory in Italy and, most importantly, in Florence. The late Middle Ages and the beginning of what was to become the Renaissance, witnessed Dante, most famous Florentine that he was, fall from grace and into relative obscurity—at least in some circles.[130]

The treatment of Dante in the *Dialogo*, while perhaps more cutting, is not out of line with those great Florentines who preceded him. Interestingly, in 1960 Grayson summed up the political and literary problems represented by Dante in the *Dialogo*, when he wrote, "It is not only the linguistic treachery of Dante that Machiavelli deplores; it is his whole attitude toward Florence, and his fundamentally different outlook."[131] The same can be said of the long list of *quattrocento* Florentine humanist writers who chose to enter into the discussion of Dante's life and political views. These writers include nearly all of Florence's most famous humanist scholars. Leonardo Bruni's writings are the most important at this stage. Bruni's early work the *Dialogi ad Petrum Paulum Histrum* contains a scathing commentary on Dante. Yet Bruni desired to reconcile Dante's views with those of *quattrocento* Florence, thereby restoring him to his former greatness. Bruni reached his conclusions by contextualizing Dante's world-view. By so doing, he was able to explain Dante's apparent hatred for Brutus. In *quattrocento* Florence, Brutus was viewed as the restorer and savior of Roman Republican virtue. By assassinating Caesar, Brutus gave Rome her freedom once again, after Caesar had taken it hostage in his tyranny.[132]

Baron cites Bruni's work among others as the reconciliation of Dante's medieval world-view with that of early *quattrocento* humanism. It is apparent from his research that many others followed Bruni, including Giannozzo Manetti, Cristoforo Landino and Marisilio Ficino.[133] However, the most important of these scholars in this present context is Cristoforo Landino. His 1481 work published in Florence, *Comento sopra la Commedia di Dante Alighieri*, a commentary on Dante's *Commedia* was the most famous and most widely read companion to Dante's poem.[134] For he, according to Baron, was able to justify, while criticizing at the same time, Dante's approach to universal monarchy.[135]

Baron's research highlights the place of prominence that Dante held in *quattrocento* and *cinquecento* Florence, even though it was not always an esteemed place. Furthermore, Baron mentions Machiavelli's interest in *quattrocento* republicanism and humanist views of Dante, but only in passing. His reference, brief though it is, highlights a certain sense of historical continuity. Machiavelli, like his Florentine predecessors, had a great interest in republican liberty and therefore he took an interest in the debates surrounding Dante's *Commedia*. The *Dialogo*'s harsh references to Dante could make Machiavelli's authorship more probable, not less. When the *Dialogo*, like the earlier works of Bruni and Landino, is viewed as part of an evolving historical continuum within a greater Florentine context, it would be hard to imagine Machiavelli treating Dante any other way than he did.

As late as 1546 Donato Giannotti wrote a small treatise entitled *Dialoghi de'giorni che Dante consumò nel cercare l'Inferno e 'l Purgatorio*.[136] In this short dialogue, Giannotti speaks with Michelangelo. Giannotti was an ardent defender of republican freedom, and thus he questions Dante's lasting fame, whereas Michelangelo appears to be "of two minds," as Baron wrote, for he strove to defend Dante, but he was also persuaded by Giannotti to sculpt a bust of Brutus.[137] The problems and complexities of the relationships between scholars, artist and patriots of the *cinquecento*, Dante and Brutus are mirrored in Michelangelo's bust of Brutus. He left the bust unfinished.[138] Michelangelo was never able completely to overcome his anxiety as to where Dante as well as Brutus fit into Florentine artistic and political history.[139] Machiavelli exhibited none of Michelangelo's uneasiness or uncertainty over where Dante fit into Florentine republican values. He had no doubts.

Baron's scholarship, while helpful, is perhaps too one-sided, failing to take into account those who continued to defend Dante during the *cinquecento*. It seems that Baron neglected to mention that Dante's acceptance or rejection in Florence was often linked to whether a not a given scholar preferred Petrarch's "humanism" to Dante's heavenly musings, or, put another way, a battle between the *Canzoniere* and the *Commedia*.

Michele Barbi's scholarship on the reception of Dante in the *cinquecento* eloquently fills the gaps which Baron created. Citing Vincenzo Borghini, Barbi noted that "Borghini dichiarava di celebrar Dante 'per un ingeno eccellente, miracoloso, divino.'"[140] Perhaps this explains why Borghini's manuscript of the *Dialogo* ends before its author criticizes Dante. Giovanni Battista Gelli, like Borghini, also viewed Dante as "gloria ed onore particolare della loro città."[141] These scholars generally conferred on Dante, a higher status than Petrarch.[142] As Baron's scholarship failed to point out, there were those who sought to praise Petrarch to the exclusion of Dante, though the most famous were not natives to Florence.

Among the latter, one may find such figures as the Venetians Pietro Bembo and Trifone Gabriele. Bembo's critique of Dante is highly unfavorable.[143] For Bembo, Barbi and Lino Pertile agree, Petrarch and Boccaccio were by far superior.[144] A less virulent example may be found in Gabriele a close friend of Bembo. He produced notes on Dante's *Commedia*, which were according to Pertile, quite independent.[145] Rather than slavishly follow Landino's famous example, Gabriele, while he expressed admiration for Dante, thought of him as "too imperial," or "troppo imperiale."[146] He made no attempt to reconcile Dante's political views, but merely tried to comment on them objectively.

In Machiavelli, then, we have strands of both schools of thought; those who followed Dante and those who lauded Petrarch. Machiavelli followed and at times mimicked Dante's *terza rima* (as in his *Decennale*), and he often carried the famous poet's works with him, while on country walks.[147] Furthermore, he quoted Petrarch at the end of *Il Principe*, in his *Esortazione alla penitenza* and in various letters.[148] However, it seems that Machiavelli's literary relationship with Petrarch was more stable, if not more fruitful, than that with Dante. And this wavering relationship with Dante may be borne out in the pages of the *Dialogo*.

Conclusion

The treatment of Dante in the *Dialogo* is not out of character with the treatment by Machiavelli and other Florentines. Both Bruni in the early *quattrocento* and Giannotti in the middle of the *cinquecento* struggled to reconcile Dante's medieval worldview with their humanistic and republican theories. Machiavelli's mockery of Dante in his *L'Asino* is an evident and telling example of his willingness to undermine Dante's authority when he thought it was necessary to illustrate a point. As Skinner's discussion of *Il Principe* highlighted, Machiavelli was willing to undermine Cicero's authority when elsewhere he praised him.[149] In other works, particularly the *Discorsi*, Machiavelli adopted Cicero's patriotic and republican theories.[150] These facts do not render *Il Principe* un-"Machiavellian" or cause scholars to doubt Machiavelli's authorship. By the same token, it is difficult to rule out Machiavelli's authorship of the *Dialogo* solely because the treatment of Dante in that work is inconsistent with what Machiavelli says elsewhere.

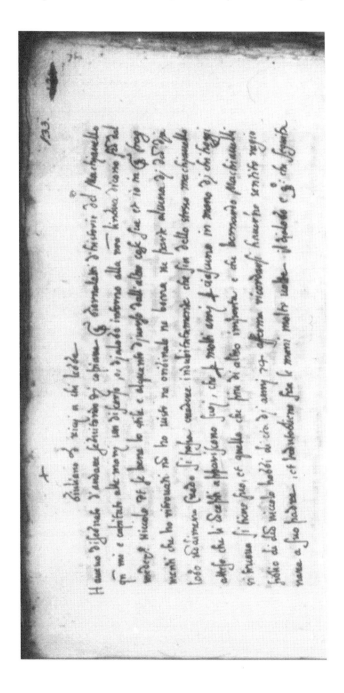

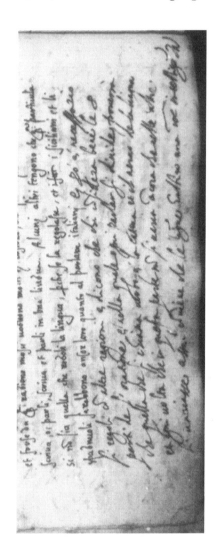

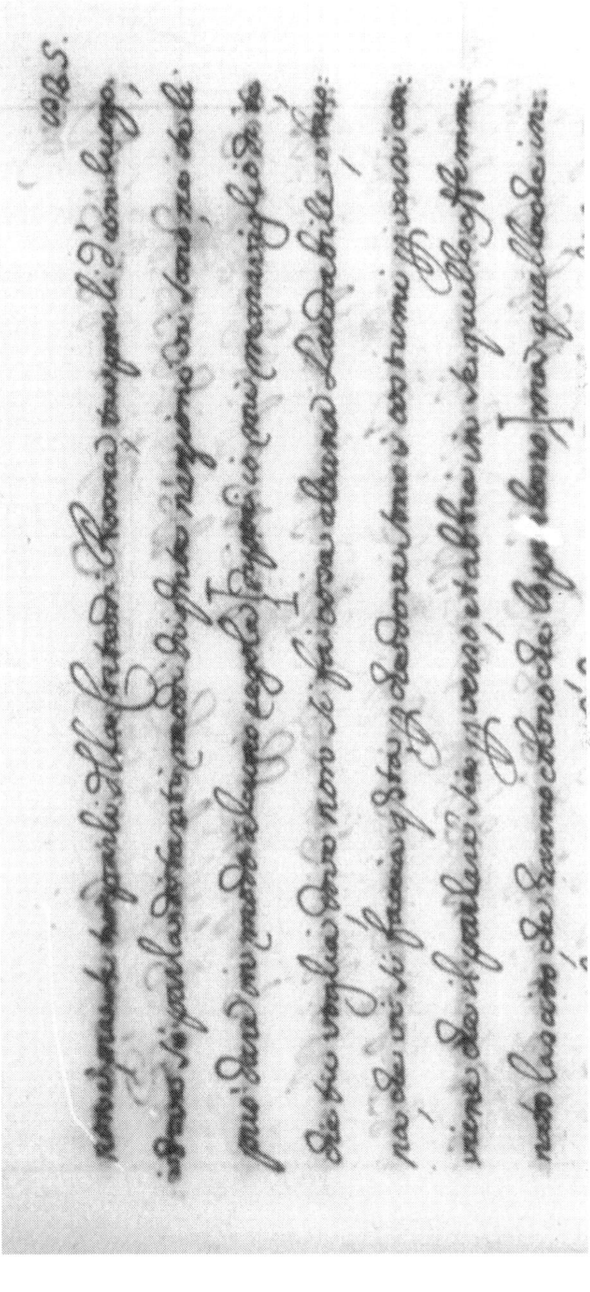

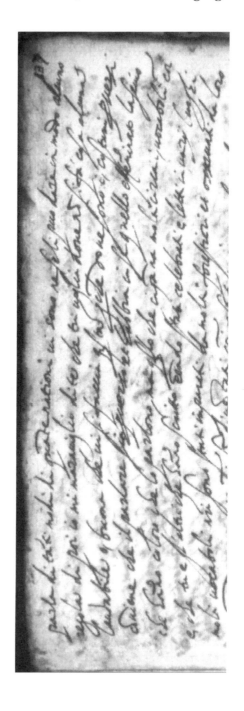

317

D I S C O R S O,

O v v e r o

D I A L O G O,

*In cui fi efamina; fe la lingua, in cui fcriffero Dante,
il Boccaccio, e il Petrarca, fi debba chiamare*

ITALIANA, TOSCANA, O FIORENTINA.

SEMPRECHE' io ho potuto onorare la patria mia,
eziandio con mio carico e pericolo, l' ho
fatto volentieri, perchè l' uomo non ha maggiore obbligo nella vita fua, che con quella; dependendo prima da effa l' effere, e dipoi tutto quello
che di buono la fortuna, e la natura ci hanno conceduto; e tanto viene ad effere maggiore in coloro, che hanno fortito patria più nobile. E veramente colui, il quale coll' animo, e coll' opera fi
fa nimico della fua patria, meritamente fi può
chiamare parricida, ancorachè da quella foffe futo
offefo. Perchè fe battere il padre, e la madre per
qualunque cagione è cofa nefanda, di neceffità
ne fegue, il lacerare la patria effere cofa nefandif-
fima, perchè da lei mai fi patifce alcuna perfecu-
zione, per la quale poffa meritare di effere da te
ingiuriata, avendo a riconofcere da quella ogni
tuo bene; talchè fe ella fi priva di parte de' fuoi

cit-

OVVERO DIALOGO.   135

za , o e' ne lievano , come *poltrone* , *poltron* . Talmentechè quelli vocaboli che fono fimili a' noftri, gli ftorpiano in modo , che gli fanno diventare un' altra cofa ; e fe tu mi allegaffi il
parlar Curiale , ti rifpondo , fe tu parli delle
Corti di Milano , o di Napoli, che tutte tengono del luogo della patria loro , e quelli hanno più di buono , che più s' accoftano al Tofca-
no , e più l' imitano : e fe tu vuoi, che e' fia
migliore l' imitatore , che l' imitato , tu vuoi
quello , che il più delle volte non è ; ma fe
tu parli della Corte di Roma , tu parli di un
luogo , dove fi parla di tanti modi, di quante
nazioni vi fono , nè fe gli può dare in modo alcuno regola . Ma quello che inganna molti circa i vocaboli comuni , è , che tu , e gli
altri che hanno fcritto, effendo ftati celebrati ,
e letti in varj luoghi, molti vocaboli noftri fono ftati imparati da molti foreftieri , ed offer-
vati da loro , talchè di proprj noftri fon diventati comuni . E fe tu vuoi conofcer quefto , arrecati innanzi un libro compofto da quelli foreftieri , che hanno fcritto dopo voi , e vedrai
quanti vocaboli egli ufano de' voftri , e come e'
cercano d' imitarvi : e per aver riprova di quefto fa lor leggere libri compofti dagli uomini
loro avantichè nafcefte voi , e fi vedrà , che in

                       quel-

DISCORSO

OVVERO

DIALOGO

SOPRA IL NOME

DELLA LINGUA VOLGARE.

415

DISCORSO

OVVERO

DIALOGO

*In cui si esamina se la lingua in cui scrissero
Dante, il Boccaccio, e il Petrarca,
si debba chiamare*

ITALIANA, TOSCANA, O FIORENTINA.

~~~~~~

SEMPRECHÈ io ho potuto onorare la patria
mia, eziandio con mio carico e pericolo,
l'ho fatto volentieri, perchè l'uomo non
ha maggiore obbligo nella vita sua che con
quella, dependendo prima da essa l'essere,
e dipoi tutto quello che di buono la fortuna, e la natura ci hanno conceduto; e
tanto viene ad essere maggiore in coloro
che hanno sortito patria più nobile. E veramente colui il quale coll'animo, e col-

433

e lauda quelli, come li primi che cominciarono ad arricchire la lingua Latina. I
Romani negli eserciti loro non avevano più
che due legioni di Romani, quali erano
circa dodici mila persone, e dipoi vi avevano venti mila dell' altre nazioni, nondimeno
perchè quelli erano con li loro capi il nervo
dell' esercito, perchè militavano tutti sotto
l' ordine, e sotto la disciplina Romana, te-
nevano quelli eserciti il nome, l' autorità,
e la dignità Romana; e tu che hai messo
ne' tuoi scritti venti legioni di vocaboli Fiorentini, ed usi i casi, i tempi, e i modi,
e le desinenze Fiorentine, vuoi che li vocaboli avventizj facciano mutar la lingua?
E se tu la chiamassi comune d' Italia, o
Cortigiana, perchè in quella si usassino tutti
li verbi ch' usano in Firenze, ti rispondo
che, se si sono usati li medesimi verbi, non
s' usano i medesimi termini, perchè si va-
riano tanto colla pronunzia, che diventano
un' altra cosa, perchè tu sai che i forestieri, o e' pervertono il *c* in *z*, come di sopra
si disse di *cianciare*, e *zanzare*, o eglino
aggiungono lettere, come *vien qua*, *vegnù
za*, o e' ne lievano, come *poltrone*, *poltron*.
Talmentechè quelli vocaboli che sono simili
a' nostri, gli storpiano in modo, che gli
fanno diventare un' altra cosa; e se tu mi
allegassi il parlar Curiale, ti rispondo, se
tu parli delle Corti di Milano, o di Napoli, che tutte tengono del luogo della patria
loro, e quelli hanno più di buono che più

434

s'accostano al Toscano , e più l'imitano , e
se tu vuoi ch' e'sia migliore l' imitatore che
l'imitato, tu vuoi quello che il più delle
volte non è; ma se tu parli della Corte di
Roma, tu parli d'un luogo dove si parla
di tanti modi, di quante nazioni vi sono,
nè segli può dare in modo alcuno regola.
Ma quello che inganna molti circa i vocaboli comuni, è, che tu, e gli altri che
hanno scritto, essendo stati celebrati, e
letti in varj luoghi, molti vocaboli nostri
sono stati imparati da molti forestieri, ed
osservati da loro, talchè di proprj nostri
son diventati comuni. E se tu vuoi conoscer
questo, arrecati innanzi un libro composto
da quelli forestieri che hanno scritto dopo
voi, e vedrai quanti vocaboli egli usano
de'vostri, e come e' cercano di imitarvi: e
per aver riprova di questo fa' lor leggere
libri composti dagli uomini loro avantichè
nasceste voi, e si vedrà che in quelli non
fia nè vocabolo, nè termine; e così apparirà
che la lingua in che essi oggi scrivono, è
la vostra, e per conseguenza la vostra non
è comune colla loro : la qual lingua ancorachè con mille sudori cerchino d'imitare,
nondimeno, se leggerai i loro scritti, vedrai,
in mille luoghi essere da loro male, e perversamente usata, perch'egli è impossibile
che l'arte possa più che la natura. Considera ancora un'altra cosa, se tu vuoi vedere la dignità della tua lingua patria, che
i forestieri che scrivono, se prendano alcu-

CHAPTER SIX

The Date of the *Dialogo* and of Machiavelli's *Exhortatio* in *Il Principe*

ಐ⊂ಐ

This Chapter is concerned with three separate yet complementary subjects: first, the date on which Machiavelli could have written the *Dialogo*; second, when Machiavelli wrote the dedicatory letter and epilogue to *Il Principe* and, third the way in which the *Dialogo* seems to prefigure the patriotism and call for unification inherent in the *Exhortatio* at the end of *Il Principe*. This Chapter is a broad historiographical survey in which primary sources play a small but decisive role. It is vital to proceed with caution, for there is serious danger that the argument becomes circular: that is to say, that establishing the date of the treatise "proves Machiavelli's authorship" while Machiavelli's authorship "establishes the date." This Chapter explores some suggestive possibilities that weave together—but it does not aspire to more than that.

In the first part of this Chapter, which focuses specifically on the date of the *Dialogo*, the analysis of the historiography ranges from Pasquale Villari's 1877 investigations to Susan Meld Shell's very recent scholarship published in 2000.[1] Careful attention is given to all of the prominent arguments concerned with the date of the *Dialogo*. What emerges is that the year 1515 seems to be the most likely year in which Machiavelli could have written the treatise. That year, 1515, was, perhaps, a unique and productive period in his life, which may also have witnessed the completion of *Il Principe* and the beginning of the *Discorsi*.

The second part of this Chapter suggests that the dedicatory letter to *Il Principe* and its epilogue can be traced to the autumn of 1515. This date may indicate that Machiavelli could have written the *Dialogo* in the same period as the epilogue to *Il Principe*. This proposed, close proximity, suggests that there may be a link between the two works.

The patriotic call in the *Dialogo* for linguistic unification contains a distinctive yet unpolished sketch. It has some similarities to Machiavelli's call for Italian unification in the epilogue to *Il Principe* (see below). The *Dialogo* may fit firmly between the body of *Il Principe* (Chapters I–XXV) and the *Discorsi*. Thus, Chapters I–XXV of *Il Principe* are from 1513, the *Dialogo* from the *vendemmial* of 1515, the dedicatory letter and epilogue to *Il Principe*, from the *vendemmial* of 1515 and the *Discorsi* from late 1515 or early 1516. There is a great deal of evidence to support these dates to which we may now proceed.

The Date of the *Dialogo*

The text of the *Dialogo* may provide evidence as to the time of year, or season in which it was written, for the author told his reader as much. He wrote the work, when "it occurred to me, in this *vendemmial* labor (negozio) of mine."[2] Does the term "negozio," a vernacular derivative of the Latin "negotium" indicate that the author of the *Dialogo*, perhaps Niccolò, had overcome his personal "otium"? Keeping this in mind, it may be helpful to define the *vendemmial* to which Machiavelli referred. John Hale translated "vendemmial" as "autumnal." More specifically, "vendemmial" is directly linked to the vintage season in Tuscany, which occurs in the autumn, but it *begins* in the late summer. The Tuscan "vendemmial" is actually linked with the ancient Roman vintage celebration of "vinalia rustica," which began as early as 19 August.[3] Additional, though later, French sources trace the *vendemmial* to as late as 21 October.[4] When all of these dates and definitions are taken into consideration it is best to define the "vendemmial" as beginning in the third week of August and ending in the third week of October.[5] The *Dialogo* is certainly a work of this period, but scholars are divided as to the year in which it was written.

It may be interesting to note here, that the scholars mentioned in the following passage all accept Machiavelli's authorship, though they disagreed about when it was written. The controversy over the *Dialogo*'s date began as early as 1877, when Pasquale Villari suggested a date, possibly "earlier than 1512."[6] Then, in 1883 Pio Rajna proposed 1514 as a more probable year.[7] However, Rajna was never completely sure that the *Dialogo* was written in 1514. Instead he added a caveat to his thesis, acknowledging that 1516 was also a possibility.[8] Interestingly, Villari was later persuaded by Rajna's 1514 date, "thus," as Baron noted, "beginning the rarely interrupted applause for Rajna's theory."[9] This lasted until 1954 when Ridolfi asserted that several of the passages in the *Dialogo* could not fit Rajna's thesis.

Ridolfi was more cautious than his predecessors. He did not ascribe a specific date to the work, but he thought that it may have come from 1522–

23, the pontificate of Adrian VI.[10] However, Ridolfi's conclusions did not sway scholars from accepting Rajna's date of 1514. In 1960, Grayson, at the time believing the work to be penned by Machiavelli, wrote that "Machiavelli's *Dialogo intorno alla lingua* was most probably written in 1514."[11] One year later, in 1961, Baron dismissed 1514 and Ridolfi's cautious dating, when he traced the *Dialogo*'s origins to 1515 or 1516, but his arguments were not enough to put an end to the controversy over the *Dialogo*'s date.[12] In 1971, Grayson, after he had re-thought his position on Machiavelli's authorship, suggested that "what appears to be no longer open to question is its composition no earlier than 1525—and probably no later than 1530."[13] More recently still, in 1988 Eric Cochrane indicated that the *Dialogo* was written in the 1540's, though not by Machiavelli.[14] Interestingly, Cochrane cites Sergio Bertelli's research as proof against Machiavelli's authorship.[15] Indicative of the complexities associated with studying the *Dialogo*, in an earlier work, particularly in his scholarly edition of Machiavelli's *opere*, Bertelli published the *Dialogo* as a work of Machiavelli written between 1513 and 1518.[16] As recently as 1998 Maurizio Viroli moved the *Dialogo*'s date to 1524–1525.[17] However, in 2000 Rajna's thesis surfaced once again, bringing the date controversy back to its starting point; Shell indicated that she, like Grayson in 1960 and Villari in 1897, subscribed to Rajna's proposed date of 1514.[18] Thus, according to the scholars who have studied the *Dialogo*, it may have been written anywhere between the years 1512 (or just before as Villari first suggested) and 1549.

Dates and Contexts

Gian Giorgio Trissino "passed through Tuscany nearly annually between 1513 and 1518."[19] It is accepted by the majority of those who study the *Dialogo* that it was written in response to a lecture given by Trissino on one of his trips through Tuscany when he stopped at the Florentine *Orti Oricellari*. Many scholars (who accept Machiavelli's authorship) trace the *Dialogo* to the years 1513 to 1518. Rajna, and later Villari, reasoned that the *Dialogo* originated in 1514.[20] This date steadfastly resisted attempts to dislodge it until Ridolfi described the work as "di data incertissima."[21] Ridolfi refused to commit to a specific date because of what he saw as irreconcilable differences between the text of the *Dialogo* and the events of the years 1513 to 1518. Most notably, Ridolfi found the author's references to Florence's "tranquillo stato" incompatible with events in Florence in 1514.[22] Thus, Ridolfi was the first to cast doubt on Rajna's 1514 date for the *Dialogo*. Furthermore, Ridolfi found the impassioned language used to criticize the papacy as unfitting with the pontificate of Leo X, which, automatically in his thesis, eliminated the years 1513 to 1521.[23] This leaves Villari's original dates of 1512 or the years just before, or the pontificate of Adrian VI, 1522–1523 as proposed by Ridolfi. Neither set of dates seems likely.

Villari does not provide evidence for the year 1512, or the years just before it. That year, it appears, was selected as a defense against attacks on Machiavelli's authorship by Polidori who thought that the reference to Florence's *tranquillo stato*, referred to princely, not republican, rule. Referring to Polidori's criticisms, Villari wrote:

> He interprets these words (*tranquillo stato*) as a favorable allusion to princely rule, and cannot think, he says, that Machiavelli would have been capable of uttering them. Nevertheless, the ex-secretary frequently praised the condition of Florence in his own time, and in fact its condition was by no means one of persistent wretchedness. There can be no allusion in the work (i.e. the *Dialogo*) to the princely rule that was only inaugurated after his death.[24]

In 1512, Villari properly reasoned, Florence was still a republic, and thus Machiavelli could have referred to its *tranquillo stato*. Villari does not mention Machiavelli's criticisms of the papacy. It seems likely that, after the *Dialogo* was accepted as Machiavelli's by many Italian scholars, Villari changed his mind, siding with Rajna's 1514 date. What then is to be made of Ridolfi's suggestion that the *Dialogo* was written in 1522–23, during the pontificate of Adrian VI?

This is answered in part by what is perceived to be a contradiction between the *Dialogo* and Machiavelli's *Arte della Guerra*—certainly written in 1519–20. In his *Arte*, Machiavelli wrote that Rome's two legions consisted of 11,000 Roman soldiers and 11,000 non-Roman soldiers, where the *Dialogo* says that Roman legions consisted of 12,000 Romans and 20,000 others.[25]

There appears to be an inconsistency between these two works, but there are also inconsistencies between Machiavelli's *Discorsi* and his *Arte*. The former relied on Livy's calculations to describe the numbers of troops in Roman legions, while the latter relied, primarily, on Polybius for such numbers. By the same token, the *Dialogo* appears to have relied on Livy for its numbers relating to the makeup of Rome's legions.[26] There is then, no consistency between two of the works known to be by Machiavelli. One might argue, then, that it may be a mistake to view the apparent inconsistencies between the *Dialogo* and the *Arte* as *proof* against Machiavelli's authorship. By the same token, one may notice that despite the differences in the numbers cited, both works are united by an interest in

Roman military organization—linking all three works, the *Discorsi*, the *Dialogo* and the *Arte*. Furthermore, it may be that Machiavelli's thought grew from one to the next, or that he gained access to different materials which caused him to change his calculations regarding the make-up of the Roman army. Indeed, his access to the work of Polybius might yet provide an explanation.

Baron, following A. Arthur Burd's thesis, illustrated that Machiavelli had recourse to *portions* of translated versions of Polybius *Histories*, Book VI as early as 1516. This assertion is corroborated by J. H. Hexter's research on Machiavelli and Polybius VI. Machiavelli cited Polybius' book extensively in the *Discorsi*, but he did not mention the makeup of the Roman armies that is included in detail in VI 19–42.[27] If he had recourse to this section of Polybius' work as early as 1516, it is at least probable, given his reliance on many other sections of Polybius VI, that it would have been inserted into his *Discorsi* and, if he authored the text, the *Dialogo*. Perhaps it was later in his research—maybe in 1519—that Machiavelli came across this section of Polybius' *Histories*? Baron's and Burd's work provides a satisfactory explanation to the problem of the "contradiction" between the *Dialogo* and the *Arte*.[28] If Machiavelli wrote the *Dialogo*, it seems unlikely that he could have done so after he began his *Arte* in 1519. Rather, it may be that the *Dialogo* was written before 1519. In arguing for this, Baron and Burd gave more weight to Rajna's earlier assessment that came to the same conclusion; the *Dialogo* could not have been written after the *Arte*. Scholars, one might suggest, have focused too much energy on the contradictions between the *Arte* and the *Dialogo*. Rather, it may be more helpful to view them in the manner in which one may view the evolution of *Il Principe* and the *Discorsi*. The first, smaller text appears to have led the author to grander and more expansive themes. Might there be a similar progression from the *Dialogo* to the *Arte*? There is further evidence that Machiavelli's ideas concerning the defense of the Florentine language were known by at least one young scholar, Lodovico Martelli, which may help to date the treatise.

Martelli published his *Risposta alla* Epistola *del Trissino*—a defense against Trissino's attack on the Florentine vernacular—in Florence in 1525.[29] This work, Rajna, Ridolfi and Baron assert, is similar in some ways to the *Dialogo*.[30] Indeed, it appears to them, that Martelli borrowed some of his ideas from that work.[31] The title of Martelli's treatise lends strength to this notion because it is obvious that he is responding to Trissino's printed work. The *Dialogo* does not mention Trissino by name and does not mention any work written by Trissino because his famous works on language were not printed until the 1520's.[32] However, Grayson finds fault with this thesis. Martelli, Grayson illustrated, "appears to have thought he was the first," to defend the Florentine language.[33] Grayson cites this passage from Martelli's *Risposta*: "E qui parrà forse nuovo a costoro che io così risoluto mi opponga a quella ch'ei dicono che ha lasciato scritto Dante nel suo libro *de vulg. eloquio*."[34] However, Grayson acknowledges in a footnote that there are "also obvious dissimilarities, especially in Martelli's uses of (Dante's) *Convivio I* and his doubts about Dante's authorship of *De vulgari eloquentia*."[35] By his own admission, Grayson chose to focus only on the similarities between the *Dialogo* and the *Risposta*, which are few. Yet, he continued to believe that Machiavelli borrowed from Martelli and not *vice versa*.[36]

It appears that Viroli also subscribed to this scenario, for he placed the *Dialogo* around 1524.[37] Unfortunately, he does not provide arguments for this date. The date he selected indicated that he was in agreement with Grayson's assumption that Machiavelli borrowed from Martelli. Yet, Grayson managed this date by a rhetorical sleight of hand; positing rather speculatively that Machiavelli would never have allowed someone to publish his ideas on language without protest.[38] It seems that Grayson not only placed too much emphasis on the apparent "similarities" between the *Dialogo* and the *Risposta*, but that he also overlooked certain historical factors linked with the *Dialogo*'s provenance.

First, as Chapter Five set out, the *Dialogo* was by no means a well-known treatise. After all, it was only discovered in 1577. Second, the work is written in the form of a personal letter. The historical record provides no evidence that it was ever delivered to its intended recipient, who remains unknown. Finally, the *Dialogo* was not published until the 18th century. These combined factors do not point to Grayson's conclusion that Machiavelli would have been upset if some of his ideas appeared in a later work. On the contrary, it seems at least as likely that he would have been flattered by the younger Martelli's emulation.[39]

Perhaps then, there is reason to think that the older and more polished Machiavelli, while at the *Orti Oricellari*, influenced the budding scholar Martelli. Or, as Brian Richardson put it, Martelli's *Risposta* "benefited from the various ideas of the *Dialogo*." (usufruì di varie idée del *Dialogo*).[40] It seems that Machiavelli's influence over Martelli is exemplified in the younger scholar's *Risposta*, not the other way around. With the years 1524 and after eliminated, and with the pontificate of Adrian VI also set aside, one is left with only a few years in which the *Dialogo* could have been written. These are the years 1513 to 1518, the years in which Gian Giorgio Trissino visited Tuscany.

In 1546, Benedetto Varchi, a Florentine scholar, wrote that in 1513, when he and Luigi Alamanni were boys, they attended, along with

Machiavelli, a lecture given by Trissino.

> I being a young boy—with Zanobi Buondelmonti, and Niccolò Machiavelli, Messer Luigi being an older boy—went to the Orti Oricellari, where we, together with Messer Cosimo and many other young men, listened to Trissino, and respected him much more as a Master, or Superior, than as a companion, or equal.[41]

Varchi was well respected and had no reason to fabricate such a story, but Baron found problems with his account. Varchi was born in 1502 or 1503, meaning that he was only 10 or 11 years old when he went to hear Trissino lecture. Varchi's word selection is interesting. By even suggesting that he, a 10 or 11 year old boy, would consider himself equal with the older scholar Trissino is odd. The fact that a boy of 10 or 11 considered himself to be of lesser standing than an older, educated scholar should go without saying. This oddity in Varchi's account led Baron to think that one so young as Varchi was in 1513 would not have been allowed to enter the *Orti*. Baron may have been correct in his assumption, but by dismissing an eyewitness account out of hand, he also damages other mid-*cinquecento* accounts that place Trissino at the *Orti* in the *vendemmial* of 1515. More will be said of this in due course. Contrary to Baron's rejection, it is better, at least at this point, to leave 1513 as a possible year for the *Dialogo*'s origin due to Varchi's account even if it is somewhat questionable. For Machiavelli, 1513 was an eventful year.

On 12 February 1513 Machiavelli was imprisoned by the restored Medici government as a conspirator against their regime. He was not released until one month later—12 March.[42] He spent the summer months in exile. His letters are without hope and he gives no indication that he was preparing formal studies of any sort. He spent most of his time writing letters to Vettori but none of these hints at any sort of scholarly pursuit.[43] That is, until 10 December 1513—long after the close of the *vendemmial*. In this letter he told Francesco Vettori about the little book he was writing—*De principatibus*—what became *Il Principe*.[44] Baron wrote, "during the autumn, he (Machiavelli) led a lonely country life and was lost in the labors on the *Prince* (*Il Principe*) so vividly described in his famous letter to Vettori."[45] This evidence provides better reasons than do the problems with Varchi's account for excluding 1513 as a possible year in which the *Dialogo* was written. It is impossible to imagine Machiavelli, even at his most ironic, referring to Florence's "tranquillo stato" in 1513; the year of his fall from grace and the year in which he was exiled from Florentine political life. Furthermore, he only returned to Florence on one or two occasions; not to hear lectures at the *Orti*, but to pay punitive taxes and fines imposed on him by the Medici.[46] Thus, 1513 can be added to the list of years in which it is unlikely that Machiavelli could have written the *Dialogo*. We may add 1514 to that list.

In 1514 Machiavelli was caught up in a love affair with a much younger woman. Just weeks before the start of the *vendemmial*, on 3 August 1514 he went as far as to say, "I have renounced, then, thoughts about matters great and grave."[47] It is difficult to imagine the *Dialogo* springing from this year. His love affair, whether genuine or contrived in order to suppress his boredom, it would appear, took up most of his free time, providing enough distraction to inhibit the writing of a treatise on language. His next letter is dated 3 December 1514, long after the end of the *vendemmial*. This year is an impossibility if Machiavelli's "*vendemmial* labors" (vendemmial negozio) is to be believed, for Trissino was nowhere near Tuscany in the *vendemmial*.[48] He only visited Tuscany once that year, between "the end of March and early April, when he traveled from Ferrara to Rome."[49] It seems unlikely that the *Dialogo* is a product of 1514.

In regard to the remaining dates 1515–1518, internal evidence in the *Dialogo* provides a possible solution. The text refers to the court of Milan. Speaking to Dante, the author said: "I respond to you, that if you speak of the courts of Milan or Naples, that they take from the place of their *patria* (or local languages), and those are best that come nearest to Tuscan and imitate it most."[50] Francis I, King of France, desired to reassert his claims to Milan and all of its territories. The French army, with Francis as their commander, crushed the Swiss and the Milanese contingent—allies of Leo X and Florence—at Marignano on 13 September.[51] Riding the wave of his success, Francis was able to seize Milan for himself. With his arrival, the Milanese court ceased to be and it did not regain its independence until 1525. As a result of the historical evidence relating to the court at Milan as well as the lack of reference to Polybius VI in the *Dialogo* discussed above, the years 1516–1518 may be excluded, leaving 1515 as the most likely year that Machiavelli could have written the *Dialogo*. The remaining problem Ridolfi raised concerning Florence's *tranquillo stato* and Machiavelli's anti-papal language can be solved as well when the circumstances and factual evidence of the year 1515 are examined.

The *tranquillo stato* of Florence and the references to the papacy highlighted by Ridolfi provide an interesting point of discussion. Like Machiavelli's works, the *Dialogo* is able to stand on its own. However, its subtleties are perhaps more pronounced when it is compared with Machiavelli's *Istorie Fiorentine*. If one thinks back to the discussion of Machiavelli's treatment of Cicero in *Il Principe* and in the *Discorsi* and the "bi-focal" attitude adopted toward the great Roman in those works, one may find that similar phenomena occur within the pages of the *Istorie*. An examination of this work, may help to illustrate that Machiavelli could have written the *Dialogo* in the year 1515.

In his *Istorie*, Machiavelli intersperses flattery with a sense of moral outrage; at once trying to restore his position with the Medici while at the same time undermining it. Viroli noted that this pattern exists throughout Machiavelli's *Istorie*.[52] The Medici Pope, Clement VII, commissioned this long work. Viroli asserted that Machiavelli's true voice is heard in the *Istorie* when anti-Mediceans speak. Machiavelli provides the dissenters with eloquent and patriotic speeches defending love of *patria* over tyranny.[53]

The strongly patriotic and perhaps autobiographical words given to Rinaldo degli Albizzi, enemy of the Medici, are very similar to a passage in *Il Principe*, Chapter XVII: "They would shed their blood for you, risk their property, their lives, their children, so long, as I said above, as danger seems remote; but when you are in danger they turn against you."[54]

In *Il Principe*, as in the *Istorie*, Machiavelli's style is, as Wayne Rebhorn noted, "marked by binary oppositions and symmetries."[55] Thus, after lambasting the Medici, in his next breath, Machiavelli was just as willing to provide Lorenzo de'Medici with stirring words, filled with patriotic sentiment.[56] Flattery tempered with disdain, or even at times disgust: these elements are often associated with the tone Machiavelli takes when writing. Machiavelli's ability to write a given statement and later completely reverse the view set forth in that statement, provides an interesting insight into his style of argument but it also provides insight into his use of irony. This use of irony is evident in the *Istorie*, as Viroli illustrated. It is likewise evident in the *Dialogo*. When read in this context, the *tranquillo stato* of Florence and the harsh criticisms of the papacy can be accounted for and justified. Keeping the *Istorie* and *Il Principe* in mind it becomes easier to justify Machiavelli's seemingly opposing views.

On 6 June 1515 Lorenzo di Piero de' Medici was installed as "capitano generale dei Fiorentini."[57] On 13 October 1515 Leo X and Francis I of France signed the Treaty of Viterbo, which guaranteed French protection for the Medici family forever. Following these grand events, November saw the first visit of Pope Leo X to Florence, a time of lavish festivals throughout the city.[58] Between the installation of Lorenzo and the papal visit, one might easily write of Florence's *tranquillo stato*, and at the same time allowing him to comment on the *costumi perversi* of the papal court.[59]

Moreover, Giovanni Battista Gelli, according to Baron, provided a "semi-contemporary source" supporting the year 1515. In 1551, Gelli wrote: "But if perhaps you do not remember it, take heed that those literati of the Rucellai Gardens, disputing the arrival of Pope Leo X, with Trissino (because he brought us his work there for the first time)."[60] Admittedly, Baron noted that Trissino and Leo X could not have been in Florence at the same time. Trissino was in Florence earlier in the autumn. Baron did not think that this problem was a problem at all.[61]

Gelli, writing in 1551, remembered Leo's visit. The magnitude of the pomp surrounding this occasion would serve as a definite historical point of reference by which Gelli remembered and associated these related events. Gelli may have mistakenly overlapped the visit of Trissino and Leo X, but it is improbable that he was wrong about the year in which both men visited Florence. It seems likely that Gelli remembered Trissino's visit precisely because he visited Florence a short time before Leo X. That said, there was clearly great political tension in Florence in the autumn of 1515.

John Stephens's, *The Fall of the Florentine Republic: 1512–1530* provides insight into the situation in Florence in 1515. He wrote, "1515 was a difficult year for the Medici. In secret everyone disparaged the government and 'almost everyone complained about the sad fate of modern times.'"[62] And as Humphrey Butters wrote concerning the Medici and the autumn of 1515:

> Ostensibly the year ended on a note of high success for the Medici: the accord with Francis I, the papal entry into Florence, the meeting between Leo X and the French Monarch. But in reality there was much discontent in the city.[63]

Amid the festivities of the autumn of 1515, Florence was, on the surface at least "tranquillo" but there was a sense of underlying disillusion and discontent among its citizenry. Butters highlighted that many people, proud though they were to have the Medici Pope return to his home city, were also upset at the cost of the festivities surrounding his entry.[64] This may go some way to dispel Ridolfi's doubts concerned with Florence's *tranquillo stato* and the *Dialogo*'s references to the *costumi perversi* of the papal court. Machiavelli's comments and their apparent contradictions echoed the prevailing sentiments of the Florentine public in the *vendemmial* of 1515. We might suggest then, that if Machiavelli wrote the *Dialogo*, he may have done so in 1515. That was the year in which Machiavelli completed *Il Principe* and, it was also the year in which he began his *Discorsi*, which was discussed in Chapter One. This chronological link is tantalizing. Could the *Dialogo* help to explain the transition between Machiavelli's works on principalities and republics? Might it even solve the mystery of the date of the last Chapter of *Il Principe*?

The Date of the Epilogue to *Il Principe*

Scholars are divided as to when the dedicatory letter to *Il Principe* and its last Chapter were written. It seems likely that the epilogue's history and origin are linked directly with the *Dialogo* and the *vendemmial* in which it was written. That in turn highlights the special *occasione* that existed in 1515 in Florence, in the form of a Medici Pope and a Medici *Capitano* in Florence. Given the festivities in Florence in 1515 which celebrated the French crown's promise to provide to Florence and the Medici eternal protection, did Machiavelli author the epilogue of *Il Principe* to exhort Leo and Lorenzo to throw off the newly fashioned yoke of foreign oppression? Indeed, this, along with the possibility of the unification of a secular Italian *patria* that this *occasione* presented may have loomed larger in Machiavelli's thinking than is usually supposed. Neither Sergio Bertelli nor Hans Baron gives the *Dialogo* any close attention in this regard. However, always acknowledging the conditions that the *Dialogo* may be by Machiavelli and that it dates from 1515—which are recalcitrant to certain proof—that small tract may yet have contained the preliminary sketches for the epilogue to *Il Principe*.

Bertelli "conjectured that the epilogue was composed together with the final dedication of the work to Lorenzo de' Medici, which occurred between September 1515 and September 1516."[65] The reason Bertelli chose September 1515 was because Lorenzo's position in Florence was at a high point. Lorenzo was *Capitano* of Florence, which gave him tremendous power over political appointments and decision making within the city and its protectorates. These factors indicate that September of 1515 was a logical time for Machiavelli to re-dedicate his *Il Principe* to Lorenzo while at the same time writing its epilogue. Bertelli also thought that September 1516 was a suitable date, for Giuliano passed away in March 1516 and Lorenzo sought to increase his political standing in the wake of his relative's recent death.[66] Gilbert supported Bertelli's argument:

> The structure of *The Prince* has always been examined in the hope of finding a solution to the much debated question whether the Italian nationalism of the last chapter formed an integral part of Machiavelli's political outlook or whether it was merely a decorative conclusion—a rhetorical ornament. If we are right in our theory that from chapter 15 onward Machiavelli was inspired by opposition to the humanists who preceded him and that, consequently, the second part of *The Prince* is very loosely composed and forms no connected unity, I believe we have to accept, as a further result that also the last chapter, which is not prepared for by any hint in the preceding sections of the book, stands by itself, mainly intended as a concluding rhetorical flourish. This conclusion must not be interpreted as a denial of national

feeling in Machiavelli, but it does show that nationalism had no definite and prescribed place in his system.[67]

However, Baron, who proposed a different date for the last Chapter of *Il Principe*, disputed the conclusions of Bertelli and Gilbert.

Baron believed that the last Chapter of *Il Principe* was written in January 1515.[68] This time was special, according to Baron, because Machiavelli became privy to Leo X's plan to form a northern Italian state, which was to be created under the guidance of Giuliano de' Medici, to whom *Il Principe* was originally dedicated.[69] Leo's plan, Baron hypothesized, caused Machiavelli's spirits to rise at the thought of a unified northern Italy, prompting him to write *Il Principe*'s epilogue.[70] The possibility for unification in the north of Italy, when Baron's research is taken to its logical conclusion, can be viewed as the *occasione* that Machiavelli hoped Leo would seize. Only later, after Giuliano's death, did Machiavelli re-dedicate the work to Lorenzo. On the surface this is a plausible answer to the problem of the date of the last Chapter and the dedicatory letter. However, an examination of the reasoning behind Baron's proposed date for the last Chapter of *Il Principe* will prove that Bertelli's suggested dates—September 1515 or 1516—are more probable.

Machiavelli learned of Pope Leo's plans for northern-Italian unification in January 1515. In his letter to Vettori he wrote:

> Your Paolo has been here with His Magnificence (Giuliano) and, among other discussions he had with me about his prospects, he told me that His Lordship promised to appoint him governor of one of those cities over which he is currently taking control. And understood—not from Paolo but from a rumor—that His Magnificence is to become lord of Parma, Piacenza, Modena, and Reggio, I think this is a rule that would be considerable and would be strong; it is such that, were it governed correctly from the outset, it can be held onto under any condition.[71]

So, Baron posited, the last Chapter of *Il Principe* must be linked to that period and no later, for in August 1515 the French began preparations for a military campaign in northern Italy. Beginning in September, under the leadership of Francis I, the French army swept southward across the Alps. Then, over two tragic days, 13–14 September, the united Italian forces were humiliated and decimated. The "French victory at Marignano put an end to all of Leo's endeavors to save Milan from foreign rule, as well as his plan to create a new power centre in northern Italy."[72] Surely, Baron posited, the special *occasione* for Italian unification died with the Italian defeat at Marignano. However, Baron overlooked the fact that Lorenzo, not Giuliano, saved the papal and Florentine armies from destruction. He kept them from the fray, thus preserving their full strength, instead sacrificing the mercenary Swiss.[73]

Despite Lorenzo's role at Marignano, Baron asserted that the epilogue to *Il Principe* could only have been written for Giuliano before Marignano. Furthermore, he posited that the last Chapter to *Il Principe* could not have been intended for Lorenzo, for the language therein, Baron believed, was not suitably adapted to an individual of Lorenzo's character. Following this logic, the epilogue must have been written to Giuliano before Marignano.

Baron contended that Machiavelli's references in *Il Principe*'s epilogue, to "your illustrious house" or "illustre casa vostra" were not suitably written for presentation to an individual like Lorenzo, whom Baron called "proud and imperious."[74] In other words, Machiavelli would have gravely offended Lorenzo by not naming him personally as Italy's savior. Therefore, it must have been written before the defeat at Marignano, with Giuliano in mind. But if the epilogue would have offended Lorenzo, as Baron asserted, then Machiavelli would have removed it before re-dedicating the book to him. There is no evidence to support such a claim. After all, given that the dedicatory letter named Lorenzo personally, would there have been a need specifically to name him in the epilogue? The answer to this question can be ascertained by examining to whom and for what purpose *Il Principe* was written.

Baron insists that the epilogue was intended for a single individual—Giuliano—with *one* specific *occasione* in mind.[75] It must have been written before Marignano, while the *occasione* for the unification of northern Italian was a possibility. However, perhaps the epilogue was intended for the eyes of two people—members of the same "casa illustre"—rather than one as Baron suggests: Leo X and Lorenzo, not Giuliano.[76] Medici Pope and Medici *Capitano* working in tandem; church and state temporarily united for the cause of unification, mirroring the earlier, successful relationship of Pope Alexander VI and his son Cesare Borgia—who are so central to the action of Chapter VII of *Il Principe*. Baron mentioned Borgia, but he surprisingly neglected to mention the role of Alexander VI.[77] So, it was entirely possible for Machiavelli to have written the dedicatory and the last Chapter for Lorenzo *and* Leo. However, one must examine Baron's definition of *occasione* in Machiavelli's *Il Principe*, in order to demonstrate that Machiavelli may have intended the epilogue for Lorenzo and Leo, not Giuliano.

It is likely that the *occasione* to which Machiavelli referred in *Il Principe* was unrelated to the *occasione* which Baron described. Contrary to Baron's assessment that the *occasione* was directly related to Giuliano and the possible creation of a strong, northern Italian state, it appears that

Machiavelli's *occasione* was rather different. His *occasione* may have been linked with the unique position in which Florence found itself between 1515 and 1516—a Medici on the papal throne and a Medici "prince" in Florence itself, for Lorenzo was in almost complete control of Florence by the latter half of 1515.[78] Peter Godman quoted from Marcello Virgilio Adriani's speech at Lorenzo's coronation to describe this special relationship: Lorenzo was "'one prince, one arbiter, one lord in war,' but in peace(time) a different and more mighty prince reigned: Leo X."[79] Therefore, Machiavelli's *occasione* existed only *after* Marignano, when Leo and Lorenzo were working together, uniting the interests of Florence and Rome. Furthermore, there is no indication in the epilogue that Machiavelli was referring to the possible unification of northern Italy. For example, Machiavelli did not mention, "northern Italians" in the epilogue. On the contrary, he wrote of the "università delli uomini di quella."[80] "Di quella" in this context refers to "Italia."[81] Thus, George Bull translated this passage as, "all and every Italian."[82] Given that Lorenzo was made *Capitano* of Florence on 6 June 1515, the letter of dedication may have followed this date as Bertelli indicated, and it is most likely that Machiavelli wrote the last Chapter of *Il Principe* with Lorenzo *and* Leo in mind. Even if January 1515 is left as a possible date for Machiavelli to have written the epilogue, as Baron suggested, with the *occasione* of northern Italian unification in mind, a question arises that cannot be answered by Baron's logic. Why would Machiavelli, given that the *occasione* no longer existed after Marignano, leave the epilogue unchanged when he re-dedicated *Il Principe* to Lorenzo? Perhaps the *occasione* referred to the unique opportunity that existed in the form of Leo and Lorenzo, and thus the special relationship that existed between Rome and Florence; which gives still greater weight to Bertelli's date of September 1515.

In September 1515 the special Florentine *occasione* was at its high point. Yet, it seems that Machiavelli realized that the *occasione* was slipping away even as he wrote his epilogue. With the "freschi esempli" of Cesare Borgia's successes and ultimate failure in mind, Machiavelli realized that when the *occasione* ceased to be, so did Italy's chance for unification.[83] Pope Leo gave Machiavelli reasons to hold on to his hope. He met and made peace with Francis I later in the autumn of 1515. By this means, the pope sought to gain standing for the Church and Florence by reaching accords with the French. He achieved both by 13 October 1515 at the Treaty of Viterbo. Francis I promised to protect the Medici and their descendants forever. After this meeting, as was illustrated earlier, Leo was accepted in Florence as a returning hero in November of 1515, even if the public resented the amount of money he spent on the festivities (this was discussed in the previous section). Furthermore, Lorenzo's political standing was at a high point around September of 1515, which only increased after he became the Duke of Urbino early in the following year. When viewed in this perspective, the *occasione* still existed in the persons and relationship between Leo and Lorenzo, even after Marignano. In his dedicatory letter the sense of urgency comes to the forefront. He let Lorenzo know just how narrow the window of opportunity was for Florence's special *occasione*.[84] Machiavelli may have thought that Italy, slim though the chance was, could still be united under the leadership of Leo and Lorenzo.

The *Dialogo* carefully defines the reason that should cause a citizen to lay down his or her life—a duty to honour the *patria*. These sentiments have much in common with the epilogue of *Il Principe*. A unifying Prince, Lorenzo, with the cooperation of his uncle Leo X, could unite every Italian *patria* into a single entity. A common *patria* and a common love of it would provide the means by which a prince could unite a citizenry and thus create an Italian national identity. If it is by Machiavelli, the *Dialogo* preceded the epilogue of *Il Principe* and it presented in a rough manner some of the ideas that became central to Machiavelli's famous closing Chapter. As a result of the reasoning set forth above, Bertelli's date of September 1515, just following the *Dialogo*, is the most likely time in which Machiavelli wrote the last Chapter and the dedicatory letter to his *Il Principe*. An examination of the similarities between the *Dialogo* and *Il Principe*'s last Chapter adds more weight to the September 1515 date of the latter's epilogue.

The *Dialogo* and *Chapter Twenty-Six*

Machiavelli's preoccupation with Italian unity and with Petrarch's patriotic "Italia mia" may have drawn conviction from the influence of Angelo Poliziano. He too devoted energy to the "Italia mia" and may have exerted some influence on Machiavelli's humanist education.[85]

Poliziano's writing offers an older yet startlingly similar approach to the history of Florentine poetic greatness that is illustrated by the author of the *Dialogo*. Indeed, Poliziano's *Raccolta Aragonese*, in which the he referred to Dante's "uncouthness" seem further to link that work with the *Dialogo*.[86] The following passages are taken from Poliziano's edition of the *Raccolta*, and from the *Dialogo*.[87] Compare Poliziano's words in the *Epistola* to his *Raccolta* with the author of the *Dialogo*.

> Fu l'uso della rima, secondo che in una latina epistola scrive il Petrarca, ancora appresso gli antichi romani assai celebrato; il quale, per molto tempo intermesso,

> cominciò poi nella Sicilia non molti secoli avanti a rifiorire, e, quindi per la Francia sparto, finalmente in Italia, quasi in un suo ostello, è pervenuto.[88]

And the author summarised:

> Perché ciascuno sa come i Provenzali cominciarono a scrivere in versi; di Provenza ne venne quest'uso in Sicilia, e di Sicilia, in Italia; e in tra le provincie d'Italia in Toscana; e di tutta Toscana in Firenze.[89]

When Poliziano's writing is compared with the knowledge of poetry illustrated in the *Dialogo*, the similarities are telling. The brief analysis in the *Dialogo* is perhaps more refined than Poliziano's, but this may be explained by the four trips that Machiavelli took to the French court, while he was an ambassador for the Ten in Florence.[90]

Poliziano was a contemporary of the young Machiavelli. He compiled and wrote the *Epistola* to the *Raccolta* at the request of Lorenzo the Magnificent in 1477, when Machiavelli was 8 years old. It is highly likely that the young Machiavelli studied Poliziano's writings as a pupil—as a part of his humanist training.[91] He most definitely gained a deeper knowledge of Poliziano's work by way of his superior, the windbag extraordinaire, Marcello Virgilio Adriani, at the Palazzo Vecchio during their years together[92]. In light of Poliziano's much earlier work, it is clear that the history of poetry and the discussion of it, was entering into the consciousness of the Florentine humanists.

The opening of Poliziano's *Epistola* to Frederick of Aragon like Chapter 26 of *Il Principe*, quotes Petrarch.

> Ripensando assai volte meco medesimo, illustrissimo signor mio Federico, quale in tra molte e infinite laudi degli antichi tempi fussi la più eccellente, una percerto sopra tutte l'altre esser gloriosissima e quasi singulare ho giudicato: che nessuna illustre e virtuosa opera *né di mano né d'ingegno* si puote immaginare, alla quale in quella prima età non fussino e in publico e in privato grandissimi premi e nobilissimi ornamenti apparecchiati. Imperocché, sì come dal mare Oceano tutti li fiumi e fonti si dice aver principio, così da quest'una egregia consuetudine tutti i famosi fatti e le maravigliose opere degli antichi uomini s'intende esser derivati.[93]

The phrase in italics is borrowed from Petrarch's famous poem "Italia mia," *Canzoniere* CXXVIII. Claudio Varese illustrated this point in his *Prosatori Volgari del Quattrocento*.[94] The passage to which Poliziano referred follows closely the section of Petrarch's *Canzoniere* made more famous by Machiavelli at the end of *Il Principe*. Only 11 lines separate the two quotations. Those passages are in italics below:

Per Dio, questo la mente
talor vi mova, e con pietà guardate
le lagrime del popol doloroso,
90 che sol da voi riposo
dopo Dio spera; e pur che voi mostriate
segno alcun di pietate,
virtú contra furore
prenderà l'arme a fia 'l combater corto:
95 *ché l'antico valore*
ne l'italici cor non è ancor morto.
Signor, mirate come 'l tempo vola
e sí come la vita
fugge e la morte n'è sovra le spalle.
100 Voi siete or qui, pensate a la partita:
ché l'alma ignuda e sola
conven ch'arrive a quel dubbioso calle.
Al passar questa valle
piacciavi porre giú l'odio e lo sdegno,
105 venti contrari a la vita serena,
e quell che 'n altrui pena
tempo si spende, in qualche atto più degno
o di mano o d'ingegno.[95]

In Poliziano's letter to Frederick, cited above, he used the words "illustre" and "virtuosa." Both of these words are central in the last Chapter of *Il Principe*. Machiavelli refers to the "illustre" house of the Medici no less than four times. Furthermore, "virtuoso," the masculine form of "virtuosa" is a pivotal term in the first sentence of the last Chapter. This may be coincidence, but it certainly adds weight to the possibility that if Machiavelli wrote the *Dialogo*, he drew on Poliziano's work and that this work in turn shaped the last Chapter of *Il Principe*.

The prefatory remarks in the *Dialogo* appear to be as patriotic as the final Chapter in *Il Principe*. The *Dialogo* states that the author's Florentine *patria* was "più nobile" or the most noble *patria*.[96] This nobility, in the larger context of the work, is afforded his *patria* by the beauty and supremacy of its language. The Florentine *patria*, was according to its author, at least where the realm of language was concerned, the most noble. *Il Principe*, on the other hand is concerned with liberation and unification as was argued in the Chapter One. It is interesting to compare the view of the Florentine *patria* in the *Dialogo* with Machiavelli's view in the last sentence of *Il Principe*. There, Machiavelli wrote,

Pigli, adunque, la illustre casa vostra questo assunto con quello animo e con quella speranza che si pigliano le imprese iuste; acciò che, sotto le sua insegna, e questa *patria ne sia nobilitata*, e sotto li sua auspizi, si verifichi quell detto del Petrarch.[97]

Then Machiavelli quotes the famous lines from Petrarch. He desired for his *patria* to be "più nobile" in the realm of political affairs just as it was superior in the realm of language. Leo and Lorenzo, working in unison, could make Florence politically, "più nobile" as it was linguistically.

Conclusion

This Chapter and the previous Chapter have sought to explore the possibility of Machiavelli's authorship of the *Dialogo* and to set out a likely year in which it was written. By so doing, distinct similarities were uncovered between works definitely attributed to Machiavelli and the *Dialogo*. Indeed, one might argue that the combination of politics and patriotism in Machiavelli's *oeuvre*, and particularly in the epilogue of *Il Principe* is mirrored in the *Dialogo*. This close relationship may be explained by what appear to be close ties between the two works, both in their patriotism and in the time they may have been written—the *vendemmial* of 1515.

When one considers the different aspects of Machiavelli's plan for Italian unification which were developed in the previous Chapters: secular patriotism, republicanism, a national military and an end to exile, a startlingly recognizable picture of "nationhood" emerges. If one adds to these components unity of language, as called for in the *Dialogo*, one might suggest that in the pages of that work and in the political works definitely attributed to Machiavelli, the seeds of the Italian nation were sown. If Lorenzo had seized the *occasione* as Machiavelli exhorted, could Florence, as a new Rome, have exerted a "benevolent" *egemonia politica e linguistica* over the Italian peninsula?[98] In seeking to answer that question, it may prove helpful to see if there is further evidence of "cross-pollination" between works definitely attributed to Machiavelli and the *Dialogo*. If, for example, one finds further similarities in the language used in these, might one suggest that the possibility of Machiavelli's authorship of the *Dialogo* is strengthened further still?

CHAPTER SEVEN

A New Translation of the
Discorso o dialogo intorno alla nostra lingua

ಏು಄

Angelo Codevilla, pointed out that translating a given work, particularly one which may be by Machiavelli, is potentially treacherous. Indeed, the *traduttore* (translator) can easily become a *traditore* (traitor) by the very act of translating[1]. Keeping this helpful and humbling anecdote in mind, the author, in this instance, the translator, strove to provide a new translation of the *Dialogo* without losing too much of its original feel.

Our translation is intentionally a little rough around the edges, in much the same way, we hope the reader will agree, the Italian is. This stands in contrast to the only other translation of the *Dialogo*, which was produced by John R. Hale in 1961[2]. Like all of his scholarship, that translation was thoughtful and elegant, though perhaps a little too much so concerning the latter. However, the author wishes to follow Hale's lead in one very important element; there are no arguments for or against Machiavelli's authorship of the work in the translation. On the contrary, the *Dialogo* is allowed to speak for itself.

In the Appendices, the reader will find an Italian edition of the *Dialogo* with references to the quotations from Dante, Virgil and Pulci among others as well as extensive intertextual notes illustrating the similarities between the *Dialogo* and a large proportion of Machiavelli's *oeuvre*. It is our hope, that this new translation and heavily annotated Italian edition, will further strengthen the case for Machiavelli's authorship of the *Dialogo*.

A Discourse or Dialogue Concerning Our Language

Whenever *I* have been able to honour *my* native country, even with *my* burden and peril *I* have done so voluntarily, because *a man* has no greater obligation in *his* life than that; first *they* depend on her for existence and then for every other good thing that fortune and nature have given *us*[3]. They all were because of her; and so much greater is the obligation for those who have been given the noblest country. And truly he, who with his spirit and labor, makes himself an enemy of his native country, deservedly ought to be called a parricide; even though he may be acting out of some legitimate grievance. For if it is an evil deed to strike one's father or mother, whatever the reason, it follows out of necessity that striking one's country is a most infamous deed, because she is never the source of any persecution powerful enough to merit your insults. You must recognize that all good things come from her; such that if she strips herself of part of her citizens you are obligated even more so to thank her for those that she left than to slander her for those that she took (or exiled). And when this is true, that is most true, I shall never be wrong in defending her and warring against those who too presumptuously seek to deprive her of her honour.

The occasion which prompted this line of reasoning is the dispute, brought up repeatedly in the past days, as to whether the language in which our Florentine poets and orators have written is Florentine, Tuscan or Italian. In this dispute I have considered how some less dishonest persons want it to be called Tuscan, some others who are most dishonest call it Italian, and others hold that it should simply be called Florentine. And every one of them is strong to defend their part; so, with the brawl remaining indecisive, it occurred to me, in this *vendemmial* labor of mine, to write to you at length about that which I think, in order to end the question or give everyone material for greater argument.

Thus if we want to see with which idiom these writers (among whom Dante, Petrarch and Boccaccio hold the highest place without any disagreement whatsoever) who are celebrated in this modern language, have written, it is necessary to put them in one place, and on the other all of Italy, to whose province (as a result of the love for the language of these three) it seems, every other region yields. For, in this regard, the Spanish and the French and the German are less presumptuous than the Lombard.

It is necessary, once this point has been made, to consider all of the Italian regions to see the difference in their speech and to give greater favor to those writers who agree more with these writers (i.e. Dante, Petrarch and Boccaccio) and to grant them a higher degree and a greater place in the language that they utilize. And, if you agree, it is good to distinguish between all of Italy and the many castles and cities that are in her. However, wanting to escape this confusion, let us divide her only into her provinces such as Lombardy, Romagna, Tuscany, the Papal States and the Kingdom of Naples.

And truly, if each of these places are thoroughly examined one will see great differences in their speech; and if one wants to know from whence this proceeds, it is necessary to examine first some of the reasons why there is so much similarity between them, that these writers today, think that those who wrote in the past employed a "common Italian language"; and why, amidst such diversity of language, we understand one another.

Some people want to believe that every language is determined by the affirmative particle which, subsequently, for all the Italians is signified with this word "*sì*," and that one understands the same spoken language throughout that province where one affirms—or says yes—by saying the same word. They cite the authority of Dante, who, wanting to signify Italy, defined it with this particle "*sì*," when he said:

> *Ah Pisa, shame of the peoples*
> *of the beautiful land where the* sì *sounds*

that is Italy. They cite France as a further example, where the whole land is called France but the language is nevertheless divided into the regions of *ui* and of *oc*, which mean for them the same thing as *sì* for the Italians. As an additional example they put forward the whole German language, which says *iò* along with the entirety of England which says *jeh*. And perhaps motivated by these reasons many of them think that everyone in Italy who writes or speaks, does so according to only one language.

Some others hold that it is not the particle *sì* which defines the language, because, should *sì* determine it, the Sicilians and the Spanish might also be considered Italians as far as language is concerned. Therefore, it is necessary to define language with other arguments. They say that where one considers carefully the eight parts of speech into which every language is divided that you will find that the verb is the chain and nerve of the language, and that every time this part is consistent, even though the other parts might vary a great deal, it follows that the language must be mutually intelligible. Because the nouns that are unfamiliar to us are made understandable by the verb which is located between them, and thus, where the verbs are different, even though there are similarities among the nouns, it becomes another language. The province of Italy—whose differences among verbs is small, but among nouns most different—may be given as an example of this sort. For every Italian says *amare* (to love), *stare* (to be, etc.) and *leggere* (to read), but not everyone says *deschetto* (dressing table, work bench), *tavola* (table) and *guastada* (specifically shaped glass or bottle). Among the most important pronouns there are variations, as with *mi* in place of *io* and *ti* for *tu*. That which makes further differences among the dialects—but none so great that they are not mutually comprehensible—are the pronunciation and the accents. The Tuscans end all their words with vowels, but the Lombards and the Romangols end almost all of them with consonants, as is *pane* (Tuscan—bread) and *pan* (Romagnol/Lombard—bread).

Once these, and all of the other differences in the Italian languages have been considered (if one wishes to see which of these takes the quill in hand and in which language the ancient writers have written) it is first necessary to see from whence Dante and the first writers came and whether or not they wrote in their native tongue. Then we will examine their writings and compare them with writings that are simply Florentine or Lombard or from another province of Italy—places where there is no art but only nature (or, it is not tempered with artifice but in its natural state); and that which is most consistent with their writings can be called, I believe, the language in which they wrote.

It is well-known from whence those first writers came (except a Bolognese, an Aretine and a Pistoiese, who among them did not piece ten poems together). They were Florentines; among whom, Dante, Petrarch and Boccaccio take the prominent place, and such a high place, that others cannot hope to join them there. Among these authors, Boccaccio declared in the *Decameron* that he wrote in the Florentine dialect; I am not aware that Petrarch said anything about the matter; but Dante, in one of his books called the *De vulgari eloquio* (the *De vulgari eloquentia*), where he damned all of the particular languages of Italy, declared not to have written in Florentine, but in a curial language. In that manner, should one trust him, I would have to wipe out the arguments that I set forth above, in order to learn from their works, where they learned the language in which they wrote and spoke.

I do not want, as far as Petrarch and Boccaccio are concerned, to repeat myself yet again, because the latter is with us and the former is neutral, but I would rather dwell upon Dante, who in every aspect showed himself to be—by his genius, by his learning and by his judgment—an excellent man, except where he discussed his native country, which he persecuted beyond all humanity and philosophical foundation, and with every type of injury. And being unable to do anything other than defame her, he accused her of every vice, condemned her men, slandered her situation, spoke poorly of her customs and of her laws; and he did this, not only in one part of his *Cantica* (the *Commedia*), but in all of it—in various places and in diverse ways. He was injured by the offence of his exile so deeply, that he longed for revenge, and therefore he exacted as much revenge as he was able. And if, by chance, the bad things that he predicted had come about, Florence would have more to lament for having nurtured that man, than of any other calamity. But Fortune, in order to make lies of and to overshadow with its glory, his false slander, has continually favored her and made Florence famous throughout the provinces of the world, and has brought her to the present in such happiness and so tranquil a state, that, if Dante were to see her, either he would accuse himself of the same crime once again, or beaten by the blows of his hateful envy, he would want, being newly resurrected, to die anew.

It is not, therefore, a marvel that this man, who in every way heaped infamy on his native country, wished once more with regard to language, to rob her of that reputation with which his writings had adorned her. And so as not to honor her in any way he wrote that work (*De vulgari eloquentia*) to demonstrate that the language in which he had written was not Florentine. Who, if he should be trusted, found Brutus in the deepest of Lucifer's throats, and five Florentine citizens among the thieves, and that his Cacciaguida should be found in Paradise and his similar passions and opinions; in those he made himself so blind, that he lost all of his dignity, learning, judgment, and he became another man altogether. To such an extent that, if he would have judged everything always in this way, either he would have continued to live in Florence or he would have been chased out like a lunatic.

But because things that are questioned with general words and conjectures may be easily criticized, I want, with vivid and true words, to demonstrate that his language is entirely Florentine and even more so than that which Boccaccio himself confesses to be Florentine—and in part I want to respond to those who hold the same opinion as Dante.

A common Italian language would be one where there was more of the common than of one's local language; and similarly one's local language would be that in which there is more of one's own than of any other language; because one will not be able to find a language that is complete unto itself without having borrowed from others. For, when men from varied provinces converse together, they borrow words one from the other. In addition to this, whenever time passes or new ideas or new arts come to a city it is necessary that new words come there also—words born in that language from whence those ideas or those arts have come; but accommodating themselves—in speech and moods and cases, with other differences and in the accents—they are made consistent with the words of that language that appropriates them, and so become its own. If this was not the case, languages would appear to be a patchwork and not well polished. Thus, foreign words are turned into Florentine, not Florentine into foreign words. Neither, therefore, can our language become anything other than Florentine.

And here it follows, that languages enrich themselves from the beginning, and become more beautiful as the they become most copious; but is it very true that with time, through the multitude of these new words, they are bastardized and become something different; but this happens over hundreds of years, which others do not perceive until it has descended into an extreme barbarism. This change is very quick when it happens that a new population comes to live in a province. In this case it makes its change in the course of an age of a man. But in whichever of these two ways the language is changed, it follows that if there is the will, the lost language can be regained by good writers who have written in that language, as has been done and is still being done with the Latin language and the Greek.

But leaving this part alone as not necessary, for our language is not yet in decline, and returning from whence I started, I say that that language ought to be called common to a province where the greatest part of its words, along with their uses, are not used in the other local dialects of that province; and a language can call itself local when the greater part of its words are not used in another language of that province.

As what I say is true—which is certainly most true—I would like to conjure Dante, so that he can show me his poem; and I will bring with me something which is written in the Florentine language. I will ask him what part of his poem was not written in Florentine. And he will respond that many words are non-Florentine, some were taken from Lombardy, some he made up himself and others taken from the Latin...

But because I would like to speak a little with Dante; in order to escape *he said* and *I responded*, I will put the speakers in front.

N. Which words did you drag in from Lombardy?
D. This:

> At the bridge-head (co del ponte) near Benevento

and this also:

> With you will be born and will with you hide (vosco)

N. Which did you borrow in from the Latins?
D. These, and many others:

> The passing beyond humanity may not be set forth in words.

N. Which words did you create?
D. These:

> If I were in you, even as you are in me.

These words, intermingled with Tuscan words, make a third language.

N. That's good, but tell me: in your work, how many of these words are foreign or of your own making, or from Latin?

D. In the first two *Canticles* there are only a few, but in the last, there are many—mostly derived from the Latins, because the varied ideas with which I reasoned, compelled me to use suitable words to express them; and this was not possible if I did not use Latin endings. So, I used them, but I changed them so that the endings became similar to the language of the rest of the work.

N. In what language is the work written?

D. Curial.

N. What does curial mean?

D. It means a language spoken by the courtesans at the Papal court, and at The Duke's (Milan), who, being learned men, speak better than those from particular regions of Italy.

N. You will speak lies. Tell me something: what does "*morse*" (he bit) mean in that curial language?

D. It means "*mori*" (he died).

N. In Florentine what does it mean?

D. It means "to squeeze with the teeth."

N. When you said, in your verses:

And when the teeth of the Lombard bit (morse).

What does that *morse* (bit) mean?

D. "Pricked," "offended" and "assaulted": that is a translation taken from the *mordere* (to bite) which the Florentines use.

N. Therefore, you speak Florentine and not the courtly tongue.

D. This is true for the most part; however, I am careful not to use certain words which are our own.

N. How are you "careful"? When you say:

He kicks (spingeva) violently with both feet.

This *spingere*, (to kick) what does it mean?

D. In Florence it means, when an animal kicks with its feet, "it jumps with a couple of kicks"; because I wanted to show how he was kicking his feet, I said, "he kicks" (*spingeva*).

N. Again, tell me: wanting to say "legs,"(*gambe*)

And he who kicks hard with the legs (zanche)

Why did you say that?

D. Because in Florence they call those stilts "legs" (*zanche*) on which the spirits go about for Saint John's Day, and because they use them as legs (*gambe*), I wanted to signify *gambe*, so I said *zanche*[4].

N. By my faith you do guard yourself well against Florentine words! But tell me when you say later on:

Do not take, mortals, vows too lightly (ciancie),

why do you say "lightly" (*ciancie*) like the Florentines and not "lightly" (*zanze*) like the Lombards, as you have said *vosco* and *co del ponte*?

D. I did not say *zanze* to avoid using a barbarous word like that; but I said *co* and *vosco*, either, because they are not such barbarous words, or, because in a lengthy work it is permissible to use some foreign words, as Virgil did when he said:

The waves and the treasures of Troy.

N. That is fine; but did Virgil not write in Latin for this reason?

D. No.

N. And so you have not left your native language just because you have said *co* and *vosco*. But we are having a vain dispute, because in your work, in many places, you confess that you speak both Tuscan and Florentine. Do you not say of one that heard you speaking in the Inferno:

And he that understood the Tuscan speech.

And in another place, Farinata is heard speaking to you:

Your way of speaking has made manifest
That you are a native of the country
Against which, perhaps, I made too many attacks.

D. It is true that I said all of these things.

N. Why then do you say that you do not speak Florentine? But I want to convince you with books in hand and by comparisons between them; and therefore we shall read your work and the *Morgante*. Read on (in your work).

D.   *In the middle of our life's walk*
        I discovered myself in a dark wood
        Where the straight way was lost.

N. That is sufficient. Read a little, now, of the *Morgante*
D. Where?
N. Wherever you want. Read here or there.
D. Here:

    He who (chi) begins has not merit yet, it is written
    In your holy Gospel, good Father.

N. Well now, what difference is there between your language and this?
D. Little.
N. I do not think there is any.
D. Here there is one thing that I do not understand.
N. What?
D. That *chi* is too Florentine.
N. You will have to retract that: or did you not say

    I do not know who (chi) you are, or by what means
    You have come down here,
    but (you do seem to me) Florentine..?

D. It is all true and I am wrong.
N. My Dante, I hope that you will amend your ways, and that you will consider better the Florentine idiom and your work, and that you will see that if anybody is to feel shame, Florence will know it better than you; because, if you will consider carefully that which you have said, you will see that in your own verses you have not escaped awkwardness, as in:

    Then we left...and we went on a while;

You have not escaped filthy words, like this:

    That makes shit of that which is eaten;

You have not escaped obscenity, such as:

He raised his hands with both the figs.

And not having fled this type of writing that dishonors all of your work, you cannot have escaped an infinite number of local words that are not used anywhere other than Florence; because art can never be completely contrary to nature.

Besides this, I want you to consider that languages cannot be simple, and that it is better that they are mixed with other languages. But a native language (such as Florentine), converts words that it has borrowed from others into its own use, and it is so powerful, that the borrowed words do not disorder it, but rather, it disorders theirs; because that which it bears from the others it pulls to itself in such a manner, that it seems to be its own.

And these men who write in such a language, like her lovers, are bound to do that which you have done, but not to say that which you have said; because if you have borrowed many words from the Latins and from foreigners, if you have made new words, you have done very well; but you have done badly to say that for this reason that which you wrote has become another language. Horace says:

When the language of Cato and Ennius
had enriched the speech of their native country;

and he lauds these as the first who began to adorn the Latin language.

In their armies, the ancient Romans did not have more than 2 legions of native Romans—these totaled roughly 12,000 persons, and then they had 20,000 from other nations. Nevertheless, because the native Romans were, along with their captains, the nerve of the army, they all fought according to Roman order and discipline. Indeed, these armies retained the name (that is Roman), and the authority along with Roman dignity. And you, Dante, who have put in your writings twenty legions of Florentine words and used cases, tenses and moods and Florentine endings, want these foreign words to change the language?

And if you called it the common Italian or courtly language, because in such a language, one uses all the verbs that are used in Florence, I respond to you, that even if the same verbs have been used, they do not use the same nouns, because they change so much with pronunciation, that they become another thing. Because you know that foreigners pervert the *c* so that it becomes *z*, like those discussed above, *cianciare* and *zanzare*, or they add letters, like *verrà* which becomes *vegnirà*, or they take them away, like *poltrone* and *poltron*; so much so that these words, which are similar to ours, are bungled so, that they turn them into something else.

And if, while speaking with me, you continue to press for the courtly language, I respond to you, that if you speak of the courts of Milan or Naples that they mirror the locale of their native countries, and those are best that come nearest to Tuscan and imitate it most. And if you want that which imitates to be better that than which is imitated, you wish for something that is almost never the case. But if you speak of the court of Rome, you speak of a place where people speak in as many ways as there are nations there, and it is not possible to provide any rule. Then I marvel that you want, where nothing praiseworthy or good is done, to do this (to elevate this court to such a high place of esteem); because where there are perverse customs it necessarily follows that the language must also be perverse; for it reflects the effeminate lasciviousness of those who speak it.

But that which deceives many regarding shared or common words is this, (you and the other writers, having been celebrated and having been read in various places) many of our words were learned by many foreigners and used by them, so that from our own they became common property. And if you want to prove this, simply bring forward a book composed by one of those foreigners who wrote after you, and you will see how many words of yours they use, and how they seek to imitate you. And to have evidence of this, make them read books written by their fellow citizens before you were born and they will see, that in these books none of our words, nor any of our terms are found. And so it appears that the language in which they write is yours, and it is due to you, and yours is not common to theirs. If you read their writing you will see, although they try to imitate your language with continual effort, that in a thousand places it is badly and perversely used— because it is impossible that art should be mightier than nature.

Consider yet another thing, if you want to see the dignity of your native tongue; when these foreign writers entertain a new subject, if they do not have an example of words learned from you, out of necessity, they must scurry back to the Tuscan. Or, if they use their own native words, they smooth them out and change them according to the Tuscan usage. Otherwise neither they nor other persons would approve of it.

And as a result, they say that all of the native languages are ugly unless they have been mixed, so that none need be brutish. But, I say furthermore, that the language which has to be mixed the least is the most praiseworthy— and without a doubt the one which has the least need of admixture is Florentine.

I say once again that since many things are written, which are written without words and expressions from their own native tongues, they cannot be beautiful. An example of this sort are comedies; because, although the end of a comedy is to raise a mirror to private life, nevertheless, the way in which it does this is with a certain urbanity and with expressions that move people to laughter so that men, racing to this delight, taste afterwards the useful example that is implied. Consequently the characters who are serious are difficult to deal with; because there can be no gravity in a fraudulent servant, in a lecherous old man, in a young man made insane by love, in a flattering whore, in a greedy parasite; but good comes from comic compositions for they produce men who are gravely effected along with other uses for our daily lives. But because these things are dealt with ridiculously, it is necessary to use terms and words that bring about these effects; if these sayings and expressions are not derived from their own local or native words, where they are popular and well-known, they do not move nor can ever combine to produce these desired effects.

Therefore, one who is born as a non-Tuscan can never play this part well, because if he wants to use jests from his native country he will make a patchwork garment. Indeed, he will make a composition half-Tuscan and half-foreign; and this will illustrate which language he has used, and whether it is communal or his own local language. And if he does not want to use them, not knowing the Tuscan, he will produce a work which is lacking—far from possessing perfection.

And to prove this I would have you read a comedy written by one of the Ariosti from Ferrara. You will find a refined composition, well ordered with an ornate style; you will see a tightly woven knot (plot or intrigue) well adjusted and even better loosened (plot resolution); but you will see it stripped of those salts that such a comedy requires, for no other reason than that stated before. He did not like the Ferrarese words and he did not know the Florentine words, so he left them out. He used one common word, and I also believe that it was made common by way of Florence, saying that a doctor of theology would pay one of his women in *doppioni*. Then, he used one of his own local words, which proves how bad it is to mingle the Ferrarese with the Tuscan; one of Ariosto's characters, saying that she did not want to speak where there were ears that could hear her, is made to respond that she would not speak where there were *bigonzoni*. And, a refined palate knows how offensive *bigonzoni* is both when read and when heard. And you can easily see here and in many other places with what difficulty he maintained the decorum of the language that he had borrowed.

Consequently, I conclude that there are many things that cannot be written well without understanding the local and particular elements of that language, which is most highly regarded (i.e. Florentine); and wanting to use local words one should go to the source—the place from whence the language has its origin. Otherwise you will make a work where one part does not correspond to the other.

And the importance of this language in which you, Dante, wrote—the same language that the others who came before and after you have written—owes its preeminence to Florence. This is demonstrated by the fact that you were Florentine, born into a native country that spoke in such a way, that it was able to accommodate better than any other, writing in verse and in prose—which is not possible with the other languages of Italy. Everyone knows that the Provençaux were the first to write in verse; from Provence the use of verse traveled to Sicily, and from Sicily to Italy; and from among the provinces of Italy to Tuscany; and from all of Tuscany to Florence, for no other reason than its language was most suited to it. Florence did not merit being the first to beget these writers as a result of the comfort of her situation, or for the genius of her people, or for any other particular occasion, but her language was best accommodated—before that of any other city—to take on the discipline of writing in verse.

One sees in these times that this is true, in that there are many Ferrarese, Neapolitans, Vicentines and Venetians who write well and who possess the ingenious capacities necessary to be a writer. This could not have happened before you, Petrarch and Boccaccio had written. For, wanting to reach this place of esteem, but being hindered by their native tongue, it was necessary that first, one should come to teach them by his example—to teach them how to forget the natural barbarism in which their native tongues drowned them.

I will conclude, therefore that there is no language, which can be called common to Italy or a courtly tongue, because all those that might be called thus, have their foundation in Florentine writers and their language. To whom, as their true fount and their foundation, foreign writers must apply for all of their deficiencies. And not wanting to be truly stubborn, they have to confess that Florentine is their source and foundation.

After Dante listened to these things he confessed that I was correct and he departed. I remained, completely contented with myself at having undeceived him. But, I do not know whether I will undeceive those who are so little learned of the benefits that they have themselves received from our native country, that they wish to unite her with the Milanese language, Venice, Romagna, and all the blasphemies of Lombardy.

Conclusion

The *Discourse or Dialogue Concerning our Language* may provide interesting insight into Machiavelli's plan for Italian unification. While we do not possess enough evidence to attribute the work to the famous Florentine with certainty, given the work's obsession with Florentine greatness and linguistic supremacy, it is safe to say that Machiavelli could have written the *Dialogue* and that the ideas contained in it were far from alien to Niccolò. If he did author the text, which we suggest is a distinct possibility, the *Dialogue* may be one part of Machiavelli's tri-partite design for Italian political and cultural unity.

Conclusion

ꙮ

Niccolò Machiavelli's plan for Italian liberation and unification, detailed in the pages of *Il Principe* and the *Discorsi*, highlights his genius. Indeed, his concept of the "secular *patria*," when linked with the idea of a national "citizen army" and an end to the practice of exile within the peninsula encompasses startlingly familiar elements—to the contemporary eye at least—of an Italian "national identity." In seeking to bring out these different aspects of Machiavelli's plan, several longstanding issues related to the interpretation of *Il Principe* and the *Discorsi* were brought to the fore and shown to be less "damaging" to his political thought than many scholars were willing to admit.

The Florentine's conception of an Italian *patria*, as that which he desired to be founded in *Il Principe* and consolidated under a republican regime in the *Discorsi* provides continuity to Machiavelli's political thought. By the same token, the presence of the term *patria* in both works seems to reconcile the other well-documented differences in their vocabulary and genre. *Il Principe*'s focus on the person of the prince and the *Discorsi*'s focus, in general terms, on republican government are drawn together by a consistency in Machiavelli's use of *patria* as Chapter One illustrated. Indeed, it seems that in the latter, Machiavelli's concept of the "secular *patria*" took on a broader definition. It was something that was fundamental, something that a republican government should strive to protect and maintain. In other words, the considerations on *patria* in *Il Principe* which focused on the prince's role in founding and uniting a *patria*, were expanded upon in the *Discorsi*, to include the maintenance of the "bene comune" and the "comune patria." There is then, in Machiavelli's concept of the "secular *patria*" an evolution from the individual's responsibility to the corporate responsibility of the citizenry as a whole to protect and defend their communal *patria*. But what led Machiavelli to come to such conclusions?

This study argued that in the autumn of 1515, with a Medici *Capitano* in Florence and a Medici Pope in Rome, Machiavelli saw a unique opportunity. This *occasione*—the link between Florence and Rome that briefly united their interests—Machiavelli argued in the epilogue of *Il Principe*, could see the unification and liberation of Italy. Following the example of Cesare Borgia and his father, Pope Alexander VI, Lorenzo and Leo X could use their familial bond and the prestige this afforded to establish a "national" citizen army, expel the barbarians and then, out of duty to the united *patria* which they helped to create, immediately end their union. Then, following the example of the Roman dictators, Lorenzo would magnanimously lay aside his all-powerful office allowing not only for the creation of a republican government, but for the separation of Church and *patria*.

Machiavelli's plan never made it off the ground. It is arguable whether Lorenzo ever saw, let alone took the time to read, the work so earnestly dedicated to him or its companion work on republicanism.[1] Indeed, with Lorenzo's death in 1519, all of Machiavelli's hopes for Italian greatness perished. Lorenzo, his would-be prince, following the precedent set by Giuliano de'Medici (Lorenzo's predecessor) had no time for the outspoken republican patriotism of an exiled has-been. Francesco Guicciardini, Machiavelli's friend and confidant in the last years of his life was more accessible, and though he had read Machiavelli's work, he was scathingly critical.

Guicciardini's commentary on Machiavelli's *Discorsi*, the *Considerazioni intorno ai Discorsi del Machiavelli sopra la prima deca di Tito Livio* illustrates a recognition of Machiavelli's plan for the liberation and unification of Italy. In Book One, Chapter 12 of that work, Guicciardini even discussed the transition from the government of one ("una monarchia") to government by the many ("republiche"). In theory, Guicciardini argued such a transition was possible, but in practice, laughable. As Chapters Two, Three and Four illustrated, Guicciardini's criticisms of Machiavelli crossed the length and breadth of his political theory.

Guicciardini argued that a prince (Lorenzo in this case) would never willingly lay aside his dictatorial power after unification. In theory, love of *patria* and the duty to honor it may have been enough to cause him to quit his office, but in practice it is hard to imagine Lorenzo acting with such selfless magnanimity. By the same token, Machiavelli's gross misunderstanding of Italian warfare—which led him to deride not only all mercenary soldiers, but also artillery—caused Guicciardini to chide his friend. One can imagine Guicciardini's dismay at his friend's refusal to see the "real truth." Machiavelli, the master of the "verità effettuale" was taken to school by his younger and more politically savvy friend.[2] The picture painted by Guicciardini's commentary on Machiavelli is a comment on a theory which was woefully unsuited to its time. However, the unsuitability of Machiavelli's call for liberation and unification of Italy which sounded so out of touch in the *cinquecento* was taken up and expounded upon by the historians and politicians of the *Risorgimento* era.

Standing in stark contrast to the reprimands of Guicciardini, Francesco de Sanctis, recognizing Machiavelli's idealism, sounded the praises of his call of unification. Encapsulating the spirit of his generation, de Sanctis wrote[3]:

> The scheme that Machiavelli proposed was nothing less than a great Italian state, to be the bulwark of Italy against the foreigner. So the conception of the fatherland was no longer the little commune, but was the whole of the nation. In Dante's Utopia Italy was the "garden of the empire"; in Machiavelli's Utopia Italy is the *patria*, the fatherland, an independent autonomous nation[...] Country to Machiavelli was a god, higher even than morality, and higher than law. Just as the ascetics saw the individual as absorbed into the Godhead, and just as the Inquisitors burned heretics in the name of God, so for one's country everything was lawful—actions that in private life would be crimes, when done for the sake of country became magnanimous[...] God had come out of Heaven and descended to earth, and had changed his name to "Fatherland" but was no less terrible."[4]

Machiavelli's precocious idealism which de Sanctis found fitted in so well in nineteenth-century Italy, may also have been reflected in a work which many scholars attribute to the famous Florentine—the *Discorso o dialogo intorno all nostra lingua*.

The arguments for Machiavelli's authorship of that work appear to outweigh those that deny it as Chapters Five and Six illustrated. While there are too many holes in the provenance of the *Dialogo* to attribute definitively the work to Machiavelli, the call for political unification in *Il Principe* and the *Discorsi* seems to be complemented in the *Dialogo*'s call for linguistic unification. Working in combination, the secular patriotism of *Il Principe* and the *Discorsi* called for a new prince to rise, unite Italy and then resign his all-powerful office, allowing the peoples of Italy to form a republican government. The *Dialogo* and its call for Florentine linguistic dominance may complement the secular patriotism of Machiavelli's two most famous works. Politics, secular patriotism and perhaps language, defended by a "national citizen" army; are these the ingredients for an Italian national identity? This examination argued that for Machiavelli, at least, they were.

Those same elements, for which Machiavelli was maligned in the *cinquecento*, appear to have enjoyed a renewed topicality in the *Risorgimento*. In conclusion, while Machiavelli's authorship of *Il Principe* and the *Discorsi* is incontestable, the *Dialogo* is another story. One cannot know for sure whether Niccolò Machiavelli authored the *Dialogo*, but it is tempting to ask, what if he did?

At the very least, a comparison of Machiavelli's best-known works with a short treatise which he may have written may add to our understanding of the complexities of national identities in Italy and elsewhere since the Renaissance. Moreover, one might surmise, that the suspicion with which Machiavelli's political theory was viewed in the *cinquecento*, ultimately resulting in his work being banned by the Church—his time in purgatory— gave way in the *Risorgimento* era to his vindication and restoration.

APPENDIX ONE

Supplement to Chapter One:
Occurrences of *Patria* in Machiavelli's
Il Principe and the *Discorsi*

౭౦౧౩

This Appendix, and the Appendices that follow, relied on electronic sources to locate "patria" and related terms in the works of Machiavelli, Guicciardini, Livy and Cicero. The website which the Author found to be most helpful in this, is the "Intratext Digital Library" (http://www.intratext.com). Having used "Intratext's" concordance to locate the desired terms—*patria* most importantly—the author utilized the best available scholarly printed editions on which to base the quotations below. One will notice that there are no references to Machiavelli's, Cicero's or Guicciardini's private correspondence in either Appendix. This is because those works have yet to be produced in electronic format. Not wanting to include an incomplete or imperfect record of *patria* in those works, the Author has left them out. More work, therefore, needs to be done on *patria* in Machiavelli's personal writings, his sources and his contemporaries.

In order to aid the reader, one will find the work from which the references are drawn with appropriate page numbers as guides. This method is followed throughout this Appendix and the others that follow.

Patria in *Il Principe*. All references are to Niccolò Machiavelli, *Il Principe e Altre Opere Politiche*. Introduzione di Delio Cantimori, Note di Stefano Andretta. Milano: Garzanti Libri, 1999.

1.   Roma e fondatore di quella *patria*. Bisognava che Ciro trovassi (*Il Principe*; Capitolo 6, pp. 29–30).

2.   donde la loro *patria* ne fu nobilitata e diventò felicissima.   (*Il Principe*; Capitolo 6, p. 30).

3.   uno privato cittadino con il favore delli altri della sua *patria*.   E, parlando del primo modo(*Il Principe*; Capitolo 8, p. 38).

4.   la libertà della loro *patria*, e con il favore vitellesco, di occupare Fermo (*Il Principe*; Capitolo 8, p. 40).

5.   possé vivere lungamente sicuro nella sua *patria* e defendersi dalli inimici esterni (*Il Principe*; Capitolo 8, p. 41).

6.   cittadini diventa principe della sua *patria*, il quale si può chiamare principato civile (*Il Principe*; Capitolo 9, p. 41).

7.   e difese contro a quelli la *patria* sua et il suo stato: e li bastò solo (*Il Principe*; Capitolo 9, p. 44).

8.   acciò che, sotto la sua insegna, e questa *patria* ne sia nobilitata (*Il Principe*; Capitolo 26, p. 98).

Patria in the *Discorsi*. All References are to Niccolò Machiavelli. *Discorsi Sopra la Prima Deca di Tito Livio*: Introduzione di Gennaro Sasso, Note di Giorgio Inglese. Milano: Biblioteca Universale Rizzoli, 1999.

1.   che si sono per la loro *patria* affaticati, essere più tosto (*Discorsi*, Libro I. Proemio, pp 55–56).

2.   successione ma alla comune *patria*, debbe ingegnarsi di avere l'autorità solo (*Discorsi*, Libro I. 9, p. 86).

3.   fare questo bene alla sua *patria* se non diventava solo di autorità (*Discorsi*, Libro I, Capitolo 9, p. 87).

4.   regno loro o quello della *patria*. A questi si (*Discorsi*, Libro I, Capitolo 10, p. 88).

5.   privati vivere nella loro *patria* più tosto Scipioni che Cesari

(*Discorsi*, Libro I, Capitolo 10, p. 89).

6. gli altri non ebbono nella *patria* loro meno autorità che si (*Discorsi*, Libro I, Capitolo 10, p. 89).

7. insieme, e, sbigottiti della *patria* si erano convenuti abbandonare la Italia (*Discorsi*, Libro I, Capitolo 11, p. 92).

8. giurare di non abbandonare la *patria*. Lucio Manlio padre di Tito Manlio (*Discorsi*, Libro I, Capitolo 11, p. 92).

9. e così quelli cittadini i quali lo amore della *patria*, le leggi di quella non ritenevano in Italia (*Discorsi*, Libro I, Capitoli 11, p. 92).

10. a congiurare contro alla *patria* per altro se non perché (*Discorsi*, Libro I, Capitolo 16, p. 104).

11. sono diventati della loro *patria* tiranni, dico ch'ei debbe esaminare prima quello che il popolo desidera (*Discorsi*, Libro I, Capitolo 16, pp. 104–105).

12. commissono la fortuna tutta della *patria* loro e la virtù di tanti uomini (*Discorsi*, Libro I, Capitolo 23, p. 116).

13. volle più tosto vedere il disonore della *patria* sua e la rovina di quello esercito che soccorrerlo (*Discorsi*, Libro I, Capitolo 31, pp. 129–130).

14 la rovina della loro *patria*, andati ad abitare a Veio (*Discorsi*, Libro I, Capitolo 57, p. 178).

15. bene commune della sua *patria*; vedrà tanti esempli usati da lui (*Discorsi*, Libro I, Capitolo 58, p. 182).

16. uno consiglio da fare alla loro *patria* grande utilità, ma non lo poteva dire per non lo scoprire (*Discorsi*, Libro I, Capitolo 59, pp. 185–186).

17. della quale in quella età la *patria* sua si poteva valere (*Discorsi*, Libro I, Capitolo 60, p. 187).

18.   giudicando non essere bene difendere la *patria* di coloro che l'avevano di già sottomessa a altrui (*Discorsi*, Libro II, Capitolo 2, p. 296).

19.   Talché de' suoi acquisti solo egli ne profitta e non la sua *patria*. E chi volessi confermare (*Discorsi*, Libro II, Capitolo 2, p. 297).

20.   la esaltazione e la difesa della *patria*, vedrebbono come la vuole che noi (*Discorsi*, Libro II, Capitolo 2, p. 299).

21.   aveva i suoi costumi e la sua lingua *patria*: il che tutto è suto spento dalla potenza romana. (*Discorsi*, Libro II, Capitolo 5, p. 309).

22.   non impoverisca il paese e la *patria* sua. È necessario, dunque (*Discorsi*, Libro II, Capitolo 6, p. 309).

23.   abbandonare la loro *patria* non sono molti (*Discorsi*, Libro II, Capitolo 8, p. 314).

24.   tanto che, dimenticata la *patria* e la reverenza del Senato (*Discorsi*, Libro II, Capitolo 20, p. 348).

25.   tornato nella sua *patria* donde era esule (*Discorsi*, Libro II, Capitolo 24, p. 361).

26.   Ma vegnamo alle republiche che fanno le fortezze non nella *patria*; ma nelle terre che le acquistano. (*Discorsi*, Libro II, Capitolo 24, p. 362).

27.   per tenere la *patria* propria, la fortezza è dannosa; per tenere le terre che si acquistono (*Discorsi*, Libro II, Capitolo 24, p. 362).

28.   a soccorrere la *patria*, trovò rotto Asdrubale e Siface (*Discorsi*, Libro II, Capitolo 27, pp. 369–370).

29.   era l'ultima posta della sua *patria*, non volle prima metterla a rischio (*Discorsi*, Libro II, Capitolo 27, p. 370).

30.   se alcuno rimedio aveva la sua *patria*, era in quella e non nella guerra (*Discorsi*, Libro II, Capitolo 27, p. 370).

31. che perdendo quella la sua *patria* diveniva serva (*Discorsi*, Libro II, Capitolo 27, p. 370).

32. e intero nella sua riputazione per la recuperazione della *patria* sua. (*Discorsi*, Libro II, Capitolo 29, p. 374).

33. credere a quelli che sono cacciati dalla *patria* sua, (*Discorsi*, Libro II, Capitolo 31, p. 378).

34. sendo loro promessa la ritornata nella *patria* dai loro cittadini se lo ammazzavano (*Discorsi*, Libro II, Capitolo 31, p. 378).

35. Debbesi considerare pertanto quanto sia vana e la fede e le promesse di quelli che si truovano privi della loro *patria*. Perché, quanto alla fede (*Discorsi*, Libro II, Capitolo 31, p. 378).

36. che per gli tuoi rientrare nella *patria* loro, che lasceranno te e accosterannosi ad altri (*Discorsi*, Libro II, Capitolo 31, p. 378).

37. i Re e di liberare la sua *patria*, qualunque volta gliele fosse data occasione (*Discorsi*, Libro III, Capitolo 2, p. 466).

38. stato ne' dì nostri e nella nostra *patria* memorabile. (*Discorsi*, Libro III, Capitolo 3, p. 467).

39. come quello aveva fatto era per salute della *patria*, e non per ambizione sua (*Discorsi*, Libro III, Capitolo 3, p. 468).

40. e' perdé insieme con la *patria* sua, lo stato e la riputazione (*Discorsi*, Libro III, Capitolo 3, p. 468).

41. figliuoli di Bruto contro alla *patria*, e di quelle fatte contro a Tarquinio Prisco (*Discorsi*, Libro III, Capitolo 5, p. 471).

42. il più delle volte rovina sé e la sua *patria*. Dobbiamo adunque (*Discorsi*, Libro III, Capitolo 6, p. 472).

43. contro alla *patria*, o contro a uno principe (*Discorsi*, Libro III, Capitolo 6, p. 472).

44. la quale è il desiderio di liberare la *patria*, stata da quello occupata (*Discorsi*, Libro III, Capitolo 6, p. 473).

45. questa ha mosso molti altri contro a' Falari, Dionisii e altri occupatori della *patria* loro. Né può da questo (*Discorsi*, Libro III, Capitolo 6, p. 473).

46. e confortatogli a liberare la *patria*, alcuni di loro (*Discorsi*, Libro III, Capitolo 6, p. 478).

47. perché non si fa bene nè a sé nè alla *patria* nè ad alcuno (*Discorsi*, Libro III, Capitolo 6, pp. 484–485).

48. È vero che la congiura che Pelopida fece per liberare Tebe sua *patria*, ebbe tutte le difficultà (*Discorsi*, Libro III, Capitolo 6, p. 485).

49. ammazzare i tiranni e liberare la *patria*. Pure nondimanco, fece tutto (*Discorsi*, Libro III, Capitolo 6, p. 485).

50. Le congiure che si fanno contro alla *patria* sono meno pericolose, (*Discorsi*, Libro III, Capitolo 6, p. 487).

51. È bene vero, che nello eseguire una congiura contro alla *patria* vi è difficultà più e maggiori pericolo (*Discorsi*, Libro III, Capitolo 6, p. 488).

52. che hanno ad un tratto e con le forze loro occupato la *patria*. Perché a simili (*Discorsi*, Libro III, Capitolo 6, p. 488).

53. o con eserciti esterni hanno congiurato per occupare la *patria*, hanno avuti varii eventi, secondo la fortuna. (*Discorsi*, Libro III, Capitolo 6, p. 489).

54. Tanto che, esaminate tutte le congiure fatte contro alla *patria*, non ne troverrai alcuna (*Discorsi*, Libro III, Capitolo 6, p. 489).

55. quante buone opere fatte in favore della *patria*, cancella dipoi una brutta cupidità di regnare. (*Discorsi*, Libro III, Capitolo 8, p. 492).

56. lo amore della *patria* che alcuno altro rispetto (*Discorsi*, Libro III, Capitolo 8, p. 493).

57. Prosperò egli e la sua *patria* mentre che i tempi (*Discorsi*, Libro III, Capitolo 9, p. 496).

58. non lo seppe fare; talché insieme con la sua *patria* rovinò (*Discorsi*, Libro III, Capitolo 9, p. 496).

59. per la salute della *patria* contro all'ambizione de' Tribuni (*Discorsi*, Libro III, Capitolo 11, p. 502).

60. gli ebbono tratta Tebe loro *patria* della servitù degli Spartani (*Discorsi*, Libro III, Capitolo 13, p. 507).

61. pietoso verso il padre e verso la *patria*, e reverentissimo a' suoi maggiori. (*Discorsi*, Libro III, Capitolo 22, pp. 523–524).

62. non solamente alla *patria* ma a sé (*Discorsi*, Libro III, Capitolo 22, p. 527).

63. ed in uno cittadino utile, e massime alla *patria*; ed ancora rade volte offende (*Discorsi*, Libro III, Capitolo 22, p. 527).

64. noi abbiamo conchiuso di sopra come, procedendo come Valerio, si nuoce alla *patria* ed a sé, e, procedendo come Manlio (*Discorsi*, Libro III, Capitolo 23, p. 528).

65. si giova alla *patria* e nuocesi qualche volta a sé. (*Discorsi*, Libro III, Capitolo 23, p. 528).

66. per questo Cesare potette occupare la *patria*. Che se mai (*Discorsi*, Libro III, Capitolo 24, p. 530).

67. in modo furono quegli tribuni, in quelli tempi per la salute della *patria* disposti a comandare e a ubbidire. (*Discorsi*, Libro III, Capitolo 30, p. 539).

68. e quanto utile e' possa fare alla sua *patria*, quando mediante la sua bontà e virtù (*Discorsi*, Libro III, Capitolo 30, p. 539).

69.   sarebbero contenti vedere la rovina della loro *patria*. A vincere questa invidia (*Discorsi*, Libro III, Capitolo 30, pp. 539–540).

70.   *Che la* patria *si debbe difendere o con ignominia o con gloria, e in qualunque modo è bene difesa.* (*Discorsi*, Libro III, Titolo 41, p. 563).

71.   qualunque partito per salvare la *patria*; perché, consistendo la vita di Roma nella vita di quello esercito (*Discorsi*, Libro III, Capitolo 41, p. 563).

72.   E che la *patria* è bene difesa in qualunque modo la si difende (*Discorsi*, Libro III, Capitolo 41, p. 563).

73.   qualunque cittadino si truova a consigliare la *patria* sua; perché dove si dilibera al tutto (*Discorsi*, Libro III, Capitolo 41, p. 563).

74.   della salute della *patria*, non vi debbe cadere alcuna considerazione nè di giusto nè d'ingiusto (*Discorsi*, Libro III, Capitolo 41, p. 563).

75.   per ubbidire alle leggi e agli auspicii della loro *patria*. (*Discorsi*, Libro III, Capitolo 46, p. 569).

76.   *Che uno buono cittadino per amore della* patria *debbe dimenticare le ingiurie private.* (*Discorsi*, Libro III, Titolo 47, p. 570).

77.   mosso dalla carità della *patria*; ancora che col tacere e con molti altri modi (*Discorsi*, Libro III, Capitolo 47, p. 570).

78.   ne' petti romani che gli abbandonassono la *patria*. Quando nel 1508 (*Discorsi*, Libro III, Capitolo 48, p. 571).

Patrie in the *Discorsi*

1.   contro alle leggi *patrie*. Dove si conosce (*Discorsi*, Libro III, Capitolo 8, p. 493).

APPENDIX TWO

Supplement to Chapter Two: Occurrences of *Patria* in Cicero, Livy and Guicciardini

୨୦୯ଓ

For the sake of simplicity, this Appendix, like the others contains references and quotations to works in the original language. Also, like Appendix One, rather than include notes for each quotation, the author will provide a full reference for each volume cited. Thereafter an abbreviation will suffice.

Patria in Marcus Tullius Cicero, *De Officiis*, trans. Walter Miller. Cambridge, Mass.: Harvard University Press, 1997.

1. Sed quoniam, ut praeclare scriptum est a Platone, non nobis solum nati sumus ortusque nostri partem *patria* vindicat, partem amici, atque, ut placet Stoicis, quae in terris gignantur, ad usum hominum omnia creari, homines autem hominum causa esse generatos, ut ipsi inter se aliis alii prodesse possent, in hoc naturam debemus ducem sequi, communes utilitates in medium adferre, mutatione officiorum, dando accipiendo, tum artibus, tum opera, tum facultatibus devincire hominum inter homines societatem. (*De officiis*, Liber 1, Caput 7.20, pp. 22 and 24).

2. Sed cum omnia ratione animoque lustraris, omnium societatum nulla est gravior, nulla carior quam ea, quae cum re publica est uni cuique nostrum. Cari sunt parentes, cari liberi, propinqui, familiares, sed omnes omnium caritates *patria* una complexa est, pro qua quis bonus dubitet mortem oppetere, si ei sit profuturus? Quo est detestabilior

istorum immanitas, qui lacerarunt omni scelere *patriam* et in ea
funditus delenda occupati et sunt et fuerunt. (*De officiis*, Liber 1,
Caput 17.57, pp. 58 and 60).

3.   Sed si contentio quaedam et comparatio fiat, quibus plurimum
tribuendum sit officii, principes sint *patria* et parentes, quorum
beneficiis maximis obligati sumus proximi liberi totaque domus,
quae spectat in nos solos neque aliud ullum potest habere perfugium,
deinceps bene convenientes propinqui, quibuscum communis etiam
fortuna plerumque est. (*De officiis*, Liber 1, Caput 17.58, p. 60).

4.   Inventi autem multi sunt, qui non modo pecuniam, sed etiam vitam
profundere pro *patria* parati essent, idem gloriae iacturam ne
minimam quidem facere vellent, ne re publica quidem postulante.
(*De officiis*, Liber 1, Caput 24.84, p. 84).

5.   Non igitur *patria* praestat omnibus officiis? Immo vero, sed ipsi
patriae conducit pios habere cives in parentes. Quid? si tyrannidem
occupare, si *patriam* prodere conabitur pater, silebitne filius? Immo
vero obsecrabit patrem, ne id faciat. Si nihil proficiet, accusabit,
minabitur etiam; ad extremum, si ad perniciem *patriae* res spectabit,
patriae salutem anteponet saluti patris. (*De officiis*, Liber 3, Caput
23.90, pp. 364 and 366).

6.   Is cum Romam venisset, utilitatis speciem videbat, sed eam, ut res
declarat, falsam iudicavit; quae erat talis: manere in *patria*, esse
domui suae cum uxore, cum liberis, quam calamitatem accepisset in
bello communem fortunae bellicae iudicantem tenere consularis
dignitatis gradum. (*De officiis*, Liber 3, Caput 26.99, pp. 374 and
376).

7.   Quod maximum in eo est, id reprehenditis. Non enim suo iudicio
stetit, sed suscepit causam, ut esset iudicium senatus; cui nisi ipse
auctor fuisset, captivi profecto Poenis redditi essent. Ita incolumis in
patria Regulus restitisset. (*De officiis*, Liber 3, Caput 30.102, p.
388).

8.   Quamquam hi tibi tres libri inter Cratippi commentarios tamquam
hospites erunt recipiendi, sed, ut, si ipse venissem Athenas, quod
quidem esset factum, nisi me e medio cursu clara voce *patria*

revocasset, aliquando me quoque audires, sic, quoniam his voluminibus ad te profecta vox est mea, tribues iis temporis, quantum poteris, poteris autem quantum voles. (*De officiis*, Liber 3, Caput 33.121, p. 402).

Patriam in Cicero's *De officiis*

1. Nam qui iniuste impetum in quempiam facit aut ira aut aliqua perturbatione incitatus, is quasi manus afferre videtur socio; qui autem non defendit nec obsistit, si potest, iniuriae, tam est in vitio, quam si parentes aut amicos aut *patriam* deserat. (*De officiis*, Liber 1, Caput 7.23, p. 24).

2. Quo est detestabilior istorum immanitas, qui lacerarunt omni scelere *patriam* et in ea funditus delenda occupati et sunt et fuerunt. (*De officiis*, Liber 1, Caput 17.57, p. 60).

3. Cui cum exposuisset *patriam* se liberare velle causamque docuisset (*De officiis*, Liber 2, Caput 23.82, p. 258).

4. Utile ei videbatur plurimum posse alterius invidia; id quam iniustum in *patriam* et quam turpe esset, non videbat. (*De officiis*, Liber 3, Caput 21.82, p. 354).

5. Si tyrannidem occupare, si *patriam* prodere conabitur pater, silebitne filius? Immo vero obsecrabit patrem, ne id faciat. Si nihil proficiet, accusabit, minabitur etiam; ad extremum, si ad perniciem *patriae* res spectabit, *patriae* salutem anteponet saluti patris. (*De officiis*, Liber 3, Caput 23.90, p. 366).

Patriae in Cicero's *De officiis*

1. Quis enim est tam cupidus in perspicienda cognoscendaque rerum natura, ut, si ei tractanti contemplantique res cognitione dignissimas subito sit allatum periculum discrimenque *patriae*, cui subvenire opitularique possit, non illa omnia relinquat atque abiciat, etiamsi dinumerare se stellas aut metiri mundi magnitudinem posse arbitretur? atque hoc idem in parentis, in amici re aut periculo

fecerit. (*De officiis*, Liber 1, Caput 43.154, p. 158).

2. Illud forsitan quaerendum sit, num haec communitas, quae maxime est apta naturae ea sit etiam moderationi modestiaeque semper anteponenda. non placet; sunt enim quaedam partim ita foeda, partim ita flagitiosa, ut ea ne conservandae quidem *patriae* causa sapiens facturus sit. (*De officiis*, Liber 1, Caput 45.159, p. 162).

3. In ipsa autem communitate sunt gradus officiorum, ex quibus quid cuique praestet intellegi possit, ut prima diis immortalibus, secunda *patriae*, tertia parentibus, deinceps gradatim reliquis debeantur. (*De officiis*, Liber 1, Caput 45.160, p. 164).

4. Cum autem consilium hoc principes cepissent, cognationem Superbi nomenque Tarquiniorum et memoriam regni esse tollendam, quod erat utile, *patriae* consulere, id erat ita honestum, ut etiam ipsi Collatino placere deberet. (*De officiis*, Liber 3, Caput 10.40, p. 308).

5. Qui autem fatetur honestum non esse in ea civitate, quae libera fuerit quaeque esse debeat, regnare, sed ei, qui id facere possit, esse utile, qua hunc obiurgatione aut quo potius convitio a tanto errore coner avellere? Potest enim, di immortales, cuiquam esse utile foedissimum et taeterrimum parricidium *patriae*, quamvis is, qui se eo obstrinxerit, ab oppressis civibus parens nominetur? Honestate igitur dirigenda utilitas est, et quidem sic, ut haec duo verbo inter se discrepare, re unum sonare videantur. (*De officiis*, Liber 3, Caput 21.83, p. 356).

6–8. Non igitur patria praestat omnibus officiis? Immo vero, sed ipsi *patriae* conducit pios habere cives in parentes. Quid? si tyrannidem occupare, si *patriam* prodere conabitur pater, silebitne filius? Immo vero obsecrabit patrem, ne id faciat. Si nihil proficiet, accusabit, minabitur etiam; ad extremum, si ad perniciem *patriae* res spectabit, *patriae* salutem anteponet saluti patris. (*De officiis*, Liber 3, Caput 23.90, pp. 364 and 366).

9. Promisisse nollem et id arbitror fuisse gravitatis; quoniam promisit, si saltare in foro turpe ducet, honestius mentietur, si ex hereditate nihil ceperit, quam si ceperit, nisi forte eam pecuniam in rei publicae magnum aliquod tempus contulerit, ut vel saltare, cum *patriae*

consulturus sit, turpe non sit. (*De officiis*, Liber 3, Caput 24.93, p. 268).

10. Quid? si is, qui apud te pecuniam deposuerit, bellum inferat *patriae*, reddasne depositum? Non credo, facies enim contra rem publicam, quae debet esse carissima. (*De officiis*, Liber 3, Caput 25.95, pp. 370 and 372).

11. Cuius cum valuisset auctoritas, captivi retenti sunt, ipse Carthaginem rediit, neque eum caritas *patriae* retinuit nec suorum. (*De officiis*, Liber 3, Caput 27.100, p. 376).

12. Quod quia *patriae* non utile putavit, idcirco sibi honestum et sentire illa et pati credidit. (*De officiis*, Liber 3, Caput 30.102, p. 388).

Patria and religion in Titus Livy, *Ab urbe condita*, vol. I. (Books I–II) trans. B.O. Foster. Cambridge, Mass.: Harvard University Press, 10th edn., 1998.

1. Ibi audire iussis consul laudare fortunam collegae, quod liberata *patria*, in summo honore, pro re publica dimicans, matura gloria necdum se vertente in invidiam, mortem occubuisset: se superstitem gloriae suae ad crimen atque invidiam superesse; ex liberatore *patriae* ad Aquilios se Vitelliosque recidisse. (*Ab urbe*, Liber II, Caput 7.8, p. 240).

Patria and Religion in Titus Livy, *Ab urbe condita*, vol. II. (Books III–IV) trans. B.O. Foster. Cambridge, Mass.: Harvard University Press, 7th edn., 1997.

2. Dissolvi licentia militandi morem, nec pro communi iam *patria* Romam esse. (*Ab urbe*, Liber III, Caput 66.4, pp. 222 and 224).

3. Orare eum collegamque ut capesserent rem publicam; orare tribunos ut uno animo cum consulibus bellum ab urbe ac moenibus propulsari vellent plebemque oboedientem in re tam trepida patribus praeberent; appellare tribunos communem *patriam* auxiliumque eorum implorare vastatis agris, urbe prope oppugnata. (*Ab urbe*,

Liber III, Caput 69.5, p. 234).

Patria and Religion in, Titus Livy, *Ab urbe condita*, vol. III. (Books V–VII) trans. B.O. Foster. Cambridge, Mass: Harvard University Press, 7th edn., 1996.

4. nos tamquam cum civibus agere volumus, agique tamquam cum *patria* nobiscum aequum censemus. (*Ab urbe*, Liber V, Caput 4.8–9, p. 12).

5. Postremo se relinqui a civibus in *patria* posse: ut relinquant *patriam* atque cives nullam vim unquam subacturam, et T. Sicinium—is enim ex tribunis plebis rogationis eius lator erat—conditorem Veios sequantur, relicto deo Romulo, dei filio, parente et auctore urbis Romae. (*Ab urbe*, Liber V. Caput 24.11, p. 84).

6. sed nefas ducere desertam ac relictam ab dis immortalibus incoli urbem, et in captivo solo habitare populum Romanum et victrice *patria* victam mutari. (*Ab urbe*, Liber V, Caput 30.3, p. 106).

7. Dictator reciperata ex hostibus *patria* triumphans in urbem redit, interque iocos militares quos inconditos iaciunt, Romulus ac parens *patriae* conditorque alter urbis haud vanis laudibus appellabatur. Servatam deinde bello *patriam* iterum in pace haud dubie servavit cum prohibuit migrari Veios, et tribunis rem intentius agentibus post incensam urbem et per se inclinata magis plebe ad id consilium; eaque causa fuit non abdicandae post triumphum dictaturae, senatu obsecrante ne rem publicam in incerto relinqueret statu. (*Ab urbe*, Liber V, Caput 49.7–8, p. 166).

8. Adeo nihil tenet solum *patriae* nec haec terra quam matrem appellamus, sed in superficie tignisque caritas nobis *patriae* pendet? (*Ab urbe*, Liber V, Caput 54.2, p. 182).

9. Fuit cum hoc dici poterat: patricius enim eras et a liberatoribus *patriae* ortus, et eodem anno familia ista consulatum quo urbs haec consulem habuit: nunc iam nobis patribus vobisque plebei promiscuus consulatus patet nec generis, ut ante, sed virtutis est praemium. (*Ab urbe*, Liber VII, Caput 32.13–14, p. 470).

10. Quod deos immortales inter nuncupanda vota expoposci, eius me compotem voti vos facere potestis, si meminisse voltis non vos in Samnio nec in Volscis sed in Romano solo castra habere, si illos colles quos cernitis *patriae* vestrae esse, si hunc exercitum civium vestrorum, si me consulem vestrum, cuius ductu auspicioque priore anno bis legiones Samnitium fudistis, bis castra vi cepistis. (*Ab urbe,* Liber VII, Caput 40.5–7, p. 504).

11. Tum Volscorum legiones, quia Romanum habebant ducem, quieverunt: vos, Romanus exercitus, ne destiteritis impio bello? T. Quincti, quocumque istic loco seu volens seu invitus constitisti, si dimicandum erit, tum tu in novissimos te recipito; fugeris etiam honestius tergumque civi dederis quam pugnaveris contra *patriam.* (*Ab urbe,* Liber VII, Caput 40.12–14, p. 506).

Patria and Religion in Titus Livy, *Ab urbe condita,* vol. IV. (Books VIII–X) trans. B.O. Foster. London: William Heinemann, 1926. 1st Loeb edition.

12. sed hic *patriam* video, hic quidquid Romanarum legionum est; quae nisi pro se ipsis ad mortem ruere volunt, quid habent quod morte sua servent? tecta urbis, dicat aliquis, et moenia et eam turbam a qua urbs incolitur. Immo hercule produntur ea omnia deleto hoc exercitu, non servantur. Quis enim ea tuebitur? imbellis videlicet atque inermis multitudo. Tam hercule quam a Gallorum impetu defendit. An a Veiis exercitum. (*Ab urbe,* Liber IX, Caput 4.11–16, p. 176)

13. "Camillumque ducem implorabunt? hic omnes spes opesque sunt, quas servando *patriam* servamus, dedendo ad necem *patriam* deserimus (ac prodimus). At foeda atque ignominiosa deditio est. Sed ea caritas *patriae* est ut tam ignominia eam quam morte nostra, si opus sit, servemus. Subeatur ergo ista, quantacumque est, indignitas et pareatur necessitati, quam ne di quidem superant. Ite, consules, redimite armis civitatem, quam auro maiores vestri redemerunt."(*Ab urbe,* Liber IX, Caput 4.11–16, p. 176).

Patria in Francesco Guicciardini's *Considerazioni,* in *Opere* Volume 8, pp. 1–65, *Scritti Politici e Ricordi* (1933) of *Opere,* in 9 vols. A cura di

Roberto Palmarocchi. Bari: Laterza (1929–36).

1. Ma perché e' casi sono vari, e lo autore confonde gli esempli, bisogna considerare che rare volte occorre che chi occupa la tirannide nella *patria* libera abbia tale necessitá di farlo, o, se ha necessitá, che sia causata sanza colpa sua, talmente che gli resti colore alcuno di giustificazione. (*Considerazioni*, Libro I, Capitolo 10, Capoverso 1, p. 19).

2. Nel quale caso sarebbe molto laudabile chi preponessi l'amore della *patria* alla salute sua particulare; ma perché questo amore o questa fortezza si desidera negli uomini più presto che la si truovi, merita essere assai scusato chi è mosso da tale cagione, e tanto più se el governo contro al quale va è disordinato, perché molte sono chiamate spesso libertà che non sono. (*Considerazioni*, Libro I, Capitolo 10, Capoverso 1, p. 19).

3–5. E' quali la necessitá ha condotti o a desiderare la mutazione di uno stato che sotto nome di libertà è tirannico e distruttore della *patria*, o tacitamente lasciarsi con somma ingiustizia tôrre la *patria* e le facultá. Chi adunche è autore nella *patria* libera, di una tirannide, e lo fa per appetito di dominare, merita somma reprensione; e di questi fu Cesare, Falari, Pisistrato e simili, de' quali è più infame l'uno che l'altro, secondo che più o manco crudelmente la usorono, e secondo che furono più o meno ornati di altre virtú. (*Considerazioni*, Libro I, Capitolo 10, Capoverso 1, p. 20).

6. Di questi si truova pochissimi, o forse nessuno, che sanza necessitá l'abbino lasciata; nè è maraviglia, perché chi è nutrito in una tirannide non ha occhi da cognoscere quella gloria che si acquista di mettere la *patria* in libertà, nè considera questo caso con quello gusto che fanno gli uomini privati, perché, assuefatto a quello modo di vivere, giudica che el sommo bene sia nella potenzia, e non cognoscendo el frutto di quella gloria, nessuna altra ragione gli può persuadere a lasciare la tirannide. (*Considerazioni*, Libro I, Capitolo 10, Capoverso 2, p. 20)

7. Si può dire forse di Orazio che fu assoluto non tanto per la considerazione de' meriti suoi, quanto perché non paressi errore amazzare una sorella che si lamentava di quello che era causa della

salute e libertà della *patria*, ed insultava al fratello autore di tanto bene; ed intendendola cosí, non è maraviglia fussi chiamato in giudicio, perché di necessitá l'omicidio aveva bisogno di assoluzione, fatta non da' privati ma dal publico. (*Considerazioni*, Libro I, Capitolo 24, Capoverso 1, p. 31).

8. Di poi chi cerca la rovina della *patria* fa male a' parenti, agli amici, a tutte le cose sue medesime ed a sé proprio, e con infamia di sé medesimo; che non interviene a chi fa contro a uno principe. (*Considerazioni*, Libro III, Capitolo 17, Capoverso 1, p. 61).

APPENDIX THREE

Supplement to Chapter Three:
Patria in the *Arte della guerra*

❧

The *Arte della guerra* contains a distillation of all of Machiavelli's ideas concerning the citizen army. It is 61,408 words in length and divided into seven books. One will find that *patria* appears in the work just nine times. The first is in the work's *Proemio*, five occurrences appear in Book One; there are two occurrences in Book Four and one in Book Six. One will find that *patria* and the words linked with it in the *Arte* are familiar and similar to those occurrences in the *Discorsi*. For example, the final six occurrences of *patria* appear to have direct counterparts in the *Discorsi*. This may give greater credibility to the assertion that the *Arte* may have "arisen from the *Discorsi*" (Anglo, *Dissection*, p. 84). They are: "la mia *patria* rovinò"; "usurpando e tiranneggiando la *patria* e in ogni modo prevalendosi"; "accrebbero la loro *patria*"; "confidenza e dall'amore del capitano o della *patria*"; "l'amore della *patria* è causato dalla natura"; "erano tornati nella *patria*." "Rovinare" and its derivatives are linked with *patria* in the *Discorsi* three times; derivatives and words similar to 'tiranneggiando' appear in the *Discorsi* twice directly linked with *patria*. "Amore della patria" three times and "tornare" and its derivatives two times. These appear to illustrate a linkage between the *Arte* and the *Discorsi*. Indeed, there seems to be room for additional study on this aspect of *patria* in Machiavelli's *opere*.

Niccolò Machiavelli, *Dell'Arte della guerra*, in *Tutte le opere Storiche e Letterarie di Niccolò Machiavelli*. A cura di Guido Mazzoni e Mario Casella. Firenze: G. Barbèra, 1929: 263–374.

1.   perché in quale uomo debbe ricercare la *patria* maggiore fede, che in colui che le ha a promettere di morire per lei? (*Arte*, Proemio, p.

266).

2.   in uno cittadino dalla sua *patria* si possono disiderare. (*Arte*, Libro I, p. 266).

3.   dove quello avesse conosciuto il bene della sua *patria*. (*Arte*, Libro I, p. 266).

4.   perché, poi che questi studi piacquero ai miei Romani, la mia *patria* rovinò. (*Arte*, Libro I, p. 268).

5.   usurpando e tiranneggiando la *patria* e in ogni modo prevalendosi (*Arte*, Libro I, p. 271).

6.   con l'armi in mano, accrebbero la loro *patria*. Ma venendo tempo (*Arte*, Libro I, p. 277).

7.   dall'amore del capitano o della *patria*. La confidenza, la causa l'armi (*Arte*, Libro IV, p. 327).

8.   L'amore della *patria* è causato dalla natura (*Arte*, Libro IV, p. 327).

9.   poi ch'egli erano tornati nella *patria*, con solenni pompe e con gran dimostrazioni tra gli amici e parenti le dimostravano. (*Arte*, Libro VI, p. 345).

APPENDIX FOUR

Supplement to Chapter Seven:
A "New" Italian Edition of the
Discorso o dialogo intorno
alla nostra lingua

ഇരുഗ

This edition cannot in the proper sense be called a "new" one. Rather it is based on nineteenth-century edition which resides in the author's library; the 1843 edition referred to frequently in Chapters Five and Six.[1] However, that edition was modernized with guidance from several other editions. Primarily, these are Sergio Bertelli's 1969 edition, Bortolo Tommaso Sozzi 1976 text and Ornella Castellani Pollidori's 1978 critical edition.[2] But why bother, considering how many eminent Italian scholars have already done so, to produce another Italian edition?

First and foremost, this edition complements the new translation of the *Dialogo* found in Chapter Seven of our study—the first translation since 1961. Second and perhaps more importantly, while some scholars have cross-referred their readers to passages in Machiavelli's *opere* which seem to correspond to the *Dialogo*, such an edition has not been undertaken since the early 1980's. Our edition adds additional materials, and we hope new insight into the relationship of the *Dialogo* with Machiavelli's personal correspondence, his literary output and of course, his political considerations. In light of the conclusions of our study which argued that the ideas in the *Dialogo* certainly seem to augment those in works definitely by Machiavelli, this "new" Italian editions seeks to further strengthen our position.

Discorso o dialogo intorno alla nostra lingua

Sempre che io ho potuto onorare la patria mia eziandio *con mio carico e pericolo*[3] l'ho fatto volentieri, perché l'uomo non ha maggiore obbligo nella vita sua che con quella, dependendo prima da essa l'essere e di poi, tutto quello che di buono *la fortuna e la natura ci hanno conceduto*[4]; e tanto viene ad esser maggiore in coloro che hanno sortito patria più nobile. E veramente colui il quale con l'animo e con le opere si fa nimico della sua patria meritamente si può chiamare parricida, ancora che da quella fosse suto offeso. Perché se battere il padre e la madre, per qualunque cagione, è cosa nefanda, di necessità ne segue il lacerare la patria essere cosa nefandissima, perché da lei mai si patisce alcuna persecuzione per la quale possa meritare di essere da te ingiuriata, avendo a riconoscere da quella ogni tuo bene; tal che se ella si priva di parte de' suoi cittadini, sei più tosto obbligato ringraziarla di quelli che la si lascia che infamarla di quelli che la si toglie. E quando questo sia vero (che è verissimo) io non dubito mai di ingannarmi per difenderla e venire contro a quelli che troppo presuntuosamente cercano di privarla dell'onor suo.[5]

La cagione perché io abbia mosso questo ragionamento è la disputa nata più volte *ne' passati giorni*[6] se la lingua nella quale hanno scritto i nostri poeti e oratori fiorentini è fiorentina, toscana o italiana.[7] Nella qual disputa ho considerato come alcuni meno inonesti vogliono che la sia toscana, alcuni altri inonestissimi la chiamono italiana, e alcuni tengono che la si debba chiamare al tutto fiorentina, e ciascuno di essi si è sforzato di difendere la parte sua in forma che, restando la lite indecisa, mi è parso in questo mio vendemmial negozio scrivervi largamente quello che io ne senta, per terminare la quistione o per dare a ciascuno materia di maggior contesa.

A volere vedere, addunque, con che lingua hanno scritto gli scrittori in questa moderna lingua celebrati, delli quali tengono, senza alcuna discrepanza d'alcuno il primo luogo *Dante,*[8] il *Petrarca*[9] e il *Boccaccio,*[10] è necessario metterli da una parte, e dall'altra parte tutta Italia, alla qual provincia, per amore circa la lingua di questi tre pare che qualunque altro luogo ceda, perché *la spagnuola e la francese e la tedesca è meno in questo caso presuntuosa che la lombarda.*[11] È necessario, fatto questo, considerare tutti li luoghi di Italia e vedere la differenza del parlar loro, e a quelli dare più favore che a questi scrittori si confanno, e concedere loro più grado e più parte in quella lingua e, se voi volete, bene distinguere tutta Italia e quante castella, non che città, sono in essa. Però volendo fuggire questa confusione divideremo quella solamente nelle sue provincie, come Lombardia, Romagna, Toscana, Terra di Roma e Regno di Napoli.

E veramente, se ciascuna di dette parti saranno bene esaminate, si vedrà nel parlare di esse grandi differenzie; ma a volere conoscere donde proceda questo è prima necessario vedere qualche ragione di quelle che fanno che infra loro sia tanta similitudine, che questi che oggi scrivono vogliono che quelli che hanno scritto per lo addrieto abbino parlato in questa lingua comune italiana; e quale ragione fa che in tanta diversità di lingua noi ci intendiamo.

Vogliono alcuni che a ciascuna lingua dia termine la particula affermativa, la quale, appresso alli Italiani con questa dizione *sì* è significata e che per tutta quella provincia si intenda il medesimo parlare dove con uno medesimo vocabolo parlando si afferma; e allegano l'autorità di Dante, il quale, volendo significare Italia, la nominò sotto questa particula *sì*, quando disse:

Ahi Pisa, vitupero delle genti
del bel paese là dove il sì *suona,*[12]

cioè d'Italia. Allegano ancora l'essemplo di Francia, dove tutto il paese si chiama Francia ed è detto ancora lingua d'*uì* e d'*oc*, che significano appresso di loro quel medesimo che appresso l'Italiani *sì*. Adducono ancora in exemplo tutta la lingua tedesca che dice *iò* e tutta la Inghilterra che dice *jeh*. E forse da queste ragioni mossi vogliono molti di costoro che qualunque è in Italia che scriva e parli, scriva e parli in una lingua. Alcuni altri tengono che questa particula *sì* non sia quella che regoli la lingua, perché se la regolasse, e i Siciliani e li Spagnuoli sarebbono ancor loro quanto al parlare Italiani. E però è necessario si regoli con altre ragioni; e dicono che chi considera bene le otto parti dell'orazione nelle quali ogni parlare si divide troverrà che quella che si chiama verbo è la catena e il *nervo della lingua*,[13] e ogni volta che in questa parte non si varia, ancora che nelle altre si variasse assai, conviene che le lingue abbino una comune intelligenza. Perché quelli nomi che ci sono incogniti ce li fa intendere il verbo quale infra loro è collocato; e così per il contrario dove li verbi sono differenti, ancora che vi fusse similitudine ne' nomi, diventa quella un'altra lingua. E per esempio si può dare la provincia d'Italia, la quale è in una minima parte differente nei verbi, ma nei nomi differentissima, perché ciascuno Italiano dice *amare*, *stare* e *leggere*, ma ciascuno di loro non dice già *deschetto*, *tavola* e *guastada*. Intra i pronomi quelli che importano più sono variati, sì come è *mi* in vece d'*io* e *ti* per *tu*.

Quello che fa ancora differenti le lingue, ma non tanto che le non s'intendino, sono la pronunzia e gli accenti. Li Toscani fermano tutte le loro parole in su le vocali, ma li Lombardi e li Romagnuoli quasi tutte le sospendono su le consonanti, come è *pane* e *pan*.

Considerato adunque tutte queste e altre differenze che sono in questa lingua *italica*,[14] a voler vedere quale di queste tenga la penna in mano e in quale abbino scritto gli scrittori antichi, è prima necessario vedere donde Dante e gli primi scrittori furono e se essi scrissono nella lingua patria o non vi scrissero;[15] di poi arrecarsi innanzi i loro scritti, e appresso qualche scrittura mera fiorentina o lombarda o d'altra provincia d'Italia, dove non sia arte ma tutta natura; e quella che fia più conforme alli scritti loro, quella si potrà chiamare, credo, quella lingua nella quale essi abbino scritto. Donde quelli primi scrittori fussino (eccetto che un bolognese, un aretino e un pistolese,[16] i quali tutti non aggiunsono a dieci canzoni) è cosa notissima come e' furono fiorentini; intra li quali Dante, il Petrarca e il Boccaccio tengono il primo luogo, e tanto alto, che alcuno non spera più aggiungervi. Di questi, il Boccaccio afferma nel *Centonovelle*[17] di scrivere in vulgar fiorentino; il Petrarca non so che ne parlì cosa alcuna; Dante, in un suo libro ch'ei fa *De vulgari eloquio*,[18] dove egli danna tutta la lingua particolar d'Italia, afferma non avere scritto in fiorentino, ma in una lingua curiale; in modo che, quando e' se li avesse a credere, mi cancellerebbe, l'obbiezioni che di sopra si feciono di volere intendere da loro donde avevano quella lingua imparata. Io non voglio, in quanto s'appartenga al Petrarca e al Boccaccio, replicare cosa alcuna, essendo l'uno in nostro favore e l'altro stando neutrale; ma mi fermerò sopra di Dante, il quale in ogni parte mostrò d'esser per ingegno, per dottrina e per giudizio uomo eccellente, eccetto che dove egli ebbe a ragionar della patria sua, la quale, fuori d'ogni umanità e filosofico instituto, perseguitò con ogni specie d'ingiuria.[19] E non potendo altro fare che infamarla, accusò quella d'ogni vizio, dannò gli uomini, biasimò il sito, disse male de' costumi e delle leggi di lei; e questo fece non solo in una parte de la sua Cantica, ma in tutta, e diversamente e in diversi modi; tanto l'offese l'ingiuria dell'esilio! tanta vendetta ne desiderava! e però ne fece tanta quanta egli poté. E se, per sorte, de' mali ch'egli li predisse le ne fusse accaduto alcuno, Firenze avrebbe più da dolersi d'aver nutrito quell'uomo, che d'alcuna altra sua rovina. Ma la fortuna, per farlo mendace e per ricoprire con la gloria sua la calunnia falsa di quello, l'ha continuamente prosperata e fatta celebre per tutte le provincie del mondo, e condotta al presente in tanta felicità e sì tranquillo stato, che, se Dante la vedessi, o egli accuserebbe se stesso, o ripercosso dai colpi di quella sua innata invidia, vorrebbe, essendo risuscitato, di nuovo morire. Non è pertanto maraviglia se costui, che in ogni cosa accrebbe infamia a la sua patria, volse ancora nella lingua torle quella riputazione la quale pareva a lui d'averle data ne' suoi scritti, e per non l'onorare in alcun modo compose quell'opera, per mostrar quella lingua nella quale egli aveva scritto non esser fiorentina. Il che tanto se li debbe credere, quanto ch'ei trovassi Bruto in bocca di Lucifero maggiore,[20] e cinque cittadini fiorentini in tra i ladroni,[21] e quel suo Cacciaguida in Paradiso,[22] e simili sue passioni e oppinioni; nelle quali fu tanto cieco, che perse ogni sua gravità, dottrina e giudicio, e divenne al tutto un altro uomo; talmente che, s'egli avessi giudicato così ogni cosa, o egli sarebbe vivuto sempre a Firenze o egli ne sarebbe stato cacciato per pazzo. Ma perché le cose che s'impugnano per parole generali o per conietture possono esser facilmente riprese, io voglio a ragioni vive e vere mostrare come il suo parlare è al tutto fiorentino, e più assai che quello che il Boccaccio confessa per se stesso esser fiorentino, e in parte *rispondere a quelli che tengono la medesima oppinione di Dante.*[23]

Parlare comune d'Italia sarebbe quello dove fussi più del comune che del proprio d'alcuna lingua; e similmente parlar proprio fia quello dove è più del proprio che di alcuna altra lingua; perché non si può trovare una lingua che parli ogni cosa per sé senza avere accattato da altri; perché, nel conversare gli uomini di varie provincie insieme, prendono de' motti l'uno dell'altro. Aggiugnesi a questo che, qualunque volta viene o nuove dottrine in una città o nuove arti, è necessario che vi venghino nuovi vocaboli, e nati in quella lingua donde quelle dottrine o quelle arti son venute; ma riducendosi, nel parlare, con i modi, con i casi, con le differenze e con gli accenti, fanno una medesima consonanza con i vocaboli di quella lingua che trovano, e così diventano suoi; perché, altrimenti, le lingue parrebbono rappezzate e non tornerebbono bene. E così i vocaboli forestieri si convertono in fiorentini, non i fiorentini in forestieri; né però diventa altro la nostra lingua che fiorentina. E di qui dipende che le lingue da principio arricchiscono, e diventono più belle essendo più copiose; ma è ben vero che col tempo, per la moltitudine di questi nuovi vocaboli, imbastardiscono e diventano un'altra cosa; ma fanno questo in centinaia d'anni; di che altri non s'accorge se non poi che è rovinato in una estrema barbaria. Fa ben più presto questa mutazione quando egli avviene che una nuova populazione venisse ad abitare in una provincia. In questo caso ella fa la sua mutazione in un corso d'un'età d'un uomo. Ma in qualunque di questi duoi modi che la lingua si muti, è necessario che quella lingua persa volendo la sia riassunta per il mezzo di buoni scrittori che in quella hanno scritto, come si è fatto e fa della *lingua latina e della greca.*[24]

Ma lasciando stare questa parte come non necessaria, per non essere la nostra lingua ancora nella sua declinazione, e tornando donde io mi partii, dico che quella lingua si può chiamare comune in una provincia, dove la maggior parte de' suoi vocaboli con le loro circonstanze non si usino in alcuna lingua propria di quella provincia; e quella lingua si chiamerà propria dove la maggior parte de' suoi vocaboli non s'usino in altra lingua di quella provincia.

Quando questo ch'io dico sia vero (che è verissimo) io vorrei chiamar Dante, che mi mostrasse il suo poema; e avendo appresso alcuno scritto in lingua fiorentina, lo domanderei qual cosa è quella che nel suo poema non fussi scritta in fiorentino. E perché e' risponderebbe che molte, tratte di Lombardia, o trovate da sé, o tratte dal latino....

Ma perché io voglio parlare un poco con Dante, per fuggire e*gli disse* ed *io risposi, noterò gl'interlocutori d'avanti.*[25]

N. Quali traesti tu di Lombardia?

D. Questa:

In co del ponte presso a Benevento;[26]

e quest'altro:

Con voi nascerà e s'asconderà vosco.[27]

N. Quali traesti tu da i Latini?

D. Questi, e molti altri:

Transumanar significare per verba.[28]

N. Quali trovasti da te?

D. Questi:

S'io m'intuassi come tu ti immii.[29]

Li quali vocaboli, mescolati tutti con li toscani, fanno una terza lingua.

N. Sta bene. Ma dimmi: in questa tua opera come vi sono di questi vocaboli o forestieri o trovati da te o latini?

D. Nelle prime due Cantiche ve ne sono pochi, ma nell'ultima assai, massime dedotti da i latini, perché le dottrine varie di che io ragiono mi costringono a pigliare vocaboli atti a poterle esprimere; e non si potendo se non con termini latini, io gli usavo, ma li deducevo in modo, con le desinenze, ch'io gli facevo diventare simili a la lingua del resto de l'opera.

N. Che lingua è quella dell'opera?

D. Curiale.

N. Che vuol dir curiale?

D. Vuol dire una lingua parlata da gl'uomini di corte del Papa, del Duca i quali, per essere uomini litterati, parlono meglio che non si parla nelle terre particulari d'Italia.[30]

N. Tu dirai le bugie. Dimmi un poco: che vuol dire in quella lingua curiale, *morse*?

D. Vuol dire *morì*.

N. In fiorentino che vuol dire?

D. Vuol dire strignere uno con i denti.

N. Quando tu di' ne' tuoi versi:

> *E quando il dente longobardo morse,*[31]

che vuol dire quel *morse*?

D. *Punse, offese* e *assaltò*: che è una translazione dedotta da quel *mordere* che dicono i Fiorentini.

N. Adunque parli tu in fiorentino e non cortigiano.

D. Egli è vero in maggior parte; pure io mi riguardo di non usare certi vocaboli nostri proprii.

N. Come te ne riguardi? Quando tu di':

> *Forte spingeva con ambe le piote,*[32]

questo *spingere* che vuol dire?

D. In Firenze s'usa dire, quando una bestia trae de' calci: *ella spicca una copia di calci*; e perché io volsi mostrare come colui traeva de' calci, dissi *spingeva*.

N. Dimmi: tu di' ancora volendo dire *le gambe*,

> *e quello che spingeva con le zanche,*[33]

perché lo di' tu?

D. Perché in Firenze si chiamano *zanche* quelle aste sopra le quali vanno gli spiritelli per Santo Giovanni, e perché allora e' l'usano per *gambe*, e io volendo significare *gambe* dissi *zanche*.

N. Per mia fe' tu ti guardi assai bene dai vocaboli fiorentini! Ma dimmi, più là, quando tu di':

> *Non prendete, mortali, i voti a ciancie,*[34]

perché di' tu *ciancie* come i Fiorentini e non *zanze* come i Lombardi, avendo detto *vosco* e *co del ponte*?

D. Non dissi *zanze* per non usare un vocabolo barbaro come quello; ma dissi *co* e *vosco*, sì perché non sono vocaboli sì barbari, sì perché in una opera grande è lecito usare qualche vocabolo esterno; come fe' Virgilio quando disse:

> *Troica gaza per undas.*[35]

N. Sta bene; ma fu egli per questo che Virgilio non scrivesse in latino?

D. No.

N. E così tu ancora, per aver detto *co* e *vosco*, non hai lasciata la tua lingua. Ma noi facciamo una disputa vana, perché nella tua opera tu medesimo in più luoghi confessi di parlare toscano e fiorentino. Non di' tu di uno che ti sentì parlare nell'Inferno:

> *Ed egli ch'intese la parola tosca?*[36]

e altrove, in bocca di Farinata, parlando egli teco:

> *La tua loquela ti fa manifesto*
> *di quella dolce patria natio*
> *alla qual forse fui troppo molesto?*[37]

D. Gli è vero ch'io dico tutto cotesto.

N. Perché di' dunque di non parlar fiorentino? Ma io ti voglio convincere co i libri in mano e con il riscontro; e però leggiamo questa tua opera e il *Morgante*.[38] Leggi su.

D.   *Nel mezzo del cammin di nostra vita*
        mi ritrovai per una selva oscura,
        che la diritta via era smarrita.[39]

N. E' basta. Leggi un poco ora il *Morgante*.

D. Dove?

N. Dove tu vuoi. Leggi costì a caso.

D. Ecco:

> *Non chi comincia ha meritato è scritto*
> *nel tuo santo Vangel benigno Padre.*[40]

N. Or ben che differenza è da quella tua lingua a questa?

D. Poca.

N. Non mi ce ne par veruna.

D. Qui è pur non so che.

N. Che cosa?

D. Quel *chi* è troppo fiorentino.

N. Tu farai a ridirti: o non di' tu:

> *Io non so chi tu sia, né per qual modo*
> *venuto sei quaggiù, ma fiorentino...?*[41]

D. Egli è il vero e io ho il torto.

N. Dante mio, io voglio che tu t'emendi, e che tu consideri meglio il parlar fiorentino e la tua opera, e vedrai che se alcuno s'arà da vergognare, sarà più tosto Firenze che tu; perché se considererai bene a quel che tu hai detto, tu vedrai come ne' tuoi versi non hai fuggito il goffo, come è quello:

> *Poi ci partimmo, e n'andavamo introcque;*[42]

non hai fuggito il porco, come quello:

> *Che merda fa di quel che si trangugia;*[43]

non hai fuggito l'osceno, come è:

> *Le mani alzò con ambedue le fiche;*[44]

e non avendo fuggito questo, che disonora tutta l'opera tua, tu non puoi aver fuggito infiniti vocaboli patrii che non s'usano altrove che in quella, perché l'arte non può mai in tutto repugnare alla natura. Oltre di questo io voglio che tu consideri come le lingue non possono esser semplici, ma conviene che sieno miste con l'altre lingue. Ma quella lingua si chiama d'una patria, la quale convertisce i vocaboli ch'ella ha accattati da altri nell'uso suo, ed è sì potente, che i vocaboli accattati non la disordinano, ma ella disordina loro; perché quello ch'ella reca da altri lo tira a sé in modo, che par suo. E gli uomini che scrivono in quella lingua come amorevoli di essa debbono far quello ch'hai fatto tu, ma non dir quello ch'hai detto tu; perché se tu hai accattato da' Latini e da' forestieri assai vocaboli, se tu n'hai fatti de' nuovi, hai fatto molto bene; ma tu hai ben fatto male a dire che per questo ella sia diventata un'altra lingua. Dice Orazio:

> *... quum lingua Catonis et Ennî*
> *sermonem patrium ditaverit;*[45]

e lauda quelli come li primi che cominciorno ad arricchire la lingua latina. I Romani ne gli eserciti loro non avevono più che due legioni di Romani, quali erano circa dodicimila persone, e di poi vi avevano ventimila dell'altre nazioni; nondimeno, perché quelli erano con li loro capi *il nervo de l'esercito*,[46] perché militavano tutti sotto l'ordine e disciplina romana, teneano quelli eserciti il nome, l'autorità e dignità romana.[47] E tu che hai messo ne' tuoi scritti venti legioni di vocaboli fiorentini, e usi i casi, i tempi e i modi e le desinenze fiorentine, vuoi che li vocaboli avventizii faccino mutar la lingua? E se tu la chiamassi o comune d'Italia o cortigiana perché in quella si usassino tutti li verbi che s'usano in Firenze, ti rispondo che, se si sono usati li medesimi verbi, non s'usano i medesimi termini, perché si variono tanto con la pronunzia che diventono un'altra cosa. Perché tu sai che i forestieri o e' pervertano il *c* in *z*, come di sopra si disse di *cianciare* e *zanzare*, o eglino aggiungano le lettere, come *verrà*, *vegnirà*; o e' ne lievano, come *poltrone* e *poltron*; talmente che quegli vocaboli che son simili a' nostri, gli storpiano in modo che gli fanno diventare un'altra cosa. E se tu mi allegassi il parlar curiale, ti rispondo, se tu parli delle corti di Milano o di Napoli, che tutte tengono del luogo della patria loro, e quelli hanno più di buono che più s'accostano al toscano e più l'imitano; e se tu vuoi ch'e' sia migliore l'imitatore che l'imitato, tu vuoi quello che il più delle volte non è. Ma se tu parli della corte di Roma, tu parli d'un luogo dove si parla di tanti modi di quante nazioni vi sono, né se li può dare, in modo alcuno, regola. Di poi io mi maraviglio di te, che tu voglia, dove non si fa cosa alcuna laudabile o buona, che vi si faccia questa: perché dove sono i costumi perversi conviene che il parlare sia perverso e abbia in sé quello effeminato lascivo che hanno coloro che lo parlono. Ma quello che inganna molti circa i vocaboli comuni è che, tu e gli altri che hanno scritto essendo stati celebrati e letti in varii luoghi, molti vocaboli nostri sono stati imparati da molti forestieri e osservati da loro, tal che di proprii nostri son diventati comuni. E se tu vuoi conoscer questo, arrecati innanzi un libro composto da quelli forestieri che hanno scritto dopo voi, e vedrai quanti vocaboli egli usano de' vostri, e come e' cercano d'imitarvi. E per aver riprova di questo, fa lor leggere libri composti dagli uomini loro avanti che nasceste voi, e si vedrà che in quelli non fia né vocabolo né termine: e così apparirà che la lingua in che essi oggi scrivano, è la vostra, e, per consequenza, vostra; e la vostra non è comune con la loro. La qual lingua ancora che con mille sudori cerchino d'imitare, nondimeno, se leggerai attentamente i loro scritti, vedrai in mille luoghi essere da loro male e perversamente usata, perché gli è impossibile che l'arte possa più che la natura.

Considera ancora un'altra cosa se tu vuoi vedere la dignità della tua lingua patria: che i forestieri che scrivano, se prendano alcuno soggetto nuovo dove non abbino esempio di vocaboli imparati da voi, di necessità conviene ch'e' ricorrino in Toscana; o vero, s'e' prendano vocaboli loro, gli spianino e allarghino all'uso toscano, che altrimenti né loro né altri gli approverebbono. E perché e' dicano che tutte le lingue patrie son brutte s'elle non hanno del misto, di modo che veruna sarebbe brutta, ma dico ancora che quella che ha di esser mista men bisogno è più laudabile, e senza dubbio ne ha men bisogno la fiorentina. Dico ancora come si scrivano molte cose che senza scrivere i motti e i termini proprii patrii non sono belle. Di questa sorte sono le commedie; perché ancora che il fine d'una commedia sia proporre uno specchio d'una vita privata, nondimeno il suo modo del farlo è con certa urbanità e termini che muovino riso, acciò che gli uomini, correndo a quella delettazione, gustino poi l'esemplo utile che vi è sotto.[48] E perciò le persone con chi difficilmente possano essere persone gravi la trattano; perché non può esser gravità in un servo fraudolente, in un vecchio deriso, in un giovane impazzato d'amore, in una puttana lusinghiera, in un parasito goloso; ma ben ne risulta di questa composizione d'uomini effetti gravi e utili alla vita nostra. Ma perché le cose sono trattate ridiculamente, conviene usare termini e motti che faccino questi effetti; i quali termini, se non son proprii e patrii, dove sieno soli interi e noti, non muovono né posson muovere. Donde nasce che uno che non sia toscano non farà mai questa parte bene, perché se vorrà dire i motti de la patria sua farà una veste rattoppata, facendo una composizione mezza toscana e mezza forestiera; e qui si conoscerebbe che lingua egli avessi imparata, s'ella fusse comune o propria. Ma se non gli vorrà usare, non sappiendo quelli di Toscana, farà una cosa manca e che non arà la perfezione sua. E a provare questo io voglio che tu legga una commedia fatta da uno degli Ariosti di Ferrara;[49] e vedrai una gentil composizione e uno stilo ornato e ordinato; vedrai un nodo bene accomodato e meglio sciolto; ma la vedrai priva di quei sali che ricerca una commedia tale, non per altra cagione che per la detta, perché i motti ferraresi non gli piacevano e i fiorentini non sapeva, talmente che gli lasciò stare. Usonne uno comune, e credo ancora fatto comune per via di Firenze, dicendo che un dottore de la berretta lunga pagherebbe una sua dama di *doppioni*. Usonne uno proprio, per il quale si vede quanto sta male mescolare il ferrarese con il toscano; che dicendo una di non voler parlare dove fussino orecchie che l'udissino, le fa rispondere che non parlassino dove fossero i *bigonzoni*; e un gusto purgato sa quanto nel leggere e nell'udire dir *bigonzoni* è offeso. E vedesi facilmente e in questo e in molti altri luoghi con quanta difficultà egli mantiene il decoro di quella lingua ch'egli ha accattata.

Pertanto io concludo che molte cose sono quelle che non si possono scriver bene senza intendere le cose proprie e particolari di quella lingua che è più in prezzo; e volendolo proprii conviene andare alla fonte donde quella lingua ha auto origine, altrimenti si fa una composizione dove l'una parte non corrisponde a l'altra. E che l'importanza di questa lingua nella quale e tu,

Dante, scrivesti, e gli altri che vennono e prima e poi di te hanno scritto, sia derivata da Firenze, lo dimostra esser voi stati fiorentini, e nati in una patria che parlava in modo che si poteva, meglio che alcuna altra accomodare a scrivere in versi e in prosa. A che non si potevano accomodare gli altri parlari d'Italia. Perché ciascuno sa come i Provenzali cominciarono a scrivere in versi; di Provenza ne venne quest'uso in Sicilia e, di Sicilia, in Italia; e, intra le provincie d'Italia, in Toscana; e di tutta Toscana, in Firenze, non per altro che per esser la lingua più atta. Perché non per commodità di sito, né per ingegno, né per alcuna altra particulare occasione meritò Firenze esser la prima, e procreare questi scrittori, se non per la lingua commoda a prendere simile disciplina; il che non era nell'altre città. E che sia vero, si vede in questi tempi assai Ferraresi, Napoletani, Vicentini e *Viniziani*,[50] che scrivono bene e hanno ingegni attissimi allo scrivere; il che non potevano far prima che tu, il Petrarca e il Boccaccio avessi scritto. Perché, a volere ch'e' venissino a questo grado, disaiutandoli la lingua patria era necessario ch'e' fussi prima alcuno il quale con lo esemplo suo insegnassi com'egli avessino a dimenticare quella lor naturale barbaria, nella quale la patria lingua li sommergeva.

Concludesi, pertanto che non c'è lingua che si possa chiamare o comune d'Italia o curiale, perché tutte quelle che si potessino chiamare così, hanno il fondamento loro da gli scrittori fiorentini e dalla lingua fiorentina, alla quale in ogni defetto come a vero fonte e fondamento loro è necessario che ricorrino; e non volendo esser veri pertinaci hanno a confessarla fiorentina [.....]

Udito che Dante ebbe queste cose, le confessò vere, e si partì; e io mi restai tutto contento parendomi di averlo *sgannato*.[51] Non so già s'io mi sgannerò coloro che sono sì poco conoscitori de' beneficii ch'egli hanno auti da la nostra patria, che e' vogliono accomunare con essa lei nella lingua Milano, Vinegia e Romagna, e tutte le bestemmie di Lombardia.

Appendix Five

Other Occurrences of *Patria* in the Works of Niccolò Machiavelli

࿇ঙৎ

This Appendix provides the reader with a compendium of references to "patria" and related words in the writings of Niccolò Machiavelli which were not cited in the body of the text. Such a comprehensive list, arranged chronologically according to Sebastian de Grazia's indications, may complement the work done on *patria* in *Il Principe*, the *Discorsi* and the *Dialogo* which took centre-stage in this study. De Grazia dated the works included in this Appendix as follows: *La Prima Decennale* (1504), *Il Decennale Secondo* (1514), *La vita di Castruccio Castracani* (1520), the *Istorie fiorentine* (1520–1525) and the *Capitoli* as uncertain (De Grazia, *Hell*, pp. 23–24).

This Appendix may help scholars who wish further to examine Machiavelli's use of the term "patria." That said, one may notice that 'patria' is not used in all of Machiavelli's political and literary works. Conspicuously absent, are his plays and the majority of his short political and literary works and poetry. One might argue, as this study has, that *patria* played an important role in those works which seemed to make up his plan for Italian unification, i.e. *Il Principe*, the *Discorsi* and possibly the *Dialogo*. The *Istorie fiorentine* are an exception to this, and more work needs to be done on that work in order to assess just how important *patria* was therein.

All works cited and their corresponding page references may be found in one volume; Mario Casella's and Guido Mazzoni's 1929 edition of Machiavelli's *Opere*, titled *Tutte le Opere Storiche e Letterarie di Niccolò Machiavelli*, published by G. Barbèra.

Patria in *La Prima Decennale* (1504)

Ma perché molti temen la ruina
Veder de la lor *patria* a poco a poco
Sotto la sua profetica dottrina (ll. 160–162, p. 803).

Patriae in *La Prima Decennale*

sicut illi ac labanti *patriae* tuae non defuisti, si cupis carmina haec nostra, quae tuo invitatu edimus, non contemnenda. Vale. (Epistola, p. 799)

Patria in *Il Decennale Secondo* (1514)

Questo per la sua *patria* assai sostenne,
E di vostra milizia il suo decoro
Con gran iustizia gran tempo mantenne (ll. 37–39, p. 812).

Patria in *La vita di Castruccio Castracani da Luca* (1520)

1. e ciascuno gli prometteva lo imperio della sua *patria*, quando per suo mezzo vi rientrasse (*Castruccio*, Capoverso 17, p. 754).

2. né perdonò ad alcuno, privandogli della *patria* e della roba, e, quegli che poteva avere nelle mani, della vita (*Castruccio*, Capoverso 19, p. 757).

3. non potendo sopportare che la sua *patria* fussi serva d'uno Lucchese (*Castruccio*, Capoverso 29, p. 757).

4. in cambio di Lucca, egli avessi avuto per sua *patria* Macedonia o Roma (*Castruccio*, Capoverso 73, p. 763).

Patria in the *Istorie fiorentine* (1520–1525)

1. vedrà come la Sua *patria*, levatasi per divisione dalla ubidienzia degli imperadori (*Istorie*, Epistola, p. 377).

2. e animo loro a fare sé e la loro *patria* grande, che quelli tanti che rimanevono (*Istorie*, Proemio, p. 379).

3. Ma gli abitatori di quella, sendo spogliati della *patria* loro, diventorono per la necessità feroci (*Istorie*, Libro I, Capoverso 2, p. 382).

4. e ritornarsi nella *patria* loro; e gli Ostrogoti e i Zepidi si posono in Pannonia (*Istorie*, Libro I, Capoverso 3, p. 382).

5. il quale mescolato con la lingua *patria* di quelli nuovi popoli e con la antica romana fanno un nuovo ordine di parlare (*Istorie*, Libro I, Capoverso 5, p. 384).

6. i quali dopo la morte di Attila dicemmo essersi nella loro *patria* ritornati, e ne venne in Italia (*Istorie*, Libro I, Capoverso 8, p. 386)

7. la grandezza della città di Pisa, nella quale assai popoli, cacciati dalla *patria* sua, ricorsono (*Istorie*, Libro I, Capoverso 12, p. 390)

8. Ma poco stettano fuora, ché, per accordi fatti intra lo Imperadore e il Papa, furono restituiti nella *patria* loro (*Istorie*, Libro I, Capoverso 27, p. 399).

9. se non per potere nella sua *patria* abitare; e che non era allora per non volere quello che già aveva cerco (*Istorie*, Libro II, Capoverso 7, p. 413).

10. e se di loro alcuno temeva della sua *patria*, la rovinasse, perché sperava (*Istorie*, Libro II, Capoverso 7, p. 413).

11. e a' Ghibellini ancora fu perdonata la fresca ingiuria, e riposti nella *patria* loro (*Istorie*, Libro II, Capoverso 9, p. 414).

12. e agli amici di offendere la *patria*, deliberò di partirsi, e dare luogo

alla invidia (*Istorie*, Libro II, Capoverso 13, p. 417).

13. non era altro che volere rovinare la *patria* loro e le loro condizioni raggravare (*Istorie*, Libro II, Capoverso 14, p. 417)

14. mediante gli ordini fatti, cacciargli della *patria* loro; e però era bene mitigare quelli (*Istorie*, Libro II, Capoverso 14, p. 418).

15. messer Corso per amore della *patria* muoversi (*Istorie*, Libro II, Capoverso 21, p. 422).

16. quando disarmati pregavano di essere alla *patria* restituiti, poichè gli viddono armati (*Istorie*, Libro II, Capoverso 22, p, 423).

17. Questo fine ebbe messer Corso, dal quale la *patria* e la parte de' Neri molti beni e molti mali ricognobbe (*Istorie*, Libro II, Capoverso 23, p. 425).

18. Vero è che la sua inquietudine fece alla *patria*. E alla parte non si ricordare (*Istorie*, Libro II, Capoverso 23, p. 425).

19. a' quali aveva promesso di restituirgli alla *patria* loro. Donde a' capi del (*Istorie*, Libro II, Capoverso 24, p. 425)

20. al soccorso di Prato sarebbe dopo la impresa, alla *patria* restituito: donde più che quattromila ribelli vi concorsono (*Istorie*, Libro II, Capoverso 26, p. 427).

21. e con la servitù della *patria* dalla servitù de' loro creditori liberarsi (*Istorie*, Libro II, Capoverso 33, p. 433).

22. i signori, avvenga che molto innanzi avessero la rovina della *patria* loro preveduto (*Istorie*, Libro II, Capoverso 34, p. 433–434).

23. nondimeno per non mancare alla *patria*, animosamente gliene negorono (*Istorie*, Libro II, Capoverso 34, p. 433–434).

24. e con quelli cittadini i quali della *patria* e della libertà giudicavano amatori si ristrinsono (*Istorie*, Libro II, Capoverso 34, p. 433–434).

25.   e che a molti di quelli avesse la *patria* renduta; perché non poteva credere che i generosi animi (*Istorie*, Libro II, Capoverso 36, p. 436).

26.   gli parve avere ingannato la *patria* sua; e per emendare il fallo commesso (*Istorie*, Libro II, Capoverso 36, p. 437).

27.   intra i quali erano Sanesi con sei ambasciadori, uomini assai nella loro *patria* onorati (*Istorie*, Libro II, Capoverso 37, p. 439).

28.   Onde che molti cittadini, mossi dallo amore della *patria*, in San Piero Scheraggio si ragunorono (*Istorie*, Libro III, Capoverso 5, p. 446).

29.   Lo amore che noi portiamo, magnifici Signori, alla *patria* nostra, ci ha fatti prima ristrignere (*Istorie*, Libro III, Capoverso 5, p. 446).

30.   se non intra quelli che sono di qualche scelleratezza, o contro alla *patria* o contro ai privati commessa, consapevoli (*Istorie*, Libro III, Capoverso 5, p. 447).

31.   A che noi, mossi dalla carità della *patria*, non da alcuna privata passione, vi confortiamo (*Istorie*, Libro III, Capoverso 5, p. 448).

32.   tanto quelli cittadini stimavono allora più la *patria* che l'anima (*Istorie*, Libro III, Capoverso 7, p. 450).

33.   in loro qualche umanità, e alla loro *patria* qualche amore, prendemmo il magistrato volentieri (*Istorie*, Libro III, Capoverso 11, p. 453).

34.   sotto le spalle vostre, di rovinare la *patria* vostra (*Istorie*, Libro II, Capoveso 11, p. 454).

35.   i Signori ancora erano confusi e della salute della *patria* dubbi, vedendosi da uno di loro abbandonati (*Istorie*, Libro III, Capoverso 15, p. 459).

36.   e merita di essere annoverato intra i pochi che abbino benificata la *patria* loro; perché, se in esso fusse stato animo o maligno o ambizioso (*Istorie*, Libro III, Capoverso 17, p. 461).

37.   era messer Benedetto uomo ricchissimo, umano, severo, amatore
       della libertà della *patria* sua, e a cui dispiacevono assai i modi
       tirannici (*Istorie*, Libro III, Capoverso 20, p. 464).

38.   si fermò uno governo, per il quale alla *patria* tutti quelli che erano
       stati confinati poi che messer Salvestro de' Medici era stato
       gonfaloniere si restituirono (*Istorie*, Libro III, Capoverso 21, p. 464).

39.   Fugli pertanto alle sue buone operazioni la sua *patria* poco grata; nel
       quale errore (*Istorie*, Libro III, Capoverso 22, p. 465).

40.   Lo amore della mia *patria* mi fece accostare a messer Salvestro de'
       Medici e di poi da messer Giorgio Scali discostare (*Istorie*, Libro III,
       Capoverso 23, p. 466).

41.   di me non mi incresce, perché quegli onori che la *patria* libera mi ha
       dati la serva non mi può torre (*Istorie*, Libro III, Capoverso 23, p.
       466).

42.   duolmi bene che la mia *patria* rimanga in preda di pochi, e alla loro
       superbia ed avarizia sottoposta (*Istorie*, Libro III, Capoverso 23, p.
       466).

43.   e perciò fece pensiero di fare esperienza se poteva rendere la *patria*
       agli sbanditi, o almeno gli uffici agli ammuniti (*Istorie*, Libro III,
       Capoverso 26, p. 469).

44.   ma tutti giovani feroci e disposti, per tornare nella *patria*, a tentare
       ogni fortuna (*Istorie*, Libro II, Capoverso 27, p. 469).

45.   ma che gli era posto nello arbitrio loro rendere agli sbanditi la *patria*
       e agli ammuniti lo stato (*Istorie*, Libro II, Capoverso 27, p. 470).

46.   Pertanto affermava come ciascuno che amava la *patria* e lo onore
       suo era necessitato a risentirsi e ricordarsi della virtù di Bardo
       Mancini (*Istorie*, Libro IV, Capoverso 9, p. 477).

47.   che vivere salvo per le mani degli avversari della *patria* sua (*Istorie*,
       Libro IV, Capoverso 12, p. 479).

48.   aveva molte volte ricevuti i Guelfi che non potevono stare nella *patria* loro (*Istorie*, Libro IV, Capoverso 19, p. 485).

49.   gridando e pregando che fusse loro renduto la roba e la *patria*: e facessero restituire (poichè non si poteva l'onore) almeno le moglie a' mariti, e a' padri le figliuole (*Istorie*, Libro IV, Capoverso 21, p. 487).

50.   acciò che quelli fussero ancora più pronti a operare bene per la *patria*: e poichè in Firenze non si usava concedere loro il trionfo (*Istorie*, Libro IV, Capoverso 23, p. 488).

51.   E quando travaglio alcuno nasca, vivendo neutrale, sarai a ciascuno grato; e così gioverai a te, e non nocerai alla tua *patria* (*Istorie*, Libro IV, Capoverso 27, p. 492).

52.   che si armassero a liberare la *patria* di quello uomo che di necessità (*Istorie*, Libro IV, Capoverso 28, p. 493).

53.   chiamare il popolo in piazza, ripigliare lo stato, per rendere alla *patria* la sua libertà (*Istorie*, Libro IV, Capoverso 28, p. 493).

54.   Sta' pertanto di buona voglia prendi il cibo, e mantienti vivo agli amici e alla *patria* (*Istorie*, Libro IV, Capoverso 29, p. 494).

55.   pensando di avere tradita la *patria* loro tre volte; l'una quando salvorono Cosimo (*Istorie*, Libro IV, Capoverso 31, p. 497).

56.   La quale, come prima si ragunò, restituì Cosimo alla *patria* e gli altri che erano con quello stati confinati (*Istorie*, Libro IV, Capoverso 33, p. 498).

57.   poichè io credetti che voi, che eri stato cacciato della *patria* vostra, potessi tenere me nella mia (*Istorie*, Libro IV, Capoverso 33, p. 498).

58.   le leggi che gli uomini; perché quella *patria* è desiderabile nella quale le sustanze e gli amici si possono securamente godere (*Istorie*, Libro IV, Capoverso 33, p. 498).

59.   e sempre agli uomini savi e buoni fu meno grave udire i mali della *patria* loro, che vederli (*Istorie*, Libro IV, Capoverso 33, p. 498).

60.   tornando trionfante d'una vittoria, fusse ricevuto dalla sua *patria* con
       tanto concorso di popolo e con tanta dimostrazione di benivolenzia
       (*Istorie*, Libro IV, Capoverso 33, p. 498).

61.   con quanta fu ricevuto egli tornando dallo esilio. E da ciascuno
       voluntariamente fu salutato benefattore del popolo e padre della
       patria (*Istorie*, Libro IV, Capoverso 33, p. 498).

62.   e cognoscendo il male che da quello onesto ozio alla sua *patria* ne
       poteva risultare, provvide che niuno filosofo potesse essere in Roma
       ricevuto (*Istorie*, Libro V, Capoverso 1, p. 499).

63.   o virtù di capitano, o amore verso la *patria* di cittadino, si vedrà con
       quali inganni (*Istorie*, Libro V, Capoverso 1, p. 599).

64.   e qualunque altro si trovava ribelle, alla *patria* restituirono; tutti i
       Grandi, eccetto pochissimi, nell'ordine populare ridussono (*Istorie*,
       Libro V, Capoverso 4, p. 502).

65.   alle armi forestiere ricorrono, e quella *patria* che loro governare non
       possono allo imperio d'uno forestiero sottomettono (*Istorie*, Libro V,
       Capoverso 6, p. 503).

66.   il quale, non molto poi che egli ebbe fatta la sua *patria* serva, come
       in simili casi sempre interviene, diventò sospetto al duca (*Istorie*,
       Libro V, Capoverso 6, p. 503).

67.   perché egli non poteva credere che quello che non aveva amato la
       libertà della sua *patria* amasse lui, deliberò di tentare di nuovo la
       fortuna (*Istorie*, Libro V, Capoverso 6, p. 503)

68.   e a uno tratto rendere la libertà alla *patria*, e a sé la fama e la securtà,
       giudicando non avere con i suoi cittadini altro rimedio se non fare
       opera che (*Istorie*, Libro V, Capoverso 6, p. 504).

69.   se noi, già tuoi nimici, vegniamo ora confidentemente a supplicare
       gli aiuti tuoi per ritornare nella *patria* nostra, né tu né alcuno altro
       che considera le umane cose come le procedono (*Istorie*, Libro V,
       Capoverso 8, p. 504).

70.   per quello che già facemmo, e con la *patria*, per quello che ora

facciamo, possiamo avere manifeste e ragionevoli scuse (*Istorie*, Libro V, Capoverso 8, p. 504).

71. Niuno uomo buono riprenderà mai alcuno che cerchi di difendere la *patria* sua, in qualunque modo se la difenda (*Istorie*, Libro V, Capoverso 8, p. 504).

72. Né fu mai il fine nostro di iniuriarti, ma sibbene di guardare la *patria* nostra dalle ingiurie (*Istorie*, Libro V, Capoverso 8, p. 504).

73. Né anche la *patria* nostra si può dolere che noi ti confortiamo ora a pigliare quelle armi contro a di lei (*Istorie*, Libro V, Capoverso 8, p. 504).

74. dalle quali con tanta ostinazione la difendemmo; perché quella *patria* merita di essere da tutti i cittadini amata la quale ugualmente tutti i suoi cittadini ama, non quella che posposti tutti gli altri, pochissimi ne adora (*Istorie*, Libro V, Capoverso 8, p. 505).

75. Né sia alcuno che danni le armi in qualunque modo contro alla *patria* mosse; perché le città ancora che sieno corpi misti, hanno con i corpi semplici somiglianza (*Istorie*, Libro V, Capoverso 8, p. 505).

76. Io non so quale necessità sia maggiore che la nostra, o quale pietà possa superare quella che tragga la *patria* sua di servitù (*Istorie*, Libro V, Capoverso 8, p. 505).

77. pensate il premio della vittoria vostra essere la salute non solo della *patria*, ma delle case e de' figliuoli vostri (*Istorie*, Libro V, Capoverso 11, p. 508).

78. ma di quelli de' descendenti loro non si cancellerebbe, e che quella *patria* aveva sempre a essere comune a' Fiorentini e a loro (*Istorie*, Libro V, Capoverso 21, p. 517).

79. quelli erano dalla volontà di tornare nella loro *patria* spinti; e ciascuno aveva mosso il duca con ragioni opportune e conforme al desiderio suo (*Istorie*, Libro V, Capoverso 26, p 520).

80. De' quali messer Rinaldo elesse la sua abitazione ad Ancona; e per

guadagnarsi la celeste *patria*, poichè egli aveva perduta la terrestre (*Istorie*, Libro V, Capoverso 34, p. 528).

81.   che si faccia colui che per forza abbandona gli amici e la *patria*, dolendosi della sua malvagia sorte (*Istorie*, Libro VI, Capoverso 4, p. 533).

82.   la quale facessi ritornare i Canneschi, con la rovina della *patria* e della parte loro (*Istorie*, Libro VI, Capoverso 10, p. 537).

83.   e giudicò non potere tentare altro che vedere se potesse trarre la *patria* sua delle mani de' prelati e ridurla nello antico vivere (*Istorie*, Libro VI, Capoverso 29, p. 533).

84.   e andando circuendo Italia, sullevando i principi contro alla *patria*, fu in Lunigiana (*Istorie*, Libro VII, Capoverso 3, p. 564).

85.   perché intra tutte le altre qualità che lo feciono principe nella sua *patria*, fu lo essere, sopra tutti gli altri uomini liberale, e magnifico (*Istorie*, Libro VII, Capoverso 5, p. 565).

86.   prudenza che qualunque seco e con la sua *patria* si collegava, rimaneva o pari o superiore al nimico (*Istorie*, Libro VII, Capoverso 5, p. 566).

87.   come uomo che amasse più se medesimo che la *patria*, e più questo mondo che quell'altro (*Istorie*, Libro VII, Capoverso 6, p. 566).

88.   e per publico decreto sopra la sepultura sua PADRE DELLA *PATRIA* nominato (*Istorie*, Libro VII, Capoverso 5, p. 567).

89.   per mostrare che da quello avesse e la salute e la libertà di quella *patria* a dependere (*Istorie*, Libro VII, Capoverso 14, p. 572).

90–91. questo partito che voi pigliate farà alla *patria* nostra perdere la sua libertà, a voi lo stato e le sustanze, a me e agli altri la *patria* (*Istorie*, Libro VII, Capoverso 15, p. 574).

92.   il quale reputava a sé infelice e alla *patria* sua dannoso (*Istorie*, Libro VII, Capoverso 16, p. 574).

93.   stimando più quella ingiuria che i pericoli miei, io ne perdei la *patria*, e fui per perderne la vita (*Istorie*, Libro VII, Capoverso 18, p. 576).

94.   che io giudicai che fusse da dare tal forma allo stato, che dopo la tua morte la *patria* nostra non rovinasse (*Istorie*, Libro VII, Capoverso 18, p. 576).

95.   Da questo sono nate le cose fatte, non contro a te, ma in benifizio della *patria* mia, il che, se pure è stato errore (*Istorie*, Libro VII, Capoverso 18, p. 576).

96.   Né ti scusa lo amore della *patria*; perché non sarà mai alcuno che creda questa città essere stata meno amata e accresciuta dai Medici che dagli Acciaiuoli (*Istorie*, Libro VII, Capoverso 18, p. 576).

97.   Messer Dietisalvi dall'altra parte e Niccolò Soderini con ogni diligenza cercorono di muovere il Senato viniziano contra alla *patria* loro, giudicando che (*Istorie*, Libro VII, Capoverso 19, p. 576).

98.   il quale non per altro errore dicevano sopportare che per avere voluto che la *patria* loro con le leggi sue vivesse e che i magistrati (*Istorie*, Libro VII, Capoverso 19, p. 577).

99.   e con inganno cacciatigli poi dalla *patria*: né furono contenti a questo (*Istorie*, Libro VII, Capoverso 19, p. 577).

100.   Né ci poteva fare altri rimedi che ammunirli e pregarli dovessero civilmente vivere e godersi la loro *patria* salva più tosto che destrutta (*Istorie*, Libro VII, Capoverso 21, p. 578).

101.   e che bastasse loro vivere nella loro *patria* securi e onorati, e di più, de' loro nimici vendicati (*Istorie*, Libro VII, Capoverso 23, p. 579).

102.   Dunque questa nostra *patria* ci ha dato la vita perché noi la togliamo a lei? (*Istorie*, Libro VII, Capoverso 23, p. 580).

103.   che egli avesse tutti i fuori usciti per frenare le rapine di quelli di dentro alla *patria* restituiti (*Istorie*, Libro VII, Capoverso 23, p. 580).

104.　la virtù e bontà del quale la *patria* sua non potette interamente cognoscere (*Istorie*, Libro VII, Capoverso 23, p. 580).

105.　e narrò la cagione della impresa sua essere volere liberare loro e la *patria* sua dalla servitù (*Istorie*, Libro VII, Capoverso 26, p. 582).

106.　come per la età e' potessero, la loro *patria* dalla tirannide di quel principe libererebbono (*Istorie*, Libro VII, Capoverso 33, p. 587).

107.　liberare la loro *patria* da tanti mali, sperando che, qualunque volta riuscisse loro lo ammazzarlo (*Istorie*, Libro VII, Capoverso 33, p. 588).

108.　promettendo di rendere loro la *patria*, avevano tirati nella voglia loro (*Istorie*, Libro VIII, Capoverso 7, p. 595).

109.　né prima perderebbe quello, che loro la *patria* perdessero. E perché le opere corrispondessero alle parole (*Istorie*, Libro VIII, Capoverso 10, p. 599).

110.　sendo arrivato a Milano, morì; onde che la *patria*, per remunerare chi era rimaso di lui e per onorare la sua memoria (*Istorie*, Libro VIII, Capoverso 14, p. 601).

111.　avendo esposto la propria vita per rendere alla *patria* sua la pace (*Istorie*, Libro VIII, Capoverso 19, p. 606).

112.　dicendo che per salvare sé egli aveva venduta la sua *patria*; e come nella guerra si erano perdute le terre (*Istorie*, Libro VIII, Capoverso 22, p, 608).

113.　in modo che convenne che la sua *patria* di gran somma di danari lo suvvenisse (*Istorie*, Libro VIII, Capoverso 36, p. 620).

114.　Tenne ancora, in questi tempi pacifici, sempre la *patria* sua in festa; dove spesso giostre e rappresentazioni di fatti e trionfi antichi si vedevano (*Istorie*, Libro VIII, Capoverso 36, p. 620).

115.　Né morì mai alcuno, non solamente in Firenze, ma in Italia, con tanta fama di prudenza, né che tanto alla sua *patria* dolesse (*Istorie*, Libro

VIII, Capoverso 36, p. 621).

Ripatriare in the *Istorie fiorentine*

1. e perché era di nazione ghibellino, aveva in animo *ripatriare* gli usciti; ma volle prima guadagnarsi il popolo (*Istorie*, Libro II, Capoverso 21, p. 422).

2. Mostrorono questi nuovi ribelli a (Giovan Francesco) la facilità del *ripatriarsi*, quando e' Viniziani ne facessero impresa (*Istorie*, Libro VII, Capoverso 19, p. 576).

3. la duchessa Bona fu consigliata *ripatriasse* gli Sforzeschi, e per levare via queste civili contese, gli ricevesse in stato (*Istorie*, Libro VIII, Capoverso 18, p. 605).

4. confortò la duchessa a *ripatriare* gli Sforzeschi; la quale, seguitando i suoi consigli (*Istorie*, Libro VIII, Capoverso 18, p. 605).

Patria in *I Capitoli* (Dates of these are uncertain)

Dell'Ingratitudine

1. Come in Affrica ancor le insegne misse,
    Prima Siface, e di poi d'Anniballe
    E la fortuna e la sua *patria* afflisse (ll. 88–90, p. 843).

2. Né l'almo suo d'altra vendetta armava;
    Solo a la *patria* sua lasciar non volse
    Quell'ossa che d'aver non meritava (ll. 124–126, p. 843).

APPENDIX SIX

Patria in the Works of Francesco Guicciardini

⛤⛥

This Appendix contains all references to "patria" in the political and historical works of Guicciardini, with the exception of his *Considerazioni* which were included in the Appendix to Chapter Two. As with the earlier Appendices, which included all references to "patria" in Machiavelli that were not cited in the body of our work, this compendium, may be helpful to scholars who wish to examine "patria" and related words in Guicciardini; or who wish to undertake a more exhaustive comparison of Machiavelli and Guicciardini.

The references to "patria" are arranged according to Constantino Panigada's and Roberto Palmarocchi's complete works of Guicciardini, published between 1929 and 1936. The author utilized the helpful "Intratext Digital Library" to search the texts for "patria" and related terms (http://www.intratext.com). The combination of electronic texts and scholarly printed editions helped tremendously in the compilation of this Appendix.

The reader will find each volume of Guicciardini's *Opere* cited once in its entirety, then abbreviated throughout.

Patria in Guicciardini's *Storia d'Italia*

Storia d'Italia (Libri I–IV), in Volume I, Francesco Guicciardini, *Opere*, in 9 vols. A cura di Constantino Panigada e Roberto Palmarocchi. Bari: Laterza (1929–36).

1. acerba alla *patria*, la quale, per la riputazione e prudenza sua e per lo ingegno attissimo a tutte le cose onorate e eccellenti (*Opere* I, *Storia*

d"Italia, Libro I, Capitolo 2, p. 5).

2.   A Innocenzio succedette Roderigo Borgia, di *patria* valenziano, una delle città regie di Spagna, antico cardinale, (*Opere* I, *Storia d'Italia*, Libro I, Capitolo 2, p. 6).

3.   dominio della loro *patria* stata posseduta da Carlo suo padre (*Opere* I, *Storia d'Italia*, Libro I, Capitolo 4, p. 29).

4.   e perciò la *patria* loro, abbandonata da ognuno (*Opere* I, *Storia d'Italia*, Libro I, Capitolo 14, p. 83).

5.   non solo nella *patria* ma in molte parti del mondo (*Opere* I, *Storia d'Italia*, Libro I, Capitolo 15, p. 88).

6.   ogni favore a rimetterlo nella *patria*: né contenti di questo (*Opere* I, *Storia d'Italia*, Libro I, Capitolo 16, p. 94).

7.   Ma perché queste cose non si possono tentare senza mettere la *patria* comune in gravissimi pericoli (*Opere* I, *Storia d'Italia*, Libro I, Capitolo 19, p. 110).

8.   Benché esule e spogliato della *patria* e del regno mio (*Opere* I, *Storia d'Italia*, Libro I, Capitolo 19, p. 111).

9.   i quali v'aveva ritenuti l'amore della *patria*, perché per l'acerbe esazioni del publico (*Opere* I, *Storia d'Italia*, Libro II, Capitolo 1, p. 118).

10. avere tutti unitamente determinato d'abbandonare prima la *patria*, d'abbandonare prima la vita (*Opere* I, *Storia d'Italia*, Libro II, Capitolo 1, p. 119).

11. arebbe certamente il gusto molto corrotto chi altro governo nella *patria* nostra desiderasse. (*Opere* I, *Storia d'Italia*, Libro II, Capitolo 2, p. 127).

12. la infermità d'Italia, e particolarmente quella della *patria* nostra: però che imprudenza sarebbe (*Opere* I, *Storia d'Italia*, Libro II, Capitolo 2, p. 130).

13. la desolazione ultima di quella *patria*, la quale non arebbe causa di lamentarsi d'altro (*Opere* I, *Storia d'Italia*, Libro II, Capitolo 7, p. 156).

14. ritenendo il nome medesimo che hanno nella *patria*, sono chiamati stradiotti. (*Opere* I, *Storia d'Italia*, Libro Capitolo II, 8, p. 158).

15. capitano Consalvo Ernandes di casa d'Aghilar, di *patria* cordovese, uomo di molto valore (*Opere* I, *Storia d'Italia*, Libro II, Capitolo 10, p. 177).

16. la quale nella propria *patria* tanto amano, né il rispetto della salute comune (*Opere* I, *Storia d'Italia*, Libro III, Capitolo 4, pp. 225–226).

17. risposta se ne tornassino alla *patria*: però venuti all'ora deputata innanzi al duca (*Opere* I, *Storia d'Italia*, Libro III, Capitolo 9, p. 265).

18. il cardinale di San Piero in Vincola in Savona sua *patria* e in quelle riviere (*Opere* I, *Storia d'Italia*, Libro III, Capitolo 11, p. 271).

19. era stato cagione che da se stessi gli avessino sottomessa la propria *patria* (*Opere* I, *Storia d'Italia*, Libro IV, Capitolo 3, p. 315).

20. e lodata da molti in lui la generosità dell'animo suo e lo amore verso la *patria*. (*Opere* I, *Storia d'Italia*, Libro IV, Capitolo 6, p. 330).

21. ribelle prima e che era venuto con l'armi contro alla *patria*, fusse stata fatta senza saputa loro tale abilità. (*Opere* I, *Storia d'Italia*, Libro IV, Capitolo 7, p. 338).

22. avendo giudicato non potere fare maggiore beneficio alla *patria* e a' popoli suoi che provedere non fussino molestati dalle guerre. (*Opere* I, *Storia d'Italia*, Libro IV, Capitolo 9, p. 355).

23. Però pregargli che, alienando l'animo da i costumi barbari e inumani, si disponessino a difendere insieme la *patria* e la propria salute. (*Opere* I, *Storia d'Italia*, Libro IV, Capitolo 9, p. 355).

24. tiranni della loro *patria* e poi vicari; Faenza Furlí Imola e Rimini erano dominate da vicari particolari (*Opere* I, *Storia d'Italia*, Libro IV, Capitolo 12, pp. 381–382).

Storia d'Italia (Libri V–VIII) in Volume II, (1929) of Francesco Guicciardini, *Opere*, in 9 vols. A cura di Constantino Panigada e Roberto Palmarocchi. Bari: Laterza (1929–36).

25. una paga per ritornarsene alla *patria*, perché si erano partiti molti dí prima che avessino finito di servire lo stipendio ricevuto (*Opere* II, *Storia d'Italia*, Libro V, Capitolo 4, pp. 14–15).

26. in nome suo e de' fratelli, della restituzione alla *patria*, promettendogli quantità grandissima di danari, l'avea udito gratissimamente (*Opere* II, *Storia d'Italia*, Libro V, Capitolo 4, p. 16).

27. co' quali sapeva che Piero ritornato nella *patria* sarebbe stato congiuntissimo. (*Opere* II, *Storia d'Italia*, Libro V, Capitolo 4, p. 18).

28. alla libertà alla *patria* e a loro stati degnità e beni (*Opere* II, *Storia d'Italia*, Libro VI, Capitolo 16, p. 164).

29. non si tenendo più sicura nella *patria*, se n'uscí fuora. (*Opere* II, *Storia d'Italia*, Libro VII, Capitolo 5, p. 187).

30. antica delle parti di Savona sua *patria*, contrario a' gentiluomini e favorevole al popolo. (*Opere* II, *Storia d'Italia*, Libro VII, Capitolo 5, p. 190).

31. né hanno essi questa infelice città in luogo di *patria*. Ma la intenzione nostra (*Opere* II, *Storia d'Italia*, Libro VII, Capitolo 6, p. 198).

32. in beneficio della *patria* vostra, considerare quanta differenza sia dal muovere la guerra ad altri ad aspettare che la sia mossa a noi (*Opere* II, *Storia d'Italia*, Libro VII, Capitolo 10, pp. 222–223).

33. e il pericolo della ultima ruina della loro *patria*, in luogo di tanta

gloria e grandezza (*Opere* II, *Storia d'Italia*, Libro VIII, Capitolo 5, p. 273).

34. E che sicurtà avere che nella propria *patria*, piena di innumerabile moltitudine, non si suscitasse (*Opere* II, *Storia d'Italia*, Libro VIII, Capitolo 5, p. 274).

35. i quali, disposti a vedere prima l'ultimo esterminio della *patria* che cedere a sí orribile necessità (*Opere* II, *Storia d'Italia*, Libro VIII, Capitolo 8, p. 289).

36. l'ultima desolazione di questa *patria*, bisogna di necessità confessare che le provisioni e preparazioni fatte insino a ora (*Opere* II, *Storia d'Italia*, Libro VIII, Capitolo 10, p. 299).

37. mentre che ancora non è passato il tempo di aiutare la nostra *patria*, non debbiamo lasciare indietro opera o sforzo alcuno (*Opere* II, *Storia d'Italia*, Libro VIII, Capitolo 10, p. 300).

38. la conservazione della *patria* solamente il publico bene (*Opere* II, *Storia d'Italia*, Libro VIII, Capitolo 10, p. 300).

39. la conservazione della *patria*, non è questo premio degno de' suoi generosi cittadini? (*Opere* II, *Storia d'Italia*, Libro VIII, Capitolo 10, p. 300).

40. aiutato conservato e accresciuto la *patria* loro. (*Opere* II, *Storia d'Italia*, Libro VIII, Capitolo 10, p. 300).

41. E quale *patria* è giammai stata che meriti di essere più aiutata e conservata da' suoi figliuoli che questa (*Opere* II, *Storia d'Italia*, Libro VIII, Capitolo 10, p. 300).

42. maggiori da questa republica e dagli uomini nostri che da' romani in qua abbia fatto *patria* alcuna. (*Opere* II, *Storia d'Italia*, Libro VIII, Capitolo 10, p.301).

43. Già a quale città, a quale imperio cede di religione e di pietà verso il sommo Dio la *patria* nostra? (*Opere* II, *Storia d'Italia*, Libro VIII, Capitolo 10, p. 302).

44. È meritamente per tutte queste cose preposta la *patria* nostra a tutte l'altre (*Opere* II, *Storia d'Italia*, Libro VIII, Capitolo 10, p. 302).

45. Ebbe la *patria* nostra in uno tempo medesimo l'origine sua e la sua libertà (*Opere* II, *Storia d'Italia*, Libro VIII, Capitolo 10, p. 302).

46. Adunque a tanta e a sí gloriosa *patria*, stata moltissimi anni antimuro della fede (*Opere* II, *Storia d'Italia*, Libro VIII, Capitolo 10, pp. 302–303).

47. gli altri non essere superstite alla ruina della *patria*. Ma perché né Vinegia (*Opere* II, *Storia d'Italia*, Libro VIII, Capitolo 10, p. 303).

48. le persone de' quali in sí grave pericolo offerisco alla *patria* volentieri (*Opere* II, *Storia d'Italia*, Libro VIII, Capitolo 10, p. 304).

49. la salute della più degna *patria* e della più nobile che sia in tutto il mondo. (*Opere* II, *Storia d'Italia*, Libro VIII, Capitolo 10, p. 304).

50. tanta prontezza in soccorso della *patria*: né con minore letizia e giubilo di tutti furono ricevuti in Padova (*Opere* II, *Storia d'Italia*, Libro VIII, Capitolo 10, p. 304).

51. l'amore della *patria* alla vita propria (*Opere* II, *Storia d'Italia*, Libro VIII, Capitolo 10, p. 305).

52. e per la pietà verso la *patria*, nondimeno, per offerirsi prontamente a' pericoli e per l'esempio che faceva agli altri (*Opere* II, *Storia d'Italia*, Libro VIII, Capitolo 11, p. 309).

53. in su uno monte aspro in mezzo della *patria* (cosí chiamano il Friuli) (*Opere* II, *Storia d'Italia*, Libro VIII, Capitolo 13, p. 321).

54. fu di grandissimo giovamento alla sua *patria* nelle cose che si ebbono poi a trattare appresso a lui. (*Opere* II, *Storia d'Italia*, Libro VIII, Capitolo 16, p. 335).

Storia d'Italia (Libri IX–XII) in Volume III, (1929) of Francesco Guicciardini, *Opere*, in 9 vols. A cura di Constantino Panigada e

Roberto Palmarocchi. Bari: Laterza (1929–36).

55. figliuoli nostri e della nostra afflitta *patria*. In modo che si conosce che non alcuna malignità (*Opere* III, *Storia d'Italia*, Libro IX, Capitolo 3, p. 10).

56. ma che in altri tempi abbia veduto la *patria* nostra, a vederla di presente. (*Opere* III, *Storia d'Italia*, Libro IX, Capitolo 3, pp. 10–11).

57. di quella afflittissima nostra *patria* o la speranza di potere (*Opere* III, *Storia d'Italia*, Libro IX, Capitolo 3, p. 11).

58. la infelicissima *patria* nostra ti chiamerà sempre suo padre e suo conservatore. (*Opere* III, *Storia d'Italia*, Libro IX, Capitolo 3, p. 12).

59. da ciascuno godere quietamente la *patria*, partecipi del governo partecipi dell'entrate (*Opere* III, *Storia d'Italia*, Libro IX, Capitolo 17, p. 94).

60. cagione della liberazione e della felicità della loro *patria*. (*Opere* III, *Storia d'Italia*, Libro IX, Capitolo 17, p. 98).

61. don Ramondo di Cardona, di *patria* catelano e allora viceré del reame di Napoli. (*Opere* III, *Storia d'Italia*, Libro X, Capitolo 5, p. 128).

62. e perciò stato molto utile alla *patria* nella sua legazione. (*Opere* III, *Storia d'Italia*, Libro X, Capitolo 5, p. 129).

63. Aiutate, mentre che voi potete, cittadini, la vostra *patria* e la vostra libertà (*Opere* III, *Storia d'Italia*, Libro X, Capitolo 6, p. 137).

64. se ne tornorno alla *patria*; lasciando liberi i giudíci degli uomini se fussino scesi per assaltare lo stato di Milano (*Opere* III, *Storia d'Italia*, Libro X, Capitolo 8, p. 151).

65. in manifestissimo pericolo la libertà e la salute della *patria*. Contrario a questi era il parere del gonfaloniere (*Opere* III, *Storia d'Italia*, Libro X, Capitolo 8, p. 153).

66. secondo le leggi della *patria*, inabile a esercitare qualunque magistrato (*Opere* III, *Storia d'Italia*, Libro X, Capitolo 8, p. 155).

67. Giuliano de' Medici non erano restituiti nella *patria*: le quali cose consentite sarebbono facilmente concordi nell'altre (*Opere* III, *Storia d'Italia*, Libro XI, Capitolo 3, p. 223).

68. desiderare che i Medici potessino godere la *patria*, non come capi del governo ma come privati (*Opere* III, *Storia d'Italia*, Libro XI, Capitolo 3, p. 224).

69. laudabile la loro restituzione, acciò che la *patria* comune si unisse in un corpo comune (*Opere* III, *Storia d'Italia*, Libro XI, Capitolo 3, p. 227).

70. la salute della vostra *patria*, a me o rinunziare con animo costante e lietissimo a questo magistrato (*Opere* III, *Storia d'Italia*, Libro XI, Capitolo 3, p. 227).

71. che con le facoltà e con la vita si attendesse a difendere la libertà e la *patria* comune. (*Opere* III, *Storia d'Italia*, Libro XI, Capitolo 3, p. 228).

72. della ruina propria e delle calamità della sua *patria*, allungava artificiosamente la spedizione degli imbasciadori (*Opere* III, *Storia d'Italia*, Libro XI, Capitolo 4, p. 230).

73. e di tutti quegli che l'avevano seguitato, alla *patria*, come privati cittadini (*Opere* III, *Storia d'Italia*, Libro XI, Capitolo 4, p. 232).

74. e molto più per lo sdegno che avessino condotto l'esercito spagnuolo contro alla *patria*, stati cagione del sacco crudelissimo di Prato (*Opere* III, *Storia d'Italia*, Libro XI, Capitolo 4, p. 234).

75. secondo il costume di chi è fuori della *patria*, proponevano la impresa dovere essere molto facile (*Opere* III, *Storia d'Italia*, Libro XI, Capitolo 9, p. 263).

76. anzi gli commendò che alla salute della *patria* comune pietosamente pensassino. (*Opere* III, *Storia d'Italia*, Libro XI, Capitolo 10, p.

269).

77.   se per opera loro fussino restituiti alla *patria*, quantità di danari pari
a quella che aveva pagata il Fregoso agli spagnuoli (*Opere* III, *Storia
d'Italia*, Libro XI, Capitolo 14, p. 286).

78.   a loro che a' barbari incrudelire contro alle magnificenze e ornamenti
della *patria* comune. (*Opere* III, *Storia d'Italia*, Libro XI, Capitolo
14, p. 291).

79.   Novara con intenzione di ritornarsene alla *patria*; cosa che molti di
loro desideravano (*Opere* III, *Storia d'Italia*, Libro XII, Capitolo 14,
pp. 355–356).

80.   *Ritorno di svizzeri in* patria. *Sacco di Lodi e di Sant'Angelo*. (*Opere*
III, *Storia d'Italia*, Libro XII, Capitolo 20, Titolo, p. 385).

81.   ottenne da lui per questo la restituzione alla *patria* e in progresso di
tempo molte grazie e onori (*Opere* III, *Storia d'Italia*, Libro XII,
Capitolo 22, p. 403).

Storia d'Italia (Libri XIII–XVI) in Volume IV, (1929) of Francesco
Guicciardini, *Opere*, in 9 vols. A cura di Constantino Panigada e
Roberto Palmarocchi. Bari: Laterza (1929–36).

82.   l'uno de' quali restituito dall'esilio nella *patria*, l'altro per non gli
parere che da Cesare fussino riconosciute l'opere sue (*Opere* IV,
Storia d'Italia, Libro XIII, Capitolo 8, p. 36).

83.   restituisse alla sua *patria* la libertà, propose il cardinale de' Medici
alla amministrazione di quello stato (*Opere* IV, *Storia d'Italia*, Libro
XIII, Capitolo 12, p. 59).

84.   mossi dallo amore della *patria* comune germanica, avevano
supplicato il pontefice (*Opere* IV, *Storia d'Italia*, Libro XIII,
Capitolo 13, p. 60).

85.   il quale, stato poco felice ne' trattati che aveva fatto per sé per
rientrare nella propria *patria*, prometteva più prospero successo in

quegli che faceva per altri nelle patrie forestiere. (*Opere* IV, *Storia d'Italia*, Libro XIII, Capitolo 14, pp. 64–65).

86. il nuovo pontefice fusse inimico di Firenze *patria* sua: però, né per rispetti publici né per rispetti privati avere cagione di desiderare la grandezza della Chiesa (*Opere* IV, *Storia d'Italia*, Libro XIV, Capitolo 10, p. 136.

87. alla propria difesa e a conservare la *patria* loro libera dal giogo de' barbari inimicissimi di quella città (*Opere* IV, *Storia d'Italia*, Libro XIV, Capitolo 13, p. 151).

88. debitori alla conservazione della *patria*, per la quale se i gentili, che non aspettavano altro premio che della gloria (*Opere* IV, *Storia d'Italia*, Libro XIV, Capitolo 13, p. 151).

89. *I grigioni assoldati dai francesi giunti a Cravina ritornano in* patria. *I francesi perdono Biagrassa; la peste a Milano* (*Opere* IV, *Storia d'Italia*, Libro XV, Capitolo 8, Titolo, p. 220).

90. Risguarderà Iddio la pietà vostra verso il duca, la pietà del duca verso la *patria*; e dobbiamo tenere per certo che (*Opere* IV, *Storia d'Italia*, Libro XV, Capitolo 10, p. 233).

91. di avere avuto per *patria* più presto Spagna che Italia. (*Opere* IV, *Storia d'Italia*, Libro XVI, Capitolo 11, p. 324).

92. l'amore di Italia sua *patria* o la benivolenza che ha al duca di Milano) (*Opere* IV, *Storia d'Italia*, Libro XVI, Capitolo 14, p. 341).

Storia d'Italia (Libri XVII–XX) in Volume V, (1929) of Francesco Guicciardini, *Opere*, in 9 vols. A cura di Constantino Panigada e Roberto Palmarocchi. Bari: Laterza (1929–36).

93. casa Sforzesca o dalla compassione della sua *patria*, trattata da Fabbrizio Maramaus (*Opere* V, *Storia d'Italia*, Libro XVII, Capitolo 5, p. 26).

94. lo stato miserabile della *patria* e di ciascuno di loro, si condussero

con molte lacrime e lamenti innanzi al duca di Borbone (*Opere* V, *Storia d'Italia*, Libro XVII, Capitolo 8, p. 46).

95.   Se questa *patria* miserabile, la quale ha sempre per giustissime cagioni desiderato d'avere uno principe proprio (*Opere* V, *Storia d'Italia*, Libro XVII, Capitolo 8, p. 47).

96.   con condizione di perdere in perpetuo e la *patria* e i beni. (*Opere* V, *Storia d'Italia*, Libro XVII, Capitolo 8, p. 49).

97.   in tanto pericolo della *patria* pigliassino prontamente l'armi per difenderla (*Opere* V, *Storia d'Italia*, Libro XVIII, Capitolo 8, p. 136).

98.   per introdurre sotto nome della libertà della *patria* la sua grandezza né potendo conseguire questo fine con altro modo (*Opere* V, *Storia d'Italia*, Libro XIX, Capitolo 4, p. 222).

99.   più presto a cedere che a mettere la *patria* in sommo e manifestissimo pericolo. (*Opere* V, *Storia d'Italia*, Libro XIX, Capitolo 12, p. 266).

100.   e che fatto questo dimostrerebbe il buono animo che aveva al benefizio della *patria* comune. (*Opere* V, *Storia d'Italia*, Libro XIX, Capitolo 15, p. 278).

101.   i quali, indotti dalla ultima disperazione di non volere che senza l'eccidio della *patria* fusse la rovina loro (*Opere* V, *Storia d'Italia*, Libro XX, Capitolo 2, p. 297).

102.   né trattandosi più che essi o altri cittadini morissino per salvare la *patria* ma che (*Opere* V, *Storia d'Italia*, Libro XX, Capitolo 2, p. 297).

103.   la *patria* morisse insieme con loro, (*Opere* V, *Storia d'Italia*, Libro XX, Capitolo 2, p. 297).

104.   la acerbità grande usata contro alla *patria*, con tanti tumulti di guerra (*Opere* V, *Storia d'Italia*, Libro XX, Capitolo 3, p. 301).

105.   a godere la *patria* e i beni loro quegli del Monte de' nove (*Opere* V,
        Storia d'Italia, Libro XX, Capitolo 7, p. 303).

106.   allo essere stato cagione di tanto esterminio della sua *patria*? Morí
        odioso alla corte (*Opere* V, *Storia d'Italia*, Libro XX, Capitolo 7, p.
        303).

Patrie in Guicciardini's *Storia d'Italia*

1.   la libertà delle loro *patrie*, avesse cosí vilmente e senza la morte di
        uno uomo solo abbandonata tanta grandezza. (*Opere* I, *Storia
        d'Italia*, Libro I, Capitolo 15, p. 88).

2.   molti cittadini potenti occuporno nelle *patrie* proprie la tirannide
        (*Opere* I, *Storia d'Italia*, Libro IV, Capitolo 12, p. 379).

3.   prometteva più prospero successo in quegli che faceva per altri nelle
        patrie forestiere. (*Opere* IV, *Storia d'Italia*, Libro XIII, Capitolo 14,
        p. 64).

4.   per le terre de' svizzeri e de' grigioni, alle *patrie* loro. (*Opere* V,
        Storia d'Italia, Libro XIX, Capitolo 2, p. 213).

Patria in Guicciardini's *Storie fiorentine*, Volume VI (1932) of *Opere*, in 9 vols. A cura di Roberto Palmarocchi. Bari: Laterza (1929–36).

1.   ed intra gli altri fu per publico decreto chiamato padre della *patria*.
        Fu tenuto uomo prudentissimo (*Opere* VI, *Storie fiorentine*, Capitolo
        I, Capoverso 20, p. 11).

2.   Careggio, fuori della *patria* sua in molti luoghi (*Opere* VI, *Storie
        fiorentine*, Capitolo I, Capoverso 20, p. 11).

3.   debito universale di tutti e' cittadini verso la *patria* e pel particulare
        suo (*Opere* VI, *Storie fiorentine*, Capitolo VI, Capoverso 1, p. 50).

4.–5.   chiese nella *patria* e fuori della *patria*, e cose che avessino a essere perpetue (*Opere* VI, *Storie fiorentine*, Capitolo IX, Capoverso 13, p. 81).

6. o perché ne sperassi la restituzione nella *patria* e qualche guadagno, (*Opere* VI, *Storie fiorentine*, Capitolo XV, Capoverso 12, p. 139).

7. o veramente perderne la vita, ed almeno la *patria* e la città; e pensino bene che quando sono scoperti ed in pericolo (*Opere* VI, *Storie fiorentine*, Capitolo XV, Capoverso 21, p. 144).

8. e però essere necessario prevenire ed assicurarsene in modo col restituire e' Panciatichi alla *patria* ed alle facultà, che più non s'avessi da dubitarne. (*Opere* VI, *Storie fiorentine*, Capitolo XX, Capoverso 9, p. 205).

9. per la affezione portavano alla *patria*, volevano consiglio in che modo s'avessi a riparare (*Opere* VI, *Storie fiorentine*, Capitolo XX, Capoverso 17, p. 208).

10. lui cercò pacificamente rimettergli nella *patria*. Ma sendo ostinati gli animi de' popolani ed intendendo che el re era disposto (*Opere* VI, *Storie fiorentine*, Capitolo XXVIII, Capoverso 1, p. 294).

11. e chiedere la tornata nella *patria* amorevolmente, e di essere rimesso non come capo del governo e dello stato, ma come privato cittadino. (*Opere* VI, *Storie fiorentine*, Capitolo XXX, Capoverso 1, p. 322).

12. o per amore della *patria* o per qualche suo parente o amico gli soccorreva (*Opere* VI, *Storie fiorentine*, Capitolo XXXI, Capoverso 2, p. 335).

Patria in *Se'l Gran Capitano debbe accettare la impresa di Italia*, in *Opere*, Volume VIII, *Scritti Politici e Ricordi* (1933).

1. in una provincia dove la fama vostra è maggiore che nella *patria*, contro a una nazione ed eserciti che triemano del vostro nome per avervi altra volta provato con tanto loro danno (*Opere* VIII, *Gran Capitano*, Capitolo V, p. 105).

Patria in *Ragioni che consiglio la Signoria di Firenze ad accordarsi con Clemente VII*, in *Opere*, Volume VIII, *Scritti Politici e Ricordi* (1933).

1. arebbe atteso a beneficare ed esaltare questa sua dilettissima *patria*. Ma la mala fortuna dell'uno e dell'altro (*Opere* VIII, *Signoria di Firenze*, Capitolo XVI, p. 212).

2. che è stato el principio donde sono nati tanti mali da' quali è ora oppressa questa infelice *patria*. (*Opere* VIII, *Signoria di Firenze*, Capitolo XVI, p. 212).

3. perché più poteva in lui lo amore della *patria*, la considerazione della autoritá che ci avevano avuto (*Opere* VIII, *Signoria di Firenze*, Capitolo XVI, p. 214).

4. se la necessitá ed el desiderio di salvare la *patria* sua non l'avessi sforzato a fare altrimenti. (*Opere* VIII, *Signoria di Firenze*, Capitolo XVI, p. 214).

5. e reputandosi come cittadino di questa *patria* essere obligato a aiutarla e salvarla (*Opere* VIII, *Signoria di Firenze*, Capitolo XVI, pp. 214–215).

6. e pregandolo che per rispetto suo volessi rimettere alla sua *patria* le ingiurie ed el desiderio che aveva di vendicarsi (*Opere* VIII, *Signoria di Firenze*, Capitolo XVI, p. 215).

7. ma solo per amore e per desiderio di salvare questa *patria*, sperando che fatto questo gli fussi facile persuadere Cesare (*Opere* VIII, *Signoria di Firenze*, Capitolo XVI, p. 215).

8. di avere amato più la *patria* ed el bene suo che alcuno interesse particulare di casa sua. (*Opere* VIII, *Signoria di Firenze*, Capitolo XVI, p. 216).

9. la pietà che ha di questa povera sua *patria*. (*Opere* VIII, *Signoria di Firenze*, Capitolo XVI, p. 216).

Patria in Guicciardini's *Elogio di Lorenzo de' Medici*, in *Opere*, Volume

VIII, *Scritti Politici e Ricordi* (1933).

1. buono cittadino provedere che la *patria* per causa di lui solo non corressi tanto pericolo (*Opere* VIII, *Elogio*, Capoverso 2, p. 224).

2. liberare col suo sangue proprio la *patria* da guerra tanto pericolosa. (*Opere* VIII, *Elogio*, Capoverso 2, p. 224).

3. e lo amore che e' portava alla *patria*, ave(ndo), perché quella stessi in pace, messa la vita propria in mano degli inimici. (*Opere* VIII, *Elogio*, Capoverso 3, p. 224).

4. e che amava sí ardentemente la *patria*, fussi morto sí giovane. (*Opere* VIII, *Elogio*, Capoverso 10, p. 228).

Patria in *Se sia lecito condurre el populo alle buone legge con la forza non potendo farsi altrimenti*, in *Opere*, Volume VIII, *Scritti Politici e Rocordi* (1933).

1. in altri tempi di potere sotto lo scudo suo fare male alla *patria*. (*Opere* VIII, *Se sia lecito*, Capoverso 1, p. 230).

2. e per non vedere perdere alla *patria* sua la libertà, (*Opere* VIII, *Se sia lecito*, Capoverso 2, p. 230).

3. la perdizione della sua *patria* e conoscendo quale sia el riparo (*Opere* VIII, *Se sia lecito*, Capoverso 3, p. 231).

4. né debbe assicurarsi per averlo conosciuto ne' tempi passati buono ed amatore della *patria*, perché li omini sono fallacissimi (*Opere* VIII, *Se sia lecito*, Capoverso 4, p. 231).

Patria in *Se lo amazzarsi da sé medesimo per non perdere la libertà o per non vedere la patria in servitù procede da grandezza di animo a da viltà, e se è laudibile o no*, in *Opere*, Volume VIII, *Scritti Politici e Ricordi* (1933).

1. Se lo amazzarsi da sé medesimo per non perdere la libertà o per non

vedere la *patria* in servitù procede da grandezza di animo o da viltà, e se è laudabile o no. (*Opere* VIII, *Se lo amazzarsi*, Capitolo 3, Titolo, p. 232).

2. Verbigrazia chi si amazza per non vedere o la *patria* o la persona sua serva (*Opere* VIII, *Se lo amazzarsi*, Capitolo 2, pp. 232–233).

3. la servitù sua o della *patria*, è originalmente mosso da paura e da timore (*Opere* VIII, *Se lo amazzarsi*, Capitolo 2, p. 233).

4. venendo in servitù, o lui o la *patria*, sperassi che la libertà si potessi qualche volta recuperare (*Opere* VIII, *Se lo amazzarsi*, Capitolo 4, p. 234).

5. non vedere la servitù della sua *patria*, alla quale potrebbe molto più giovare vivendo (*Opere* VIII, *Se lo amazzarsi*, Capitolo 5, p. 235).

6. e però non so come si possa dire amatore della *patria* quello che col fare male (*Opere* VIII, *Se lo amazzarsi*, Capitolo 5, p. 235).

7. non solo per fare qualche beneficio grande alla *patria*, come feciono e' Decii (*Opere* VIII, *Se lo amazzarsi*, Capitolo 6, p. 235).

8. solo per fuggire la servitú e non volere vivere in *patria* non libera. (*Opere* VIII, *Se lo amazzarsi*, Capitolo 6, p. 235).

9. per non vivere nella *patria* serva per beneficio di altri (*Opere* VIII, *Se lo amazzarsi*, Capitolo 6, p. 235).

10. non potendo per generositá di animo soportare che la *patria* sua servissi, si fece capo della coniura contro a lui (*Opere* VIII, *Se lo amazzarsi*, Capitolo 6, p. 235).

11. che vivendo in servitú e vedendo servire la *patria*, seguire speranze incerte. (*Opere* VIII, *Se lo amazzarsi*, Capitolo 6, p. 236).

12. e che vivendo vedrebbono forse uno giorno tornare la *patria* in libertà. (*Opere* VIII, *Se lo amazzarsi*, Capitolo VIII, p. 237).

Patria in Guicciardini's *Ricordi: Serie Prima*, in *Opere*, Volume VIII,

Scritti Politici e Ricordi (1933).

1. e fare buone opere per la *patria*; e Dio volessi (*Opere* VIII, *Ricordi, Serie Prima*, Capoverso 1, p. 241).

2. ingegnatevi di non venire in malo concetto apresso a chi è superiore nella *patria* vostra, né vi fidate che el modo (*Opere* VIII, *Ricordi, Serie Prima*, Capoverso 37, p. 247).

3. non voglio già ritirare coloro che infiammati dallo amore della *patria* si metteriano in pericolo per ridurcela in libertà (*Opere* VIII, *Ricordi, Serie Prima*, Capoverso 53, p. 250).

4. A chi ha condizione nella *patria* e sia sotto uno tiranno sanguinoso e bestiale (*Opere* VIII, *Ricordi, Serie Prima*, Capoverso 82, p. 256).

5. ma non è buono questo ricordo per chi non ha condizione grande nella sua *patria*. (*Opere* VIII, *Ricordi, Serie Prima*, Capoverso 83, p. 257).

6. dalle repubbliche in fuora, nella loro *patria* e non più oltre (*Opere* VIII, *Ricordi, Serie Prima*, Capoverso 95, p. 259).

7. amatore della *patria* non solo debbe trattenersi col tiranno per sua sicurtá (*Opere* VIII, *Ricordi, Serie Prima*, Capoverso 108, p. 262).

8. ma ancora per beneficio della *patria*, perché governandosi cosí (*Opere* VIII, *Ricordi, Serie Prima*, Capoverso 108, p. 262).

9. Assai è buono cittadino chi è zelante del bene della *patria*, e alieno da tutte le cose che pregiudicano al terzo (*Opere* VIII, *Ricordi, Serie Prima*, Capoverso 179, p. 279).

Patria in the *Ricordi: Serie Seconda* in *Opere*, Volume VIII, *Scritti Politici e Ricordi* (1933).

1. non dite male della *patria*, della famiglia o parentado suo (*Opere* VIII, *Ricordi, Serie Seconda*, Capoverso 8, p. 285).

2. da quelli delle repubbliche nella *patria* propria in fuora (*Opere* VIII, *Ricordi, Serie Seconda*, Capoverso 48, p. 295).

3. si truova al fine della sua *patria*, non può tanto dolersi della disgrazia di quella e chiamarla mal fortunate (*Opere* VIII, *Ricordi, Serie Seconda*, Capoverso 189, p. 327).

4. quanto della sua propria; perché alla *patria* è accaduto quello che a ogni modo aveva a accadere (*Opere* VIII, *Ricordi, Serie Seconda*, Capoverso 189, p. 327).

5. Credo sia uficio di buoni cittadini, quando la *patria* viene in mano di tiranni (*Opere* VIII, *Ricordi, Serie Seconda*, Capoverso 220, p. 335).

Patria in Guicciardini's *Consolatoria* in *Opere*, Volume IX, *Scritti autobiografici e rari* (1936).

1. vedervi aperta la via di collocare nella tua *patria* le tue figliuole con migliori e più onorati partiti che vi fussino. (*Opere* IX, *Consolatoria*, Capoverso 1, pp. 165–166).

2. in quello che depende dalla *patria* tua, non posso credere che el dispiacere tuo non sia infinito (*Opere* IX, *Consolatoria*, Capoverso 2, pp. 166).

3. tu perda per modo di parlare la civilità e forse la *patria*, donde oltre alli altri incommodi ti si difficulta mirabilmente el maritare delle figliuole (*Opere* IX, *Consolatoria*, Capoverso 2, pp. 166).

4. perché io so quanto sempre hai amato la *patria*, e quanto capitale hai sempre fatto di avervi drento buona grazia e buona fama (*Opere* IX, *Consolatoria*, Capoverso 4, p. 167).

5. acquistato nelle provincie forestiere, ora nella *patria* tua alla quale sempre hai avuto la mira (*Opere* IX, *Consolatoria*, Capoverso 4, p. 168).

6. ma a quello che hanno e' pari tuoi nella *patria* tua; perché ti senti percosso in quello tesoro che stimavi quanto la vita (*Opere* IX, *Consolatoria*, Capoverso 10, p. 171).

7. non solo e' cittadini e sudditi della mia *patria*, ma né anche gli strani (*Opere* IX, *Consolatoria*, Capoverso 11, p. 172).

8. avendo fatto innumerabili benefici alla *patria*, non solo sono stati (*Opere* IX, *Consolatoria*, Capoverso 13, p. 173).

9. e se bene tutto è stato fuora della *patria*, nondimeno e per el grido di molti (*Opere* IX, *Consolatoria*, Capoverso 26, p. 181).

10. potere essere utile alla *patria* o agli altri (*Opere* IX, *Consolatoria*, Capoverso 27, p. 182).

11. quando n'abbia occasione o quando la *patria* ti ricerchi (*Opere* IX, *Consolatoria*, Capoverso 27, p. 182).

12. sono forse centinaia di anni che della *patria* nostra non uscì cittadino più onorato di te. (*Opere* IX, *Consolatoria*, Capoverso 28, p. 182).

13. che abbino autorità nella *patria* sua; ma chi consìdera bene, non è manco bello vivere libero dalle cupidità (*Opere* IX, *Consolatoria*, Capoverso 31, p. 184).

14. non vedere el conspetto della ingrata *patria*, fu in tanta esistimazione apresso (*Opere* IX, *Consolatoria*, Capoverso 35, p. 186).

15. potrai vivere onestamente secondo el costume della tua *patria*, ed in esse hai guadagnato quello che era da stimare più di tutto (*Opere* IX, *Consolatoria*, Capoverso 37, pp. 188–189).

16. ed altre buone qualità che hai nella *patria*, non sarà la vita tua abietta ed incognita (*Opere* IX, *Consolatoria*, Capoverso 38, p. 189).

Patria in Guicciardini's *Accusatoria* in *Opere*, Volume IX, *Scritti autobiografici e rari* (1936).

1. acciò che uno medesimo luogo fussi memoria dell'onore di chi ha conservato la *patria*, e del supplicio di chi l'ha oppressa. (*Opere* IX, *Accusatoria*, Capoverso 6, p. 197).

2. alcuna umanità, alcuna pietà alla sua *patria* ed a' suoi cittadini,

credevano portassi loro odio e gli avessi per inimici (*Opere* IX, *Accusatoria*, Capoverso 9, p. 199).

3.   come se tu fussi defensore della *patria* e non sceleratissimo predone e corsale, come se tu fussi conservatore di questa libertà e non uno immanissimo e pestifero tiranno. (*Opere* IX, *Accusatoria*, Capoverso 10, p. 200).

4.   Oh, e' non è stata offesa la *patria* sola, ma el publico, el privato (*Opere* IX, *Accusatoria*, Capoverso 12, p. 201).

5.   Oh tu sei uno esemplo di tutti e' mali che può fare uno cittadino alla *patria*. Speri tu nella nostra buona natura (*Opere* IX, *Accusatoria*, Capoverso 13, p. 201).

6.   non ti pareva debito farsi nello stato della tua *patria*? Avevavi accecati tutt'a dua tanto (*Opere* IX, *Accusatoria*, Capoverso 17, p. 204).

7.   l'abbia voluto cattivo nella *patria*; produrrà testimoni, fede, lettere di quelle comunità (*Opere* IX, *Accusatoria*, Capoverso 18, p. 205).

8.   bene universale e della libertà della sua *patria*. Ma quando mi rivolgo (*Opere* IX, *Accusatoria*, Capoverso 26, p. 211).

9.   el frutto de' quali fu poi la ruína della *patria*? Non so parlare per molto tempo degli anni che seguirono a quella età (*Opere* IX, *Accusatoria*, Capoverso 28, p. 212).

10.   operatore di tôrre la libertà della sua *patria* perché contienein sé tanti tristi effetti (*Opere* IX, *Accusatoria*, Capoverso 32, p. 215).

11.   che avendo in sì giovane età conseguito dalla *patria* sua con commune consenso (*Opere* IX, *Accusatoria*, Capoverso 33, p. 215).

12–13.   el piede in sul collo alla *patria* sua, ed a quella *patria* con la quale aveva tutte le obligazione commune (*Opere* IX, *Accusatoria*, Capoverso 33, p. 215).

14.   che siamo cittadini di una medesima *patria*, e della conversazione che in quelli primi tempi ebbi teco (Capoverso 34, p. 216).

15.   ed oscurare el nome della *patria*, farsi inimico a tutti e' cittadini (Capoverso 34, p. 216).

16.   inimico della libertà della sua *patria*; questo è stato el vinculo (*Opere* IX, *Accusatoria*, Capoverso 36, p. 218).

17.   onorato e chiamato da tutti, vendesti per schiavi, rimettesti in servitù la *patria*, te ed ognuno (*Opere* IX, *Accusatoria*, Capoverso 42, p. 221).

18.   tu solo di tutta questa *patria* rimettesti el giogo in sul collo a ognuno. (*Opere* IX, *Accusatoria*, Capoverso 42, p. 222).

19.   scritte lettere pregandolo che venissi a soccorrere la sua *patria*, che menassi alla salute nostra gli eserciti pagati da noi (*Opere* IX, *Accusatoria*, Capoverso 45, p. 223).

20.   e che non amando la *patria* sua non poteva amare la nostra (*Opere* IX, *Accusatoria*, Capoverso 45, p. 224).

21.   questo el trionfo che tu n'hai cavato, orribile inimico della tua *patria*, la quale non ti può perdonare tanta atrocità, né te la perdonerebbe tuo padre se fussi vivo. (*Opere* IX, *Accusatoria*, Capoverso 45, p. 224).

22.   come se lui fussi buono cittadino sarebbono grate ed utili alla *patria*, così essendo el contrario sono pericolose. (*Opere* IX, *Accusatoria*, Capoverso 49, p. 226).

23.   affaticato assai per la *patria*; era noto in tutta Italia, grato in Francia donde allora dependevano le cose nostre (*Opere* IX, *Accusatoria*, Capoverso 51, p. 227).

24.   perché principalmente questo è delitto contro alla *patria*, alla quale siamo più obligati che a' parenti, che al padre, che a noi medesimi. Ordinarono le legge supplicio crudelissimo a chi amazza el padre (*Opere* IX, *Accusatoria*, Capoverso 60, p. 232–233).

25.   quanto più merita chi amazza la *patria*, con la quale abbiamo maggiore vinculo (*Opere* IX, *Accusatoria*, Capoverso 60, p. 233).

26.   e con lo affaticarsi e mettersi a pericolo per la *patria*. Perché sempre
        e' savi (*Opere* IX, *Accusatoria*, Capoverso 62, p. 235).

27.   e fatto del sangue tuo quello sacrificio che si doveva alla *patria* ed
        alla nostra libertà (*Opere* IX, *Accusatoria*, Capoverso 65, p. 236).

28.   ma permesso che usi la *patria*, usi la civiltà, usi tutti e' benefici
        (*Opere* IX, *Accusatoria*, Capoverso 66, p. 237).

29.   se questa mansuetudine che tu alleghi è crudeltà contro alla *patria*,
        chi è quello che non vede che per la salute tua non si debbe
        distruggere la salute nostra? (*Opere* IX, *Accusatoria*, Capoverso 67,
        p. 238).

30.   inimico di Dio e degli uomini, inimico della *patria* e delle provincie
        forestiere (*Opere* IX, *Accusatoria*, Capoverso 75, p. 243).

31.   l'ho presa voluntariamente, non aspettava questo da me la *patria*, non
        avevo obligazione propria di farlo (*Opere* IX, *Accusatoria*,
        Capoverso 77, p. 243).

32.   della libertà, della salute di questa *patria*, che mancando del debito
        vostro (*Opere* IX, *Accusatoria*, Capoverso 79, p. 243).

Patria in Guicciardini's *Defensoria*, in *Opere*, Volume 9, *Scritti*
autobiografici e rari (1936).

1.   Benché più laudabile era cercare di mostrare alla *patria* prudenzia o
        bontà che artificio di parlare (*Opere* IX, *Defensoria*, Capoverso 13,
        p. 256).

2.   avessi imparato che la *patria* ha bisogno di cittadini buoni, (*Opere*
        IX, *Defensoria*, Capoverso 13, p. 256).

3.   Vogliono le legge che in ogni causa benché minima si sappino e'
        nomi de' testimoni, la *patria*, la origine, la vita, le dependenzie
        (*Opere* IX, *Defensoria*, Capoverso 18, p. 258).

4.   essendo negli occhi della *patria* e di tutti e' cittadini, a' quali chi non

ha desiderio di satisfare (*Opere* IX, *Defensoria*, Capoverso 29, p. 264).

5.   avevo a essere tenuto nella *patria* mia ladro publico (*Opere* IX, *Defensoria*, Capoverso 34, p. 267).

6–7.   Se io avessi perduto la roba, se io avessi perduto e' figliuoli, se avessi perduto la *patria*, non mi dorrebbe la metà (*Opere* IX, *Defensoria*, Capoverso 35, p. 267).

7.   troppo mi pare disonesto che in sullo uscio della *patria* mia mi sia caduto quello buono nome (*Opere* IX, *Defensoria*, Capoverso 35, p. 267).

8.   avessi cominciato a rubare nella *patria* sua, dove aveva a vivere e che aveva autorità di punirlo con odio infinito di ognuno (*Opere* IX, *Defensoria*, Capoverso 39, pp. 269–270).

Patrie in the *Consolatoria*

1.   mandati in esilio e qualche volta dalli ingrati popoli e *patrie* privati della vita. (*Opere* IX, *Consolatoria*, Capoverso 13, p. 173).

Patrie in the *Defensoria*

1.   e che erano lo specchio ed ornamento delle loro *patrie*; anzi pare che questa, o invidia o fortuna che la sia (*Opere* IX, *Defensoria*, Capoverso VIII, p. 254).

2.   in grandissima licenzia, in *patrie* forestieri delle quali non aveva a tenere conto (*Opere* IX, *Defensoria*, Capoverso 39, p. 269).

APPENDIX SEVEN

Patria and Related Words in the First Ten Books of Livy's *Ab urbe condita*

ℰℒℭℬ

Patria in the First Ten Books of Titus Livy's *Ab urbe condita*. See Titus Livy, *Ab urbe condita* vol I. (Books I–II) trans. B.O. Foster. Cambridge, Mass: Harvard University Press, 10th edn., 1998.

1. ducem Aeneam filium Anchisae et Veneris, cremata *patria* domo profugos, sedem condendaeque urbi locum quaerere. (Volume I, Liber I. i.6–8, p. 10).

2. Cum trigeminis agunt reges ut pro sua quisque *patria* dimicent ferro; ibi imperium fore unde victoria fuerit. (Volume I, Liber I. xxiv. 2, p. 82).

3. quae velut dis quoque simul cum *patria* relictis oblivioni dederant. (Volume I, Liber I. xxxi.3, p. 110).

4. "Iniustum esse neque ius persolvere; sed de istis rebus in *patria* maiores natu consulemus, quo pacto ius nostrum adipiscamur." (Volume I, Liber I. xxxii.10, p. 116).

5. Facile persuadet ut cupido honorum et cui Tarquinii materna tantum *patria* esset. (Volume I, Liber I. xxxiv.7, p. 124).

6. Romae se quam in vetere *patria* vixisse; domi militiaeque sub haud paenitendo magistro (Volume I, Liber I. xxxv.4, p. 128).

7. fortunam matris, quod, capta *patria* in hostium manus venerit, ut serva natus crederetur fecisse. (Volume I, Liber I. xxxix.6, p. 140).

8.   inflammatus ira "ille est vir" inquit, "qui nos extorres expulit *patria*".
        (Volume I, Liber II. vi.7, p. 236).

9.   quod liberata *patria*, in summo honore, pro re publica dimicans,
        (Volume I, Liber II. vii.8, p. 240).

10.   Iuberem macte virtut esse, si pro mea *patria* ista virtus staret; nunc
        iure belli liberum te, intactum inviolatumque hinc dimitto. (Volume
        I, Liber II. xii.14, p. 258).

11.   aut plebi honestum esse, nisi mercede prius accepta, arma pro *patria*
        non cepisse. (Volume I, Liber II. xxiv.4–5, p. 296).

12.   libertatem unicuique prius reddendam esse quam arma danda, ut pro
        patria civibusque, non pro dominis pugnent. (Volume I, Liber II.
        xxviii.6–7, p. 308).

13.   Roma non oppugnaretur; nisi filium haberem, libera in libera *patria*
        mortua essem. (Volume I, Liber II. xl.8, p. 348).

Patria in Livy Continued in Titus Livy, *Ab urbe condita* vol. II.
(Books III–IV) trans. B.O. Foster. Cambridge, Mass.: Harvard
University Press, 6th edn., 1997.

14.   Dissolvi licentia militandi morem, nec pro communi iam *patria*
        Romam esse. (Volume II, Liber III. lxvi.4, p. 222).

15.   "nec rei publicae est verecundia, *patria* maiestas altercationem istam
        dirimet". (Volume II, Liber IV. xlv.8, p. 404).

16.   effectum esse fatentibus ut nemo pro tam munifica *patria*, donec
        quicquam virium superesset, corpori aut sanguini suo parceret.
        (Volume II, Liber IV. lx.1, p. 452).

Patria in Livy Continued in Titus Livy, *Ab urbe condita* vol. III.
(Books V–VII) trans. B.O. Foster. Cambridge, Mass.: Harvard
University Press, 6th edn., 1996.

17.   Nos tamquam cum civibus agere volumus, agique tamquam cum

patria nobiscum aequum censemus. (Volume III, Liber V. iv.8, p. 12).

18. "Bello perfecto donum amplum victor ad mea templa portato, sacraque *patria*, quorum omissa cura est, instaurata ut adsolet facito." (Volume III, Liber V. xvi.11, p. 58).

19. Postremo se relinqui a civibus in *patria* posse: ut relinquant patriam atque cives nullam vim unquam subacturam. (Volume III, Liber V. xxiv.10–11, p. 84).

20. et in captivo solo habitare populum Romanum et victrice *patria* victam mutari. (Volume III, Liber V. xxx.3, p. 105).

21. Sunt qui M. Folio pontifice maximo praefante carmen devovisse eos se pro *patria* Quiritibusque Romanis tradant. (Volume III, Liber V. xli.3–4, p. 142).

22. tanto ante alios miserandi magis qui unquam obsessi sunt quod interclusi a *patria* obsidebantur, omnia sua cernentes in hostium potestate. (Volume III, Liber V. xlii.4–5, pp. 142 and 144).

23. Hac arte in *patria* steti et invictus bello, in pace ab ingratis civibus pulsus sum. (Volume III, Liber V. xliv.2–3, p. 148).

24. Dictator reciperata ex hostibus *patria* triumphans in urbem redit, interque iocos militares quos inconditos iaciunt. (Volume III, Liber V. xlix.7, p. 166).

25–27. Nec nunc me ut redirem mea voluntas mutata sed vestra fortuna perpulit; quippe ut in sua sede maneret *patria*, id agebatur, non ut ego utique in *patria* essem. Et nunc quiescerem ac tacerem libenter nisi haec quoque pro *patria* dimicatio esset; cui deesse, quoad vita suppetat, aliis turpe, Camillo etiam nefas est. (Volume III, Liber V. li.2, p. 170).

28. cum abessem, quotienscumque *patria* in mentem veniret, haec omnia occurrebant. (Volume III, Liber V. liv.2–3, p. 182).

29. Falerios Veiosque captos et in capta *patria* Gallorum legiones caesas taceam. (Volume III, Liber VI. vii.4–5, p. 218).

30. a M. Furio reciperari *patria* ex obsidione hostium non potuerit (Volume III, Liber VI. xi.4–5, p. 230).

31. quodcumque sibi cum *patria* penatibus publicis ac privatis iuris fuerit, id cum uno homine esse. (Volume III, Liber VI. xiv.8, p. 242).

32. se ita pugnaturos ut Romae pugnaverint in repetenda *patria* ut postero die ad Gabios. (Volume III, Liber VI. xxvii.9, pp. 294 and 296).

33. eoque id laudabilius erat quod animum eius tanta acerbitas *patria* nihil a pietate avertisset. (Volume III, Liber VII. v.7, p. 370).

34. Quinctius, quem armorum etiam pro *patria* satietas teneret. (Volume III, Liber VII. xl.3, pp. 502 and 504).

Patria in Livy Continued in Titus Livy, *Ab urbe condita* vol. IV. (Books VIII–X) trans. B.O. Foster. Cambridge, Mass.: Harvard University Press, 1st edn., 1926.

35. bene vertat, sit haec sane *patria* potior et Romani omnes vocemur. (Volume IV, Liber VIII. v.6, p. 16).

36. eo facto utrum ab se prodita an servata *patria* videatur, in fide Romana positum esse. (Volume IV, Liber VIII. xxv.10–11, p. 100).

37. Equidem mortem pro *patria* praeclaram esse fateor et me vel devovere pro populo Romano legionibusque vel in medios me immittere hostes paratus sum. (Volume IV, Liber IX. iv.10, p. 176).

38. cuius vi atque iniuriis compulsi, extorres *patria* Sacrum montem cepistis. (Volume IV, Liber IX. xxxiv.3, p. 290).

Patriam in Livy's *Ab urbe condita*

1. Ubi nomen patremque ac *patriam* accepit, "Iove nate, Hercules, salve." (Volume I, Liber I. vii.10, p. 28).

2. deos patrios, *patriam* ac parentes, quidquid civium domi, quidquid in

exercitu sit. (Volume I, Liber I. xxv., pp. 84 and 86).

3.　oblitaque ingenitae erga *patriam* caritatis dummodo virum honoratum videret, consilium migrandi ab Tarquiniis cepit. (Volume I, Liber I. xxxiv.5, p. 124).

4.　Illos eo potissimum anno *patriam* liberatam, patrem liberatorem, consulatum ortum ex domo Iunia. (Volume I, Liber II. v.7, p. 232).

5.　*Patriam* se regnumque suum repetere et persequi ingratos cives velle. (Volume I, Liber II. vii.3, pp. 234 and 236).

6.　precantur ut illud agmen faustum atque felix mittant, sospites brevi in *patriam* ad parentes restituant. (Volume I, Liber II. xlix.7, p. 386).

7.　ut exsules iniuria pulsos in *patriam* reduceret et servitiis grave iugum demeret. (Volume II, Liber III. xv.8–9, pp. 52 and 54).

8.　a cetero populo vestram *patriam* peculiaremque rem publicam fecistis (Volume II, Liber III. xix.9–10, pp. 66 and 68).

9.　Aventinum obsedissent belloque averso ab hostibus *patriam* suam cepissent. (Volume II, Liber III. l.15, p. 166).

10.　"Quod bonum faustum felixque sit vobis reique publicae, redite in *patriam* ad penates coniuges liberosque vestros." (Volume II, Liber III. liv.7–8, p. 178).

11.　infestus Regillum, antiquam in *patriam*, se contulerat, is magno iam natu cum ad pericula eius deprecanda redisset cuius vitia fugerat. (Volume II, Liber III. lviii.1, p. 194).

12.　Ecquando unam urbem habere, ecquando communem hanc esse *patriam* licebit? (Volume II, Liber III. lxvii.10, p. 228).

13.　appellare tribunos communem *patriam* auxiliumque eorum implorare vastatis agris, urbe prope oppugnata. (Volume II, Liber III. lxix.5, p. 234).

14.　Quid esse aliud quam minari se proditurum *patriam*, oppugnari atque capi passurum! (Volume II, Liber IV. ii.13, p. 262).

15.   si non easdem opes habere, eandem tamen *patriam* incolere?
       (Volume II, Liber IV iii.1–2, pp. 262 and 264).

16.   memorem pietatis eorum erga *patriam* dicerent senatum fore.
       (Volume III, Liber V. vii.11, p. 26).

17.   Postremo se relinqui a civibus in patria posse: ut relinquant *patriam*
       atque cives nullam vim unquam subacturam, et T. Sicinium.
       (Volume III, Liber V. xxiv.10–11, p. 84).

18.   orare cum lacrimis coepere ne eam *patriam* pro qua fortissime
       felicissimeque. (Volume III, Liber V. xxx.4–5, p. 106).

19.   quibus non arma ferre, non tueri *patriam* possent, oneraturos
       inopiam armatorum. (Volume III, Liber V. xxxix.13, pp. 134 and
       136).

20.   maturum iam videbatur repeti *patriam* eripique ex hostium manibus;
       sed corpori valido caput deerat. (Volume III, Liber V. xlvi.4, p. 154).

21.   Suos in acervum conicere sarcinas et arma aptare ferroque non auro
       reciperare *patriam* iubet, in conspectu habentes fana deum et
       coniuges et liberos. (Volume III, Liber V. xlix.2–3, p. 164).

22.   Servatam deinde bello *patriam* iterum in pace haud dubie servavit
       cum prohibuit migrari Veios. (Volume III, Liber V. xlix.7, p. 166).

23.   Reddidere igitur *patriam* et victoriam et antiquum belli decus
       amissum. (Volume III, Liber V. li.10, p. 172).

24.   Non enim reliquisse victores, sed amisisse victi *patriam* videbimur:
       hoc ad Alliam fuga. (Volume III, Liber V. liii.5, p. 180).

25–26. vel felicitate qua restitutus in *patriam* secum *patriam* ipsam restituit.
       (Volume III, Liber VII. i.9–11, p. 358).

27.   Etiam ad Alliam fusae legiones eandem quam per pavorem
       amiserant *patriam* profectae postea a Veiis virtute reciperavere.
       (Volume III, Liber VII. xiii.5, p. 398).

28.   Quinctius, quem armorum etiam pro patria satietas teneret nedum

adversus *patriam*, Corvinus omnes caritate cives. (Volume III, Liber VII. xl.3–4, pp. 502 and 504).

29.   fugeris etiam honestius tergumque civi dederis quam pugnaveris contra *patriam*. (Volume III, Liber VII. xl.12–13, pp. 506).

30.   T. Manli, neque imperium consulare neque maiestatem *patriam* veritus, adversus edictum nostrum extra ordinem in hostem pugnasti et. (Volume IV, Liber VIII. vii.15–17, p. 26).

31.   Vitruvium iudicasse, cum receptaculum fugae Privernum habuerit non *patriam* (Fundanos). (Volume IV, Liber VIII. xix.10, p. 76).

32–34. Sed hic *patriam* video, hic quidquid Romanarum legionum est....hic omnes spes opesque sunt, quas servando *patriam* servamus, dedendo ad necem *patriam* deserimus (ac prodimus). (Volume IV, Liber IX. iv.11–16, p. 176).

35.   inde foedi agminis miserabilem viam per sociorum urbes, reditum in *patriam* ad parentes, quo saepe ipsi maioresque eorum triumphantes venissent: se solos sine volnere, sine ferro, sine acie victos. (Volume IV, Liber IX. v.8–9, pp. 178 and 180).

36.   Non enim tamquam in *patriam* revertentes ex insperato incolumes sed captorum habitu voltuque. (Volume IV, Liber IX. vii.10–11, p. 186).

Patriae in Livy's *Ab urbe condita*

1.   servitiumque obversatur animo futuraque ea deinde *patriae* fortuna quam ipsi fecissent. (Volume I, Liber I. xxv.3, p. 86).

2.   "oblita fratrum mortuorum vivique, oblita *patriae*." (Volume I, Liber I. xxvi.3–4, p. 90).

3.   "Si ego iniuste impieque illos homines illasque res dedier mihi eco, tum *patriae* compotem me nunquam siris esse." (Volume I, Liber I. xxxii.7, p. 116).

4.   ni scelus intestinum liberandae *patriae* consilia agitanti intervenisset.

(Volume I, Liber I. xlviii.9, p. 170).

5.   ex liberatore *patriae* ad Aquilios se Vitelliosque recidisse. (Volume I, Liber II. vii.8, p. 240).

6.   Damnatus absens in Volscos exsulatum abiit, minitans *patriae* hostilesque iam tum spiritus gerens. (Volume I, Liber II. xxxv.6, p. 334).

7.   velut contacta civitate rabie duorum iuvenum funestas nuptias ex occasu *patriae* petentium. (Volume II, Liber IV. ix.8–9, p. 288).

8.   anno sororis filios regis et liberos consulis, liberatoris *patriae*, propter pactionem indicatam recipiendorum. (Volume II, Liber IV. xv.3–4, pp. 306 and 308).

9.   Adeo, quidquid tribunus plebi loquitur, etsi prodendae *patriae* dissolvendae rei publicae est. (Volume III, Liber V. vi.15, p. 22).

10.   Veienti populo illo fuisse die quo sibi eam mentem obiecissent ut excidium *patriae* fatale proderet. (Volume III, Liber V. xv.8–9, p. 54).

11.   excidium illius urbis servandaeque *patriae*, M. Furius Camillus, dictator dictus magistrum. (Volume III, Liber V. xix.2–3, pp. 64 and 66).

12.   Victamne ut quisquam victrici *patriae* praeferret sineretque maiorem fortunam captis esse Veiis quam incolumibus fuerit? (Volume III, Liber V. xxiv.10, p. 84).

13.   Nam quod ad se privatim attineat, si suae gloriae sibi inter dimicationem *patriae* meminisse sit fas. (Volume III, Liber V. xxx.2–3, p. 84).

14.   velut ad spectaculum a fortuna positi occidentis *patriae* nec ullius rerum suarum relicti praeterquam corporum vindices. (Volume III, Liber V. xlii.4–5, pp. 142 and 144).

15.   in conspectu habentes fana deum et coniuges et liberos et solum *patriae* deforme belli malis et omnia quae defendi. (Volume III,

Liber V. xlix.3, p. 164).

16. Romulus ac parens *patriae* conditorque alter urbis haud vanis laudibus appellabatur. (Volume III, Liber V. xlix.7, p. 166).

17–18. Adeo nihil tenet solum *patriae* nec haec terra quam matrem appellamus, sed in superficie tignisque caritas nobis *patriae* pendet? (Volume III, Liber V. liv.2, p. 182).

19. Selibrisne farris gratiam servatori *patriae* relatam? (Volume III, Liber VI. xvii.5, p. 252).

20. tristia responsa reddita, tristiora colonis quod cives Romani *patriae* oppugnandae nefanda consilia inissent. (Volume III, Liber VI. xvii.7, p. 254).

21. Fuit cum hoc dici poterat: patricius enim eras et a liberatoribus *patriae* ortus, et eodem anno familia ista consulatum quo urbs haec consulem habuit. (Volume III, Liber VII. xxxii.13–14, p. 470).

22. animos avertit a memoria *patriae*, inibanturque consilia in hibernis. (Volume III, Liber VII. xxxviii.5–6, pp. 494 and 496).

23. Ubi primum in conspectum ventum est (et) arma signaque agnovere, extemplo omnibus memoria *patriae* iras permulsit. (Volume III, Liber VII. xl.1, p. 502).

24. Samnio nec in Volscis sed in Romano solo castra habere, si illos colles quos cernitis *patriae* vestrae esse, si hunc exercitum civium vestrorum, si me consulem vestrum. (Volume III, Liber VII. xl.5–6, p. 504).

25. eodem haec imperiosa dictatura geretur; ut neque in hos meos et *patriae* meae milites (sim) mitior quam in vos. (Volume III, Liber VII. xl.9–10, p. 506).

26. "integri adversus fessos, memores *patriae* parentumque et coniugum ac liberorum, memores consulis pro vestra victoria morte occubantis." (Volume IV, Liber VIII. x.3–5, pp. 38 and 40).

27. et ipsi aut suarum rerum aut partium in re publica magis quam

patriae memores. (Volume IV, Liber VIII. xii.2–3, p. 48).

28.   populi Romani quaerendos persequendosque esse, qui simul a Fundanis ac Romanis utriusque *patriae* immemores defecerint. (Volume IV, Liber VIII. xix.10–12, p. 76).

29.   At foeda atque ignominiosa deditio est. Sed ea caritas *patriae* est ut tam ignominia eam quam morte nostra, si opus sit, servemus. (Volume IV, Liber IX. iv.15–16, p. 176).

30.   non publica solum auctoritate moverent ut memoriam simultatium *patriae* remitteret. (Volume IV, Liber IX. xxxviii.10–12, p. 176).

Patriamque in Livy's *Ab urbe*

1.   Ea quo maiore pugnabat ira ob erepta bona *patriamque* ademptam, pugnam parumper restituit. (Volume I, Liber II. xix.10, p. 280).

2.   Tum dictator "macte virtute" inquit "ac pietate in patrem *patriamque*, T. Manli, esto". (Volume III, Liber VII. x.4, p. 384).

Patriaeque in Livy's *Ab urbe*

1.   cum suam vicem functus officio sit, parentium etiam *patriaeque* expleat desiderium. (Volume I, Liber I. ix.15, p. 38).

2.   fletusque ob omni turba mulierum ortus et comploratio sui *patriaeque* fregere tandem virum. (Volume I, Liber II. xl.9–10, p. 350).

Notes

ಬುಐಲ

Introduction

1. Federico Chabod, *"The Prince*: Myth and Reality" in *Machiavelli and the Renaissance* trans. David Moore (London: Bowes and Bowes, 1958): 30–125. See p. 61.

2. De Lamar Jensen, ed., *Machiavelli, Cynic, Patriot or Political Scientist?* (Boston: D.C. Heath and Co., 1960). This is an interesting collection of essays and extracts that deals with these aspects of Machiavelli's posthumous persona.

3. For comparison, see A. Richard Turner, *Inventing Leonardo* (New York: Knopf, 1993) and Peter Burke, *The Fortunes of the "Courtier"* (Cambridge: Polity Press, 1995).

4. Christopher Marlowe, *The Jew of Malta* ed. James R. Siemon (London: A. and C. Black, 1997), 9. Act One, opening lines. "Albeit the world think Machevill is dead, Yet was his soul but flown beyond the Alps, And now the Guise is dead, is come from France To view this land, and frolic with his friends. To some perhaps my name is odious, But such as love me, guard me from their tongues, And let them know that I am Machevill, And weigh not men, and therefore not men's words."

5. William Shakespeare, "Henry VI, Part III," *The Complete Signet Classic Shakespeare*, ed. Sylvan Barnet (New York: Harcourt Brace Jovanovich, 1972), 190–232. See III. ii. 182–195, pp. 215–216. "Why, I can smile, and murder whiles I smile, And cry, "Content" to that which grieves my heart, And wet my cheeks with artificial tears, And frame my face to all occasions. I'll drown more sailors than the mermaid shall; I'll slay more gazers than the basilisk; I'll play the orator as well as Nestor, Deceive more slyly than Ulysses could, And, like a Sinon, take another Troy. I can add colors to the chameleon, Change shapes with Proteus for advantages, And set the murderous Machiavel to school. Can I do this, and cannot get a crown? Tut, were it farther off, I'll pluck it down."

6. Niccolò Machiavelli, *Nicholas Machiavel's Prince: Also "The Life of Castruccio Castracani of Luca" and "The Means Duke Valentino us'd to put to death Vitellozzo Vitelli, Oliverotto of Fermo, Paul and the Duke of Gravina"* trans. Edward Dacres (Amsterdam: Da Capo, 1969—facsimile of 1640 edition printed in London by Bishop and Hils). And, Peter Godman, *From Poliziano to Machiavelli: Florentine Humanism in the High Renaissance* (Princeton: Princeton University Press, 1998), 303–333 for an overview of Machiavelli's works and the Inquisition and the Index. If one wishes to know why Machiavelli's *opere* was dragged before the Inquisition, Chapter 15 of *Il Principe*, titled "Di quelle cose per le quali li uomini, e specialmente i principi sono laudati o vituperate," provides an example. See Niccolò Machiavelli, *Il Principe e Altre Opere Politiche* Introduzione di Delio

Cantimori, Note di Stefano Andretta (Milano: Garzanti Libri, 1999), 60–61.

7.   Allan H. Gilbert, *Machiavelli's "Prince" and Its Forerunners: "The Prince" as a Typical Book "de Regimine Principum"* (Durham, N.C.: Duke University Press, 1938), 231–237. See also Quentin Skinner, *Machiavelli* (Oxford: Oxford University Press, 1996), 40–47.

8.   For a fine example of Machiavelli's attitude toward the church, at least in *Il Principe*, see *Il Principe, 1999*, 47–49. That Chapter, 11, is titled, "De principati ecclesiastici."

9.   Jean-Jacques Rousseau, *Le Contrat Social* (Paris, 1782). See Book III, Chapter 6. The translation is by Maurizio Viroli, *Machiavelli* (Oxford: Oxford University Press, 1998), 209, n. 6. "Machiavelli was a decent man and a good citizen. But, being attached to the court of the Medicis, he could not help veiling his love of liberty in the midst of his country's oppression. The choice of his detestable hero, Caesar Borgia, clearly shows his hidden aim; and the contradiction between the teaching of *The Prince* and that of the *Discourses on Livy* and the *History of Florence* shows that this profound political thinker has so far been studied only by superficial or corrupt readers. The Court of Rome sternly prohibited his Book. I can believe it; for it is that court that it most clearly portrays."

10.   See Chabod, "Myth and Reality," 115, where he cites Francisco Quevedo, "Lince de Italia," in *Obras* (Madrid, 1880), 237. "El duque de Saboya ha tomado por sì la eshortacion lisonjera que Nicolas Maquiavelo hace al fin del libro del tirano, que el llama Principe: para librar à Italia de los barbaros, hàse dado por entendido de las sutilezas del Bocalino, y de las malicias y susposciones de la Pietra del Paragone; y determinò edificarse liberatador de Italia, titulo dificil cuanto magnifico."

11.   Francesco de Sanctis, *Storia della letteratura Italiana, nuove edizione* 2 Vols. A cura di Benedetto Croce (Bari: Laterza e Figli, 1912). See Vol. 1, pp. 421–422. "Il concetto del Machiavelli è questo, che bisogna considerare le cose nella loro verità «effettuale», cioè come son porte dall'esperienza ed osservate dall'intelletto; che era proprio il rovescio del sillogismo e la base dottrinale del medio evo capovolta: concetto ben altrimenti rivoluzionario che non è quel ritorno al puro spirito della Riforma e che sarà la leva da cui uscirà la scienza moderna...Questo concetto applicato all'uomo ti dà *Il Principe* e i *Discorsi*, e la *Storia di firenze* e i *Dialoghi sulla milizia*. E il Machiavelli non ha bisogno di dimostrarlo: te lo dà come evidente. Era la parola del secolo ch'egli trovava e che tutti riconoscevano...Così nasce la scienza dell'uomo, non quale può o dee essere, ma quale è... La «divina commedia» diviene la «commedia umana» e si rappresenta in terra: si chiama storia, politica, filosofia della storia, la scienza nuova...Non è il caso di disputare sulla verità o falsità delle dottrine. Non fo una storia e meno un trattato di filosofia. Scrivo la storia delle lettere. Ed è mio obbligo notare ciò che si move nel pensiero italiano; perchè quello solo è vivo nella letteratura che è vivo nella coscienza."

12.   Chabod, "Myth and Reality," 61–62. "The primordial, the ultimate character of this world—devoid of great moral and political motifs, uninfluenced by the masses, having its being solely in the isolated virtue of scattered individuals, who left their own imprint on material that was flabby and incoherent—finds its true expression in *The Prince*. The latter is not exactly a history of the Seigniories and Principates, if by history we mean the detailed examination and the minute and constant assessment of specific events.   Rather does it summarize and illustrate the

consequences of history, revealing them in broad outline, stripped of all irrelevancy. Naturally, it does not go into details—Machiavelli is not at all concerned now with writing history—and these must be sought elsewhere, just as we have to look elsewhere for a precise, factual account of the course which Italian life pursued in the fourteenth and fifteenth centuries. Here we have merely the fundamental principle which determines and informs various immediate manifestations of that life—a principle that is at the same time a consequence."

13. Ibid. See the subheading "The Errors in Machiavelli's Assessment of History," 85–93.

14. Ernst Cassirer, *The Myth of the State: A reduced photographic reprint of the 1946 edition* (New Haven: Yale University Press, 1961), 142.

15. For example, Benito Mussolini's infatuation with Machiavelli's *Il Principe* is just one reason why Cassirer's views were framed thus. See the excerpt from Emil Ludwig's "Talks with Mussolini" in *Italy from the Risorgimento to Fascism: An Enquiry into the Origins of the Totalitarian State* ed. A. William Salomone (Devon: Redwood Press, 1971), 206–207. There Mussolini details his affinity for Machiavelli. "My father used to read the book aloud in the evenings, when we were warming ourselves beside the smithy fire and were drinking the *vin ordinaire* produced from our own vineyard. It made a deep impression on me. When, at the age of forty, I read Machiavelli once again, the effect was reinforced."

16. J.H. Whitfield, *Discourses on Machiavelli* (Cambridge, Heffer, 1969); Felix Gilbert, *Machiavelli and Guicciardini: Politics and History in Sixteenth-Century Florence* (Princeton: Princeton University Press, 1965); and Hans Baron, "Machiavelli the Republican Citizen and Author of The Prince," in Hans Baron, *In Search of Florentine Civic Humanism: Essays on the Transition from Medieval to Modern Thought* Vol. 2 (Princeton: Princeton University Press, 1988), 101–157.

17. Maurizio Viroli, *From Politics to Reason of State: The Acquisition and Transformation of the Language of Politics, 1250–1600* (Cambridge: Cambridge University Press, 1992). See Chapter Three, "Machiavelli and the republican concept of politics," 126–177. By the same author see *Machiavelli*.

18. Viroli, *Reason of State*, 128–130.

19. Francesco Guicciardini, *Considerazioni intorno ai Discorsi del Machiavelli sopra la Primi Deca di Tito Livio* in *Opere 8: Scritti politici e ricordi* A cura di Roberto Palmarocchi (Bari: Laterza, 1933), 1–65.

20. Baron, "Machiavelli the Republican," 101–157.

21. Maurizio Viroli, *Jean-Jacques Rousseau and the "well-ordered society"* trans. Derek Hanson (Cambridge: Cambridge University Press, 1988), 11. Viroli summarized that the crux of Machiavelli's political thought was "to work out how it (a republican government) can be brought into being."

22. *Considerazioni*, 1.10, p. 20. "Di questi si truova pochissimi, o forse nessuno, che sanza necessitá l'abbino lasciata; né è maraviglia, perché chi è nutrito in una tirannide non ha occhi da cognoscere quella gloria che si acquista di mettere la *patria* in libertá, né considera questo caso con quello gusto che fanno gli uomini privati, perché, assuefatto a quello modo di vivere, giudica che el sommo bene sia nella potenzia, e non cognoscendo el frutto di quella gloria, nessuna altra ragione gli può persuadere a lasciare la tirannide." For an interesting examination of Guicciardini's political thought, see Athanasios Moulakis, *Republican Realism in*

Renaissance Florence: Francesco Guicciardini's "Discorso di logrogno" (Rowan and Littlefield: Lanham, Maryland, 1998).

23. Sydney Anglo, *Machiavelli: A Dissection* (London: Victor Gollancz, 1969). By the same author see "Machiavelli as a Military Authority. Some Early Sources," in *Florence and Italy: Renaissance Studies in Honour of Nicolai Rubinstein* eds. Peter Denley and Caroline Elam (London: Committee for Medieval Studies, Westfield College, 1988), 321–334. And Michael Mallett, "The Theory and Practice of Warfare in Machiavelli's Republic," in *Machiavelli and Republicanism* eds. Gisela Bock, Quentin Skinner and Maurizio Viroli (Cambridge: Cambridge University Press, 1993), 173–180.

24. Sergio Bertelli, "Egemonia linguistica come egemonia culturale e politica nella Firenze cosmiana," in *Bibliotèque d'Humanisme et Renaissance*, 38 (1976): 249–281. Fredi Chiappelli, *Studi sul Linguaggio del Machiavelli* (Firenze, 1952); and *Machiavelli e la "La Lingua Fiorentina"* (Bologna: Massimiliano Boni, 1974). Niccolò Machiavelli, *Discorso o dialogo intorno alla nostra lingua: Edizione critica* A cura di Bortolo Tommaso Sozzi (Torino: G. Einaudi, 1976).

25. Susan Meld Shell, "Machiavelli's Discourse on Language," *The Comedy and Tragedy of Machiavelli: Essays on the Literary Works*, ed. Vickie B Sullivan (New Haven: Yale University Press, 2000), 78–101. Maurizio Viroli, *For Love of Country: An Essay on Patriotism and Nationalism* (New York: Clarendon Press, 1997), 32–33 for references to the *Dialogo*. Niccolò Machiavelli, *The Prince*, trans. Angelo M. Codevilla (New Haven: Yale University Press, 1997), xxi–xxv.

26. Shell, "Discourse on Language," 93.

Chapter One

1. Hans Baron, "Machiavelli the Republican Citizen and Author of *The Prince*," in Hans Baron, *In Search of Florentine Civic Humanism: Essays on the Transition from Medieval to Modern Thought* Vol. 2 (Princeton: Princeton University Press, 1988): 101–157, 101.

2. Maurizio Viroli, *From Politics to Reason of State: The Acquisition and Transformation of the Language of Politics, 1250–1600* (Cambridge: Cambridge University Press, 1992), 128–133.

3. Generally, *patria* is relegated to footnotes or endnotes and paid no real attention. For example, see Niccolò Machiavelli, *The Prince*, eds. Quentin Skinner and Russell Price (Cambridge: Cambridge University Press, 10th edn., 1998), 103. J.H. Hexter, "Il principe and lo stato," *Studies in the Renaissance* 4 (1957): 113–38. Nicolai Rubinstein, "Notes on the word *stato* in Florence before Machiavelli," *Florilegium Historiale: Essays presented to Wallace K. Ferguson*, eds. J.G. Rowe and W.H. Stockdale (Toronto: University of Toronto Press, 1971), 314–326. Quentin Skinner, "The State," in T. Ball, J. Farr and R.L. Hanson, eds., *Political Innovation and Conceptual Change* (Cambridge: Cambridge University Press, 1989), 90–131. Fredi Chiappelli, *Studi sul Linguaggio del Machiavelli* (Firenze, 1952).

4. Hexter, "*Lo Stato*," 30. Particular attention must be given to Maurizio Viroli's *For Love of Country: An Essay on Patriotism and Nationalism* (Oxford: Clarendon,

1997), 29–36; by the same author *Machiavelli* (Oxford: Oxford University Press, 1998), 156–174.

5. These are discussed in the Appendices.

6. Ottavio Condorelli, "Per la storia del nome *Stato*," *Archivio Giuridico* LXXXIX (1923): 223–235. This apparent problem is discussed in detail by Hans Baron, Felix Gilbert and J. H. Hexter in the following articles. See Baron, "Machiavelli the Republican." Also see the following articles by the same author: "Machiavelli on the Eve of the *Discourses*: The Date and Place of the *Dialogo intorno alla nostra lingua*," *Bibliothèque d'Humanisme et Renaissance* 23 (1961): 449–76; "The *Principe* and the Puzzle of the Date of the *Discorsi*," *Bibliothèque d'Humanisme et Renaissance* 18 (1956): 405–428; and "The *Principe* and the Puzzle of the Date of Chapter 26," *Journal of Medieval and Renaissance Studies* 21 (1991): 83–102. This topic is also discussed in Felix Gilbert, "Review-Discussion: The Composition of Machiavelli's *Discorsi*," *Journal of the History of Ideas* 14 (1953): 136–156; and J.H. Hexter, "Seyssel, Machiavelli, and Polybius VI: the Mystery of the Missing Translation," *Studies in the Renaissance* 3 (1956): 75–96.

7. Niccolò Machiavelli, *The Prince*, eds. Quentin Skinner and Russell Price (Cambridge: Cambridge University Press, 1998), xxvi. Niccolò Machiavelli, *The Prince*, trans. and ed. Stephen J. Milner (London: J.M. Dent, 2000), xi. Niccolò Machiavelli, *The Prince*, trans. Harvey C. Mansfield (Chicago: University of Chicago Press, 1985), xxvi. Niccolò Machiavelli, *Il Principe e Altre Opere Politiche* Introduzione di Delio Cantimori, Note di Stefano Andretta (Milano: Garzanti Libri, 1999), viii. Sebastian De Grazia, *Machiavelli in Hell* (New York: Vintage Books, 1994), 23. John Hale, *Machiavelli and Renaissance Italy* (London: The English Universities Press Ltd, 1966), 146.

8. Baron, "Date of the *Discorsi*," 405–428.

9. For Italian original see *Principe, 1999*, 15. "Io lascerò indrieto el ragionare delle republiche, perché altra volta ne ragionai a lungo." Translation is the Author's.

10. Hexter, "The Missing Translation," 75–96. Also see Gilbert, "Machiavelli's *Discorsi*," 136–156. The Author's argument is a combination of Hexter and Gilbert's arguments. Hexter poses the problem of Polybius VI and Gilbert proposes that the *Discorsi* were written in two stages, the first of which relied completely upon Livy and the second relied upon Polybius.

11. Baron, "Date of the *Discorsi*." Also see Hale, *Machiavelli and Renaissance*, 146 and 168.

12. Baron, "Date of the *Discorsi*," 405–428. Baron argues that *Il Principe* was written before the *Discorsi* and that Machiavelli added segments of the *Prince* after working on, if not completing the *Discorsi*.

13. Gilbert, "Machiavelli's *Discorsi*," 150 "it seems possible to suggest that Machiavelli had been working on a treatise on republics when he was composing *The Prince*, and that he used this manuscript when he gave the *Discorsi* their final version and realized the necessity of providing them with a fuller introduction."

14. Ibid, 151. "The[...] second stage, which was a rearrangement of previously gathered material, resulted in the version which we have today, and the analysis which we have previously made of the chronological references in the *Discorsi* permits the conclusion that this work of rearrangement and revision took place in the year 1517."

15. J.H. Whitfield, "Gilbert, Hexter and Baron" in Whitfield's *Discourses on Machiavelli* (Cambridge, Heffer, 1969), 181–206.

16. Hexter, "Missing Translation," 75.

17.   Ibid, 75–96.
18.   Whitfield, "Gilbert, Hexter and Baron," 206. Whitfield attempts, with some success, to pick apart Hexter and Baron, as well as Gilbert. However, he does not postulate a theory to replace those set forth by the aforementioned scholars. Rather, he wrote concerning the date problem, "That must remain, as far as I can see, still at present, a puzzle with no proved answer."
19.   Baron, "Date of the *Discorsi*," 423. "Indeed, our analysis of the first few chapters of the *Principe* demonstrated that the passage which contains the "altra volta" reference is not an indispensable part of the text, and even obstructs the flow of the argument. And by reviewing the genesis of the *Discorsi*, we ascertained that Machiavelli composed the version which discusses republics "at length," precisely in 1516, and that as early as the beginning of that year many cultured people in Florence not only new that Machiavelli was preparing such a work, but had conversed with the author about his subject, and possibly had seen, or listened to, portions of the book, even though semi-publication through dedication did not take place until about two years later. Late in 1515 or in 1516, therefore, nothing would have been more natural for Machiavelli than to insert in the *Principe* the somewhat vague and mystifying cross reference to his more recent but not yet "published" work: *"altra volta* ne ragionai a lungo."
20.   Hale, *Machiavelli and Renaissance Italy*, 146 and 168. Baron, "Machiavelli the Republican," 141–151.
21.   Baron, "Date of the *Discorsi*," 428.
22.   The Author's translation. Niccolò Machiavelli, *Discorsi Sopra la Prima Deca di Tito Livio*. Introduzione di Gennaro Sasso, Note di Giorgio Inglese (Milano: Biblioteca Universale Rizzoli, 1999), 53. "Il che essendo, non so quale di noi si abbia ad essere meno obligato all'altro: o io a voi, che mi avete forzato a scrivere quello che io mai per me medesimo non arei scritto; o voi a me, quando, scrivendo non vi abbi sodisfatto."
23.   For discussions of Machiavelli's time at the "Orti" see Gilbert, "Machiavelli's *Discorsi*," 136–156; and Hexter, "Missing Translation," 75–96. For a history of the "Orti" before Machiavelli's involvement, see Felix Gilbert, "Bernardo Rucellai and the Orti Oricellari: A Study on the Origins of Modern Political Thought," in *Journal of the Warburg and Courtauld Institutes*, 12 (1949): 101–131.
24.   The Author's translation. Niccolò Machiavelli, *Opere di Niccolò Machiavelli, Volume Terzo, Lettere*, A cura di Franco Gaeta (Torino: Unione Tipografico-Editrice Torinese, 1984), Letter 254, December 17, 1517, pp. 498–499. "So che vi trovate costì tutto el giorno insieme con Rv.mo de'Salviati, Filippo Nerli, Cosimo Rucellai, Cristofano Carnesechi, e qualche volta Antonio Francesco delli Albizi, e attendete a fare buona cera, e vi ricordate poco di noi qui, poveri sgraziati, morti di gielo e di sono. Pur, per parere vivi, ci troviamo qualche volta, Zanobi Buondelmonte, Amerigo Morelli, Batista della Palla et io, e ragioniamo di quella gita di Fiandra con tanta efficacia…"
25.   There is "semi-contemporary evidence" which suggests that Machiavelli did indeed attend the Orti in 1515 or earlier. See Hans Baron, "Machiavelli on the Eve of the *Discourses*: The Date and Place of the *Dialogo intorno alla nostra lingua*," *Bibliotheque d'Humanisme et Renaissance* 23 (1961): 449–76, p. 465, n. 2.
26.   Hans Baron, "The *Principe* and the Puzzle of the Date of Chapter 26," *Journal of Medieval and Renaissance Studies* 21 (1991): 83–102. We shall return to this subject in a later Chapter where it will be of central importance to our argument.
27.   Peter Laven, *Renaissance Italy: 1464–1534* (London: B.T. Batsford, 1966), 155.

28. *Discorsi, 1999*, I. 58, p. 180. "Io non so se io mi prenderò una provincia dura e piena di tanta difficultà, che mi convenga o abbandonarla con vergogna, o seguirla con carico; volendo difendere una cosa, la quale, come ho detto, da tutti gli scrittori è accusata. Ma, comunque si sia, io non giudico né giudicherò mai essere difetto difendere alcuna opinione con le ragioni, sanza volervi usare o l'autorità o la forza."

29. John Najemy, *Between Friends: Discourses of Power and Desire in the Machiavelli-Vettori Letters of 1513–1515*, (Princeton: Princeton University Press, 1993), 176–214. Therein, Najemy discusses the evolution of *Il Principe* in the context of the Machiavelli-Vettori letters of 1513. For further interesting discussion of these exchanges see Peter Godman's *From Poliziano to Machiavelli: Florentine Humanism in the High Renaissance*, (Princeton: Princeton University Press, 1998), 256–258. Also see Brian Richardson, "The *Prince* and its Early Italian Readers," in *Niccolò Machiavelli's "The Prince": New Interdisciplinary Essays*, ed. Martin Coyle (Manchester: Manchester University Press, 1995), 19–39.

30. Allan H. Gilbert, *Machiavelli's "Prince" and Its Forerunners: "The Prince" as a Typical Book "de Regimine Principum"* (Durham, N.C.: Duke University Press, 1938).

31. Ibid. For Gilbert's discussion of possibly devaluing Machiavelli's genius, see his "Conclusion," 231–237.

32. Maurizio Viroli, *From Politics to Reason of State: The Acquisition and Transformation of the Language of Politics, 1250–1600* (Cambridge: Cambridge University Press, 1992), 128–133.

33. Ibid, 128–129.

34. J.H. Whitfield, "Machiavelli and the Problem of the *Prince*" in *Discourses on Machiavelli* (Cambridge, Heffer, 1969), 17–35.

35. Machiavelli's use of the term "stato" has been often written about; did he refer to the "status" of the prince or the "modern state?" Following Viroli's argument, we suggest that at times it may mean both, but given the genre of the work, most frequently, it is linked with the person of the prince. See note 3 above for articles relating to Machiavelli's use of "stato" in *Il Principe*.

36. Viroli, *Reason of State*, 129.

37. Denys Hay, "The Italian view of Renaissance Italy," in *Florilegium Historiale: Essays Presented to Wallace K. Ferguson*, (Toronto: University of Toronto Press, 1971), 3–17. See p. 4. Hay's insightful comment provides a potent distillation of Roman republican and "Renaissance" Italian patriotic theory in a mere three sentences. For example, see Marcus Cicero, *De re publica et De legibus*, trans. Clinton Walker Keyes (Cambridge, Mass.: Harvard University Press, 11th edn., 1994). "De legibus," II. 2.5, pp. 374–375 "Surely I think that he and all natives of Italian towns have tow fatherlands, one by nature and the other by citizenship." "Ego mehercule et illi omnibus municipibus duas esse censeo patrias, unam naturae, alteram civitatis…"

38. Hay, "Renaissance Italy," 13

39. Garrett Mattingly, *Renaissance Diplomacy* (New York: Dover, 1988), 142.

40. This topic will be developed in detail in the following Chapter.

41. Niccolò Machiavelli, *The Prince* trans. George Bull (London: Penguin Group, 4th ed., 1995), p. 18. For Italian see *Principe, 1999*, 30. "Queste occasioni, per tanto, feciono questi uomini felici, e la eccellente virtù loro fece quella occasione esser conosciuta."

42. Francesco Guicciardini, "Considerazioni intorno ai Discorsi del Machiavelli sopra la Primi Deca di Tito Livio," in *Opere 7: Scritti politici e ricordi* A cura di Roberto

Palmarocchi (Bari: Laterza, 1933), 1–65.

43. For an interesting discussion of Machiavelli's view of and approach to history see Felix Gilbert, *Machiavelli and Guicciardini: Politics and History in Sixteenth-Century Florence* (Princeton: Princeton University Press, 1965), 153–235.

44. Viroli, *Reason of State*, 128–129 and 201.

45. Viroli, *Love of Country*, 31. for an excellent discussion relating the "bene comune" to *patria* in the *Discorsi*.

46. *Discorsi, 1999*, II. 2, p. 297. "perché non il bene particulare ma il bene comune è quello che fa grandi le città. E senza dubbio questo bene commune non è osservato se non nelle republiche; perché tutto quello che fa a proposito suo si esequisce e, quantunque e' torni in danno di questo o di quello privato, e' sono tanti quegli per chi detto bene fa, che lo possono tirare innanzi contro alla disposizione di quegli pochi che ne fussono oppressi."

47. *Discorsi, 1999*, I. 9, p. 86. "Però, uno prudente ordinatore d'una republica, e che abbia questo animo, di volere giovare non a sé ma al *bene comune*, non alla sua propria successione ma alla *comune patria*, debbe ingegnarsi di avere l'autorità, solo; né mai uno ingegno savio riprenderà alcuno di alcuna azione straordinaria, che, per ordinare un regno o constituire una republica, usasse."

48. For Machiavelli's ideas concerning constitutions, see *Discorsi, 1999*, I. 2.2; I. 3.1; I. 9.1 and 4.; I. 34.1 and 2.; I. 55.8; II. Preface, 4.; II. 19.2; III. 22.9; III. 1.1.

49. See the *Discorsi, 1999*, I. 2–4, pp. 64–72 for Machiavelli's discourses on the Roman republic, its constituent parts and the tensions between these. *Discorsi, 1999*, I. 4, pp. 71–72. "E se alcuno dicessi: i modi erano straordinarii, e quasi efferati, vedere il popolo insieme gridare contro al Senato, il Senato contro al Popolo, correre tumultuariamente per le strade, serrare le botteghe, partirsi tutta la plebe di Roma, le quali cose tutte spaventano, non che altro, chi le legge; dico come ogni città debbe avere i suoi modi con i quali il popolo possa sfogare l'ambizione sua, e massime quelle città che nelle cose importanti si vogliono valere del popolo: intra le quali, la città di Roma aveva questo modo, che, quando il popolo voleva ottenere una legge, o e' faceva alcuna delle predette cose, o e' non voleva dare il nome per andare alla guerra, tanto che a placarlo bisognava in qualche parte sodisfarli... Debbesi, adunque, più parcamente biasimare il governo romano; e considerare che tanti buoni effetti, quanti uscivano di quella republica, non erano causati se non da ottime cagioni. E se i tumulti furano cagione della creazione de' Tribuni, meritano somma laude, perché, oltre al dare la parte sua all'amministrazione popolare, furano constituiti per guardia della libertà romana, come nel seguente capitolo si mostrerà."

50. *Discorsi, 1999*, I. 3, pp. 69–70.

51. Ibid. I. 4, pp. 70–72

52. *Discorsi, 1999*, 134–137 for Machiavelli's discussions regarding the creation of the dictator and the benefits this office bestowed upon Rome as well as the eventual harm it caused.

Chapter Two

1. Peter Godman, *From Poliziano to Machiavelli: Florentine Humanism in the High Renaissance* (Princeton: Princeton University Press, 1998), 303–333. Godman provides a concise, though detailed history of Machiavelli's works and their relationship with the Roman Inquisition in the sixteenth century.

2.	Nicholas Machiavel's *Prince: Also "The Life of Castruccio Castracani of Luca"* *and "The Means Duke Valentino us'd to put to death Vitellozzo Vitelli, Oliverotto of* *Fermo, Paul and the Duke of Gravina"* trans. Edward Dacres (Amsterdam: Da Capo, 1969—facsimile of 1640 edition printed in London by Bishop and Hils). See pp. A3–A4.

3.	Niccolò Machiavelli, *The Discourses of Niccolò Machiavelli* 2 Vols. trans. Lesley J. Walker (London: Routledge, 1950). See Vol. 1, p. 6	For a similar view of Machiavelli's paganism it may be useful to read Giuseppe Prezzolini's *Machiavelli anticristo* (Rome: G. Casini, 1954).

4.	J.H. Whitfield, *Discourses on Machiavelli* (Cambridge: W. Heffer and Sons, 1969). In this collection of essays Whitfield provided a revised reading of Machiavelli which seeks to contextualise and "excuse" his "immorality." Whitfield bases a good deal of his observation on Roberto Ridolfi's reading of Machiavelli in *Vita di Niccolò Machiavelli* (Roma: A. Belardetti 1st edn., 1954). Maurizio Viroli, *Republicanism* trans. Antony Shugaar (New York: Farrar, Straus and Giroux), 80–81.

5.	Francesco Guicciardini, *Opere* 9 Vols. A cura di Roberto Palmarocchi (Bari: Laterza, 1929–36). See *Considerazioni intorno ai Discorsi del Machiavelli sopra la prima deca di Tito Livio* in Volume 8, *Scritti Politici e Ricordi* (1933), 1–65. For a recent English translation see Francesco Guicciardini, *Considerations* in, *The Sweetness of Power: Machiavelli's "Discourses" and Guicciardini's "Considerations"* trans. James B. Atkinson and David Sices (DeKalb: Northern Illinois University Press, 2002), I.12, pp. 404–405.

6.	Felix Gilbert, *Machiavelli and Guicciardini: Politics and History in Sixteenth-Century Florence* (Princeton: Princeton University Press, 1965). See Gilbert's "Bibliographical Essays," 305–338 for a compendium of Italian scholarship on Machiavelli and Guicciardini.

7.	J.H. Whitfield, "Three Reviews: 'Machiavelli and Guicciardini, Politics and History in Sixteenth-Century Florence,'" in *Discourses on Machiavelli* (Cambridge, Heffer, 1969), 241–243.

8.	Niccolò Machiavelli, *Il Principe e Altre Opere Politiche* Introduzione di Delio Cantimori, Note di Stefano Andretta (Milano: Garzanti Libri, 1999), 67. "Per tanto a uno principe è necessario sapere bene usare la bestia e lo uomo...Sendo adunque uno principe necessitato sapere bene usare la bestia, debbe di quelle pigliare la golpe (volpe) et il lione."

9.	Marcus Tullius Cicero, *De Officiis* trans. Walter Miller (Cambridge, Mass.: Harvard University Press, 1997), I. 42, pp. 44–47.

10.	Quentin Skinner, *Machiavelli* (Oxford: Oxford University Press, 1996), 40–47 for Skinner's discussion of Machiavelli's attitude toward Cicero in *Il Principe*.

11.	Bernardo Machiavelli, Niccolò's father, possessed a copy of Cicero's *De officiis* at their family home when Niccolò was doing his Latin studies. It is likely that this early familiarity helped to shape Machiavelli's republican theory, but also honed his anti-humanist rhetoric. See Catherine Atkinson's interesting account of Bernardo Machiavelli's life and time which deals with these subjects. *Debts, Dowries, Donkey: The Diary of Niccolò Machiavelli's Father, Messer Bernardo, in Quattrocento Florence* (Frankfurt am Main: Peter Lang, 2002), 137–152.

12.	Marcus Tullius Cicero, *De Officiis* trans. Walter Miller (Cambridge, Mass.: Harvard

University Press, 1997), III.23.90, pp. 364–367. "Non igitur *patria* praestat omnibus officiis? Immo vero, sed ipsi patriae conducit pios habere cives in parentes. Quid? si tyrannidem occupare, si *patriam* prodere conabitur pater, silebitne filius? Immo vero obsecrabit patrem, ne id faciat. Si nihil proficiet, accusabit, minabitur etiam; ad extremum, si ad perniciem *patriae* res spectabit, *patriae* salutem anteponet saluti patris." And, "Well, then, are not the claims of country paramount to all other duties?" "Aye, verily; but it is to our country's interests to have citizens who are loyal to their parents." "But once more—if a father attempts to make himself kind, or to betray his country, shall the son hold his peace?" "Nay, verily; he will plead with his father not to do so. If that accomplishes nothing, he will take him to task; he will threaten; and in the end, if things point to the destruction of the state, he will sacrifice his father to the safety of the country."

13. See *Principe, 1999*, Chapter 15, p. 60.

14. *Prince, 1640*, 117; Niccolò Machiavelli, *The Prince* trans. George Bull (London: Penguin Group, 4th ed., 1995), 48; Niccolò Machiavelli, *The Prince* eds. Quentin Skinner and Russell Price (Cambridge: Cambridge University Press, 10th edn., 1998), 54 and Niccolò Machiavelli, *The Prince*, trans. Angelo M. Codevilla (New Haven: Yale University Press, 1997), 57.

15. *De Officiis*. I. 45.160., pp. 164–165. "In ipsa autem communitate sunt gradus officiorum, ex quibus quid cuique praestet intellegi possit, ut prima diis immortalibus, secunda *patriae*, tertia parentibus, deinceps gradatim reliquis debeantur." And, "Moreover, even in the social relations themselves there are gradations of duty so well defined that it can easily be seen which duty takes precedence over any other: our first duty is to the immortal gods; our second, to country; our third, to parents; and son, in a descending scale, to the rest."

16. See Chapter 8 of *Il Principe* for a good example of this sentiment.

17. *Principe, 1999*, 98. "questa patria ne sia nobilitata." "this country may be ennobled."

18. Atkinson, *Debts*, 126–152. See Atkinson's interesting discussion of Bernardo's library and its contents. He owned Livy *Ab urbe condita*. Livy's books may have been an "addentellatto" for the young Machiavelli. For this term see *The Prince, 1995*, 6, note.

19. Lesley J. Walker, "The Structure of the 'Discourses,'" in Niccolò Machiavelli *The Discourses of Niccolò Machiavelli* Vol. 1. trans. Lesley J. Walker (London: Routledge, 1950), 59–65; Felix Gilbert, "Review-Discussion: The Composition of Machiavelli's *Discorsi*," *Journal of the History of Ideas* 14 (1953): 136–156; and J.H. Whitfield, "Gilbert, Hexter and Baron" in Whitfield's *Discourses on Machiavelli* (Cambridge, Heffer, 1969), 181–206.

20. J.H. Whitfield, "Machiavelli and the Problem of the *Prince*," in *Discourses on Machiavelli* (Cambridge, Heffer, 1969), 17–35. Maurizio Viroli, *From Politics to Reason of State: The Acquisition and Transformation of the Language of Politics, 1250–1600* (Cambridge: Cambridge University Press, 1992), 128–133.

21. Viroli, *Reason of State*, 128–133. And for a more expansive treatment of the same subject see, Maurizio Viroli, *Machiavelli* (Oxford: Oxford University Press, 1998), 148–174.

22. *Discorsi, 1999*, II. 2, p. 299. "Perché, se considerassono come la religione ci permette la esaltazione e la difesa della *patria*, vedrebbono come la vuole che noi

l'amiamo ed onoriamo, e prepariamoci a essere tali che noi la possiamo difendere."

23. Maurizio Viroli, *Republicanism* trans. Antony Shugaar (New York: Farrar, Straus and Giroux, 2002), 80–81.

24. Maurizio Viroli, *Machiavelli* (Oxford: Oxford University Press, 1998), 166. "(Machiavelli) reiterates another distinctive theme of Florentine patriotism— namely, the idea that our obligation to our country comes before our obligations to the Church's commands."

25. See "Machiavelli and Religion," in Federico Chabod, *Machiavelli and the Renaissance* trans. David Moore (London: Bowes and Bowes, 1958), 93–94.

26. Polybius, *The Rise of the Roman Empire (Selections)*, trans. Ian Scott-Kilvert (London: Penguin Books Ltd, 1979), VI. 56, p. 349. The Author does not possess a working knowledge of Greek, so the translation, here, must suffice.

27. For Machiavelli's advocacy of such a practice, see *Principe, 1999*, Chapter 21, p. 83. Discussed below.

28. Twenty-seven of their letters survive. These span a time beginning on 17 May 1521 and ending on 12 November 1526. The best complete edition of Machiavelli's correspondence was compiled and edited by Franco Gaeta. See his Niccolò Machiavelli, *Opere di Niccolò Machiavelli, Volume Terzo, Lettere* A cura di Franco Gaeta (Torino: Unione Tipografico-Editrice, 1984). Giorgio Inglese's edtion, though limited in the letters it contains is also good. See Niccolò Machiavelli, *Lettere a Francesco Vettori e a Francesco Guicciardini* A cura di Giorgio Inglese (Milano: R.C.S. Libri & Grandi Opere, 1996).

29. Felix Gilbert, *Machiavelli and Guicciardini: Politics and History in Sixteenth-Century Florence* (Princeton: Princeton University Press, 1965), 274–275. "At the time of the great crisis of Guicciardini's life, after the *Sacco di Roma* and the liberation of Florence from the Medici rule, when he did not have position or influence with either the Pope or the Florentines, he imagined that he might be called before the court which had been established by the Florentines to judge the enemies of the republic." According to Gilbert, Guicciardini overestimated his own importance in Florence; see note 12 on p. 275 in Gilbert's work. Citing Roberto Ridolfi, Gilbert noted that, "In 1530, Guicciardini was called into the court, and, in absentia condemned." See Roberto Ridolfi, *Vita di Niccolò Machiavelli* (Roma: A. Belardetti, 1954), 332 ff.

30. John Larner, *Lords of the Romagna* (Ithaca, NY: Cornell University Press, 1965). Larner's work provides an excellent history of the Romanga's troubles and internal conflicts.

31. Sydney Anglo, "Machiavelli as a Military Authority. Some Early Sources," in *Florence and Italy: Renaissance Studies in Honour of Nicolai Rubinstein* eds. Peter Denley and Caroline Elam (London: Committee for Medieval Studies, Westfield College, 1988), 321–334. See p. 328 where Anglo discusses Guicciardini's *Considerazioni* as a "commentary" on Machiavelli's *Discorsi*.

32. *Considerations*. I. 12, p. 404. For Italian, see *Considerazioni*, I. 12, pp. 22–23. "Non si può dire tanto male della corte romana che non meriti se ne dica più, perché è una infamia, uno esemplo di tutti e' vitupèri ed obbrobri del mondo. Ed anche credo sia vero che la grandezza della Chiesa, cioè la autoritá che gli ha data la religione, sia stata causa che Italia non sia caduta in una monarchia; perché da uno canto ha avuto tanto credito che ha potuto farsi capo, e convocare quando è

bisognato príncipi esterni contro a chi era per opprimere Italia, da altro essendo spogliata di arme proprie, non ha avuto tante forze che abbia potuto stabilire dominio temporale, altro che quello che volontariamente gli è stato dato da altri. Ma non so giá se el non venire in una monarchia sia stata felicità o infelicità di questa provincia, perché se sotto una republica questo poteva essere glorioso al nome di Italia e felicità a quella cittá che dominassi, era all'altre tutte calamità, perché oppresse dalla ombra di quella, non avevano facultà di pervenire a grandezza alcuna, essendo el costume delle republiche non participare e' frutti della sua libertá ed imperio a altri che a' suoi cittadini propri."

33.   Viroli, *Machiavelli*, 156. Viroli states, "we can see that he (Machiavelli) endorsed and kept alive some of the important features of the conventional language of patriotism, particularly the interpretation of love of country as a charitable love of the common good of the republic." Also see by the same author, *Love of Country*, 19 for a discussion of the historical precedents that linked the common good and the *patria*.

34.   See Chapters 21 and 7 of *Il Principe* for a description of Ferdinand's and Cesare's actions.

35.   For Machiavelli's coverage of these, see *Principe, 1999*, Chapter 21, p. 83. For translation see *Prince, 1995*, 70. Bull's translation, one will find, includes a reference to "Moriscos," which is not as accurate as Codevilla's translation. See Niccolò Machiavelli, *The Prince* trans. Angelo M. Codevilla (New Haven: Yale University Press, 1997), 81, n. 361. "Marranos means pigs. Ferdinand rid himself of those who would not eat pig, that is, of the Muslims and Jews. These were the subjects of his 'pious cruelty.'"

36.   Garrett Mattingly, *Renaissance Diplomacy* (New York: Dover, 1988), 119–124. There, Mattingly provides background to Ferdinand's diplomatic and military successes.

37.   *Principe, 1999*, 60–61. Again, Chapter 8 of *Il Principe* provides one of the most potent examples of this.

38.   Gennaro Sasso, *Machiavelli e Cesare Borgia: Storia di un giudizio* (Roma: Edizioni ell'Anteneo, 1966). This book is a compilation of Sasso's work on Borgia and Machiavelli. It provides a good all-round history and context to Borgia, Machiavelli and the Romanga.

39.   *Principe, 1999*, Chapter 7, p. 35. For the episode recounting the rather bloody dispatching of Remirro, see Chapter Seven.

40.   *Principe, 1999*, 37.

41.   Vickie B. Sullivan, *Machiavelli's Three Romes: Religion, Human Liberty, and Politics Reformed.* (DeKalb: Northern Illinois University Press, 1996), 190.

42.   Ibid, 181–190, "Machiavelli's Praise of Necessity."

43.   *Discorsi, 1999*, III. 12, p. 502. For translation, see Walker's edition, *Discourses, 1950*, III.12, p. 505.

44.   Sullivan, *Three Romes*, 188.

45.   *Discorsi, 1999*, I. 9, p. 86. Cited above in full.

46.   Again, see Chapter 8 of *Il Principe*, in *Principe, 1999*, 60–61.

47.   *Discorsi, 1999*, I. 12, p. 97. "Non essendo adunque stata la Chiesa potente da potere occupare la Italia, né avendo permesso che un altro la occupi, è stata cagione che la non è potuta venire sotto uno capo, ma è stata sotto più principe e signori, da' quali

è nata tanta disunione e tanta debolezza che la si è condotta a essere stata preda, non solamente de' barbari potenti, ma di qualunque l'assalta."

48. Mattingly, *Renaissance Diplomacy*, 142.

49. *Principe, 1999*, Chapter 11, p. 49.

50. *Principe, 1999*, Chapter 26, p. 95. Here one will find Machiavelli's call to unite Church and Medici interests.

51. *Principe, 1999*, 95. For translation see *Prince, 1995*, 81.

52. *Discorsi, 1999*, I. 34, p. 134. "E sono stati dannati da alcuno scrittore quelli Romani che trovarono in quella città il modo di creare il Dittatore, come cosa che fosse cagione col tempo della tirannide di Roma, allegando come il primo tiranno che fosse in quella città la comandò sotto questo titolo dittatorio, dicendo che, se non vi fusse stato questo, Cesare non arebbe potuto sotto alcuno titolo publico adonestare la sua tirannide. La quale cosa non fu bene, da colui che tiene questa opinione, esaminata, e fu fuori d'ogni ragione creduta."

53. *Discorsi, 1999*, I. 34, pp. 134–135. And *Discourses, 1950*, I. 34, p. 289. Walker's translation is fine here.

54. *Discorsi, 1999*, I. 34, p. 135. "E si vede che 'l Dittatore, mentre fu dato secondo gli ordini publici e non per autorità propria, fece sempre bene alla città. Perché e' nuocono alle republiche i magistrati che si fanno e l'autoritadi che si danno per vie istraordinarie, non quelle che vengono per vie ordinarie: come si vede che seguì in Roma in tanto processo di tempo, che mai alcuno Dittatore fece se non bene alla republica."

55. *Discorsi, 1999*, I. 34, p. 135.

56. Marcus Tullius Cicero, *De Officiis* trans. Walter Miller (Cambridge, Mass.: Harvard University Press, 1997), I. 17, pp. 58–61. "Sed cum omnia ratione animoque lustraris, omnium societatum nulla est gravior, nulla carior quam ea, quae cum re publica est uni cuique nostrum. Cari sunt parentes, cari liberi, propinqui, familiares, sed omnes omnium caritates *patria* una complexa est, pro qua quis bonus dubitet mortem oppetere, si ei sit profuturus? Quo est detestabilior istorum immanitas, qui lacerarunt omni scelere (patriam) et in ea funditus delenda occupati et sunt et fuerunt." Ibid. I. 17.57, pp. 58–61. "But when with a rational spirit you have surveyed the whole field, there is no social relation among them all more close, none more dear than that which links each one of us with our country. Parents are dear; dear are children, relatives, friends; but one native land embraces all our loves; and who that is true would hesitate to give his life for her, if by his death he could render her a service? So much the more execrable are those monsters who have torn their fatherland to pieces with every form of outrage and who are and have been engaged in compassing her utter destruction." Compare that quotation with Machiavelli's own writings: *Discorsi, 1999*, I. 9, p. 86. This quotation is drawn from The Appendix to Chapter One and it was cited above.

57. *Discorsi, 1999*, I. 34, p. 135. "Di che ce ne sono ragioni evidentissime. Prima, perché a volere che un cittadino possa offendere e pigliarsi autorità istraordinaria, conviene ch'egli abbia molte qualità le quali in una republica non corrotta non può mai avere: perché gli bisogna esere ricchissimo e avere assai aderenti e partigiani, i quali non può avere dove le leggi si osservano."

58. See Machiavelli's *Florentine Histories*, particularly Book 4, where he described the tumults in Florence in the early "quattrocento" that allowed the Medici to gain

control of Florence.
59.	John Hale, *Florence and the Medici: The Pattern of Control* (London: Thames and Hudson, 1977).

Chapter Three

1.	See Chapter One, note 1.
2.	Maurizio Viroli, *From Politics to Reason of State: The Acquisition and Transformation of the Language of Politics, 1250–1600* (Cambridge: Cambridge University Press, 1992), 128–133 for Viroli's discussion of political vocabulary.
3.	Sydney Anglo, *Machiavelli: A Dissection* (London: Victor Gollancz, 1969). By the same author see "Machiavelli as a Military Authority. Some Early Sources," in *Florence and Italy: Renaissance Studies in Honour of Nicolai Rubinstein* eds. Peter Denley and Caroline Elam (London: Committee for Medieval Studies, Westfield College, 1988), 321–334. This Chapter will use the following edition of Machiavelli's treatise. Niccolò Machiavelli, *Dell'Arte della guerra in Tutte le opere Storiche e Letterarie di Niccolò Machiavelli* A cura di Guido Mazzoni e Mario Casella (Firenze: G. Barbèra, 1929), 263–374.
4.	Michael Mallett, *Mercenaries and their Masters: Warfare in Renaissance Europe* (London: Bodley Head, 1074); Michael Mallett, "The Theory and Practice of Warfare in Machiavelli's Republic," in *Machiavelli and Republicanism* eds. Gisela Bock, Quentin Skinner and Maurizio Viroli (Cambridge: Cambridge University Press, 1993), 173–180. Anglo, *Dissection*; Anglo, "Military Authority." And, Francesco Guicciardini, *Considerations* in, *The Sweetness of Power: Machiavelli's "Discourses" and Guicciardini's "Considerations"* trans. James B. Atkinson and David Sices (DeKalb: Northern Illinois University Press, 2002).
5.	For discussions of Machiavelli's involvement in the creation of a citizen army at Florence, the fall of Prato and the Florentine Republic, see John Hale, *Machiavelli and Renaissance Italy* (London: Lowe and Brydon, 3rd edition, 1966), 88–96, 127–140. Roberto Ridolfi, *Vita di Niccolò Machiavelli* (Roma: A. Belardetti, 1954), 117–134, 183–201. Maurizio Viroli, *Niccolò's Smile: A Biography of Machiavelli* trans. Antony Shugaar (New York: Farrar, Straus and Giroux, 2000), 77–86, 119–130. For Machiavelli's description of the sack of Prato see Niccolò Machiavelli, *Opere di Niccolò Machiavelli, Volume Terzo, Lettere* A cura di Franco Gaeta (Torino: Unione Tipografico-Editrice, 1984), 357. "Tanto che l'altro giorno poi venne la nuova essere perso Prato, e come li Spagnuoli, rotto alquanto di muro, comonciorno a sforzare chi difendeva e a sbigottirgli, in tanto che dopo non molto di resistenza tutti fuggirno, e li Spagnoli, occupata la terra, la saccheggiorno, et ammazorno li uomini di quella con miserabile spettocolo di calamità. Né a V.S. ne referirò i particolari per non dare questa molestia d'animo; dirò solo che vi morirno meglio che quattromila uomini, e le altri rimasono presi e con diversi modi costretti a riscattarsi; né peronarono a vergini rinchiuse ne' luoghi sacri, i quali si riempierono tutti di stupri e di sacrilegi." For translation see Niccolò Machiavelli, *Machiavelli and his Friends: Their Personal Correspondences* trans. James B. Atkinson and David Sices (DeKalb: Northern Illinois University Press, 1996), 215–216, Letter 203 of 16 September 1512. "The news of Prato's capture arrived…and the

Spaniards, having broken through some of the walls, began to force the defenders back to terrify them. So that, after slight resistance, they all fled and the Spaniards took possession of the city, put it to sack, and massacred the city's population in a pitiable spectacle of calamity. In order to spare your Ladyship cause for worry in your spirit, I shall not report on the details. I shall merely say that better than four thousand died; the remainder were captured and, through various means, were obliged to pay ransom. Nor did they spare the virgins cloistered in the holy sites, which were all filled with acts of rape and pillage."

6. Niccolò Machiavelli, *The Prince* trans. George Bull (London: Penguin Group, 4th ed., 1995), 43.

7. *Lettere*, 367–368, Letter 208, 9 April 1513. "the head with little castles," or "castles in the air." The author's translation.

8. Niccolò Machiavelli, *Il Principe e Altre Opere Politiche: Introduzione di Delio Cantimori, Note di Stefano Andretta* (Milano: Garzanti Libri, 1999), 32. For translation see *Prince, 1995*, 20.

9. *Principe, 1999*, 34. The whole of Chapter Seven asserts that Borgia became successful only after he relied on his own troops.

10. *Principe, 1999*, 37. " la Romagna l'aspettò più d'uno mese."

11. For an interesting discussion of Cesare's downfall see J. Lucas-Dubreton, *The Borgias* trans. Philip John Stead (London: Staples Press, 1954), 220–252.

12. *Principe, 1999*, 50. "La cagione di questo è, che le non hanno altro amore né altra cagione che le tenga in campo, che un poco di stipendio, il quale non è sufficiente a fare che voglino morire per te."

13. *Principe, 1999*, 56. "In somma, nelle mercennarie è più pericolosa la ignavia, nella ausiliarie la virtù." See Richard Mackenney, *Sixteenth-Century Europe: Expansion and Conflict* (London: Macmillan, 1993), 237 for a brief history of the Italian battles and wars in which mercenary troops played a decisive role.

14. *Principe, 1999*, 54. "L'arme ausiliarie, che sono l'altre arme inutili, sono quando si chaiama uno potente, che con le arme sua ti venga ad aiutare e defendere."

15. *Principe, 1999*, 56. "Io non dubiterò mai di allegare Cesare Borgia e le sue azioni. Questo duca intrò in Romagna con le arme ausiliarie, conducendovi tutte gente franzese, e con quelle prese Imola e Furlì. Ma, non li parendo poi tale arme sicure, si volse alle mercennarie, iudicando in quelle manco periculo; e soldò li Orsini e Vitelli. Le quali poi nel meneggiare trovando dubbie et infideli e periculose, le spense, e volsesi alla proprie. E puossi facilmente vedere che differenzia è infra l'una e l'altra di queste arme, considerato che differenzia fu dalla reputazione del duca, quando aveva Franzesi soli e quando aveva li Orisini e Vitelli, a quando rimase con li soldati sua e sopr'a sé stesso e sempre si troverrà accresciuta; né mai fu stimato assai, se non quando ciascuno vidde che lui era intero possessore delle sue arme."

16. *Principe, 1999*, 50. "E'principali fondamenti che abbino tutti li stati, così nuovi, come vecchi o misti, sono le buone legge e le buone arme. E, perché non può essere buone legge dove non sono buone arme."

17. For Italian, see *Principe, 1999*, 51. "E per esperienza si vede a' principe soli e republiche armate fare progressi grandissimi, et alle arme mercennarie non fare mai se non danno. E con più difficultà viene alla obedienza di uno suo cittadino una repubblica armata di arme proprie, che una armata di arme di esterne."

18.   *Principe, 1999*, 96. "E non è maravaglia se alcuno de' prenominati Italiani non ha possuto fare quello che si può sperare facci la illustre casa vostra, e se, in tante revoluzioni di Italia, et in tanti maneggi di guerra, e' pare sempre che in quella la virtù militare sia spenta. Questo nasce, che il ordini antichi di essa non erano buoni, e non ci è suto alcuno che abbia saputo trovare de' nuovi: e veruna cosa fa tanto onore a uno uomo che di nuovo surga, quanto fa le nuove legge e li nuovi ordini trovati do lui. Queste cose, quando sono bene fondate et abbino in loro grandezza, lo fanno reverendo e mirabile: et in Italia non manca material da introdurvi ogni forma."

19.   *Principe, 1999*, 96–97. "Wanting, therefore, your illustrious House, to follow those excellent men who saved their counties. It is necessary, before all other things, as the true foundation of every undertaking, to provide yourself with arms of your own; because one is not able to have more faithful or better soldiers. And even though each one of them is good, all together, they become the best, when they find themselves under the command of their prince, and by him honoured and maintained. It is also necessary, therefore, to prepare these armies, to be able, with the ancient Italian *virtù* (or, *virtù Italica*) to defend (Italy) from the foreigners."

20.   "Italica" is used in a dialogue which most scholars attribute to Machiavelli. Perhaps this strengthens the case for his authorship? This topic and others are discussed in Chapter Five, Six and the Appendix to Chapter Seven.

21.   *Principe, 1999*, 97–98. This is Chapter 27's rousing conclusion.

22.   *Principe, 1999*, 37–38. "Solamente si può accusarlo nella creazione di Iulio pontefice, nella quale lui ebbe mala elezione; perché, come è detto, non possendo fare uno papa a suo modo, poteva tenere che uno non fussi papa; e non doveva mai consentire al papato di quelli cardinali che lui avessi offesi, o che, diventati papi, avessino ad avere paura di lui. Perché li uomini offendono o per paura o per odio... Errò adunque el duca in questa elezione, e fu cagione dell'ultima ruina sua."

23.   Hale, *Machiavelli*, 53–74.

24.   See Christine Shaw's insightful study on the pontificate of Julius II for an overview of this period; *Julius II: The Warrior Pope* (Oxford: Basil Blackwell, 1993).

25.   Niccolò Machiavelli, *Discorsi Sopra la Prima Deca di Tito Livio*. Introduzione di Gennaro Sasso, Note di Giorgio Inglese., (Milano: Biblioteca Universale Rizzoli, 1999), II. 10, p. 316.

26.   *Discorsi, 1999*, II. 10, p. 318. "Dico pertanto non l'oro, come grida la comune opinione, essere il nervo della guerra, ma i buoni soldati; perché l'oro non è sufficiente a trovare i buoni soldati, ma i buoni soldati sono bene sufficienti a trovare l'oro."

27.   For the passage to which Machiavelli refers, see Titus Livy, *Ab urbe condita* Vol. 4. trans. B.O. Foster (Cambridge, Mass: Harvard University Press, 1926). pp. 224–231. Book IX. 17. 1–17. Also see, *Discorsi, 1999*, II. 10, p. 319. "Ma Tito Livio è di questa opinione più vero testimone che alcuno altro, dove, discorrendo, se Alessandro Magno fussi venuto in Italia, s'egli avesse vinto i Romani, mostra essere tre cose necessarie nella guerra; assai soldati e buoni, capitani prudenti e buona fortuna; dove, esaminando quali o i Romani o Alessandro prevalessero in queste cose, fa dipoi la sua conclusione sanza ricordare mai i danari."

28.   Anglo, *Dissection*, 84.

29.   *Arte*, 299, column B. "E quando uno principe o una republica durerà fatica e metterà

diligenza in questi ordini e in queste esercitazioni, sempre avverrà che nel paese suo saranno buoni soldati; ed essi fieno superiori a' loro vicini e saranno quegli che daranno e non riceveranno le leggi dagli altri uomini. Ma, come io vi ho detto, il disordine nel quale si vive fa che si straccurano e non si istimano queste cose; e però gli eserciti nostri non son buoni; e se pure ci fusse o capi o membra naturalmente virtuosi, non la possono dimostrare."

30. *Arte*, 367, columns A–B. "E io vi affermo che qualunque di quelli che tengono oggi stati in Italia prima entrerrà per questa via, fia, prima che alcuno altro, signore di questa provincia; e interverrà allo stato suo come al regno de' Macedoni, il quale, venendo sotto a Filippo che aveva imparato il modo dello ordinare gli eserciti da Epaminonda tebano, diventò, con questo ordine e con questi esercizi, mentre che l'altra Grecia stava in ozio e attendeva a recitare commedie, tanto potente che potette in pochi anni tutta occuparla, e al figliuolo lasciare tale fondamento, che potéo farsi principe di tutto il mondo. Colui adunque che dispregia questi pensieri, s'egli è principe, dispregia il principato suo; s'egli è cittadino, la sua città. E io mi dolgo della natura, la quale o ella non mi dovea fare conoscitore di questo, o ella mi doveva dare facultà a poterlo eseguire. Né penso oggimai, essendo vecchio, poterne avere alcuna occasione; e per questo io ne sono stato con voi liberale, che, essendo giovani e qualificati, potrete, quando le cose dette da me vi piacciano, ai debiti tempi, in favore de' vostri principi, aiutarle e consigliarle. Di che non voglio vi sbigottiate o diffidiate, perché questa provincia pare nata per risuscitare le cose morte, come si è visto della poesia, della pittura e della scultura. Ma quanto a me si aspetta, per essere in là con gli anni, me ne diffido. E veramente, se la fortuna mi avesse conceduto per lo addietro tanto stato quanto basta a una simile impresa, io crederei, in brevissimo tempo, avere dimostro al mondo quanto gli antichi ordini vagliono; e sanza dubbio o io l'arei accresciuto con gloria o perduto sanza vergogna."

31. Franco Fido, "The Politician as Writer," in *The Comedy and Tragedy of Machiavelli* ed. Vickie B. Sullivan (New Haven: Yale University Press, 2000), 138–158. See p. 145.

32. See note 5 in this Chapter.

33. *Arte*. See Book I, p. 277, column A–B.

34. Mallett, *Mercenaries*: 196–197.

35. Ibid, 259.

36. *Considerations*, II. 10, pp. 426–427. For Italian, see *Considerazioni*, II. 10, pp. 50–51. "Chi fu autore di quella sentenzia che e' danari siano el nervo della guerra, e chi l'ha poi seguitata, non intese che e' danari soli bastassino a fare la guerra, né che e' fussino più necessari che e' soldati, perché sarebbe stata opinione non solo falsa, ma ancora molto ridicula; ma intese che chi faceva guerra aveva bisogno grandissimo di danari, e che sanza quelli era impossibile a sostenerla, perché non solo sono necessari per pagare e' soldati, ma per provedere le arme, le vettovaglie, le spie, le munizione e tanti instrumenti che si adoperano nella guerra; e' quali ne ricercano tanto profluvio, che a chi non l'ha provato è impossibile a immaginarlo. E se bene qualche volta uno esercito carestioso di danari con la virtú sua e col favore delle vittorie gli provede, nondimeno a' tempi nostri massime sono esempli rarissimi; ed in ogni caso ed in ogni tempo non corrono e' danari drieto agli eserciti se non dappoi che hanno vinto. Confesso che chi ha soldati propri fa la guerra con manco danari

che non fa chi ha soldati mercennari, nondimeno ed anche danari bisognano a chi fa guerra co' soldati propri, ed ognuno non ha soldati propri; ed è molto più facile co' danari trovare soldati che co' soldati trovare danari. Chi adunche interpreterrá quella sentenzia secondo el senso di chi la disse e secondo che communemente è intesa, non se ne maraviglierá, né la dannerá in modo alcuno."

37.　　Anglo, "Military Authority," 328. There Anglo discusses the *Considerazioni* as a "commentary" on Machiavelli.

38.　　Anglo, *Dissection*, 129.

39.　　Anglo, "Military Authority," 132.

40.　　Anglo, *Dissection*, 131–132.

41.　　Ibid, 152.

42.　　*Arte*. Book III. p. 311, column A. "E' non è cosa che facci maggiore confusione in uno esercito che impedirgli la vista; onde che molti gagliardissimi eserciti sono stati rotti, per essere loro stato impedito il vedere o dalla polvere o dal sole. Non è ancora cosa che più impedisca la vista che 'l fumo che fa l'artiglieria nel trarla; però io crederrei che fusse più prudenza lasciare accecarsi il nimico da se stesso, che volere tu, cieco, andarlo a trovare. Però o io non la trarrei, o (perchè questo non sarebbe approvato, rispetto alla riputazione che ha l'artiglieria) io la metterei in su' corni dell'esercito, acciò che, traendola, con il fumo ella non accecasse la fronte di quello; che è la importanza delle mie genti."

43.　　*Art*, 99. For Italian, see *Arte*. Book III. p. 312, column B. "Con ciò sia cosa che niuno ordine può fare che noi temiamo tanto quella, quanto quegli che stringono gli uomini insieme. Oltre a questo, se non mi sbigottisce l'artiglieria de' nimici nel pormi col campo a una terra dov'ella mi offende con più sua sicurtà (non la potendo io occupare per essere difesa dalle mura, ma solo col tempo con la mia artiglieria impedire di modo ch'ella può raddoppiare i colpi a suo modo), perchè la ho io a temere in campagna dove io la posso tosto occupare? Tanto che io vi conchiudo questo: che l'artiglierie, secondo l'opinione mia, non impediscono che non si possano usare gli antichi modi e mostrare l'antica virtù."

44.　　"(Machiavelli's) judgment was that of a scientist and a technician of political life." See Ernst Cassirer's *Myth of the State* (Garden City: Doubleday Anchor, 1955), 194. Also see Fredi Chiappelli, *Studi sul Linguaggio del Machiavelli* (Florence: Bibliotechina del saggiatore, 1952), 59–73, where Chiappelli discusses Machiavelli's scientific nature.

45.　　Barbara Spackman, "Politics on the Warpath: Machiavelli's '*Art of War*,'" in *Machiavelli and the Discourse of Literature* eds. Albert Russell Ascoli and Victoria Kahn (Ithaca: Cornell University Press, 1993), 179–193.

46.　　For translation see Machiavelli, *The Chief Works and Others*, Volume 2, trans., Allan Gilbert, (Durham, 1965). See p. 738. For Italian, see Niccolò Machiavelli, *I capitoli: Dell'ambizione*, in *Tutte le opere Storiche e Letterarie di Niccolò Machiavelli* A cura di Guido Mazzoni e Mario Casella (Firenze: G. Barbèra, 1929), 849–853. For quotation see p. 852. "130 Rivoglia gli occhi in qua chi veder vuole/ L'altrui fatiche, e riguardi se ancora/ Cotanta crudeltà mai vidde il sole./ 133 Chi 'l padre morte e chi 'l marito plora;/ Quell'altro mesto del/ suo proprio tetto,/ Battuto e nudo, trar si vede fora./ 136 O quante volte, avendo il padre stretto/ In braccio il figlio, con un colpo solo/ È suto rotto a l'uno e l'altro il petto!/ 139 Quello abbandona il suo paterno solo/ Accusando gli Dei crudeli e ingrati,/ Con la brigata sua piena di dolo./ 142 O esempli mai più nel mondo stati!/ Perchè si vede ogni di parti assai/ Per le ferite del lor ventre nati./ 145   Drieto a la figlia sua piena di guai/ Dice la madre: <<A che infelici nozze,/ A che crudel marito ti servai!>>/ 148 Di sangue son le fosse e l'acque sozze,/ Piene di teschi, di gambe e di mani,/ E d'altre membra laniate e mozze./ 151 Rapaci uccei, fere silvestri, cani/ Son poi le lor paterne sepolture:/ O sepulcri crudei, feroci e strani!/ 154 Sempre son le lor faccie orride e scure,/ A guisa d'uom che sbigottito ammiri/ Per nuovi danni o sùbite paure./ 157 Dovunche gli occhi tu rivolti, miri/ Di lacrime la terra e sangue pregna,/ E l'aria d'urla, singulti e sospiri.." Cited in Maurizio Viroli, *Machiavelli* (Oxford: Oxford University Press, 1998), 16, n. 19. Also cited by Sebastian De Grazia in his *Machiavelli in Hell* (New York: Vintage Books, Random House, 1994), 165–166.

47.   Anglo, "Military Authority," p. 321 and note 1 on p. 331. There Anglo cites Ridolfi's *The Life of Niccolò Machiavelli* (London, 1963), 229–230 where Ridolfi discusses Matteo Bandello's description of Machiavelli's handling of Giovanni's troops.

48.   Anglo, "Military Authority," 321 where Anglo refers to Machiavelli as an "armchair" soldier. Also see Mallett, "Machiavelli's Republic," 174, where Mallet wrote "Machiavelli was never present at a serious battle nor had he been on campaign with a large army."

Chapter Four

1.   Randolph Starn, *Contrary Commonwealth: The Theme of Exile in Medieval and Renaissance Italy* (Berkeley: University of California Press, 1982); and Christine Shaw, *The Politics of Exile in Renaissance Italy* (Cambridge: Cambridge University Press, 2000).

2.   John M. Najemy, *Between Friends: Discourses of Power and Desire in the Machiavelli–Vettori Letters of 1513–1515* (Princeton: Princeton University Press, 1993).

3.   That period was central to Najemy's considerations.

4.   Najemy, *Between Friends*, 176–214. Najemy focuses on *Il Principe* as one example of this. See p. 176 particularly where he wrote, "It has long been recognized that *The Prince* echoes and amplifies many of the themes Machiavelli addressed in the letters to Vettori."

5.   Godman, *Poliziano to Machiavelli*. His research is the most recent and perhaps the most insightful in this regard.

6.   Roberto Ridolfi, *The Life of Niccolò Machiavelli* trans. Cecil Grayson (London: Routledge and K. Paul, 1963), 18ff. Also see Giuseppe Prezzolini, *Vita di Niccolo Machiavelli Fiorentino* (Milano: Rusconi, 2nd edn., 1982), 31–33 for a brief description of Marcello di Virgilio Adriani's role in the Florentine Chancellery. Prezzolini's view of Adriani is similar to that of Ridolfi. More recently, Sebastian de Grazia completely neglected Adriani in his *Machiavelli in Hell* (New York: Vintage Books, Random House, 1994). Maurizio Viroli, in the most recent biography of Machiavelli, only mentioned Adriani four times and each of these is in a positive light. See Viroli's *Niccolò's Smile: A Biography of Niccolò Machiavelli* trans. Antony Shugaar (New York: Farrar, Straus and Giroux, 2000), 30, 31, 105

and 120.

7.   Nicolai Rubinstein, *The Palazzo Vecchio: 1298–1532: Government, Architecture, and Imagery in the Civic Palace of the Florentine Republic* (Oxford: Clarendon Press, 1995).

8.   Godman, *Poliziano to Machiavelli*, 145. Godman uses the terms "Chancellor" and "Segretario" interchangeably.

9.   Ridolfi, *Life of Niccolò*, 131.

10.   Giuseppe Prezzolini, *Niccolò Machiavelli: The Florentine* trans. Ralph Roeder (London: G. Putnam's Sons, 1928), 31–32. The quotation above is Prezzolini's own vivid portrayal of Marcello Virgilio Adriani.

11.   Godman, *Poliziano to Machiavelli*, Chapter V: 180–234 for Godman's discussion of Virgilio's cunning.

12.   Ibid, 181.

13.   John Hale, *Florence and the Medici: The Pattern of Control* (London: Thames and Hudson, 1977), 92.

14.   Niccolò Machiavelli, *Machiavelli and his Friends: Their Personal Correspondences* trans. James B. Atkinson and David Sices (DeKalb: Northern Illinois University Press, 1996), 49, Letter 33, 14 October 1502. For Italian, see Niccolò Machiavelli, *Opere di Niccolò Machiavelli, Volume Terzo: Lettere* A cura di Franco Gaeta, (Torino: Unione tipografico-editrice Torinese, 1984), 121, Letter 33, 14 October 1502. "Nicholae, salve. Scribam ne an non scribam, nescio: si non, neglientia obest; si scripsero, vereor ne maledicus habear, et presertim in Marcellum et Riccium."

15.   *Personal Correspondences*, 49, Letter 33, 14 October 1502. And, *Lettere*, 121, Letter 33, 14 October 1502. "Marcellus tanquam rei, hoc est officii tui, neglector, onus scribendi reiecit."

16.   *Personal Correspondences*: 66–67, Letter 51, 7 November 1502. And, *Lettere*, 146, Letter 51, 7 November 1502. "Spectabilis vir etc. Il Gonfalonieri stamani mi ha detto che non li pare a verun modo che tu ti parta, per non li parere ancor tempo, e lasciare cotesto luogo vacuo di qualche segno di questi città; per avervi a mandare un altro, non sa chi si potessi essere più a proposito, rispetto a molte cose. Però mi ha detto ch'io ti scriva così, e ti avvertisca a non partire; e se io lo fo volentieri, Dio lo sa, che mi truovo con le faccende mie, *con le tue e con la lezione addosso*. E se tu arai a sequire il Duca o non, andando a Rimine, per la publica ti si dirà più appunto. Vale." Portions of this letter are also cited in Godman *Poliziano to Machiavelli*, 182, n. 4.

17.   Godman, *Poliziano to Machiavelli*, 239.

18.   Ibid: 239–240.

19.   Ibid, 241.

20.   Ibid, 241. Machiavelli's merciless attack on Florence's leading citizens caused Giuliano de' Ricci and Niccolò the younger to suppress *Le Maschere*.

21.   Giuliano de' Ricci was Niccolò's grandson. Ricci was given the task of preparing and purging the complete works of Machiavelli by the Inquisition in the 1570's. He and his role in editing Machiavelli are discussed in detail in the following Chapter. His *Priorista*, with the exception of a few relatively short passages, remains unpublished. Perhaps an edition of this work would prove helpful to Machiavelli studies? Giuliano de'Ricci, *Priorista* MS. Palatino E.B. 14.1. in the Biblioteca Nazionale Centrale di Firenze.

22.   Villari's biography and assessment of Machiavelli, despite its age, remains helpful. For translation see Pasquale Villari, *Niccolò Machiavelli and his Times* 4 Vols. Trans. Linda Villari (London: Kegan Paul, 1878–83). See Vol. II, pp. 223–224. For

Italian, see Pasquale Villari, *Niccolò Machiavelli e i suoi tempi* 3 Volumi (Milano: Ulrico Hoepli, 2nd edn., 1895). See Vol. 1, p. 492. "Pare che il Machiavelli si dilettasse in quegli anni d'accoppiare spesso l'ironia e la satira al quotidiano lavoro degli affari, ed alle severe meditazioni politiche; giacchè è assai probabile che allora appunto componesse anche un secondo lavoro letterario, il quale sfortunatamente andò perduto. Era un'imitazione delle *Nuvole* e di altre commedie d'Aristofane, intitolata *Le Maschere*. Tutto quello che ne sappiamo è che la scrisse ad instigazione di Marcello Virgilio, e che pervenne con altre sue carte e lavori nelle mani di Giuliano de'Ricci, il quale non volle copiarla, come aveva fatto di tante altre cose inedite del suo illustre antenato, perchè era ridotta in frammenti appena leggebili, e perchè l'autore << sotto nomi finti va lacerando e maltrattando molti di quelli cittadini, che nel 1504 vivevano.>> Dopo di che lo stesso scrittore aggiunge: << Fu Niccolò in tutte quante le sue composizioni assai licenzioso, sì nel tassare persone grandi, ecclesiastiche e secolari, come anche nel ridurre tutte le cose a cause naturali o fortuite.>> E veramente questo spirito satirico e mordente fu quello che gli procure molti nemici, molti dispiaceri nella vita...."

23. Godman, *Poliziano to Machiavelli*, 181. Adriani was appointed to Poliziano's Chair at the Florentine Studio in 1495. Also See n. 16 above for the text of Adriani's letter to Machiavelli, where he wrote concerning the "lezione addosso."

24. Ibid, 193.

25. Ibid, 180. "Princes formed the audience to which Marcello Virgilio's lectures were addressed: "Princes and kings who, at home and abroad, were to administer the Florentine Republic." An education less for scholars than for statesmen was offered, to the sons of the ruling elite, by the First Chancellor at the Studio, from which his successful and sustained career had been launched." Godman cited a line from one of Adriani's lectures at the Studio; in double quotation marks within the quotation from Godman. Also see p. 180, n. 1, *N* fols. 65r and 51r: "reipublice nostre futuri . . . principes et reges," "qui rempublicam domi forisque administraturi sunt."

26. Ibid, 188.

27. Ibid, 241.

28. Francesco Guicciardini, *Ricordi* trans. Ninian Hill Thomson (New York: S.F. Vanni, 1949): 66–67. For Italian see same volume and pages. "Dico che uno buono cittadino ed amatore della patria non solo debbe intrattenersi col tiranno per sua sicurtà, perché è in pericolo quando è avuto a sospetto, ma ancora per beneficio della patria, perché governandosi cosí gli viene occasione co' consigli e con le opere di favorire molti beni e disfavorire molti mali; e questi che gli biasimano sono pazzi, perché sarebbe fresca la cittá e loro, se el tiranno non avessi intorno altro che tristi!" In this case, the Author translated the text.

29. Niccolò Machiavelli, *Il Principe e Altre Opere Politiche: Introduzione di Delio Cantimori, Note di Stefano Andretta* (Milano: Garzanti Libri, 1999), 89. "Perché questa è una regola generale che non falla mai: che uno principe, il quale non sia savio per sé stesso, non può essere consigliato bene, se già a sorte non si rimettessi in uno solo che al tutto lo governassi, che fussi uomo prudentissimo. In questo caso, potria bene essere, ma durerebbe poco, perché quello governatore in breve tempo li torrebbe lo stato."

30. Evidenced in the quotations just cited.

31. Machiavelli was given this position of authority because he was instrumental in organizing the militia at Florence in 1506. For a discussion of the citizen army at Florence see Viroli, *Smile*, 82.

32. Ridolfi, *Life of Niccolò*, 129.

33. Ibid, 133.

34. Ibid, 133. According to Ridolfi, the names of Machiavelli's 3 friends remain unknown.

35. Pasquale Villari, *The Life and Times of Niccolò Machiavelli* 4 Vols. trans. Linda Villari (Unwin: London, 1892), Volume II, 169.

36. Ibid, 169

37. Ibid, 170.

38. Marino Sanuto, *I Diarii, Volume XV* (Reprint of Venezia: F Visentini, 1879–1903) (Bologna: Forni, 1969), Column 573–574. Sanuto transcribed a letter written by "Julianus (Giuliano) de' Medici, Florentiae, die 19 Februarii 1513" These names are included in Giuliano's letter are: Nicolò Valori, Agostino Capponi, Giovanni Folchi, Lodovico de Nobili, Francesco Serragli, Nicolò de missier Bernardo Machiavelli, Andrea Marsuppini, Piero Orlandini, Daniele Stroze, Cechotto Tosinghi, El prete de' Martini.

39. Godman, *Poliziano to Machiavelli*, 242.

40. Villari, *Life and Times, II*, 170.

41. Ridolfi, *Life of Niccolò*, 136.

42. Godman, *Poliziano to Machiavelli*, 181. "The wonder is not that he lost his job in 1512, but that he held it for so long. The qualities of insight and outspokenness for which he is celebrated today, dangerous during the Republic, were his undoing at the restoration. Apart from his work in the organization or the militia, there is little evidence that Machiavelli, the political theorist, was especially astute in the practice of Florentine politics." Might one ask whether Machiavelli understood the "verità effettuale" of politics in Florence?

43. Ridolfi, *Life of Niccolò*, 138.

44. Shaw, *Politics of Exile*, 87.

45. Ridolfi, *Life of Niccolò*, 145.

46. Starn, *Contrary Commonwealth*, 125. For Petrarch's view of exile see by the same author "Petrarch's Consolation on Exile: a Humanist Use of Adversity," in Volume 1 of *Essays Presented to Myron P. Gilmore*, 2 Vols. eds. Sergio Bertelli and Gloria Ramakus (Firenze: La Nuova Italia Editrice, 2978), 241–254.

47. Starn, *Contrary Commonwealth*, 121. Starn is not referring directly to Machiavelli, but he ties Machiavelli as an exile, to this theme of "finding a voice."

48. Ibid, 146.

49. Najemy, *Between Friends*. See "Formerly Secretary" pp. 95–135.

50. Starn, *Contrary Commonwealth*, 98 n. 39.

51. Ibid, 3

52. Samuel Cohn, *Creating the Florentine State: Peasants and Rebellions, 1348–1434* (Cambridge: Cambridge University Press, 1999), 7–8 for his discussion of the "city-contado" dichotomy.

53. Ibid, 8. Where Cohn writes of the "plains," he is referring to Florence and its "suburbs."

54. The Author's translation. *Lettere*: 367–368, Letter 208, 9 April 1513. "Pure, se io vi potessi parlare, non potre' fare che io non vi empiessi il capo di castellucci, perché la Fortuna ha fatto che, non sapendo ragionare né dell'arte della seta e dell'arte lana, né de' guadagni né delle perdite, e' mi conviene ragionare dello stato, e mi bisogna o botarmi di stare cheto, o ragionare di questo. Se io potessi sbucare del dominio, io vorrei pure anch'io sino costì a domandare se il papa è in casa." Cited in Najemy, *Between Friends*, 107–108.

55. *Personal Correspondences*, 225, Letter 208, 9 April 1513. And, *Lettere*, 368, Letter 208, 9 April 1513. "Ma fra tante grazie, la mia per mia straccuratiggine restò in terra. Aspetterò il settembre."

56. *Personal Correspondences*, 225–226, Letter 208, 9 April 1513. For Italian, see *Lettere*, 368, Letter 208, 9 April 1513. "Io intendo che il cardinale de' Soderini fa un gran dimenarsi col pontefice. Vorrei che mi consgliassi, se vi paressi che fosse a proposito gli scrivessi una lettera, che mi raccomandassi a sua Santità; o se fosse meglio che voi facessi a bocca questo offizio per mia parte con il cardinale."

57. Najemy, *Between Friends*, 221. "By the fall (autumn) of 1513 Machiavelli probably realized that the rehabilitation he so longed for would not occur as the result of any words Vettori had spoken or might yet be willing to speak to Leo, Giulio, or Giuliano."

58. *Personal Correspondences*, 227, Letter 210, 16 April 1513. Also see *Lettere*, 370, Letter 210, 16 April 1513.

59. Shaw, *Politics of Exile*, 143–171 where she discusses in great detail the extent to which regimes would go in order to keep track of their exiles.

60. Najemy, *Between Friends*, 114–116.

61. *Personal Correspondences*, 231, Letter 211, 21 April 1513. For Italian, see *Lettere*, 376, Letter 211, 21 April 1513. "Levami e scrissi, perché quando vi viene a proposito mi diciate quello credete sia stata la fantasia di Spagna in questa triegua; et io approverrò il guidizio vostro, perché, a dirvi il vero senza adulazione, l'ho trovato in queste cose più saldo che di altro uomo, con il quale abbia parlato."

62. Machiavelli either forgot that Vettori had written him on 12 July or he had ignored Vettori's letter because of his grief at the loss of a child.

63. *Personal Correspondences*, 244, Letter 217, 4 August 1513. For Italian, see *Lettere*, 395, Letter 217, 4 August 1513. "Ho dipoi auta una littera tua de' dì 26 maggio, alla quale non mi occorre che dirti altro, se non che noi siamo tuti sani; e la Marietta fece una bambina, la quale si morì in capo di 3 dì. E Marietta sta bene."

64. *Personal Correspondences*, 257–260, Letter 222, 26 August 1513. And, *Lettere*: 414–419, Letter 222, 26 August 1513. "Signore ambasciadore. Questa vostra lettera de' 20 mi ha sbigottio, perché l'ordine di essa, la moltitudine della ragioni, e tutte le altre sue qualità mi hanno in modo implicato, che io restai nel principio smarrito e confuse."

65. The first 3 lines of Dante's *Inferno*. "Nel mezzo del cammin di nostra vita / Mi ritrovai per una selva oscura / Che la diritta via era smarrita." The translation is the Author's.

66. *Personal Correspondences*, 257, Letter 222, 26 August 1513. For Italian, see *Lettere*: 414–415, Letter 222, 26 August 1513. "E se io non mi fossi nel rileggerla un poco rassicurato, io davo cartaccia, e rispondevovi a qualche altra cosa. Ma nel particarla mi è intervenuto come alla volpe, quando la vedde il leone, che la prima volta fu per morire di paura, la seconda si fermò a guardarlo drieto ad un cespuglio, la terza gli favellò; e così io, rassicuratomi nel pratricarla, vi risponderò."

67. Najemy, *Between Friends*, 168. "Given Vettori's letter of the twentieth, although impressive in its reasoning and organized presentation of information, contained arguments consistent with those of his earlier letters, Machiavelli's "confession" of initial bewilderment and confusion seems oddly out of place."

68. Discussed in Chapter 18 of *Il Principe*. This subject is developed in the following Chapter.

69. Garrett Mattingly, "Machiavelli's *Prince*: Political Science or Political Satire?" in *The American Scholar* 27 (1958): 482–491. This article addresses that subject as

70.   well as those indicated by its title.
      Personal Correspondences, 264, Letter 224, 10 December 1513. For Italian, see
      Lettere, 426, Letter 224, 10 December 1513. "Venuta la sera, mi ritorno in casa, et
      entro nel mio scrittoio; et in su l'uscio mi spoglio quella veste cotidiana, piena di
      fango e di loto, e mi metto panni reali e curiali; e rivestito condecentemente entro
      nelle antique corti degli antiqui uomini, dove, da loro ricevuto amorevolmente, mi
      pasco di quel cibo, che solum è mio, e che io nacqui per lui; dove io non mi
      vergogno parlare con loro, e domandarli della ragione delle loro azioni; e quelli per
      loro umanità mi rispondono; e non sento per 4 ore di tempo alcuna noia, sdimentico
      ogni affano, non temo la povertà, non mi sbigottisce la morte: tutto mi transferisco
      in loro. E perché Dante dice che non fa scienza sanza lo ritenere lo avere inteso, io
      ho notato quello di che per la loro conversazione ho fatto capitale, e composto uno
      opusculo *De principatibus*."
71.   Godman, *Poliziano to Machiavelli*, 257.
72.   Najemy, *Between Friends*, 235.
73.   *L'Asino, Belfagor*, a "novella" and *Andria* written in 1517; *Mandragola*, written in
      1518.   These are only a few of the works that Machiavelli wrote after the
      "vendemmial" of 1515. The dates for these works are cited in Grazia, *Hell*, 23–24.
74.   For Italian, see *Principe, 1999*, 14.   "Né voglio sia reputata presunzione se uno
      uomo di basso et infimo stato ardisce discorrere e regolare e' governi de' principi;
      perché, così come coloro che disegnono e' paesi si pongano bassi nel piano a
      considerare la natura de' monti e de' luoghi alti, e per considerare quella de' bassi si
      pongano alto sopra monti, similmente, a conoscere bene la natura de' populi,
      bisogna esser principe, et a conoscere bene quella de' principi bisogna esser
      populare."
75.   *Principe, 1999*, 14. "Pigli adunque vostra Magnificenzia questo piccolo dono con
      quello animo che io lo mando; il quale se da quella fia diligentemente considerato e
      letto, vi conoscerà drento uno estremo mio desiderio, che Lei pervenga a quella
      grandezza che la fortuna e le altre sue qualità li promettano. E, se vostra
      Magnificenzia dallo apice della sua altezza qualche volta volgerà li occhi in questi
      luoghi bassi, conoscerà quanto io indegnamente sopporti una grande e continua
      malignità di fortuna."
76.   Machiavelli's familiarity with Petrarch appears to have been more than superficial.
      For example, he quoted Petrarch at the end of *Il Principe*; he cites Petrarch in the
      famous letter to Vettori dated 10 December 1513 among others. All references to
      Petrarch in Machiavelli are noted in the commentary to Chapter Seven of this study.
77.   Francesco Petrarch, *Letters from Petrarch* trans. and ed. Morris Bishop
      (Bloomington: Indiana University Press, 1966), 47, "The Ascent of Mont Ventoux,"
      written 26; April 1336. For Latin, see Francesco Petrarca, *Le Familiari: Edizione
      Critica: Volume Primo* Per cura di Vittorio Rossi (Firenze: Sansoni, 1933), 155–
      156, Liber Quartus, I, 12–15, 89–110. "Sic sepe delusus quadam in valle consedi.
      Illic a corporeis ad incorporeal volucri cogitatione transiliens, his aut talibus me
      ipsum compellabam verbis: "Quod totiens hodie in ascensu montis huius expertus
      es, id scito et tibi accidere et multis, accedentibus ad beatam vitam; sed idcirco tam
      facile ad hominibus non perpendi, quod corporis motus in aperto sunt, animorum
      vero invisibiles et occulti. Equidem vita, quam beatam dicimus, celso loco sita est;
      areta, ut aiunt, ad illam ducit via. Mutli quoque colles intereminent et de virtute in
      virtutem preclaris gradibus ambulandum est; in summo finis est omnium et vie
      terminus ad quem peregrinatio nostra disponitur. Eo pervinire volunt omnes, sed ut
      ait Naso, "Velle parum est; cupias, ut re potiaris, oportet." Tu certe—nisi, ut in

multis, in hoc quoque te fallis—non solum vis sed etiam cupis. Quid ergo te retinet? Nimirum nichil aliud, nisi per terrenas et infimas voluptates planior et un prima fronte videtur, expeditior via; veruntamen, ubi multum erraveris, aut sub pondere male dilati laboris ad ipsius te beate vite culmen oportet ascendere aut in convallibus peccatorum tuorum segnem procumbere; et si—quod ominari horreo—ibi te tenebre et umbra mortis invenerint, eternam noctem in perpetuis cruciatibus agree."

78.   *Familiari*, Liber Quartus, I, 26, 190. "Que dum mirarer singula et nunc terrenum alquid saperem, nunc exemplo corporis animum ad altiora subveherem, visum est michi *Confessionum* Augistini librum [...] habeoque semper in manibus." *Letters from Petrarch*, 49 where Petrarch wrote: "While admiring all these features, now recognizing some earthly object, now uplifting my soul, like my body, it occurred to me to look at the *Confessions* of Augustine [...] I keep it with me always."

79.   *Principe, 1999*, 94–95. "E se, come io dissi, era necessario, volendo vedere la virtù di Moisé, che il populo d'Isdrael fussi stiavo in Egitto, et a conoscere la grandezza dello animo di Ciro, ch'e' Persi fussino oppressati da' Medi e la eccellenzia di Teseo, che li Ateniensi fussino dispersi; così al presente, volendo conoscere la virtù d'uno spirito italiano, era necessario che la Italia si riducessi nel termine che ell'è di presente, e che la fussi più stiava che li Ebrei, più serva ch'e' Persi, più dispersa che li Ateniensi, sanza capo, sanza ordine; battuta, spogliata, lacera, corsa, et avessi sopportato d'ogni sorte ruina."

80.   Donald Weinstein, *Savonarola and Florence: Prophecy and Patriotism in the Renaissance* (Princeton: Princeton University Press, 1970); Lorenzo Polizotto, *The Elect Nation: The Savonarolan Movement in Florence, 1494–1545* (Oxford: Clarendon Press, 1994); Roberto Ridolfi, *Vita di Girolamo Savonarola* 2 Vols. (Firenze: Tipografia Giuntina, 1952). Ridolfi's biography has yet to be surpassed. For more background on religion, prophecy and politics see Ottavia Niccoli, *Prophecy and People in Renaissance Italy* trans. Lydia G. Cochrane (Princeton: Princeton University Press, 1990).

81.   Niccolò Machiavelli, *The Discourses of Niccolò Machiavelli* 2 Vol. Trans. Lesley J. Walker (London, Routledge, 1950), Vol. 1, II. 31, p. 450. For Italian, see Niccolò Machiavelli, *Discorsi Sopra la Prima Deca di Tito Livio*. Introduzione di Gennaro Sasso, Note di Giorgio Inglese., (Milano: Biblioteca Universale Rizzoli, 1999), II. 31, p. 378. "E' non mi pare fuori di proposito ragionare, intra questi altri discorsi, quanto sia cosa pericolosa credere a quelli che sono cacciati della *patria* sua, essendo cose che ciascuno dì si hanno a praticare da coloro che tengono stati... Debbesi considerare pertanto quanto sia vana e la fede e le promesse di quelli che si truovano privi della loro *patria*. Perché, quanto alla fede, si ha a estimare che, qualunque volta e' possano per altri mezzi che per gli tuoi rientrare nella *patria* loro, che lasceranno te e accosterannosi ad altri, nonostante qualunque promesse ti avessono fatte. E quanto alle vane promesse e speranze, egli è tanta la voglia estrema che è in loro di ritornare in casa, che ei credono naturalmente molte cose che sono false e molte ad arte ne aggiungano: talché, tra quello che ei credono e quello che ei dicono di credere ti riempiono di speranza, talmente che fondandoti in su quella o tu fai una spesa in vano, o tu fai una impresa dove tu rovini." Cited in Starn, *Contrary Commonwealth*: 94, 182, n. 26.

82.   Villari, *Life and Times, II*, 170.

Chapter Five

1. Maurizio Viroli and Susan Meld Shell are two such scholars. Their work is discussed below.

2. Dante Alighieri, *De Vulgari Eloquentia* trans. Warman Welliver (Ravenna: Ravenna Longo, 1981).

3. This is corroborated by Giovanni Battista Gelli in *Ragionamento...sopra le difficoltà di mettere in regole la nostra lingua* (Florence, 1551), 27. Cited by Hans Baron in Hans Baron, "Machiavelli on the Eve of the *Discourses*: The Date and Place of the *Dialogo intorno alla nostra lingua,*" *Bibliotheque d'Humanisme et Renaissance* 23 (1961): 449–76. See p. 465, n. 1. Also argued thoroughly by Pio Rajna. See his article: "La Data del "Dialogo int. alla lingua" di N. Machiavelli," *Rendiconti dell R. Accad. dei Lincei, Classe Scienze Morali* Memorie, serie V. II (1893): 203–222.

4. As in the Appendices, the references here were compiled with the aid of "intratext.com."

5. See Appendix Four for Italian.

6. The reader will find these references in Appendix Four.

7. Niccolò Machiavelli, *Il Principe e Altre Opere Politiche*: Introduzione di Delio Cantimori, Note di Stefano Andretta (Milano: Garzanti Libri, 1999), 61. "This is, that some who are held to be liberal (or generous), some miserly (using a Tuscan term, because *avaro* (or avaricious) in our language, is one who steals what he desires to have, and we call one *misero* (or miserly) who keeps more than he uses himself).

8. Niccolò Machiavelli, *Discorsi Sopra la Prima Deca di Tito Livio* Introduzione di Gennaro Sasso, Note di Giorgio Inglese (Milano: Biblioteca Universale Rizzoli, 1999), II. 5., p. 309. "Having its own customs and own native tongue." The author's translation.

9. Niccolò Machiavelli, *Istorie fiorentine*, in *Tutte le Opere Storiche e Letterarie di Niccolò Machiavelli* A cura di Guido Mazzoni e Mario Casella (Firenze: G. Barbèra, 1929), 375–621. See p. 384 for quotation. "Intra queste rovine e questi nuovi popoli sursono nuove lingue, come apparisce nel parlare che in Francia, in Ispagna e in Italia si costuma; il quale mescolato con la lingua patria di quelli nuovi popoli e con la antica romana fanno un nuovo ordine di parlare." For translation see Niccolò Machiavelli, *Florentine Histories* trans. Laura F. Banfield and Harvey C. Mansfield, Jr. (Princeton: Princeton University Press, 1990), 14.

10. See the translation of the *Dialogo* in Chapter Seven. For Italian, see Appendix Four.

11. Peter Godman, *From Poliziano to Machiavelli: Florentine Humanism in the High Renaissance* (Princeton: Princeton University Press, 1998), 304, n. 11.

12. MS *E.B.* 15–10 della Biblioteca Nazionale di Firenze (11 pp., da c. 133*r* a c. 138*r*). See the first page of the MS for Ricci's letter. Also see "Figure 1."

13. John A. Tedeschi, "Florentine Documents for a History of the *Index of Prohibited Books,*" *Renaissance Studies in Honor of Hans Baron*, ed. Anthony Molho and John A. Tedeschi (DeKalb: Northern Illinois University Press, 1971), 577–605, 581, n.11. "They (Ricci and Niccolò the younger) would not publish," their edited text, "with Rome's condition that it should appear without Machiavelli's name or a substitute." Also see John Tedeschi, *The Prosecution of Heresy: Collected Studies on the*

Inquisition in Early Modern Italy (Binghamton: Medieval & Renaissance Texts & Studies, 1991), 310–311, n. 15.

14. MS Palatino 815 della Biblioteca Nazionale di Firenze, 820–39.

15. The *Dialogo* in Benedetto Varchi, *L'Hercolano, dialogo ...nel qual si ragiona generalmente delle lingue, et in particolare della Toscana, e della Fiorentina; composto...sulla occasione della disputa occorsa tra'l Commendator Caro, e M. L. Castelvetro. Nuovamente stampato* A cura di Giovanni Bottari (Florence: Tartini e Franchi, 1730), 449–467.

16. Niccolò Machiavelli, *Discorso, overro dialogo, in cui si esamina, se la lingua, in cui scrissero Dante, il Boccaccio, e il Petrarca, si debba chiamare Italiana, Toscana, o Fiorentina, in Opere: Volume Otto: Commedie, terzine ed altre opere* (Cosmopoli, 1769).

17. Niccolò Machiavelli, *Discorso o dialogo intorno alla lingua, in Tutte le Opere Storiche e Letterarie di Niccolò Machiavelli* A cura di Guido Mazzoni e Mario Casella (Firenze: G. Barbèra, 1929), 770–778.

18. Baron, "Place of the *Dialogo*," 449–473. Also see Cecil Grayson, "Lorenzo, Machiavelli and the Italian Language," *Italian Studies*, ed. E.F. Jacob (London: Faber and Faber, 1960), 410–432.

19. Cecil Grayson, "Machiavelli and Dante," *Renaissance Studies in Honor of Hans Baron*, eds. Anthony Molho and John A. Tedeschi (DeKalb: Northern Illinois University Press, 1971), 361–384, 369, n. 17. Also see Filippo Luigi Polidori, *Opere minori di Niccolò Machiavelli rivedute sulle migliori edizioni* (Firenze, 1852), 589. Cited in Grayson, "Machiavelli and Dante," 369. Also see Oreste Tommasini, *La vita e gli scritti di Niccolo Machiavelli nella loro relazione col machiavellismo* I (Torino, 1883), 100. Cited in Grayson, "Machiavelli and Dante," 363.

20. Grayson, "Machiavelli and Dante," 362, prefatory n.

21. Ibid.

22. Carlo Dionisotti, *Machiavellerie* (Torino: G. Einaudi, 1980), 267–363. Also see Carlo Dionisotti, "Machiavelli, Man of Letters," *Machiavelli and the Discourse of Literature*, eds. Albert Russell Ascoli and Victoria Kahn (Ithaca: Cornell University Press, 1993): 17–51, 17 where Dionisotti noted, "The title and gist of this paper repeat a talk with this title that I gave in the fall of 1969 at the Villa i Tatti in Florence in honour of the fifth centennial of Machiavelli's birth, which has been published in various times and in various forms: in the *Notiziario culturale dell'Istituto Italiano di Cultura di Parigi* 4 (1969): 15–26, in *Studies on Machiavelli*, ed. Myron P. Gilmore (Florence, 1972), 101–143; and in *Machiavelli nel quinto centenario della nascita* (Bologna, 1973), 93–109."

23. Susan Meld Shell, "Machiavelli's Discourse on Language," *The Comedy and Tragedy of Machiavelli: Essays on the Literary Works*, ed. Vickie B Sullivan (New Haven: Yale University Press, 2000), 78–101. Maurizio Viroli, *For Love of Country: An Essay on Patriotism and Nationalism* (New York: Clarendon Press, 1997), 32–33 for references to the *Dialogo*.

24. Niccolò Machiavelli, *Discorso o dialogo intorno alla nostra lingua: Edizione critica* A cura di Bortolo Tommaso Sozzi (Torino: G. Einaudi, 1976); and the *Dialogo* in Ornella Castellani Pollidori, ed., *Niccolò Machiavelli e il "Dialogo intorno alla nostra lingua" con una edizione critica del testo* (Firenze: Olschki, 1978); and the

Dialogo in Ornella Castellani Pollidori, ed., *Nuove Riflessioni sul discorso o dialogo Intorno alla nostra lingua di Niccolò Machiavelli* (Roma: Solerno Editrice, 1981).

25. For a good study of Dante's political thought see Alexander Passerin D'Entrèves, *Dante as a Political Thinker* (Oxford: Clarendon, 1952); and George Holmes, *Dante* (Oxford: Clarendon, 1980).

26. Of the third complete MS, the author will say little. This is due, first and foremost, to the fact that the author was not able to examine this work in person and does not wish to speculate about that which remains unread. Furthermore, little has been written on that MS. See Rosetta Migliorini Fissi, "Per la Fortuna del "De vulgari eloquentia," un Nuovo Codice del "Discorso o dialogo intorno alla nostra lingua": Approcci per una Edizione Critica," *Studi danteschi*, XLIX (1972): 135–214. Also, see Ornella Castellani Pollidori, ed., *Niccolò Machiavelli e il "Dialogo intorno alla nostra lingua" con una edizione critica del testo* (Firenze: Olschki, 1978), p. 192. That MS is titled "Machiavelli. *Dialogo sulla lingua*," and it is found in the Biblioteca Medicea Laurenziana, Ashburnham 674 (605) (Prov. Libri—A).

27. *Dialogo, 1976.*

28. MS *E.B.* 15–10 della Biblioteca Nazionale di Firenze (11 pp., da c. 133r a c. 138r). Further information concerning the history of this MS may be found in *Dialogo, 1976*, X–XII.

29. *Dialogo, 1976*, X–XI. "Havevo disegnato d'andare seguitando di copiare questi giornaletti d'historie del Machiavello, quando mi è capitato alle mani un discorso o dialogo intorno alla nostra lingua, dicono fatto dal medisimo Niccolò, et se bene lo stile è alquanto diverso dall'altre cose sue, et io in questi fragmenti che ho ritrovati non ho visto né originale, né bozza, né parte alcuna di detto dialogo, nondimento credo si possa credere indubitatamente che sia della stesso Machiavello, atteso che li concepti appariscono suoi, che per molti anni per ciascuno in mano di chi hoggi si truova si tiene suo, et quello che più di altro importa è che Bernardo Machiavelli, figlio di detto Niccolò, hoggi di età di anni 74, afferma ricordarsi haverne sentito ragionare a suo padre, et vedutogliene fra le mani molte volte. Il dialogo e questo che seguita." Translation is the Author's. "I had intended to copy these following small history journals by Machiavelli, when, a discourse or dialogue concerning our language, which they said was written by Niccolò, fell into my hands, and even though the style is somewhat different from his other works, and I, in these fragments, which I have found, have not seen the original, neither a rough draft nor other part of the said dialogue, nevertheless, think one is able indubitably to know whether it is from the same Machiavelli, (because) I bear witness that the concepts appear to be his, that for many years, whoever has had it in hand and whoever has it now is of the opinion that it is his, and of greater importance than anything else, Bernardo Machiavelli, son of the said Niccolò, today he was 74 years of age, affirmed and recalled having heard his father reason about it, and seeing it in his hands many times. The dialogue is that which follows." This excellent quotation from Giuliano de' Ricci; Ricci's note, first appeared in Pasquale Villari, *Machiavelli e i suoi tempi* (Le Monnier: Firenze 1877). Cecil Grayson also notes Ricci's comment in his article, "Machiavelli and Dante," 369, n. 16. See "Figure 1" for a copy of Ricci's opening letter.

30. *Dialogo, 1976*, X. "Ma per il *Discorso* la trascrizione del Ricci, in bella e chiara scrittura corsiva di tipo cancelleresco, non si estende a tutta l'opera, ma copre soltanto la prima e quasi intera la seconda facciata; il rimanente, in scrittura corsiva

atipica, quasi certamente tardo-cinquecentesca, è di altra mano." See "Figure 2" which illustrates this dramatic change.

31. Ibid, XIV–XV. "Il Grayson (Cecil) lo assegna al secolo XVII; il Ridolfi (Roberto) si limita a dirlo <<tarda copia>>."

32. MS *Vat. Barb. Lat.* 5368. cc. 44–53. Titolo: *Messer Niccolò di Bernardo Machiavelli: Discorso over dialogo circa la lingua fiorentina.* More information concerning this MS may be found in *Dialogo, 1976*, XIV–XVI.

33. *Dialogo, 1976*, XV–XVI. "Il Casella (Mario), come s'è detto, lo associa a *R* (apografo Ricci] come suo parallelo e gemello nella derivazione da *y* (tesi respinta dalla Migliorini Fissi, che lo considera dipendente da *R)* e lo assume come complentare di *R* nella formazione del testo critico.

34. Ornella Castellani Pollidori suggests that Niccolò the younger copied the Vatican MS. If true, this corroborates the author's suggestion that Niccolò the younger is the "altro mano" in the Ricci MS. An examination of the Vatican MS and the latter portions of the Ricci MS, seem to bear this out. See Pollidori's 1978 edition of the *Dialogo*, p. 192.

35. MS segnatura Miscell. Borghini III, Filze Rinucinni 22, 9 pp., c 1*r* a c. 5*r*. Titolo: *Discorso di Nic0. Machiavelli nel quale si tratta [della lingua].* The words in brackets are in another's handwriting. This manuscript is discussed in greater detail in *Dialogo, 1976*, XIII–XIV.

36. For translation, see Chapter Seven of this book, p. 169. For Italian, see Appendix Four, p. 205. Also see p. XIII in *Dialogo, 1976* where Sozzi mentions that this is the last line of the Borghini MS. Also see Grayson, "Machiavelli and Dante," 368, n. 14.

37. See note 35 above for MS's full details

38. *Dialogo, 1976*, XIII. "La specificazione ultima è di altra e più tarda mano."

39. Grayson, "Machiavelli and Dante," 368, n. 14.

40. Godman, *Poliziano to Machiavelli*, 303–333 for an overview.

41. Ibid, 303.

42. Niccolò Machiavelli, *Florentine Histories* trans. Laura Banfield and Harvey C. Mansfield, Jr. (Princeton: Princeton University Press, 1988), xii

43. Godman, *Poliziano to Machiavelli*, 304.

44. Ibid, 304.

45. Ibid, 308. Ricci and Niccolò the younger centred their early efforts on the preparation of the *Istorie* in 1551. In this edition they removed offensive references to the papacy and they published the work without the author's name attached. This version of the *Istorie* was not deemed acceptable by the Congregation.

46. Tedeschi, "Prohibited Books." In this essay Tedeschi edited letters written by the Inquisitors at Florence. For a detailed discussions of the *Index*, see J.M. de Bujanda, ed., *Index de Rome 1557, 1559, 1564: Les premiers Index romains et l'Index du Concile de Trent Index de Livres interdicts* 8 (Sherbrooke, 1990).

47. Godman, *Poliziano to Machiavelli*, 304.

48. Ibid, 308.

49. Ricci's role in suppressing *Le Maschere* was discussed in the previous Chapter.

50. Godman, *Poliziano to Machiavelli*, 304.

51. Ibid, 305–307.

52. Ibid, 308.

53. Ibid, 305–307.

54.   Borghini's edition was printed without the "e" at the end of *Decameron*.
55.   Tedeschi, *Heresy*, 310, n. 15. The Author had the opportunity to examine Borghini's 1573 edition which is in the National Library of Scotland. See Giovanni Boccaccio, *Il Decameron.../ricorretto in Roma et emendato secondo l'ordine del Sacro Conc. di Trento, et riscontrato in Firenze con testi antichi & alla sua vera lezione ridotto da' deputati di loro Alt. Ser. (i.e. Vincezo M. Borghini, Pier F. Cambi and Sebastiono Antinori)* (Fiorenza: I Giunti, 1573).
56.   Tedeschi, *Heresy*, 310, n. 15.
57.   Godman, *Saint as Censor*, 31.
58.   Tedeschi, *Heresy*, 310, n. 15.
59.   Godman, *Poliziano to Machiavelli*, 307.
60.   Giuliano de' Ricci, *Cronaca: 1532–1606* A cura di Giuliano Sapori (Milano: Riccardo Ricciardi, 1972), 94, [352 r.] and 309, [462 r.] where Ricci notes the death of Borghini. He wrote "Morì don Vincenzo Borghini spedalingo dello spedale delli Innocenti, persona conosciuta per le annotationi fatte al Boccaccio."
61.   Tedeschi, *Heresy*, 310, n. 14.
62.   Ibid, 302–305. Also see, in the same work, 318–319, ns. 61–62. "Reverendo Padre. In risposta alla lettera di V.R. delli 4 di Dicembre le dico, che questi Ill.mi e R.mi Sig.ri Cardinali non hanno voluto conceder licenza al Regente dell'Accademia de' Spensierati di tennere e leggere l'opere del Machiavelli, Boccaccio e Castelvetro ad effetto di correggerle, e farle ristampare di nuovo..."
63.   Tedeschi, *Heresy*, 310, n. 14.
64.   Ibid. Also see, 324–329 in the same volume, for a representative sentence passed on an individual for possessing works deemed heretical by the Congregation.
65.   There are a total of four MSS if the Ashburnham MS, which the author could not examine, is included.
66.   MS Palatino 815 della Biblioteca Nazionale di Firenze, 820–39. See *Dialogo, 1976*, XVI.
67.   *Dialogo, 1730*. This is the full title of Bottari's edition. In the collection of the British Library, London, Shelf Mark: 1560/1859.
68.   The *Dialogo* in Benedetto Varchi, *L'Ercolano: dialogo di Benedetto Varchi nel quale si ragiona delle lingue, ed inparticolare della Toscana e della Fiorentina* (Milano: Società Tipografica de'Classici Italiani, Contrada di S. Margherita, N.o 1118, 1804). "Figures 7, 8, 9 and 10" below show this edition's title page as well as the passages that illustrate Bottari's omissions.
69.   *Dialogo, 1976*, XVI. "*Editio princeps*, a cura di Giovanni Bottari, in appendice all'*Ercolano* di B. Varchi, Tartini e Franchi, Firenze 1730."
70.   Ibid, XVI. "the addition of many arbitrary judgments and errors." The author's translation.
71.   Ibid, XVII. "Tra gli arbitrii più cospicui del Bottari è da annoverare la soppressione del passo relativo alla curia papale."
72.   For Italian edition, see Appendix Four, p. 226. Also see Niccolò Machiavelli, *Opere Complete di Niccolò Machiavelli, con molte correzione e giunte rinvenute sui manoscritti originali* (Florence, 1843), 582. "Ma se tu parli della corte di Roma, tu parli di un luogo dove si parla di tanti modi di quante nazioni vi sono, ne se gli puo dare regola. (Reference to the papacy would have been here) Ma quello che inganna molti, circa i vocaboli comuni stati celebrati e letti in varj luoghi, molti vocaboli

nostri sono stati imparati da molti forestieri, ed osservati da loro, tale che di proprj nostri son diventati comuni." Citing this edition may seem random, but it is in the author's collection. Having noticed that the references to the papacy were omitted, the author checked other editions published within 10–15 years of his edition. The same section was missing. For translation, see Chapter Seven of this work, p. 181.

73. Dante Alighieri, *De Vulgari Eloquentia* trans. Warman Welliver (Ravenna: Ravenna Longo, 1981), I. XVI for English translation: "And so, having found what I was seeking, I proclaim an illustrious, cardinal, royal, and courtly vernacular in Italy, which is of every Latin city and seems to be of none, and by which all the municipal vernaculars of Latins are measured and weighed and compared"; 80 for Latin original: "Itaque, adepti quod querebamus, dicimus illustre, cardinale, aulicum et curiale vulgare in Latio, quod omnis latie civitatis est nullis esse videtur, et quo municipalia vulgaria omnia Latinorum mensurantur et ponderantur et comparantur."

74. Ricci's Apograph, the Vatican MS and the Palatino MS.

75. The 1929 edition in *Tutte le Opere*, 770–778.

76. Unfortunately, the author was unable to obtain the necessary permission to print the underlined portion of the Vatican MS, but the reader will find the reference to the papal court in the Palatino MS in "Figure 3."

77. The first edition to do so is Niccolò Machiavelli, *Discorso, overro dialogo, in cui si esamina, se la lingua, in cui scrissero Dante, il Boccaccio, e il Petrarca, si debba chiamare Italiana, Toscana, o Fiorentina* in *Opere: Volume Otto: Commedie, terzine ed altre opere* (Cosmopoli, 1769). .

78. *Tutte le Opere, 1929*.

79. *Opere, 1769*. Cited in Grayson, "Machiavelli and Dante," 369, n. 16. The Glasgow University Library has this edition in its Special Collections Department. The author had the opportunity to examine it. Its title as well as its omissions mirrors those of Bottari's text. "Figures 5 and 6" illustrate this point.

80. This edition was printed in Florence in 1843. See Niccolò Machiavelli, *Opere Complete di Niccolò Machiavelli, con molte correzione e giunte rinvenute sui manoscritti originali* (Florence, 1843).

81. Niccolò Machiavelli, *Opere di Niccolò Machiavelli* A cura di Giuseppe Zirardini (Parigi, 1851).

82. *Opere Complete, 1843*. The brackets around the "o" are the author's, highlighting the only change to Bottari's title. The editors of 1843 edition added the "o."

83. Harry Hearder, *Italy in the Age of the Risorgimento:1790–1870* (London: Longman, 1983), 287.

84. The title of the 1843 edition is a good example of this. *Opere Complete di Niccolò Machiavelli, con molte correzioni e giunte rinvenute sui manoscritti originali.*

85. *Tutte le Opere, 1929*, 770–778.

86. Ibid, LXX. "'The Dialogo concerning the Florentine language' is here given for the first time in its entirety, with the passage against the Roman court that Bottari had suppressed in his edition of 1730." The author's translation. Mazzoni and Casella refer to "Il Dialogo" as "Discorso o Dialogo Intorno Alla Nostra Lingua," following the Ricci/Machiavelli apograph, as the proper title of the short treatise; on p. 770. Also see *Dialogo, 1976*, XVII.

87. Grayson, "Machiavelli and Dante," 365. "At no point (anywhere in his writings) does he seem at all critically engaged with Dante either as a man or as a poet in any

unfavorable sense."

88. Shell, "Machiavelli's Discourse." Shell discusses the authenticity of the work, throughout this article.

89. Tommasini, *Vita*, 100.

90. Grayson, "Machiavelli and Dante," 363–364.

91. Niccolò Machiavelli, *The First Decennale: A Facsimile of the First Edition of February, 1506* (Cambridge, Mass.: Harvard University Press, 1969). See the article used as an introduction, William A. Jackson, Richard H. Rouse and Ernest Hatch Wilkins, "The Early Editions of Machiavelli's First *Decennale*," 1.

92. Michael Harvey, "Lost in the Wilderness: Love and Longing in L'Asino," *The Comedy and Tragedy of Machiavelli: Essays on the Literary Works*, ed. Vickie B Sullivan (New Haven: Yale University Press, 2000), 120–137, see p. 123 where Harvey writes, "The work (L'Asino) draws most overtly from the *Metamorphoses* or the *Golden Ass* of Apuleius."

93. Grayson, "Machiavelli and Dante," 365–366. "If one agrees that the parody of Dante in the *Asino* is unintentional, the references and quotations and imitation of Dante in Machiavelli's works suggests respect and at times admiration for the poet." Grayson's is an awfully big "if." What if the parody is intentional?

94. Harvey, "L'Asino," 122. Also see "L'Asino d'oro," in *Tutte le Opere, 1929*, 817. "I vari casi, la pena e la doglia/ Che sotto forma d'un Asin soffersi,/ Canterò io, pur che fortuna volgia" [ll.1–3]

95. Roberto Ridolfi, *The Life of Niccolò Machiavelli* trans. Cecil Grayson (London: Routledge and K. Paul, 1963), 166.

96. John Hale, *Machiavelli and Renaissance Italy* (London: The English Universities Press Ltd, 1966), 168.

97. Harvey, "L'Asino," 123.

98. Niccolò Machiavelli, "L'Asino d'oro," in *Tutte le Opere Storiche e Letterarie di Niccolò Machiavelli* A cura di Guido Mazzoni e Mario Casella (Firenze: G. Barbèra, 1929): 817–840. See p. 823. "Dietro a le piante da la mia duchessa…"

99. Shell, "Machiavelli's Discourse," 80.

100. Niccolò Machiavelli, *The Ass* in *The Chief Works and Others* Vol. 3, trans. Allan Gilbert (Durham: Duke University Press, 1965): 769–770. For Italian, see *L'Asino*, 837. "Alzò quel porco al giunger nostro il grifo/ Tutto vergato di meta e di loto,/ Tal che mi venne nel guardarlo a schifo,/ E perch'io fui già gran tempo suo noto,/ Ver me si mosse mostrandomi i denti,/ Stando col resto fermo e senza moto./ Ond'io li dissi, pur con grati accenti:/ "Dio ti dia miglior sorte, se ti pare;/ Dio ti mantegna, se tu ti contenti." [Capitolo VIII, ll. 1–9].

101. Dante Alighieri, *The Divine Comedy: Inferno* trans. Charles Singleton (Princeton: Princeton University Press, 1989), 346–347. Canto XXXII.126–139. "ch'io vidi due ghiacciati in una buca,/ sì che l'un capo all'altro era cappello;/ e come 'l pan per fame si manduca,/ così 'l sovran li denti a l'altro pose/ là 've 'l cervel s'aggiugne con la nuca:/ non altrimenti Tideo si rose/ le tempie a Menalippo per disdegno,/ che quei faceva il teschio e l'altre cose./ "O tu che mostri per sì bestial segno/ odio sovra colui che tu ti mangi,/ dimmi 'l perchè," diss' io "per tal convegno,/ che se tu a ragion di lui ti piangi,/ sappiendo chi voi siete e la sua pecca,/ nel mondo suso ancora io te ne cangi,/ se quella con ch' io parlo non si secca.'" [Canto XXXII, ll. 125–139

102.   *Inferno, 1989*, 348–355, Canto XXXIII.1–91 for Ugolino's speech.

103.   *The Ass*, 770. For Italian, see *L'Asino*, 838. 8.19–33 and 43–44 "Vuole ancor da sua parte ch'io ti dica/ Che ti libererà da tanto male,/ Se tornar vuoi ne la tua forma antica."/ Levossi allora in piè dritto il cignale,/ Udendo quello; e fe' questa risposta,/ Tutto turbato, il fangoso animale:/ "Non so d'onde tu venga, o di qual costa;/ Ma se per altro tu non se'venuto/ Che per trarmi di qui, vanne a tua posta./ Viver con voi io non volgio, e rifiuto;/ E veggo ben che tu se'in quello errore,/ Che me più tempo ancor ebbe tenuto./ Tanto v'inganna il proprio vostro amore,/ Che altro ben non credete che sia Fuor de l'umana essenza e del valore[...]/ Senz'alcun dubbio, io affermo o confesso/ Esser superior la parte nostra;/ E ancor tu nol negherai appresso."

104.   Harvey, "L'Asino," 131

105.   Shell, "Machiavelli's Discourse," 80.

106.   Harvey, "L'Asino," 123.

107.   Barbara Godorecci, *After Machiavelli: "Re-writing" and the "Hermeneutic Attitude"* (West Lafayette: Purdue University Press, 1993), 78. As the title indicates this work is written from the perspective of a literary critic and theorist. One of Godorecci's central arguments is that Machiavelli subverts and re-appropriates the writings of others through re-writing their texts within his own.

108.   Quentin Skinner, *Machiavelli* (Oxford: Oxford University Press, 1996), 40–47 for Skinner's discussion of Machiavelli's attitude toward Cicero in *Il Principe*. See p. 40 for quotation.

109.   Marcus Tullius Cicero, *De Officiis* trans. Walter Miller (Cambridge, Mass.: Harvard University Press, 1997), pp. 44–47. I. 42, pp. 44 and 46 for the Latin original. "Cum autem duobus modis, id est aut vi aut fraude, fiat iniuria, fraus quasi vulpeculae, vis leonis videtur; utrumque homine alienissimum, sed fraus odio digna maiore. Totius autem iniustitiae nulla capitalior quam eorum, qui tum, cum maxime fallunt, id agunt, ut viri boni esse videantur."

110.   Skinner, *Machiavelli*, 40.

111.   *Principe, 1999*, 67–68. "Dovete adunque sapere come sono dua generazione di combattere: l'uno con le leggi, l'altro con la forza: quel primo è proprio dello uomo, quel secondo delle bestie: ma, perché el primo molte volte non basta, conviene ricorrere al secondo. Per tanto a uno principe è necessario sapere bene usare la bestia e lo uomo...Sendo adunque uno principe necessitato sapere bene usare la bestia, debbe di quelle pigliare la golpe (volpe) et il lione; perché il lione non si difende da' lacci, la golpe non si difende da' lupi. Bisogna adunque essere golpe a conoscere e' lacci, e lione a sbigottire e' lupi. Coloro che stanno semplicemente in sul lione, non se ne intendano. Non può per tanto uno signore prudente, né debbe, osservare la fede, quando tale osservanzia li torni contro, e che sono spente le cagioni che la feciono promettere."

112.   *Principe, 1999*, 68 "Alessandro VI non fece mai altro, non pensò mai ad altro che ad ingannare uomini, e sempre trovò subietto da poterlo fare. E non fu mai uomo che avessi maggiore efficacia in asseverare, e con maggiori giuramenti affermassi una cosa, che l'osservassi meno."

113.   Viroli, *Love of Country*, 31–40. Here, Viroli examines the Roman, and particularly Ciceronian influences in Machiavelli's *Discorsi*, *Il Principe* and *Dialogo* which he attributes to Machiavelli.

114. Ibid, 31–40.
115. This is particularly true of Cecil Grayson. He made this supposed problem central to his article "Machiavelli and Dante." Ibid, 366–367. The author has taken the editorial decision not to include the quotation for the *Dialogo* here, as the work is included in full in Chapters 7.
116. Ridolfi, *Life of Niccolò*, 137–139; Viroli, *Niccolò's Smile: A Biography of Machiavelli* trans. Antony Shugaar (New York: Farrar, Straus and Giroux, 2000), 148.
117. Grayson quotes this passage in "Machiavelli, Dante," 368. See Appendix Four, p. 207 for Italian. There, the references to Dante are also noted. For translation, see Chapter Seven of this work, pp. 170–171.
118. For an example of this, see *Lettere*, 190–191, Letter 178, 8 December 1509.
119. Viroli, *Niccolò's Smile*, 171. "We are now somewhat more familiar with the meaning of Niccolò's smile. We know it is a smile that dies on the lips and conceals his pain. Machiavelli smiled at mankind, at the constant to-and-fro of men driven by passions and unaware of how ridiculous they were. He felt neither detached from nor superior to this but instead part of the human comedy. And so he could laugh at himself, at his laughter and his tears, with men and his women friends."
120. Ibid, 138.
121. Niccolò Machiavelli, *First Prison Sonnet*, cited in Sebastian De Grazia, *Machiavelli in Hell* (New York: Vintage Books, 1994), 34–38. In the same book see pp. 392–393, endnotes numbered 34, 36 and 38 for the Italian original. "Io ho, Giuliano, in gamba un paio di geti/ Con sei tratti di fune in su le spalle:/ L'altre miserie mie no vo'contalle,/ Poichè così si trattano e poeti!/ Menon pidocchi queste parieti/ Bolsi spaccati, che paion farfalle;/ Né fu mai tanto puzzo in Roncisvalle,/ O in Sardigna fra quegli alboreta,/ Quanto nel mio sì delicato ostello;/ Con un rumor, che proprio par che'n terra/ Fùlgori Giove e tutto Mongibello./ L'un si incatena e l'altro si disferra,/ Con batter toppe, chiavi e chiavistelli:/ Un altro grida è troppo alto terra!/ Quel che mi fe' più guerra/ Fu che, dormendo presso a la aurora,/ Cantando sentii dire: "Pro eis ora."/ Or vadin in buona ora/ Purchè vostra pietà ver me si voglia/ Buon padre e questi rei lacciuol ne scoglia."
122. Cited in De Grazia, *In Hell*, 36–37. Also see *Personal Correspondences*, 222, Letter 206, 18 March 1513. For Italian original see *Lettere*, 363, Letter 206, 18 March 1513. "Che gli ho portati tanto francamente, che io stesso me ne voglio bene, et parmi essere da più che non credetti."
123. Viroli, *Niccolò's Smile*, 148.
124. De Grazia, *In Hell*, 247.
125. Hans Baron, *The Crisis of the Early Italian Renaissance: Civic Humanism and Republican Liberty in an Age of Classicism and Tyranny* (Princeton: Princeton University Press, 1966).
126. Ibid, 47–75. This section of Hans Baron's work details the transition from the medieval to renaissance view of empire and republic. See p. 48 in particular.
127. Ibid, 12–19. Here, Baron describes the Florentine Guelph cause as that which centred upon the medieval church that eventually became equated with civic freedom and city-state independence.
128. Quentin Skinner, *The Foundations of Modern Political Thought: Volume One: The*

Renaissance (Cambridge: Cambridge University Press, 1978), 12–22.

129.   Skinner, *Foundations*, 14–28 for a good discussion of the Guelph/Ghibelline dispute in Florence.

130.   Baron, *Crisis, 1966*, 47–64. In this section Baron illustrates the varied acceptance of Dante's work, based upon the then, current view of history.

131.   Grayson, "Lorenzo, Machiavelli," 425. In this early article, Grayson still believed that Machiavelli authored the "Dialogo."

132.   Leonardo Bruni, *Dialogi ad Petrum Paulum Histrum*; Cited in Baron, *Crisis 1966*, 49–50, "Or are we to believe that Dante, the most learned man of his age, did not know in what manner Caesar achieved his dominion—that he did not know of the rape of liberty, the abject fear of the people when Marc Anthony placed the crown on Caesar's head? Do you believe he did not know what *virtus* Brutus possessed in the judgement of all historical tradition? ...Dante knew it well, he knew it precisely —but he presented to us, in the image of Caesar, the legitimate prince and most just monarch of the world, and, in the image of Brutus, the rebellious troublesome villain who criminally murdered this prince. Not because Brutus was a just man; had he been such a one, how could he have been praised by the Senate as the restorer of liberty? But the poet took this material as the subject of the poem because Caesar, in whatever manner, had wielded royal power, and because Brutus, together with more than sixty of the noblest citizens, had slain him"; and 473–474 in Baron, *Crisis, 1966* for Latin original. "An tu putas Dantem, virum omnium aetatis doctissimum, ignorasse quo pacto Caesar dominium adeptus fuerit? Ignorasse libertatem sublatem et ingemiscente populo Romano diadema a M Antonio capiti Caesaris impositum? . . . Non ignoravit haec Dantes, non se legitumum principem et mundanarum rerum iustissimum monarcham in Caesare finxit; in Bruto autem seditiosum, turbulentum ac nefarium in hominen, qui hunc principem per scelus trucidaret; non quod Brutus eiusmodi fuerit; nam si hoc esset, qua ratione a senatu laudatus fuisset tamquam libertatis recuperator? Sed cum Caesar quocumque modo regnasset, Brutus autem [Garin: enim] una cum amplius sexaginta noblilissimis civibus eum interfecisset [Garin: interfecissent], sumpsit poeta ex hoc fingendi materiam." For a detailed analysis of Bruni's *Dialogi* see Hans Baron, *Humanistic and Political Literature in Florence and Venice at the Beginning of the Quattrocento* (Cambridge, Mass.: Harvard University Press, 1955), 126–165. The best edition of Bruni's *Dialogi* is *Dialogi ad Petrum Paulum Histrum* A cura di Stefano Ugo Baldassari (Firenze: Olschki, 1994).

133.   Baron, *Crisis, 1966*, 49–50.

134.   Ibid, 51. Here Baron wrote that Landino's commentary was "read by practically every literate Florentine of the later Renaissance."

135.   Ibid, 51. Also see Baron, *Crisis, 1955*, 455–456, nts. 4–7. Here Baron provides excellent quotations from Landino's commentary to back up his point.

136.   Baron, *Crisis, 1966*, 51–53 for his discussion of Giannotti's *Dialoghi*. Also see Baron, *Crisis, 1955*. In this "Appendices" Volume Baron compiles all of his references in full, 456–458 for Giannotti's original Italian, which Baron cites from Redig D. Campos' critical edition from *Raccolta di Fonti per la Storia dell'Arte*, Volume II (Firenze, 1939), 25–29, 40, 88–98, 90f., 95f., 96.

137.   Baron, *Crisis, 1966*, 53.

138.   Interestingly, after Michelangelo's death, someone attached an inscription to his

unfinished work. It reads: "Dum Bruti effigiem sculptor de marmore ducit, in mentem sceleris venit et abstinuit" which translates as: "While the sculptor was hewing the effigy of Brutus out of the marble, he came upon the spirit of crime and desisted." The quotation and translation are from Ludwig Goldscheider, ed., *Michelangelo: Paintings, Sculptures, Architecture* (4th edn., London, 1962), 21. Goldscheider suggests that Pietro Bembo may have added the inscription. Vasari, on the other hand (Goldscheider wrote) attributed the inscription to Donato Giannotti.

139.   Baron, *Crisis, 1966*, 474, endnote 10.

140.   Michele Barbi, *Dante nel Cinquecento* (Pisa: Tip. T. Nistri e. c., 1890), 4. Barbi cites Borghini's *Prose fiorentine* (Firenze, 1745). IV, IV, 161.

141.   Barbi, *Dante*, p. 4. Bardi cites Gelli's *Letture edite e inedite sopra la C. di D.* (Firenze: Bocca, 1887), Vol. I. p. 11.

142.   Interestingly, in regard to Dante and Machiavelli's authorship of the *Dialogo*, Carlo Lenzoni wrote *In difesa della lingua fiorentina, e di Dante*. In that work, a brief dialogue takes place between "Machiavelli and a certain Messer Maffio from Venice, in which the former, in reference to Bembo, points out the audacity of any attempt by non-Florentines to dictate rules for a language not their own." Might this be further evidence that those Florentines who took up the linguistic debates in the middle of *Cinquecento*—Gelli, Lenzoni, etc.—were familiar with the stance on the Florentine/Tuscan language as set forth in the *Dialogo*, possibly by Machiavelli? For more on the "Accademia fiorentina" and the Florentine/Tuscan dialect, see the very recent article by Michael Sherberg, "The *Accademia Fiorentina* and the Question of Language: the Politics of Theory in Ducal Florence," in *Renaissance Quarterly* LVI. 1. Spring 2003 (Renaissance Society of America, New York, 2003), 26–55. For quotation above, see p. 29, n. 12. Also see Dionisotti, *Machiavellerie*, 266, 319 for brief, though interesting discussions of Lenzoni and Machiavelli.

143.   Lino Pertile, "Trifone Gabriele's commentary on Dante and Bembo's *Prose della vulgar lingua*" in *Italian Studies* 40 (1985), 17–30. See p. 17 n. 1 where Pertile cites Pietro Bembo, *Prose della volgar lingua* a cura di Carlo Dionisotti (Torino, 1966), 178. "Affine di poter di qualunque cosa scrivere, che ad animo gli veniva, quantunque poco acconcia e malagevole a caper nel verso, egli molto spresso ora le latine voci, ora le staniere, che non sono state Toscana ricevute, ora le vecchie del tutto e tralasciate, ora le non usate e rozze, ora immonde e brutte, ora le durissime usando, e allo 'ncontro le pure e gentili alcuna volta mutando e guastando, e talora, senza alcuna scielta o regola, da sé formadnone, ha in maniera operato, che si più la sua *Commedia* giustamente rassomigliare ad un bello e spazio campo di grano, che sia tutto d'avene e di logli e d'erbe sterili e dannose mescolato, o ad alcuna non potata vite al suo tempo, la quale si vede essere poscia la state sí foglie e di pampini e di viticci ripiena, che se ne offendono le belle uve."

144.   Barbi, *Dante*. pp. 10–13. In Pertile, "Trifone," p. 17.

145.   Trifon Gabriele, *Annotationi nel Dante fatte con M. Trifon Gabriele in Bassano: Edizione critica* A cura di Lino Pertile (Bologna: Carducci, 1993).

146.   Pertile, "Trifone," 21.

147.   Niccolò Machiavelli, *Opere di Niccolò Machiavelli, Volume Terzo: Lettere* A cura di Franco Gaeta, (Torino: Unione tipografico-editrice Torinese, 1984). Letter 224, 10 December 1513, p. 425. "Ho un libro sotto, o Dante o Petrarca, o un di questi

poeti minori, come Tibullo, Ovvidio e simili."

148. *Esortazione alla penitenza*, in *Tutte le Opere Storiche e Letterarie di Niccolò Machiavelli* A cura di Guido Mazzoni e Mario Casella (Firenze: G. Barbèra, 1929): 778–780. For the quotation from Petrarch see p. 780.
149. Skinner, *Machiavelli*, 40–47.
150. Viroli, *Love of Country*, 31–40.

Chapter Six

1. Pasquale Villari, *Niccolò Machiavelli e i suoi tempi* (Firenze, Le Monnier, 1877–1882); Susan Meld Shell, "Machiavelli's Discourse on Language," *The Comedy and Tragedy of Machiavelli: Essays on the Literary Works*, ed. Vickie B. Sullivan (New Haven: Yale University Press, 2000), 78–101. (Hereafter abbreviated as Shell, "Machiavelli's Discourse").
2. For translation, see Chapter Seven. For Italian see Appendix Four.
3. See Hale's translation of the *Dialogo*, in *The Literary Works of Machiavelli* (London: Oxford University Press, 1961), 175. For further discussion of the term, see Hans Baron, "Machiavelli on the Eve of the *Discourses*: The Date and Place of the *Dialogo intorno alla nostra lingua*," *Bibliotheque d'Humanisme et Renaissance* 23 (1961), 449–476, 456.
4. Ibid, 456, n. 1.
5. Ibid, 456.
6. Pasquale Villari, *Niccolò Machiavelli: His Life and Times* Vol. 4 trans. Linda Villari (London: Unwin, 1883).
7. Pio Rajna, "La Data del '*Dialogo int. alla lingua*' di N. Machiavelli," *Rendiconti dell R. Accad. dei Lincei, Classe Scienze Morali, Memorie*, serie V. II (1893): 203–222. Cited first by Roberto Ridolfi in *Vita di Niccolò Machiavelli* (Roma: A. Belardetti, 1954), 446. Later cited in Cecil Grayson, "Lorenzo, Machiavelli and the Italian Language," *Italian Studies*, ed. E.F. Jacob (London: Faber and Faber, 1960): 410–432, 425, n. 2, (Hereafter abbreviated as Grayson, "Lorenzo, Machiavelli"). Cited later still in Baron, "Place of the *Dialogo*," 449, n. 1.
8. Ridolfi, *Vita*,. 446. Ridolfi wrote, "quanto alla cronologia, lo assegna all'autunno del 1514, certo non più tardi del 1516 nè prima del 1514." Also cited in Baron, "Place of the *Dialogo*," 449, n. 2.
9. Baron, "Place of the *Dialogo*," 449, n. 2. See Pasquale Villari's Second edition of *Niccolò Machiavelli e i suoi tempi* (Firenze: Le Monnier, 1897) Volume 3, 186.
10. Baron, "Place of the *Dialogo*," 450 where Baron refers to Ridofli's comments.
11. Grayson, "Lorenzo, Machiavelli," 425.
12. Baron, "Place of the *Dialogo*," 476.
13. Cecil Grayson, "Machiavelli and Dante," *Renaissance Studies in Honor of Hans Baron*, eds. Anthony Molho and John A. Tedeschi (DeKalb: Northern Illinois University Press, 1971), 361–384, p. 383. Grayson's punctuation is used in the citation.
14. Eric Cochrane, *Italy: 1530–1630* ed. Julius Kirshner, (London: Longman, 1988), 22.
15. Sergio Bertelli, "Egemonia linguistica come egemonia culturale e politica nella

Firenze cosmiana," in *Bibliothèque d'Humanisme et Renaissance*, 38 (1976): 249–281.

16. Niccolò Machiavelli, *Opere di Niccolò Machiavelli* 11 Vols. (Milano: Giovanni Salerno, 1968–82). See Volume 4, pp. 261–277 for the *Dialogo*. Specifically see p. 277 where Bertelli wrote, "si ha in tal modo un arco cronologico possibile: il 1513–1518, entro le quali fissare la composizione dello scritto."

17. Maurizio Viroli, *Machiavelli* (Oxford: Oxford University Press, 1998), 169. Viroli wrote, "Machiavelli also recognizes Florence's excellence. In his "Discourse on Our Language," composed around 1524, he writes that since Florence is nobler (più nobile) than other countries, its citizens have a greater obligation to it."

18. Shell, "Machiavelli's Discourse," 80.

19. Baron, "Place of the *Dialogo*," 452.

20. Ibid, 449 n. 1.

21. Ibid, 450.

22. Ibid, 449. Also see Ridolfi, *Vita*, 261 and particularly 446. Referring to Rajna's date of 1514 or 1516, Ridolfi wrote, "Devo semmai osservare che la "tanta felicità e sì tranquillo stato" in cui, secondo l'autore del Dialogo, Firenze s'era condotta mentre lo componeva, può benissimo riferirsi al pontificato di Leone X; ma il passo sulla corte romana che dice "mi maraviglio di te tu volgia, dove non si fa cosa alcuna laudibile o buona, che vi si faccia questa; perchè dove sono i costumi perversi, conviene che il parlare sia perverso": questo passo non so io già se il M. lo avrebbe scritto vivendo e regnando Leone. Viene fatto di pensare al pontificato di Adriano (1522–1523) che andrebbe bene anche per il passo relativo alla felicità di Firenze; e sebbene non ignori, sulla scorta del Raina, le ragioni che contrastano a questo prolungamento restando ferma l'attribuzione al M., non mi sembrano però più forti quelle che si oppongono ad assengare il *Dialogo* al tempo di papa Leone."

23. Baron, "Place of the *Dialogo*" 449–450. Pontificate of Leo X 1513–1521.

24. Villari, *Life and Times*, 4, 218.

25. Niccolò Machiavelli, *Dell'Arte della guerra*, in *Tutte le Opere Storiche e Letterarie di Niccolò Machiavelli* A cura di Guido Mazzoni e Mario Casella (Firenze: G. Barbèra, 1929), 306, column A. For reference to the *Dialogo*, see Appendix Four.

26. For an interesting of the similarities and differences between the *Discorsi*, the *Dialogo* and the *Arte*, see Baron's, "Place of the *Dialogo*," 454 and note 1; 455 and note 1.

27. Baron, "Place of the *Dialogo*," 453, n. 3 where Baron focuses on Burd's research in relation to the Polybius VI, the *Discorsi* and the *Arte*.

28. Hexter, "Missing Translation": 75–96.

29. Lodovico Martelli, *Risposta alla* Epistola *del Trissino*, in *Trattati sull'Ortografia del Volgare, 1524–1526* A cura di Brian Richardson (Exeter: Exeter University Press, 1984): 37–75, XLIII, where Richardson discusses the date of the *Risposta*.

30. Grayson, "Machiavelli and Dante," 374–375, nts. 26–27. Grayson summarized the views set forth by Rajna, Ridolfi and Baron.

31. Ibid: 374–375.

32. For example, Gian Giorgio Trissino, *Dialogo intitulato: Il Castellano, nel quale si tratta della lingua italiana* (Venezia, 1528).

33. Grayson, "Machiavelli and Dante," 375.

34. Ibid, 375. "And this will perhaps appear new to them, that I thus resolved to oppose

what they say Dante left written in his book *De vulgari eloquentia.*"
35. Ibid, 375, n. 27.
36. Ibid: 374–375.
37. Viroli, *Machiavelli,* 169. Concerning the 1524–1525 date for the *Dialogo,* it appears that Viroli is in agreement with Grayson, Carlo Dionisotti and Brian Richardson. See Dionisotti's *Machiavellerie* (Torino: G.Einaudi, 1980): 324–334 and Ornella Castellani Pollidori, ed. *Nuove Riflessioni sul Discorso o Dialogo Intorno Alla Nostra Lingua di Niccolò Machiavelli* (Roma, 1981), 83; and Brian Richardson, "Prose" in *The Cambridge History of Italian Literature* Revised edition, eds. Peter Brand and Lino Pertile (Cambridge: Cambridge University Press, 1999), 179–232. See 184 in particular where Richardson mentions that the *Dialogo* was written in 1524–1525. He gives no arguments for this date. All five choose this later date because of the "problem" represented by Martelli's *Risposta.*
38. Grayson, "Machiavelli and Dante," 374.
39. Grayson also overlooks the fact that Machiavelli's *Il Principe* was plagiarized countless times while he was still alive. See Peter Godman, *From Poliziano to Machiavelli: Florentine Humanism in the High Renaissance* (Princeton: Princeton University Press, 1998): 252–255. One might find Brian Richardson's comments on Martelli's *Risposta* helpful. In *Trattati sull'ortografia del volgare, 1524–1526* (Exeter: University of Exeter Press, 1984), p. XXXVII, Richardson wrote, "usufruì di varie idée del *Dialogo.* Il Martelli, come il Machiavelli, pianse la morte di Cosimo Rucellai (nella canzone "Quando l'alma gentile"), e dovete quindi anch'egli essere vicino all'ambiente degli Orti Oricellari. Egli aveva però trenta anni di meno del Machiavelli, ed era stato educato in un clima intellettuale molto diverso. Nel 1515, dopo un intervallo di più dieci anni, Filippo Giunta ricominciò a stampare Libri greci. Tre volumi di grammatica greca che apparvero nel corso di quelli anno furono dedicate ciascuno a tre giovani e promettenti Fiorentini: Luigi Alamanni, Pier Vettori, e Ludovico Martelli."
40. See p. XXXVII in Richardson's *Trattati.*
41. Benedetto Varchi, "Della poesia," from his lecture delivered in the Florentine Academy October-December, 1553, in *Lezioni...nell'Accademia Fiorentina* (Florence, 1590), 647. Cited in Baron, "The Place of the *Dialogo,*" 457, n. 3. "Essendo io fanciullo, con Zanobi Buondelmonti, e Nicolò Machiavegli, messer Luigi essendo garzone andava all'horto de Ruscellai, dove insieme con messer Cosimo, e più altri giovani udivano il Trissino, e l'osservavano più tosto come Maestro, o Superiore, che come compagno, o eguale." The author's translation.
42. Sebastian De Grazia, *Machiavelli in Hell* (New York: Vintage Books, 1994), 34.
43. For a recent account of this period, analyzed through Machiavelli's letters, see John M. Najemy, *Between Friends: Discourses of Power and Desire in the Machiavelli–Vettori Letters of 1513–1515* (Princeton: Princeton University Press, 1993). Specifically, refer to Chapter Three, "Formerly Secretary," 95–135.
44. Niccolò Machiavelli, *Machiavelli and his Friends: Their Personal Correspondences* trans. James B. Atkinson and David Sices (DeKalb: Northern Illinois University Press, 1996): 262–265.
45. Baron, "The Place of the *Dialogo,*" 457.
46. Ibid, 457.
47. *Personal Correspondences,* 292, Letter 238, 3 August 1514. For Italian, see

Niccolò Machiavelli, *Opere di Niccolò Machiavelli, Volume Terzo: Lettere* A cura di Franco Gaeta (Torino: Unione tipografico-editrice Torinese, 1984), 465, Letter 238, 3 August 1514. "'Ho lasciato dunque i pensieri delle cose grandi e gravi."

48.   Baron, "Place of the *Dialogo*," 461. Here Baron discusses Trissino's travels.

49.   Ibid, 461.

50.   See Chapter Seven of this Volume, p. 172 and Appendix Four, p. 208 for Italian.

51.   *Personal Correspondences*, 309.

52.   Maurizio Viroli, *For Love of Country: An Essay on Patriotism and Nationalism* (New York: Clarendon, 1997), 33 and n. 53 .

53.   Viroli, *Love of Country*, 33 Viroli quotes from the *Istorie Fiorentina*. "I shall esteem it little to live in a city where the laws can do no less than men. For that *patria* is desirable in which property and friends can be safely enjoyed, and not that in which property can be taken from you, nor friends, out of fear for their own, abandon you in your greatest necessity." Viroli cites Machiavelli's *Istorie* as it appears in *Opere di Niccolò Machiavelli* ed. A. Montevecchi (Torino, 1986), 33, Book IV. "Io stimerò sempre poco vivere in una città dove possino meno le leggi che gli uomini; perchè quella patria è desiderabile nella quale le sustanze e gli amici si possono sicuramente godere, non quella dove ti possino essere quelle tolte facilmente, e gli amici per paura di loro propri nelle tue maggiori necessità t'abbandono."

54.   Niccolò Machiavelli, *The Prince* trans. George Bull (London: Penguin Group, 4th ed., 1995), 52. For Italian original see Niccolò Machiavelli, *Il Principe e Altre Opere Politiche* Introduzione di Delio Cantimori Note di Stefano Andretta (Milano: Garzanti Libri, 1999), 65. "Offeronti el sangue, la roba, la vita, e' figliuoli, come di sopra dissi, quando el bisogno è discosto; ma, quando ti si appressa, e' si rivoltano."

55.   Wayne Rebhorn, *Foxes and Lions: Machiavelli's Confidence Men* (Ithaca: Cornell University Press, 1988), 204–205.

56.   Viroli, *Love of Country*, 39. And, Viroli, *Love of Country*, 39. He cites Niccolò Machiavelli, *Florentine Histories* trans. Laura F. Banfield and Harvey C. Mansfield, Jr. (Princeton: Princeton University Press, 1990), 302. "Nor do I believe that in all Italy are there so many examples of violence and avarice as in this city. Then did this fatherland of ours give us life so that we might take life from it? Make us victorious so that we might destroy it? Honour us so that we might insult it?" For Italian, see Viroli cites *Istorie, Montevecchi.* VII. 23. "Nè credo che sia in tutta Italia tanti esempli di violenza e di avarizia, quanti sono in questa città. Dunque questa nostra patria ci ha dato la vita perchè noi la togliamo a lei? Ci ha fatti vittoriosi perchè noi la destruggiamo? Ci onora perchè noi la vituperiamo?"

57.   John Stephens, *The Fall of the Florentine Republic: 1512–1530* (Oxford: Clarendon, 1983), 99.

58.   Ibid, 74. Also see Baron "Place of the *Dialogo*," 464. Baron carefully illustrates the importance of the Autumn of 1515.

59.   See Appendix Four, p. 218 for "tranquillo stato" and p. 227 for "costumi perversi."

60.   Baron, "Place of the *Dialogo*," 465, n. 1: Gelli cited. "Ma se voi forse non ve ne ricordate, advertite che que' litteratti dell' Orto de Rucellai, disputando nella venuta di Papa Leone, co'l Tressino (perche egli fu che ci condusse la prima volta questa opere)."

61.   Baron, "Place of the *Dialogo*," 466.

62. Stephens, *Florentine Republic*, 100. The quotation within Stephens's quotation is from Pietro Parenti, *Historia fiorentina*, Biblioteca Nazionale Centrale di Firenze, *Fondo Principale*, II, IV, 171, fol 114r.

63. Humphrey Butters, *Governors and Government in the Early Sixteenth-Century Florence: 1502–1519* (Oxford: Clarendon, 1985), 273.

64. Butters, *Governors*, 273.

65. Hans Baron, "The *Principe* and the Puzzle of the Date of Chapter 26." *Journal of Medieval and Renaissance Studies* 21 (1991): 83–102, p. 90. (Hereafter abbreviated as Baron, "Date of Chapter 26"). For Bertelli's edition see Niccolò Machiavelli, *Il Principe e Discorsi sopra la prima deca di Tito Livio*, A cura di Sergio Bertelli (Milano: Feltrinelli, 1960; reprint 1977), 109–110.

66. Stephens, *Florentine Republic*, 102.

67. Felix Gilbert, *Machiavelli e i suoi tempi* (Bologna, 1977), 340 where Gilbert wrote, "E sono convinto che l'ultimo capitolo del *Principe* era una storia di secondo pensiero: talche ho notato con grande interesse l'ipotesi di Bertelli...che quest'ultimo capitolo l'*exhoratio*, si connette strettamente alla *Dedicatio* e deve pertanto essere datato tral il settembre 1515 e il settembre 1516. Questo tesio mi sembra risolvere le difficoltà in discussione." Cited in Baron "Date of Chapter 26," 90, n. 16. For an earlier interpretation see Felix Gilbert, "The Humanist Concept of the Prince and *The Prince* of Machiavelli," in Gilbert's *History: Choice and Commitment* ed. Arno M. Mayer, (Cambridge, Mass.: Belknap Press of Harvard, 1977), 91–114, specifically 114.

68. Baron, "The Date of Chapter 26," 90.

69. Ibid, 89.

70. Ibid, 100.

71. *Personal Correspondences*: 312–313, Letter 247 dated 31 January 1515. For Italian, see *Lettere*, 490, Letter 247, 31 January 1515. "Pagolo vostro è suto qui con il Magnifico, et intra qualche ragionamento ha avuto meco delle speranze sue, mi ha detto come sua Signoria gli ha promesso farlo governatore di una di quelle terre, della quali prende ora la signoria. Et avendo io inteso, non da Pagolo, ma da una commune voce, che egli diventa signore di Parma, Piacenza, Modena et Reggio, mi pare che questa signoria fosse bella et forte, et da poterla in ogni evento tenere, quando nel principio la fosse governata bene."

72. Baron, "The Date of Chapter 26," 95.

73. *Personal Correspondences*, 309.

74. Baron, "The Date of Chapter 26," 91.

75. Ibid, 84. "Chapter 26 directs an exhortation to some *member* of the House of Medici."

76. Peter Laven, *Renaissance Italy: 1464–1534*, (London: B.T. Batsford, 1966), 155.

77. Baron, "The Date of Chapter 26," 85.

78. *Personal Correspondences*, 308. "By 1515 Lorenzo was the virtual ruler of Florence and he was elected the Florentine captain general in May. He understood the military; furthermore, he had a military aura about him that Machiavelli respected."

79. Godman, *Poliziano to Machiavelli*, 243, n. 51 on the same page, where Godman cites Virgilio from *BFR*, Folio 60r. "Vocatoque ad militare imperium uno et cive hoc vestro rempublicam tueri simul et ornare cogitis...Unum oportet esse principem

in bello, unum arbitrum, unum dominum."

80.		*Principe, 1999*, 94.

81.		Ibid, 94.

82.		*Prince, 1995*, 80.

83.		*Principe, 1999*, Chapter 7, p. 37. "Freschi esempli" is almost impossible to translate into English. While it literally translates as "fresh examples," its painterly connotations are lost. "Freschi esempli" are things which have happened so recently that, if the events were part of a painted fresco, their paint would still be drying.

84.		Ibid, Introductory Epistle, p. 14. "Pigli adunque vostra Magnificenzia questo piccolo dono con quello animo che io lo mando; il quale se da quella fia diligentemente considerato e letto, vi conoscerà drento uno estremo mio desiderio, che Lei pervenga a quella grandezza che la fortuna e le altre sua qualità li promettano."

85.		Carlo Dionisotti, "Machiavelli, Man of Letters," *Machiavelli and the Discourse of Literature*, eds. Albert Russell Ascoli and Victoria Kahn (Ithaca: Cornell University Press, 1993), 23–33, where Dionisotti elegantly details Machiavelli's relationship to humanistic studies and training. Poliziano's writings definitely figured in Machiavelli's education.

86.		Godman, *Poliziano to Machiavelli*, 75 and note 232 at the bottom of that page.

87.		The *Raccolta* was edited and compiled by Poliziano at the request of Lorenzo de' Medici. Therefore, it is usually included in the *Opere* of Lorenzo. See Lorenzo de' Medici, *Opere* A cura di Tiziano Zanato (Torino: Einaudi, 1992), 353 for portions of the *Raccolta*. For a good summary of the importance of the work carried out by Poliziano and Lorenzo, see Letizia Panizza "The Quattrocento" in *The Cambridge History of Italian Literature*, Revised edition, eds. Peter Brand and Lino Pertile (Cambridge: Cambridge University Press, 1999), 129–177. See 164–165 particularly.

88.		Angelo Poliziano, "First Anthology of Vernacular Poetry," *Images of Quattrocento Florence*, eds. Stefano Ugo Baldassari and Arielle Saiber (New Haven: Yale University Press, 2000), 169–174 for the entire section of Poliziano's work: p. 172 for the English translation cited above. "The use of verse, as Petrarch writes in a Latin epistle, was held in high esteem by the ancient Romans. After having been abandoned for a long time, it began to flourish again in Sicily, just a few centuries ago. It then reached France, and finally Italy, as if that were its home." For Italian original see Claudio Varese, ed., *Prosatori Volgari del Quattrocento* (Milano: Riccardo Ricciardi, 1957), 987. In the same work, also see p. 987, n. 5.

		Here Varese details that Poliziano is referring to Petrarch's *Familium Rerum* I. I. See Francesco Petrarca, *Le Familiari: Edizione Critica Volume Primo: Introduzione e Libri I–IV* A cura di Vittorio Rossi (Firenze: G.C. Sansoni, 1933), 4. "Quod genus, apud Siculos, ut fama est, non multis ante seculis renatum, brevi per omnem Italiam ac longius manavit, apud Grecorum olim ac Latinorum vetustissimos celebratum."

89.		For Italian, see Appendix Four, p. 210. For translation, see Chapter Seven, p. 174. "Everyone knows that the Provençaux were the first to begin to write in verses; from Provence it went, this use of verse, to Sicily, and from Sicily to Italy; and from among the provinces of Italy to Tuscany; and from all of Tuscany to Florence, for no other (reason) than because it was the most suitable language."

90.   Roberto Ridolfi, *The Life of Niccolò Machiavelli* trans. Cecil Grayson (London: Routledge and K. Paul, 1963), 34–119, for Machiavelli's missions to France. Also see Niccolò Machiavelli, *Ritratti e Rapporti Diplomatici* (Roma: Riuniti, 2000): 43–48 for an excellent summation of the important dates in Machiavelli's life up to 1511. This includes specific details concerned with his diplomatic journeys in France.

91.   Dionisotti, "Man of Letters," 23–33.

92.   Ibid, 25.   Where Dionisotti illustrates that Adriani was personally taught by Poliziano. For a similar perspective see Godman, *Poliziano to Machiavelli*, 145 and 180–181. Adriani and Machiavelli served as First and Second Chancellors to the Florentine Republic. They worked together from 1498–1512; the year of Machiavelli's exile.

93.   Baldassari, Saiber, *Images*, 170. "My most illustrious Lord Frederick, I have often debated with myself which among the many and innumerable good customs of ancient times was most excellent. I finally chose one that I believe should be considered the most glorious of all: that in those times, no illustrious and virtuous work produced by either hands or intellect lacked for rewards and grand tributes, both in private and in public. Consequently, as all rivers and springs are said to originate in the Ocean, so all famous deeds and wondrous works of the Ancients are held to have derived from worthy custom." Also see Varese, *Prosatori Volgari*, 985.

94.   Varese, *Prosatori Volgari*, 985, n. 1. Here Varese illustrates that Poliziano is borrowing from Petrarch, particularly from line 108 of *Canzoniere* CXXVIII.

95.   Francesco Petrarch, *The Canzoniere, (rerum vulgarium fragmenta)* 2 Vols. trans. Frederic J. Jones (Hull: Troubadour and Hull Italian Texts, 2000–2001), Volume One: 158–159. "Oh God! Let your minds be led/ To this at times, and with pity contemplate/ The weeping of a people lost in grief,/ 90 who, after God, in you relief/ and hope now seek; and should you demonstrate/ some sign of pity for their fate,/ virtue against blind rage/ will take up arms, and short will be the fray/ 95 for age-old courage/ in (Italian) breasts has not yet passed away./ Lords, see how quickly time is borne,/ And just how life thereafter/ Flees, while death already thunders at our heels./ 100 Now you're on earth, but think of your departure,/ at which the soul, naked and forlorn,/ must perforce arrive, as to that grim pass it steals./ When beyond this vale it wheels,/ 105 Winds contrary to life's more peaceful flow;/ and the time which to others' woe/ you spend, apply to finer forms of work/ which in your hands and spirits lurk." Also see: Francesco Petrarca, *Canzoniere, Trionfi, Rime Varie e Una Scelta di Versi Latini* A cura di Carla Muscetta e Daniele Ponchiroli (Torino: Giulio Einaudi: Torino, 1958), 179.   Also see Francesco Petrarca, *Canzoniere* Introduzione e note di Piero Cudini (Milano: Aldo Garzanti, 1974), 186–187

96.   See Chapter Seven, p. 163 for translation. For Italian, see Appendix Four, p. 199.

97.   *Principe, 1999*, 98.

98.   Bertelli, "Egemonia linguistica," cited above. That article explores the Florentine notion of linguistic and cultural supremacy in the *cinquecento*.

Chapter Seven

1. Niccolò Machiavelli, *The Prince*, trans. Angelo M. Codevilla (New Haven: Yale University Press, 1997), xix.
2. Niccolò Machiavelli, the "Dialogue concerning our language" in, *The Literary Works of Machiavelli* trans. John R. Hale (Oxford: Oxford University Press, 1961). The author owes a great debt to the late John Hale. For, it was his translation of the *Dialogo*, that first caught our attention and sparked our interest in this overlooked treatise.
3. The reader will find the various pronouns in the opening sentence of the *Dialogo* highlighted. When translating this important opening paragraph, one could have changed the pronouns so that it read more consistently. However, this would have undermined the universal obligation to the *patria*, which the *Dialogo*'s author attempted to convey. This important point was highlighted by Barbara Godorecci in *After Machiavelli: "Re-writing" and the "Hermeneutic Attitude"* (West Lafeyette, IN: Purdue University Press, 1993), 68–69.
4. The author of the *Dialogo* catches Dante red-handed, using the Florentine *zanche* rather than the non-Florentine *gambe*.

Conclusion

1. Peter Godman, *From Poliziano to Machiavelli: Florentine Humanism in the High Renaissance* (Princeton: Princeton University Press, 1998), 237. "...Lorenzo was more interested in the gift of a pair of dogs than in the presentation of Machiavelli's book, there is no evidence that it ever reached the duke of Urbino or any other Medicean magnate at Florence."
2. Niccolò Machiavelli, *Il Principe e Altre Opere Politiche* Introduzione di Delio Cantimori, Note di Stefano Andretta (Milano: Garzanti Libri, 1999), 60.
3. One could also cite Giuseppe Mazzini or Francesco Crispi as other examples. See Roland Sarti, *Mazzini: A Life for the Religion of Politics* (West Port, Conn.: Praeger, 1997), 150; and Federico Chabod, *Italian Foreign Policy: The Statecraft of the Founders* trans. William McCuaig (Princeton: Princeton University Press, 1996), 418.
4. Francesco de Sanctis, *History of Italian Literature* 2 Vols. trans. Joan Redfern (London: Humphrey Milford, 1930). See Vol. 2, p. 547. For Italian, see Francesco de Sanctis, *Storia della letteratura Italiana, nuove edizione* 2 Vols. A cura di Benedetto Croce (Bari: Laterza e Figli, 1912). See Vol. 2, p. 68. "Niccolò propone addirittura la costituzione di un grande Stato italiano, che sia baluardo d'Italia contro lo straniero. Il concetto di *patria* gli si allarga. *Patria* non è solo il piccolo comune, ma è tutta la nazione. L'Italia nell'utopia dantesca è il "giardino dell'impero"; nell'utopia del Machiavelli è la *patria*, nazione autonoma e indipendente[...] La *patria* del Machiavelli è una divinità, superiore anche alla moralità e alla legge. A quel modo che il Dio degli ascetici assorbiva in sè l'individuo, e in nome di Dio gl'inquisitori bruciavano gli eretici; per la *patria* tutto era lecito, e le azioni, che nella vita privata sono delitti, diventavano magnanime nella vita pubblica[...] La divinità era scesa di cielo in terra e si chiamava la *patria*, ed era non meno terribile."

Appendix Four

1. The *Dialogo,* in Niccolò Machiavelli, *Opere Complete di Niccolò Machiavelli, con molte correzione e giunte rinvenute sui manoscritti originali* (Firenze, 1843), 578–584.

2. Niccolò Machiavelli, *Discorso o dialogo intorno alla nostra lingua* in *Opere di Niccolò Machiavelli.* A cura di Sergio Bertelli. 11 vols. Milano: Giovanni Salerno, 1968–82. See Volume 4, pp. 261–277; Niccolò Machiavelli, *Discorso o dialogo intorno alla nostra lingua: Edizione critica* A cura di Bortolo Tommaso Sozzi (Torino: G. Einaudi, 1976); Ornella Castellani Pollidori, ed., *Niccolò Machiavelli e il "Dialogo intorno alla nostra lingua" con una edizione critica del testo* (Firenze: Olschki, 1978).

3. "con...carico e pericolo" This phase is used in Niccolò Machiavelli, *Istorie fiorentine* in *Tutte le Opere Storiche e Letterarie di Niccolò Machiavelli* A cura di Guido Mazzoni e Mario Casella (Firenze: G. Barbèra, 1929): 375–621. See II. 13, p. 417. "E mentre che si praticava la causa sua, il popolo si armò, e corse alle sue case, offerendogli contro ai Signori e suoi nimici la difesa. Non volle Giano fare esperienza di questi popolari favori, né commettere la vita sua a' magistrati, perché temeva la malignità di questi e la instabilità di quegli; tale che, per torre occasione a' nimici di ingiuriare lui, e agli amici di offendere la *patria,* deliberò di partirsi, e dare luogo alla invidia, e liberare i cittadini dal timore che eglino avevono di lui, e lasciare quella città, la quale *con suo carico e pericolo* aveva libera dalla servitù de' potenti; e si elesse voluntario esilio." Note also that Machiavelli discusses these in relation to "voluntary exile"—a theme in the *Dialogo.*

4. "fortuna e natura." The secularism of the writer is evident in that there is no mention of things divine.

5. See Maurizio Viroli, *For Love of Country: An Essay on Patriotism and Nationalism* (Oxford: Clarendon, 1997): 32–33 where Viroli discusses Machiavelli's use of Ciceronian themes in the *Dialogo,* (which he attributes to Machiavelli). Might this Ciceronian tradition link the *Dialogo* further with the *Discorsi?*

6. "Ne' passati giorni." See Niccolò Machiavelli, *Discorso o dialogo intorno alla nostra lingua: Edizione critica* A cura di Bortolo Tommaso Sozzi (Torino: G. Einaudi, 1976), 4. n. 26, where Sozzi wrote "probabile allusione alle discussioni linguistiche tenutesi negli Orti Oricellari, cioè nel dotto circolo di Palazzo Rucellai."

7. Niccolò Machiavelli, *Il Principe e Altre Opere Politiche*: Introduzione di Delio Cantimori, Note di Stefano Andretta (Milano: Garzanti Libri, 1999), 61. "E questo è, che alcuno è tenuto liberale, alcuno misero (usando uno termine toscano, perché *avaro* in nostra lingua è ancora colui che per rapina desidera di avere, *misero* chiamiamo noi quello che si astiene troppo di usare il suo)." Machiavelli recognized his language as "Tuscan" and the author of the *Dialogo* uses Florentine and Tuscan interchangeably in the course of the text. The author of the *Dialogo* seems to be referring to Pietro Bembo (Florentine and Tuscan); Gian Giorgio Trissino and Baldassar Castiglione (Italian or courtly tongue). See Bembo's *Prose della Vulgar Lingua,* (1525); Castiglione's *Il Libro del Cortegiano* (1528) and Trissino's *Dialogo intitulato: Il Castellano, nel quale si tratta della lingua italiana*

(1528). See J.R. Woodhouse, *Baldesar Castiglione: A Reassessment of "The Courtier"* (Edinburgh: Edinburgh University Press, 1978): 80–83.

8. As Chapters Five and Six discussed, Machiavelli was familiar with the works of Dante, as was the author of the *Dialogo*. For references to Dante in Machiavelli see Niccolò Machiavelli, *Opere di Niccolò Machiavelli, Volume Terzo: Lettere* A cura di Franco Gaeta, (Torino: Unione tipografico-editrice torinese, 1984). Letter 224, 10 December 1513, p. 425. "Ho un libro sotto, o Dante o Petrarca, o un di questi poeti minori, come Tibullo, Ovvidio e simili."

For references to Dante in the *Discorsi* see Niccolò Machiavelli, *Discorsi Sopra la Prima Deca di Tito Livio*. Introduzione di Gennaro Sasso, Note di Giorgio Inglese (Milano: Biblioteca Universale Rizzoli, 1999), I.11, pp. 93–94. "Donde nasce che gli regni i quali dipendono solo dalla virtù d'uno uomo sono poco durabili, perché quella virtù manca con la vita di quello; e rade volte accade che la sia rinfrescata con la successione, come prudentemente Dante dice: "Rade volte *discende* per li rami/ L'umana probitate, e questo vuole/ Quei che la dà, perché da lui si chiami." Here Machiavelli quotes Dante's *Purgatorio*, VII. 121–123. Dante's text says "risurge" rather than "discende." For a good bilingual edition of Dante's work, see *Purgatorio* trans. Charles Singleton (Princeton: Princeton University Press, 1973), 74. Also in the *Discorsi, 1999* see I. 53, p. 169. "E Dante dice a questo proposito, nel discorso suo che fa *De Monarchia*, che il popolo molte volte grida <<Viva>> la sua morte e <<Muoia>> la sua vita." See Cecil Grayson, "Machiavelli and Dante," 364, where Grayson illustrates that Machiavelli is in actuality citing Dante's *Convivio* I. 9, not the *Monarchia*. In note 6 on the same page in Grayson, he wrote, "The context of *Convivio* I, 9 is linguistic. Machiavelli's applies the quotation to politics." Might the *Dialogo* be an equally political text? One must note that Grayson also makes a mistake, for the quotation Machiavelli used is actually in *Convivio*, I. 11. See Dante Alighieri, *Convivio: Edizione Critica* A cura di Maria Simonelli (Bologna: Casa Editrice Prof. Riccardo Pàtron, 1966), I. 11.8, p. 23. There, Dante wrote, <<Viva la loro morte>>, e <<Muoia la loro vita>>.

Dante in the *Istorie*: II. 2, pp. 408–409 "Egli è cosa verissima, secondo che Dante e Giovanni Villani dimostrano, che la città di Fiesole, sendo posta sopra la sommità del monte, per fare che i mercati suoi fussero più frequentati, e dare più commodità a quelli che vi volessero con le loro mercanzie venire, aveva ordinato il luogo di quelli, non sopra il poggio, ma nel piano intra le radice del monte e del fiume d'Arno." II. 2, p. 410. "Ma come ne' corpi nostri quanto più sono tarde le infirmità, tanto più sono pericolose e mortali; così Florenzia, quanto ella fu più tarda a seguitare le sette di Italia, tanto di poi fu afflitta più da quelle. La cagione della prima divisione è notissima, perché è da Dante e da molti altri scrittori celebrata." *Istorie* II. 18, p. 420. "E trovandosi in arme ambedue le parti, i Signori, de' quali era in quel tempo Dante, per il consiglio e prudenza sua presono animo e feciono armare il popolo, al quale molti del contado aggiunsono." *Istorie* II. 20, p. 422. "Furono pertanto confinati tutti i Cerchi con i loro seguaci di parte Bianca, intra i quali fu Dante poeta, e i loro beni publicati e le loro case disfatte." *Istorie* II. 24, p.

425. "Donde che restarono fuori la maggior parte de' Ghibellini e alcuni di quegli di parte Bianca, intra i quali furono Dante Aldighieri, i figliuoli di messer Veri de' Cerchi e di Giano della Bella."

9. For references to Petrarch see *Lettere*: p. 371, letter 210 dated 16 April 1513. Machiavelli quotes Petrarch: "Però se alcuna volta io rido o canto/ Follo perché io non ho se non questa una/ Via da sfogare il mio acerbo pianto." Gaeta notes that this is from *Canzoniere* CII. ll. 12–14. "L'ultimo verso suona però: << via da celare il mio angoscioso pianto>>. For a good edition of Petrarch's porty, see *Canzoniere, Trionfi, Rime Varie e una scelta di versi latini* A cura di Carlo Muscetta e Daniele Ponchirolo (Torino: Einaudi, 1958), p. 137 for quotation. Also see p. 423 in *Lettere*, letter 224 dated 10 December 1513. "<<Tarda non furon mai grazie divine>>. Dico questo, perché mi pareva aver perduta no, ma smarrita la grazia vostra, sendo stato voi assai tempo senza scrivermi, et ero dubbio donde potessi nascere la cagione." Machiavelli cited Petrarch's *Tionfo dell'Eternità*, 13. See *Trionfo dell'Eternità*, p. 542. In the same letter in *Lettere*, also see p. 425 where Machiavelli mentions carrying a book by Dante or Petrarch with him on his country walks (Cited above). Also see *Lettere*, letter 229, dated 4 February 1514, p. 443 where Machiavelli cited Petrarch's *Trionfo d'Amore*, I. 150–160. See *Trionfo d'Amore*, p. 471. And *Lettere*, letter 230 dated 9 February 1514, p. 445 where he cites the *Trionfo d'Amore*, III, 91–93. See *Trionfo d'Amore*, p. 483. These are detailed by Gaeta.

Petrarch in *Il Principe*, 98. "Pigli, adunque, la illustre casa vostra questo assunto, con quello animo e con quella speranza che si pigliano le imprese iuste; acciò che, sotto la sua insegna, e questa *patria* ne sia nobilitata, e sotto li sua auspizii si verifichi quel detto del Petrarca: *Virtù contro a furore/ Prenderà l'arme; e fia el combatter corto:/ Ché l'antico valore/ Nelli italici cor non è ancor morto.*" At the end of *Il Principe*, Machiavelli cited Petrarch. See *Canzoniere*, CXXVII, 93–96, p. 179.

Petrarch in *Istorie*. VI. 29, p. 553. "Ma sopra tutto gliene davano speranza quelli versi del Petrarca, nella canzona che comincia: "Spirto gentil, che quelle membra reggi," dove dice: Sopra il monte Tarpeio, canzon, vedrai/ Un cavalier che Italia tutta onora,/ Pensoso più d'altrui che di se stesso." Machiavelli quotes from *Canzoniere* LIII, ll. 99–101. See *Canzoniere*, p. 77. And *Istorie*. VI. 29, p. 553. "Sapeva messer Stefano i poeti molte volte essere di spirito divino e profetico ripieni; tal che giudicava dovere ad ogni modo intervenire quella cosa che il Petrarca in quella canzona profetizzava, ed essere egli quello che dovesse essere di sì gloriosa impresa esecutore; parendogli, per eloquenzia, per dottrina, per grazia e per amici, essere superiore ad ogni altro romano.

See the *Esortazione alla penitenza* in *Tutte le opere Storiche e Letterarie di Niccolò Machiavelli* A cura di Guido Mazzoni e Mario Casella (Firenze: G. Barbèra, 1929): 778–780. For the quotation from Petrarch see p. 780.

10. For references to Boccaccio in Machiavelli's letters see *Lettere*, Letter 231, dated 25 February 1514, p. 450. "Priegovi seguitate la vostra stella, e non ne lasciate andare un iota per cosa del mondo, perché io credo, credetti, e crederrò sempre che sia vero

quello che dice il Boccaccio: che gli è meglio fare e pentirsi, che non fare e pentirsi." Gaeta noted that Machiavelli was citing the *Decamerone*, III, 5; and that Machiavelli slightly altered Boccaccio's words from "è egli meglio fare e pentere che starsi e pentersi."

There is also a reference to Boccaccio in the *Istorie* II. 42, p. 443. "Mantennesi la città, dopo questa rovina, quieta infino all'anno 1353; nel corso del qual tempo seguì quella memorabile pestilenza da messer Giovanni Boccaccio con tanta eloquenzia celebrata, per la quale in Firenze più che novantaseimila anime mancarono." Here, Machiavelli is referring to Boccaccio's masterful description of the plague in Florence. See Boccaccio's *The Decameron* ed. Jonathan Usher, trans. Guido Waldman (Oxford: Oxford University Press, 1998), 6–23.

11.   Niccolò Machiavelli, *The Prince*, trans. Angelo M. Codevilla (New Haven: Yale University Press, 1997), xxiii. Codevilla's interpretation of this passage is of some interest. "Language, therefore, is a most powerful weapon in the struggle for primacy, and particularly suited to the unarmed. In the *Discourse upon Our Language*, Machiavelli notes that the most powerful nations of modern Europe— Spain, France and Germany—"yield" not only to Italy, which did not exist politically, but even to its despised part, Lombardy, for the sake of the language in which Dante, Petrarch and Boccaccio wrote." One might also note that Venice is conspicuously absent.

12.   For a good bilingual edition see Dante Alighieri, *Inferno* trans. Charles Singleton (Princeton: Princeton University Press, 1970), XXXIII, 79–80, p. 354. The author of the *Dialogo* cites Dante's *Commedia*, frequently. References to Dante are included as a guide to the reader.

13.   "Il nervo della lingua." Might this be reciprocal with Machiavelli's use of "nervo" in relation to military considerations? These are discussed below where the author of the *Dialogo* also uses "nervo" in relation to military make-up.

14.   "italica." The only time that the term "italica" appears in Machiavelli's works is in the epilogue of *Il Principe*. See pp. 96–97 "Volendo dunque la illustre casa vostra seguitare quelli eccellenti uomini che redimirno le provincie loro, è necessario, innanzi a tutte l'altre cose, come vero fondamento d'ogni impresa, provvedersi d'arme proprie; perché non si può avere né più fidi né più migliori soldati. E, benché ciascuno di essi sia buono, tutti insieme diventeranno migliori, quando si vedranno comandare dal loro principe, e da quello onorare et intrattenere. È necessario, per tanto, prepararsi a queste arme, per potere con la *virtù italica* defendersi dalli esterni." Chronologically, may this seldom used word, link the *Dialogo* to 1515; to the time Machiavelli wrote the epilogue of *Il Principe*?

15.   "Lingua patria." Machiavelli, unlike his contemporary Guicciardini, used this term. For examples, see *Discorsi, 1999*, II. 5, p. 309. "Era dunque, come di sopra è detto, già la Toscana potente, piena di religione e di virtù; aveva i suoi costumi e la sua *lingua patria*; il che tutto è stato spento dalla potenza romana. Talché, come si è detto, di lei ne rimane solo la memoria del nome." Machiavelli also uses this term in the *Istorie*. I.5., p. 384. "Intra queste rovine e questi nuovi popoli sursono nuove

lingue, come apparisce nel parlare che in Francia, in Ispagna e in Italia si costuma; il quale mescolato con la *lingua patria* di quelli nuovi popoli e con la antica romana fanno un nuovo ordine di parlare."

16. *Dialogo, 1976*, 8, n. 5. Sozzi noted that the Bolognese, Aretine and Pistoese are "Guido Guinizelli, Guittone d'Arezzo and Cino da Pistoia' respectively.

17. "Centonovelle." The author is referring to Giovanni Boccaccio, *Il Decameron: Edizione Critica* A cura di Aldo Rossi (Bologna: Cappelli, 1977), 215. "Giornata IV," "Introduzione," where Boccaccio wrote "le presenti novellette...sono...in fiorentin volgare." The author of the *Dialogo* overlooked, or purposely neglected the words that came between the above quotation, which read as follows; "le presenti novellette riguarda, le quali non solamente in fioretin volgare ed in prosa scritta per me sono senza titolo."

18. "De vulgari eloquio." See *Dialogo, 1976*, 9. n. 29, where Sozzi noted, "titolo improprio, dato dal codice Trivulziano usufruito dal Trissino, e da altri manoscritti ed edizioni, e presente ancora nel Manzoni. Il titolo essatto *De vulgari eloquentia*, dato dal codice Berlinese scoperto dal Bertalot nel 1917, era già noto al Villani e al Boccaccio.—Circa la deformazione della tesi linguistica dantesca da parte del Trissino, e circa polemica antitrissiniana e antidantesca del Machiavelli."

19. Dante Alighieri, *Dante in Hell, the De Vulgari Eloquentia* trans. Warman Welliver (Ravenna: Ravenna Longo, 1981), I. XIII., p. 72 for the Latin original. "Post hec veniamus ad Tuscos, qui propter amentiam suam infrontit titulum sibi vulgaris illustris arrogare videntur"; and I. VI, p. 52 for the Latin original. "Et quamvis ad voluptatem nostram sive nostre sensualitatis quietem in terris amenior locus quam Florentia non existat, revolventes et poetarum et aliorum scriptorum volumina, quibus mundus universaliter et membratim describitur, ratiocinantesque in nobis situationes varias mundi locorum et eorum habitudinem ad utrunque polum et circulum equatorem, multas esse perpendimus firmiterque censemus et magis nobiles et magis delitiosas et regiones et urbes quam Tusciam et Florentiam, unde sumus oriundus et civis, et plerasque nationes et gentes delectabiliori atque utiliori sermone uti quam Latinos."

20. *Inferno*. Canto XXXIV, 61–66, p. 364.

21. *Inferno*. Canto XXIV, pp. 246–257 and Canto XXV, pp. 258–269. These are filled with references to Florentine citizens.

22. Dante Alighieri, *Paradiso* trans. Charles Singleton (Princeton: Princeton University Press, 4th edn, 1991), Canto XV, 130–138, p. 170.

23. "rispondere a quelli." See *Dialogo, 1976*, p. 11, nts. 773b, 4–5, where Sozzi argued that, "è evidente che la polemica del Machiavelli contro Dante è in funzione della polemica linguistica contro i contemporanei. (Trissino in primo luogo); la quale a sua volta muove da una sollecitudine prevalentemente politica (il primato linguistico di Firenze come coefficiente del suo primato politico).

24. "Lingua Latina." See *Discorsi, 1999*, II. 5, p. 308. "Vero è che non gli è riuscito spegnere in tutto la notizia delle cose fatte dagli uomini eccellenti di quella: il che è nato per avere quella mantenuta la lingua latina." See *Istorie* VII. 33, p. 587.

"Insegnava in Milano la latina lingua a' primi giovani di quella città Cola Montano, uomo litterato e ambizioso"; and VII. 34, p. 589. "Era Girolamo di età di ventitrè anni: nè fu nel morire meno animoso che nello operare si fusse stato; perchè trovandosi ignudo e con il carnefice davanti, che aveva il coltello in mano per ferirlo, disse queste parole in lingua latina, perchè litterato era: <<Mors acerba, fama perpetua, stabit vetus memoria facti>>; and VIII. 4, p.593. "De' forestieri, oltre a' prenominati, messer Antonio da Volterra e uno Stefano sacerdote, il quale nelle case di messer Iacopo alla sua figliuola la lingua latina insegnava, v'intervennono." For "Lingua greca," see Machiavelli's *Istorie*. See VI. 6, p. 567. "Fu ancora Cosimo degli uomini litterati amatore ed esaltatore; e perciò condusse in Firenze lo Argilopolo, uomo di nazione greca e in quelli tempi litteratissimo, acciò che da quello la gioventù fiorentina la lingua greca e l'altre sue dottrine potesse apprendere. Nutrì nelle sue case Marsilio Ficino, secondo padre della platonica filosofia, il quale sommamente amò; e perchè potesse più commodamente seguitare gli studi delle lettere, e per poterlo con più sua commodità usare, una possessione propinqua alla sua di Careggi gli donò."

25. Machiavelli used a similar device in his *Arte*. See Niccolò Machiavelli, *Dell'Arte della guerra*, in *Tutte le opere Storiche e Letterarie di Niccolò Machiavelli* A cura di Guido Mazzoni e Mario Casella (Firenze: G. Barbèra, 1929): 263–374. See p. 268; there Machiavelli wrote "Ma per fuggire i fastidi d'avere a repetere tante volte *quel disse e quello altro soggiunse*, si noteranno solamente i nomi di chi parli, sanza replicarne altro." Is this a further possible evidence of Machiavelli's authorship of the *Dialogo*?

26. *Purgatorio*. III, 128, p. 30.

27. *Paradiso*. XXII, 115, p. 252. This line reads "con voi nasceva e s'ascondeva vosco" in Dante.

28. *Paradiso*. I, 70, p. 6.

29. *Paradiso*. IX, 81, p. 100. In Dante, this line reads "s'io m'intuassi, come tu t'inmii."

30. *De Vulgari, 1981*. I.XVI, p. 80. "Itque, adepti quod querebamus, dicimus illustre, cardinale, aulicum et curiale vulgare in Latio, quod omnis latie civitatis est et nullius esse videtur, et quo municipalia vulargia omnia Latinorum mensurantur et ponderantur et comparantur."

31. *Paradiso*. VI, 94, p. 64.

32. *Inferno*. XIX, 120. p. 200. Dante wrote "ambo" rather than "ambe."

33. *Inferno*. XIX, 45, p. 194. Dante wrote "di quel che si piangeva con la zanca."

34. *Paradiso*. V, 64, p. 52. There, Dante wrote, "Non prendan li mortali il voto a ciancia."

35. Virgil, *The Aeneid of Virgil (Books I–VI)* ed. R.D. Williams (Glasgow: MacMillan, 1972), Book I, 119, p. 4. The whole line reads "arma virum tabulaque et Troia gaza per undas."

36. *Inferno*. XXIII, 76, p. 238. Dante wrote "E un che 'ntese la parola tosca."

37. *Inferno*. X, 25–27, p. 100. Dante wrote "nobil patria."

38.   Luigi Pulci, *Morgante e Lettere* A cura di Domenico de Robertis (Firenze: Sansoni, n.d.).

39.   *Inferno*. I, 1–3, p. 2.

40.   *Morgante*. 656, XXIV.

41   *Inferno*, XXXIII, 10, p. 348.   Dante wrote, "Io non so chi tu se' né per che modo/ venuto se' qua giù; ma fiorentino."

42.   See Niccolò Machiavelli, the "Dialogue concerning our language" in, *The Literary Works of Machiavelli* trans. John R. Hale (Oxford: Oxford University Press, 1961), 185, n. 1, where John Hale noted that "Machiavelli is confusing two lines, one from *Inferno*, XXVI. 13, "Then we set out..." and the other from *Inferno*, XX. 130, "...and we went on our way." The translations are Hale's.

43.   *Inferno*. XXVIII, 27, p. 294.

44.   *Inferno*. XXV, 2, p. 258.

45.   Horace, *Satires, Epistles and Ars poetica* trans. H. Rushton Fairclough (Cambridge, Mass.: Harvard University Press, 6th edn., 1947).   See *Ars poetica*, 454, 56–57. "Cum lingua Catonis et Enni sermonem patriam ditaverit."

46.   "il nervo dell'esercito."   This phrase in the *Dialogo* is mirrored in Machiavelli's *Il Principe*, the *Discorsi* and the *Arte della guerra*.   See *Il Principe*, p. 46 "...et oltre a questo, per potere tenere la plebe pasciuta, e sanza perdita del pubblico, hanno sempre in comune per uno anno da potere dare loro da lavorare in quelli esercizii, che sieno el nervo e la vita di quella città, e delle industrie de' quali la plebe pasca"; the *Discorsi, 1999*, II. 10, p. 318.   "Dico pertanto non l'oro, come grida la commune opinione, essere il nervo della guerra, ma i buoni soldati; perché l'oro non è sufficiente a trovare i buoni soldati, ma i buoni soldati sono bene sufficienti a trovare l'oro"; and II. 18, p. 341.   "...ma il fondamento e il nervo dello esercito, e quello che si debbe più stimare, debbano essere le fanterie."   Also see the *Arte*, I, p. 272, "Dove ancora da' re deono esser temuti quegli che prendono per loro arte la guerra, perché il nervo degli eserciti, sanza alcun dubbio, sono le fanterie"; also in *Arte* I, p. 280.   "Perché era costume che qualunque di loro avesse due legioni d'uomini romani, le quali erano il nervo degli eserciti loro"; and in the same treatise, II, p. 303; "perché il nervo e la importanza dello esercito è la fanteria; l'altra, perché questa parte di milizia è meno corrotta che quella de' fanti; perché, s'ella non è più forte dell'antica, ell'è al pari."

47.   Some commentators seize on the discrepancy between the descriptions of the Roman military in the *Arte* and the *Dialogo* as evidence against Machiavelli's authorship of the latter.   There appears to be an inconsistency between these two works, but there are also inconsistencies between Machiavelli's *Discorsi* and his *Arte*.   The former relied on Livy's calculations to describe the numbers of troops in Roman legions, while the latter relied, primarily, on Polybius for such numbers.   By the same token, the *Dialogo* appears to have relied on Livy for its numbers relating to the makeup of Rome's legions.   For example, see *Discorsi, 1999*, II. 16, p. 330, where Machiavelli follows Livy's example, without providing a number of troops. "E di questa opinione è Tito Livio, perché in ogni parte fa gli eserciti pari, di ordine,

di virtù, d'ostinazione e di numero; solo vi fa differenza, che i capi dello esercito romano furono più virtuosi che quelli dello esercito latino." See Livy's *Ab urbe condita*. VIII. vi. 14–16, and XXXV. xx and xli, where Livy uses "20,000" troops, the same number used by the author of the *Dialogo*. The passage in the *Arte*, relies on Polybius, see Book III, 306 in the former. "Voi avete a intendere come in uno esercito romano ordinario, il quale chiamavano esercito consolare, non erano più che due legioni di cittadini romani, che erano secento cavagli e circa undicimila fanti. Avevano di poi altrettanti fanti e cavagli, che erano loro mandati dagli amici e confederati loro;[...] Nè mai permettevano che questi fanti ausiliari passassero il numero de'fanti delle legioni loro[...] Con questo esercito, che era di ventiduemila fanti e circa dumila cavagli utili, faceva uno consolo ogni fazione e andava a ogni impresa." For an interesting discussion of these "inconsistencies," see Hans Baron, "Machiavelli on the Eve of the *Discourses*: The Date and Place of the *Dialogo intorno alla nostra lingua*," *Bibliotheque d'Humanisme et Renaissance* 23 (1961): 449–76, 454 and note 1; 455 and note 1. Regarding the use of "l'autorità...romana" in the *Dialogo*—this also may be reflected in the *Discorsi, 1999*, II. 18, p. 340. See the title of that discourse which links Roman authority with their military organization. "Come per *l'autorità de' Romani* e per lo esemplo della antica milizia si debbe stimare più le fanterie che i cavagli."

48.   One might suggest that there is a similarity between this passage in the *Dialogo* and one of Machiavelli's plays. See Niccolò Machiavelli, *Clizia* A cura di Guido Davico Bonino (Torino: Einaudi, 1977), 5. "Sono trovate le commedie, per giovare e per dilettare alli spettatori. Giova veramente assai a qualunque uomo, e massimamente a' giovanetti, cognescere la avarizia d'uno vechio, il furore d'uno innamorato, l'inganni d'uno servo, la gola d'uno parassito, la miseria d'uno povero, l'ambizione d'uno ricco, le lusinghe d'una meretrice, la poca fede di tutti gli uomini. De'quali essempli le comedie sono piene, e possonsi tutte queste cose con onestà grandissima rappresentare. Ma, volendo dilettare, è necesario muovere gli spettatori a riso: il che non si può fare mantenendo il parlare grave e severo, perché le parole, che fanno ridere, sono o sciocche, o iniuriose, o amorose: è necessario, pertanto, rappresentare persone sciocche, malediche, o innamorate: e perciò quelle comedie, che sono piene di queste tre qualità di parole, sono piene di risa; quelle che ne mancano, non truovano chi con il ridere la accompagni."

49.   The author of the *Dialogo* is referring to Lodovico Ariosto's poem *Orlando furioso*, circulated in manuscript form in 1515 and published in 1516, 1521 and 1532. The pressure to "Tuscanize" literary works was so great that Ariosto re-wrote his 1532 version of the *Furioso* to conform to Tuscan Italian. See John Hale, *A Concise Encyclopaedia of the Italian Renaissance* (London: Thames and Hudson, 1981): 34–35 for a brief history of Ariosto's career.

50.   It is interesting that the author of the *Dialogo* should include Venice here, while leaving it out earlier.

51.   *The Prince, 1997*. See Codevilla's interesting introduction, xxii–xxiii. "At the end [of the *Dialogo*] he claims to have *sgannato* Dante and promises to do the same to

all who show insufficient reverence to Florence. *Sgannare* appears to be a pun. *Ingannare* means "to deceive." *Sgannare* is a rare, contrived way to say "undeceive." That is, Machiavelli claims to have set Dante straight. However, the very common word *scannare* means to kill by bleeding to death. Even Machiavelli's jokes tell us that he plays for keeps."

Bibliography

ഌൗരൂ

Primary Sources

Manuscripts of the *Dialogo*

(All attributed to Machiavelli) Machiavelli, Niccolò. *Discorso di Nic⁰.*
  Machiavelli nel quale si tratta [della lingua]. Manoscritto Miscell.
  Borghini III, Filze Rinuccini 22, 9 pp, da c. 1r a c. 5r.
_____. *Discorso o dialogo intorno alla nostra lingua.* Manoscritto E.B. 15
  10 della Biblioteca Nazionale di Firenze (11 pp., da c. 133r a 138r).
_____. *Discorso o dialogo Intorno alla nostra lingua.* Manoscritto Palatino
  815 della Biblioteca Nazionale di Firenze, pp. 820-839.
_____. *Machiavelli. Dialogo sulla lingua.* Biblioteca Medicea Laurenziana.
  Ashburnham 674 (605). Nel vol. 2 (di 8), cc. 211 a 221.
_____. *Messer Niccolò di Bernardo Machiavelli: Discorso over dialogo
  circa la lingua fiorentina.* Manoscritto Vat. Barb. Lat. *5368,* cc. 44-53.

Other Manuscripts

Parenti, Pietro. *Historia fiorentina,* Biblioteca Nazionale di Firenze, *Fondo
  Principale,* II, IV, 171, fol. 114ʳ.
Ricci, Giuliano de'. *Priorista.* Manoscritto Palatino E.B. 14.1. Biblioteca
  Nazionale di Firenze.

Printed Italian Editions of the *Dialogo*

_____. The *Dialogo* in: Varchi, Benedetto. *L'Ercolano: dialogo di Messer
  Benedetto Varchi nel quale si ragiona delle lingue, ed in particolare
  della Toscana e della Fiorentina.* Milano: Società Tipografica
  de'Classici Italiani, Contrada di S. Margherita, N.° 1118, 1804.
  (Unknown editor).
_____. The *Dialogo* in: Varchi, Benedetto. *L'Hercolano, dialogo ... nel qual*

si ragioni generalmente delle lingue, et in particolare della Toscana, e della Fiorentina; composto ... *sulla occasione della disputa occorsa tra 'l Commendator Caro, e M.L. Castelvetro. Nuovamente stampato.* 2 vols. A cura di Giovanni Bottari. Firenze: Tartini e Franchi, 1730.

_____. *Discorso o Dialogo Intorno Alla Nostra Lingua: Edizione Critica.* A cura di Bortolo Tommaso Sozzi. Torino: G. Einaudi, 1976.

_____. *Discorso o dialogo intorno alla nostra lingua* in *Opere di Niccolò Machiavelli.* A cura di Sergio Bertelli. 11 vols. Milano: Giovanni Salerno, 1968-82. See Volume 4, pp. 261-277

_____. *Discorso o dialogo intorno alla lingua* in *Tutte le Opere Storiche e Letterarie di Niccolò Machiavelli.* A cura di Guido Mazzoni e Mario Casella. Firenze: G. Barbèra, 1929: 770-778.

_____. *Discorso, overro dialogo, in cui si esamina, se la lingua, in cui scrissero Dante, il Boccaccio, e il Petrarca, si debba chiamare Italiana, Toscana, o Fiorentina,* in *Opere: Volume Otto: Commedie, terzine ed altre opere.* Cosmopoli, 1769.

_____. The *Dialogo* in *Opere minori di Niccolò Machiavelli: Rivedute sul migliori edizioni.* Con note filologiche e critiche di F.-. Polidori. Firenze: Le Monnier, 1852: 589-603.

_____. *Niccolò Machiavelli e il 'Dialogo intorno alla nostra lingua',* con *una edizione del testo* A cura di Ornella Castellani Pollidori. Firenze: Olschki, 1978.

_____. *Nuove Riflessioni sul Discorso o Dialogo Intorno Alla Nostra Lingua di Niccolò Machiavelli.* A cura di Ornella Castellani Pollidori. Roma: Salerno editrice, 1981.

Translated Edition of the *Dialogo*

Machiavelli, Niccolò. The *Dialogo* in: *The Literary Works of Machiavelli.* Trans. John R. Hale. London: Oxford University Press, 1961: 173-190.

Editions of Works of Machiavelli in Italian

Machiavelli, Niccolò. *Opere.* 8 vols. Cosmopoli, 1769.

_____. *Opere di Niccolò Machiavelli cittadino e segretario fiorentino.* 10 vols. Milano: Società tipografica de' classici italiani, 1804.

_____. *Opere complete di Niccolò Machiavelli, con molte correzioni e giunte rinvenute sui manoscritti originali.* Firenze: S.I., 1843.

_____. *Opere di Niccolò Machiavelli.* Scelte da Giuseppe Zirardini. Parigi,

1851.

_____. *Opere minori di Niccolò Machiavelli rivedute sulle migliori edizioni.* A cura di Filippo Luigi Polidori. Firenze: F. Le Monnier, 1852.

_____. *Tutte le Opere Storiche e Letterarie di Niccolò Machiavelli.* A cura di Guido Mazzoni e Mario Casella. Firenze: G. Barbèra, 1929.

_____. *Opere di Niccolò Machiavelli.* 3 vols. A cura di Franco Gaeta. Torino: Unione tipografico-editrice Torinese, 1984.

Political and Literary Works
of Machiavelli in Italian

Machiavelli, Niccolò. *Clizia.* A cura di Guido Davico Bonino. Torino: Einaudi, 1977.

_____. *Lettere a Francesco Vettori e a Francesco Guicciardini.* A cura di Giorgio Inglese. Milano: R.C.S. Libri & Grandi Opere, 1996.

_____. *Il Principe e Altre Opere Politiche.* Introduzione di Delio Cantimori, Note di Stefano Andretta. Milano: Garzanti Libri, 1999.

_____. *Il Principe e Discorsi sopra la prima deca di Tito Livio.* A cura di Sergio Bertelli. Milano: Feltrinelli, 2nd edn., 1977.

_____. *Discorsi Sopra la Prima Deca di Tito Livio.* Introduzione di Gennaro Sasso, Note di Giorgio Inglese. Milano: Biblioteca Universale Rizzoli, 1999.

_____. *Istorie fiorentine* in *Opere di Niccolò Machiavelli.* Vol. 2. A cura di A. Montevecchi. Torino, 1986.

_____. *Opere di Niccolò Machiavelli, Volume Terzo, Lettere.* A cura di Franco Gaeta. Torino: Unione Tipografico-Editrice Torinese, 1984.

_____. *The First Decennale: A Facsimile of the First Edition of February, 1506.* Cambridge, Mass.: Harvard University Press, 1969.

_____. *Ritratti e Rapporti Diplomatici.* Roma: Riuniti, 2000.

Political and Literary Works
of Machiavelli in Translation

Machiavelli, Niccolò, *The Art of War.* Trans. Ellis Farneworth. New York: Da Capo Press, 1990.

_____. *The Chief Works and Others.* 3 Vols. Trans. Allan Gilbert. Durham: Duke University Press, 1965.

_____. *The Discourses of Niccolò Machiavelli.* 2 Vols. Trans. Lesley J. Walker. London, Routledge, 1950.

_____. *Florentine Histories*. Trans. Laura Banfield and Harvey C. Mansfield, Jr. Princeton: Princeton University Press, 1988.

_____. *The Prince*. Eds. Quentin Skinner and Russell Price. Cambridge: Cambridge University Press, 10ᵗʰ edn., 1998.

_____. *The Prince*. Trans. Harvey C. Mansfield. Chicago: University of Chicago Press, 1985.

_____. *The Prince*. Trans. George Bull. London: Penguin Group, 4ᵗʰ ed., 1995.

_____. *The Prince*. Trans. and Ed. Stephen J. Milner. London: J.M. Dent, 2000.

_____. *Machiavelli and His Friends: Their Personal Correspondence*. Trans. and Eds. James B. Atkinson and David Sices. DeKalb: Northern Illinois University Press, 1996.

_____. *The Prince: Also "The Life of Castruccio Castracani of Luca" and "The Means Duke Valentino us'd to put to death Vitellozzo Vitelli, Oliverotto of Fermo, Paul and the Duke of Gravina."* Trans. Edward Dacres. Amsterdam: Da Capo, 1969 – a facsimile of 1640 edition printed in London by R. Bishop for Wil. Hils.

_____. *The Prince*. Trans. Angelo M. Codevilla. New Haven: Yale University Press, 1997.

Other Primary Sources

Alighieri, Dante. *De Vulgari Eloquentia*. Trans. Warman Welliver. Ravenna: Ravenna Longo, 1981.

_____. *The Divine Comedy: Inferno*. Trans. Charles Singleton. Princeton: Princeton University Press, 1970.

_____. *The Divine Comedy: Purgatorio*. Trans. Charles Singleton. Princeton: Princeton University Press, 1973.

_____. *The Divine Comedy: Paradiso*. Trans. Charles Singleton. Princeton: Princeton University Press, 4ᵗʰ edn., 1991.

Bembo, Pietro. *Prose della volgar lingua*. A cura di Carlo Dionisotti. Torino: Classici Italiani, 1966.

Boccaccio, Giovanni. *Il Decameron.../ricorretto in Roma et emendato secondo l'ordine del Sacro Conc. di Trento, et riscontrato in Firenze con testi antichi & alla sua vera lezione ridotto da' deputati di loro Alt. Ser.* [i.e. Vincezo M. Borghini, Pier F. Cambi and Sebastiono Antinori]. Fiorenza: I Giunti, 1573.

_____. *Il Decameron: Edizione Critica*. A cura di Aldo Rossi. Bologna: Cappelli, 1977.

_____ *The Decameron*. Ed. Jonathan Usher and Trans. Guido Waldman. Oxford: Oxford University Press, 1998.

Borghini, Vincenzo, *Prose fiorentine*. Firenze, 1745.

Bruni, Leonardo. *Dialogi ad Petrum Paulum Histrum*. A cura di Stefano Ugo Baldassari. Firenze: Olschki, 1994.

Cicero, Marcus Tullius. *De re publica et De legibus*. Trans. Clinton Walker Keyes. Cambridge, Mass.: Harvard University Press, 11th edn., 1994.

_____. *De Officiis*. Trans. Walter Miller. Cambridge, Mass.: Harvard University Press, 1997.

Gabriele, Trifon. *Annotationi nel Dante fatte con M. Trifon Gabriele in Bassano: Edizione critica*. A cura di Lino Pertile. Bologna: Carducci, 1993.

Gelli, Giovanni Battista. *Ragionamento...sopra le difficoltà di mettere in regole la nostra lingua*. Florence, 1551.

_____. *Letture edite e inedite sopra la Commedia di Dante*. Firenze: Bocca, 1887.

Guicciardini, Francesco. *Considerations on the "Discourses of Niccolò Machiavelli"* in, *The Sweetness of Power: Machiavelli's "Discourses" and Guicciardini's "Considerations."* Trans. James B. Atkinson and David Sices. DeKalb: Northern Illinois University Press, 2002.

_____. *Opere*. 9 Vols. A cura di Constantino Panigada e Roberto Palmarocchi. Bari: Laterza, 1929-36.

_____. *Ricordi*. Trans. Ninian Hill Thomson. New York: S.F. Vanni, 1949.

Horace. *Satires, Epistles and Ars poetica*. Trans. H. Rushton Fairclough. Cambridge, Mass.: Harvard University Press, 6th edn., 1947.

Lenzoni, Carlo. *In difesa della lingua fiorentina, e di Dante*. Fiorenza: [appresso L. Torrentino], 1556.

Livy, Titus. *Ab urbe condita*. Vol I. (Books I-II). Trans. B.O. Foster. Cambridge, Mass: Harvard University Press, 10th edn., 1998.

_____. *Ab urbe condita*. Vol. II. (Books III-IV). Trans. B.O. Foster. Cambridge, Mass: Harvard University Press, 6th edn., 1997.

_____. *Ab urbe condita* Vol. III. (Books V-VII). Trans. B.O. Foster. Cambridge, Mass: Harvard University Press, 7th edn., 1996.

_____. *Ab urbe condita*. Vol IV. (Books VIII-X). Trans. B.O. Foster. Cambridge, Mass: Harvard University Press, 1926.

Marlowe, Christopher. *The Jew of Malta*. Ed. James R. Siemon. London: A. and C. Black, 1997.

Martelli, Lodovico. "Risposta alla *Epistola* del Trissino." *Trattati sull'Ortografia del Volgare, 1524-1526*. A cura di Brian Richardson. Exeter: University of Exeter Press, 1984: 37-75.

Medici, Lorenzo de'. *Opere*. A cura di Tiziano Zanato. Torino: Einaudi,

1992.

Petrarca, Francesco. *Canzoniere, Trionfi, Rime Varie e Una Scelta di Versi Latini*. A cura di Carla Muscetta e Daniele Ponchiroli. Torino: Giulio Einaudi: Torino, 1958.

_____. *Canzoniere*. Introduzione e note di Piero Cudini. Milano: Aldo Garzanti, 1974.

_____. *Le Familiari: Edizione Critica: Volume Primo*. A cura di Vittorio Rossi. Firenze: Sansoni, 1933.

_____. *Letters from Petrarch*. Trans. and Ed. Morris Bishop. Bloomington: Indiana University Press, 1966.

_____. *The Canzoniere, (Rerum vulgarium fragmenta)*. 2 Vols. Trans. Frederic J. Jones Hull: Troubadour and Hull Italian Texts, 2000-2001

Poliziano, Angelo. "First Anthology of Vernacular Poetry." *Images of Quattrocento Florence*. Eds. Stefano Ugo Baldassari and Arielle Saiber, New Haven: Yale University Press, 2000: 169-174

Polybius. *The Rise of the Roman Empire (Selections)*. Trans. Ian Scott Kilvert. London: Penguin Books Ltd, 1979.

Pulci, Luigi. *Morgante e Lettere*. A cura di Domenico de Robertis. Firenze: Sansoni, n.d.

Ricci, Giuliano de'. *Cronaca: 1532-1606*. A cura di Giuliano Sapori. Milano: Riccardo Ricciardi, 1972.

Rousseau, Jean-Jacques. *Le Contrat Social*. Paris, 1782.

Sanuto, Marino. *I Diarii, Volume XV* . Reprint of Venezia: F Visentini, 1879-1903; Bologna: Forni, 1969.

Shakespeare, William. "Henry VI, Part III." *The Complete Signet Classic Shakespeare*. Ed. Sylvan Barnet. New York: Harcourt Brace Jovanovich, 1972: 190-232.

Trissino, Gian Giorgio. *Dialogo intitulato: Il Castellano, nel quale si tratta della lingua italiana*. Venezia, 1528.

Varchi, Benedetto. "Della poesia", from his lectures delivered in the Florentine Academy October-December, 1553, in *Lezioni di M. Benedetto Varchi, accademico fiorentino : lette da lui publicamente nell'Accademia Fiorentina, sopra diverse materie, poetiche, e filosofiche, raccolte nuovamenta, e la maggior parte non più date in luce, con due tavole, vna delle materie, l'altra delle cose più notabili / con la vita del l'autore*. Fiorenza: Filippo Giunti,1590.

Virgil. *The Aeneid of Virgil (Books I-VI)*. Ed. R.D. Williams. Glasgow: MacMillan,1972.

Collections of Primary Sources

Baldassari, Stefano Ugo, and Arielle Saiber, eds. *Images of Quattrocento Florence*. New Haven: Yale University Press, 2000.

Varese, Claudio, ed. *Prosatori Volgari del Quattrocento*. Milano: Riccardo Ricciardi, 1957.

Secondary Sources

Anglo, Sydney. "Machiavelli as a Military Authority. Some Early Sources." *Florence and Italy: Renaissance Studies in Honour of Nicolai Rubinstein*. Eds. Peter Denley and Caroline Elam. London: Committee for Medieval Studies, Westfield College, 1988: 321-334.

_____. *Machiavelli: A Dissection*. London: Victor Gollancz, 1969.

Atkinson, Catherine. *Debts, Dowries, Donkey: The Diary of Niccolò Machiavelli's Father, Messer Bernardo, in Quattrocento Florence*. Frankfurt am Main: Peter Lang, 2002.

Barbi, Michele. *Dante nel Cinquecento*. Pisa: Tip. T. Nistri e. c., 1890.

Baron, Hans. *The Crisis of the Early Italian Renaissance: Civic Humanism and Republican Liberty in an Age of Classicism and Tyranny, Volume 2, Appendices*. Princeton: Princeton University Press, 1955

_____. *The Crisis of the Early Italian Renaissance: Civic Humanism and Republican Liberty in an Age of Classicism and Tyranny*. Princeton: Princeton University Press, 1966.

_____. *Humanistic and Political Literature in Florence and Venice at the Beginning of the Quattrocento*. Cambridge, Mass: Harvard University Press, 1955.

_____. "Machiavelli on the Eve of the *Discourses*: The Date and Place of the *Dialogo intorno alla nostra lingua*." *Bibliothèque d'Humanisme et Renaissance* 23 (1961): 449-76.

_____. "Machiavelli the Republican Citizen and Author of The Prince" Hans Baron. *In Search of Florentine Civic Humanism: Essays on the Transition from Medieval to Modern Thought*. Vol. 2. Princeton: Princeton University Press, 1988: 101-157.

_____. "The *Principe* and the Puzzle of the Date of Chapter 26." *Journal of Medieval and Renaissance Studies* 21 (1991): 83-102.

_____. "The *Principe* and the Puzzle of the Date of the *Discorsi*" *Bibliothèque d'Humanisme et Renaissance* 18 (1956): 405-428.

Bertelli, Sergio. "Egemonia linguistica come egemonia culturale e politica nella Firenze cosmiana." *Bibliothèque d'Humanisme et Renaissance* 38

(1976): 249-281.

Bock, Gisella, Quentin Skinner and Maurizio Viroli, eds. *Machiavelli and Republicanism*. New York: Cambridge University Press,1999.

Brand, Peter and Lino Pertile, eds., *The Cambridge History of Italian Literature*. Revised ed. Cambridge: Cambridge University Press, 1999.

Bujunda, J.M. de, ed. *Index de Rome 1557, 1559, 1564: Les premier Index romains et l'Index du Concile de Trent. Index de Livres interdicts 8.* Sherbrooke, 1990.

Burke, Peter. *The Fortunes of the Courtier*. Cambridge: Polity Press, 1995.

Butters, Humphrey. *Governors and Government in Early Sixteenth-Century Florence: 1502-1519*. Oxford: Clarendon, 1985.

Cassirer, Ernst. *The Myth of the State: A reduced photographic reprint of the 1946 edition*. New Haven: Yale University Press, 1961.

_____. "Science and Political Theory." *Machiavelli, Cynic, Patriot or Political Scientist?* Ed. De Lamar Jensen. Boston: D.C. Heath and Co., 1960.

Chabod, Federico. *Italian Foreign Policy: The Statecraft of the Founders*. Trans. William McCuaig. Princeton: Princeton University Press, 1996.

_____. *Machiavelli and the Renaissance*. Trans. David Moore. London: Bowes and Bowes, 1958.

Chiappelli, Fredi. *Studi sul Linguaggio del Machiavelli*. Firenze, 1952.

Cochrane, Eric. *Italy: 1530-1630*. Ed. Julius Kirshner. London: Longman, 1988.

Cohn, Samuel K., Jr. *Creating the Florentine State: Peasants and Rebellions, 1348-1434*. Cambridge, Cambridge University Press, 1999.

Condorelli, Ottavio. "Per la storia del nome "Stato, (il nome "Stato" in Machiavelli)". *Archivio Giuridico* 89 (1923): 223-235.

Dionisotti, Carlo. *Machiavellerie*. Torino: G. Einaudi, 1980: 267-363.

_____. "Machiavelli, Man of Letters." *Machiavelli and the Discourse of Literature*. Eds. Albert Russell Ascoli and Victoria Kahn Ithaca: Cornell University Press, 1993: 17-51.

D'Entrèves, Alexander Passerin. *Dante as a Political Thinker*. Oxford: Clarendon, 1952.

Fido, Franco. "The Politician as Writer." *The Comedy and Tragedy of Machiavelli*. Ed. Vickie B. Sullivan. New Haven: Yale University Press, 2000: 138-158.

Fissi, Rosetta Migliorini. "Per la Fortuna del 'De vulgari eloquentia,' un Nuovo Codice del 'Discorso o dialogo intorno alla nostra lingua': Approcci per una Edizione Critica." *Studi danteschi*, XLIX (1972): 135-214.

Gilbert, Allan H. *Machiavelli's "Prince" and Its Forerunners: "The Prince" as a Typical Book "de Regimine Principum."* Durham, N.C.: Duke University Press, 1938.

Gilbert, Felix. "Bernardo Rucellai and the Orti Oricellari: A Study on the Origins of Modern Political Thought." *Journal of the Warburg and Courtauld Institutes* 12 (1949): 101-131.

_____. *Machiavelli and Guicciardini: Politics and History in Sixteenth Century Florence.* Princeton: Princeton University Press, 1965.

_____. *Machiavelli e i suoi tempi.* Bologna, 1977.

_____. "Review-Discussion: The Composition of Machiavelli's *Discorsi.*" *Journal of the History of Ideas* 14 (1953): 136-156.

_____. "The Humanist Concept of the Prince and *The Prince* of Machiavelli." Felix Gilbert. *History: Choice and Commitment.* Ed. Arno M. Mayer. Cambridge, Mass.: Belknap Press of Harvard, 1977: 91-114.

Godman, Peter. *From Poliziano to Machiavelli: Florentine Humanism in the High Renaissance.* Princeton: Princeton University Press, 1998.

_____. *The Saint as Censor: Robert Bellarmine Between the Inquisition and Index.* Leiden: Brill, 2000.

Godorecci, Barbara J. *After Machiavelli: "Re-writing" and the "Hermeneutic Attitude."* West Lafayette: Purdue University Press, 1993.

Goldscheider, Ludwig. ed. *Michelangelo: Paintings, Sculptures, Architecture.* 4th edn. London, 1962.

Grayson, Cecil. "Lorenzo, Machiavelli and the Italian Language." *Italian Renaissance Studies: A Tribute to Cecilia M. Ady.* Ed. E.F. Jacob. London: Faber and Faber, 1960: 410-432.

_____. "Machiavelli and Dante." *Renaissance Studies in Honor of Hans Baron.* Eds. Anthony Molho and John A. Tedeschi. Dekalb: Northern Illinois University Press, 1971: 362-384.

Grazia, Sebastian de. *Machiavelli in Hell.* New York: Vintage Books, 1994.

Hale, John R. ed. *A Concise Encyclopaedia of the Italian Renaissance.* London: Thames and Hudson, 1981.

_____. *Florence and the Medici: The Pattern of Control.* London: Thames and Hudson, 1977.

_____. *Machiavelli and Renaissance Italy.* London: The English Universities Press Ltd, 1966.

Harvey, Michael. "Lost in the Wilderness: Love and Longing in *L'Asino.*" *The Comedy and Tragedy of Machiavelli: Essays on the Literary Works.* Ed. Vickie B. Sullivan. New Haven: Yale University Press, 2000: 120-137.

Hay, Denys. "The Italian view of Renaissance Italy." *Florilegium Historiale: Essays Presented to Wallace K. Ferguson.* Eds. J.G. Rowe and W.H. Stockdale. Toronto: University of Toronto Press, 1971: 3-17.

Hearder, Harry. *Italy in the Age of the Risorgimento: 1790-1870.* London: Longman,1983.

Hexter, J.H. *"Il principe* and *lo stato."* *Studies in the Renaissance* 4 (1957): 113-38.

_____. "Seyssel, Machiavelli, and Polybius VI: the Mystery of the Missing Translation." *Studies in the Renaissance* 3 (1956): 75-96.

Holmes, George. *Dante.* Oxford: Clarendon, 1980

Jensen, De Lamar, ed. *Machiavelli: Cynic, Patriot, or Political Scientist?* Boston: D.C. Heath, 1960.

Larner, John. *Lords of the Romagna.* Ithaca, NY: Cornell University Press, 1965.

Laven, Peter. *Renaissance Italy: 1464-1534.* London: B.T. Batsford, 1966.

Mackenney, Richard. *Sixteenth-Century Europe: Expansion and Conflict.* London: Macmillan, 1993.

Mallett, Michael. *Mercenaries and their Masters: Warfare in Renaissance Italy.* London: Bodley Head, 1974.

_____. "The Theory and Practice of Warfare in Machiavelli's Republic." *Machiavelli and Republicanism.* Eds. Gisela Bock, Quentin Skinner and Maurizio Viroli Cambridge: Cambridge University Press, 1993: 173-180.

Mattingly, Garrett. *Renaissance Diplomacy.* New York: Dover, 1988.

Mayor, Arno M., ed., *History: Choice and Commitment.* Cambridge, Mass.: Belknap Press of Harvard, 1977.

Moulakis, Athanasios. *Republican Realism in Renaissance Florence: Francesco Guicciardini's "Discorso di logrogno"* (Rowan and Littlefield: Lanham, Maryland, 1998).

Najemy, John. *Between Friends: Discourses of Power and Desire in the Machiavelli Vettori Letters of 1513-1515.* Princeton: Princeton University Press, 1993.

Niccoli, Ottavia. *Prophecy and People in Renaissance Italy.* Trans. Lydia G. Cochrane. Princeton: Princeton University Press, 1990.

Panizza, Letizia. "The Quattrocento." *The Cambridge History of Italian Literature, Revised edition.* Eds. Peter Brand and Lino Pertile. Cambridge: Cambridge University Press, 1999: 129-177.

Pertile, Lino "Trifone Gabriele's commentary on Dante and Bembo's *Prose della vulgar lingua."* *Italian Studies* 40 (1985): 17-30.

Polizotto, Lorenzo. *The Elect Nation: The Savonarolan Movement in Florence, 1494-1545.* Oxford: Clarendon Press, 1994

Prezzolini, Giuseppe. *Machiavelli anticristo.* Rome: G. Casini, 1954.

_____. *Niccolò Machiavelli: The Florentine.* Trans. Ralph Roeder. London: G. Putnam's Sons, 1928.

_____. *Vita di Niccolò Machiavelli Fiorentino*. Milano: Rusconi, 2nd edn. 1982.

Quevedo, Francesco. "Lince de Italia." *Obras*. Madrid, 1880.

Rajna, Pio. "La Data del *Dialogo int. alla lingua* di N. Machiavelli." *Rendiconti dell R. Accad. dei Lincei, Classe Scienze Morali*. Serie V. II (1893): 203-222.

Rebhorn, Wayne A. *Foxes and Lions: Machiavelli's Confidence Men*. Ithaca: Cornell University Press, 1988.

Richardson, Brian. "The *Prince* and its Early Italian Readers." *Niccolò Machiavelli's "The Prince": New Interdisciplinary Essays*. Ed. Martin Coyle. Manchester: Manchester University Press, 1995: 19-39.

_____. "Prose." *The Cambridge History of Italian Literature*. Revised edition. Eds. Peter Brand and Lino Pertile. Cambridge: Cambridge University Press, 1999: 179-232.

Ridolfi, Roberto. *Vita di Girolamo Savonarola*. 2 Vols. Roma: A. Belardetti, 1952.

_____. *The Life of Niccolò Machiavelli*. Trans. Cecil Grayson. London: Routledge and K. Paul, 1963.

_____. *Vita di Niccolò Machiavelli*. Roma: A. Belardetti, 1954.

Rowe, J.G. and W.H. Stockdale, eds. *Florilegium Historiale: Essays Presented to Wallace K. Ferguson*. Toronto: University of Toronto Press, 1971.

Rubinstein, Nicolai. "Notes on the word *stato* in Florence before Machiavelli." *Florilegium Historiale: Essays Presented to Wallace K. Ferguson*. Eds. Rowe, J.G. and W.H. Stockdale. Toronto: University of Toronto Press, 1971: 314-326.

_____. *The Palazzo Vecchio, 1298-1532: Government, Architecture, and Imagery in the Civic Palace of the Florentine Republic*. Oxford Warburg Studies. Oxford: Oxford University Press, 1995.

Salmone, A. William. ed. *Italy: From the Risorgimento to Fascism, an Inquiry into the Origins of the Totalitarian State*. Devon: Redwood Press, 1971.

Sanctis, Francesco de. *Storia della letteratura Italiana, nuova edizione*. 2 Vols. A cura di Benedetto Croce. Bari: Laterza e Figli, 1912.

_____. *History of Italian Literature*. 2 Vols. Trans. Joan Redfern. London: Humphrey Milford, 1930.

Sarti, Roland. *Mazzini: A Life for the Religion of Politics*. West Port, Conn.: Praeger, 1997.

Sasso, Gennaro. *Machiavelli e Cesare Borgia: Storia di un giudizio*. Roma: Edizioni dell'Ateneo, 1966.

Shaw, Christine. *The Politics of Exile in Renaissance Italy*. Cambridge:

Cambridge University Press, 2000.

Shell, Susan Meld. "Machiavelli's Discourse on Language." *The Comedy and Tragedy of Machiavelli: Essays on the Literary Works*. Ed. Vickie B Sullivan. New Haven: Yale University Press, 2000: 78-101.

Sherberg, Michael. "The *Accademia Fiorentina* and the Question of Language: the Politics of Theory in Ducal Florence." *Renaissance Quarterly* LVI. 1. Spring 2003 Renaissance Society of America, New York, 2003: 26-55.

Skinner, Quentin. "The State." *Political Innovation and Conceptual Change*. Eds. T. Ball, J. Farr and R.L. Hanson. Cambridge: Cambridge University Press, 1989: 90-131.

_____. *Machiavelli*. Oxford: Oxford University Press, 1996.

_____. *The Foundations of Modern Political Thought: Volume One: The Renaissance*. Cambridge: Cambridge University Press, 1978.

Spackman, Barbara. "Politics on the Warpath: Machiavelli's *Art of War*." *Machiavelli and the Discourse of Literature*. Eds. Albert Russell Ascoli and Victoria Kahn. Ithaca: Cornell University Press, 1993: 179-193.

Starn, Randolph. *Contrary Commonwealth: The Theme of Exile in Medieval and Renaissance Italy*. Berkeley: University of California Press, 1982.

_____. "Petrarch's Consolation on Exile: a Humanist Use of Adversity." *Essays Presented to Myron P. Gilmore* Vol. 1. Eds. Sergio Bertelli and Gloria Ramakus. Firenze: La Nuova Italia Editrice, 1978: 241-254.

Stephens, John. *The Fall of the Florentine Republic: 1512-1530*. Oxford: Clarendon, 1983.

Sullivan, Vickie B. *Machiavelli's Three Romes: Religion, Human Liberty, and Politics Reformed*. DeKalb: Northern Illinois University Press, 1996.

_____. Ed. *The Comedy and Tragedy of Machiavelli: Essays on the Literary Works*. New Haven: Yale University Press, 2000.

Tedeschi, John. "Florentine Documents for a History of the *Index of Prohibited Books*." *Renaissance Studies in Honor of Hans Baron*. Eds. Anthony Molho and John A. Tedeschi. DeKalb: Northern Illinois University Press, 1971: 577-605.

_____. *The Prosecution of Heresy: Collected Studies on the Inquisition in Early Modern Italy*. Binghamton, NY: Medieval & Renaissance Texts Studies, 1991.

Tommasini, Oreste. *La vita e gli scritti di Niccolo Machiavelli nella loro relazione col machiavellismo*. Vol. I. Torino: E. Loescher, 1883.

Turner, A. Richard. *Inventing Leonardo*. New York: Knopf, 1993.

Villari, Pasquale. *Niccolò Machiavelli e i suoi tempi*. 3 Vols. Milano: Ulrico Hoepli, 2nd edn., 1895.

_____. *Machiavelli e i suoi tempi*. 3 Vols. Le Monnier: Firenze 1877.

_____. *Niccolò Machiavelli and his Times*. 4 Vols. Trans. Linda Villari. London: Routledge and Kegan Paul, 1878-83.

Viroli, Maurizio. *For Love of Country: An Essay on Patriotism and Nationalism*. New York: Clarendon Press, 1997.

_____. *From Politics to Reason of State: The Acquisition and Transformation of the Language of Politics: 1250-1600*. Cambridge: Cambridge University Press, 1992.

_____. *Jean-Jacques Rousseau and the "well-ordered society"* Trans. Derek Hanson. Cambridge: Cambridge University Press, 1988.

_____. *Machiavelli*. Oxford: Oxford University Press, 1998.

_____. *Niccolò's Smile: A Biography of Niccolò Machiavelli*. Trans. Antony Shugaar. New York: Farrar, Straus and Giroux, 2000.

_____. *Republicanism*. Trans. Antony Shugaar. New York: Farrar, Straus and Giroux, 2002.

Weinstein, Donald. *Savonarola and Florence: Prophecy and Patriotism in the Renaissance*. Princeton: Princeton University Press, 1970.

Whitfield, J.H. *Discourses on Machiavelli*. Cambridge: Heffer, 1969.

_____. *Machiavelli*. Oxford: Basil Blackwell, 1947.

Woodhouse, J.R. *Baldesar Castiglione: A Reassessment of "The Courtier."* Edinburgh: Edinburgh University Press, 1978.

INDEX

Studies in Modern European History

The monographs in this series focus upon aspects of the political, social, economic, cultural, and religious history of Europe from the Renaissance to the present. Emphasis is placed on the states of Western Europe, especially Great Britain, France, Italy, and Germany. While some of the volumes treat internal developments, others deal with movements such as liberalism, socialism, and industrialization, which transcend a particular country.

The series editor is:

> Frank J. Coppa
> Director, Doctor of Arts Program
> in Modern World History
> Department of History
> St. John's University
> Jamaica, New York 11439

To order other books in this series, please contact our Customer Service Department:

> (800) 770-LANG (within the U.S.)
> (212) 647-7706 (outside the U.S.)
> (212) 647-7707 FAX

or browse online by series at:

> WWW.PETERLANGUSA.COM